ESSENTIALS FOR design

JAVASCRIPT

comprehensive

Michael Brooks

PEARSON
Prentice Hall

Prentice Hall
Upper Saddle River, New Jersey 07458

Library of Congress Cataloging-in-Publication Data

Brooks, Michael.
  Javascript comprehensive / Michael Brooks. — 2nd ed.
    p.   cm. — (Essentials for design)
  Includes index.
  ISBN 0-13-187897-2
  1. JavaScript (Computer program language).
    I. Title. II. Series.
  QA76.73.J39B75 2007
  005.13'3 — dc22   2005032660

Vice President and Publisher: Natalie E. Anderson
Executive Acquisitions Editor: Chris Katsaropoulos
Editorial Supervisor: Brian Hoehl
Editorial Assistant: Kaitlin O'Shaughnessy
Executive Producer: Lisa Strite
Content Development Manager: Cathi Profitko
Senior Media Project Manager: Steve Gagliostro
Media Project Manager: Alana Meyers
Director of Marketing: Sarah Loomis
Senior Marketing Manager: Jason Sakos
Marketing Assistant: Ann Baranov

Sr. Customer Service Representative: Joseph Pascale
Managing Editor: Lynda Castillo
Production Project Manager/Manufacturing Buyer: Lynne Breitfeller
Art Director/Cover Design: Blair Brown
Interior Design: Thistle Hill Publishing Services, LLC.
Cover Illustration/Photo: FoodPix®
Composition/Full-Service Project Management: Progressive Publishing Alternatives
Cover Printer: Coral Graphics
Printer/Binder: Von Hoffman Press

Credits and acknowledgments borrowed from other sources and reproduced, with permission, in this textbook appear on the appropriate page within the text.

Macromedia Flash, Generator, FreeHand, Dreamweaver, Fireworks, and Director are registered trademarks of Macromedia, Inc. Photoshop, PageMaker, Acrobat, Adobe Type Manager, Illustrator, InDesign, Premiere, and PostScript are trademarks of Adobe Systems Incorporated. QuarkXPress is a registered trademark of Quark, Inc. Macintosh is a trademark of Apple Computer, Inc. CorelDRAW!, procreate Painter, and WordPerfect are trademarks of Corel Corporation. FrontPage, Publisher, PowerPoint, Word, Excel, Office, Microsoft, MS-DOS, and Windows are either registered trademarks or trademarks of Microsoft Corporation.

Other product and company names mentioned herein may be the trademarks of their respective owners.

10 9 8 7 6 5 4 3 2 1

ISBN 0-13-187897-2

ABOUT THE AUTHOR

Michael Brooks is a senior instructional designer with Lowe's Companies and an instructor in the Interactive Media Department at the Art Institute of Charlotte; he is also a co-owner of Web-Answers, a multimedia design firm.

Michael has an MPA from Appalachian State University. His professional duties require a great deal of time working in JavaScript and Flash. He has an intimate knowledge of the business and strategic aspects of interactive media.

Raised in the foothills of Western North Carolina, Michael enjoys photography and occasionally teaches classes in business management and political science.

ACKNOWLEDGMENTS

I would like to thank the professional writers, artists, editors, students, and educators who have worked long and hard on the *Essentials for Design* series.

Ellen Behoriam and the entire crew of Against The Clock, Inc. made substantial contributions to this text. Thanks to the dedicated teaching professionals: Dean Bagley, Dan Workman, Lynn Bowen, Ric Heishman, Warren Kendrick, Janice Potter, Ph.D., Drew Kinney, and Kyle Tait—your insightful comments and expertise have certainly contributed to the success of the *Essentials for Design* series.

And to Melissa Sabella, Anne Garcia, Eileen Calabro, Crystal Clifton, and Linda Kern — I appreciate your contribution to the continued success of this wonderful series.

CONTENTS AT A GLANCE

TABLE OF CONTENTS

HOW TO USE THIS BOOK

Essentials for Design courseware from Prentice Hall is anchored in the practical and professional needs of all types of students. The *Essentials for Design* series presents a learning-by-doing approach that encourages you to grasp application-related concepts as you expand your skills through hands-on tutorials. As such, it consists of modular lessons that are built around a series of numbered step-by-step procedures that are clear, concise, and easy to review.

Essentials for Design books are divided into chapters. A chapter covers one area (or a few closely related areas) of application functionality. Each chapter consists of several lessons that are related to that topic. Each lesson presents a specific task or closely related set of tasks in a manageable portion that is easy to assimilate and retain.

Each element in the *Essentials for Design* book is designed to maximize your learning experience. A list of the *Essentials for Design* chapter elements, and a description of how each element can help you, begins on the next page. To find out more about the rationale behind each book element and how to use each to your maximum benefit, take the following walk-through.

WALK-THROUGH

Chapter Objectives. Starting with an objective gives you short-term, attainable goals. Each chapter begins with a list of objectives that closely match the titles of the step-by-step tutorials. ▶

OBJECTIVES

In this chapter, you learn how to:

- Add Boolean values
- Use if statements
- Compare mathematical values
- Contrast string values
- React to user choices
- Work with logical operators
- Create complex decision statements

Chapter 5 Using Pop-Up Windows

Why Would I Do This?

HTML allows programmers to link to other documents as well as open new browser windows using the `_blank` option of the `target` attribute of an `<a>` tag — not a very impressive variety of features from which to choose. JavaScript, however, offers extensive control over various aspects of browser windows. In fact, manipulating windows is one of the most common uses of JavaScript.

Windows created in JavaScript are commonly referred to as *pop-up windows*. Pop-up windows are widely used in Web development, most commonly as online advertisements. It is important to remember that a pop-up window is simply another browser window that can show any URL.

Consider the following pop-up window, which was taken from a Web site on laser vision correction. Several The pop-up window demonstrates the various steps in the laser-vision-correction process. Several features of the browser were turned off in the pop-up window, and the window was sized to the proper width and height.

FIGURE 5.1

When a pop-up window appears on the screen, it draws focus away from the main window. This is often undesirable for Web site designers who use pop-up windows to display advertisements but do not want users to lose interest in the main page. Using various JavaScript techniques — which are aptly called create pop-up windows that display *behind* the main browser window — which are aptly called

Why Would I Do This? ◀ Introductory material at the beginning of each chapter provides an overview of why these tasks and procedures are important.

Visual Summary. A series of illustrations introduces the new tools, dialog boxes, and windows you will explore in each chapter. ▼

Chapter 3 Understanding the JavaScript Object Model

If the `myCar` object had a horn, you could write the following statement to call for the `honk()` method.

```
myCar.horn.honk();
```

Using an actual JavaScript method, you could write the following statement using dot syntax.

```
window.document.write("hello");
```

The document object is a subordinate object of the window object. The `write()` method belongs to the document object.

Use Dot Syntax

1 Copy the content of the Chapter_03 folder to the WIP_03 folder.

You use these files for the exercises in this chapter.

2 Open WIP_03>scenic.html in your browser and text editor.

FIGURE 3.2

This simple HTML file displays a photo.

3 Find the following code in the HTML file.

```
<img src="scenic.jpg" alt="Little River, SC" name="LittleRiver"
width="350" height="206" id="LittleRiver"/>
```

You should recognize this as the source of the image on your screen. When you use an `<img>` tag in HTML, an image object is also created in JavaScript.

4 Before the `</body>` tag, insert the following code to start a script.

VISUAL SUMMARY

Pop-up windows are simply browser windows created in JavaScript. Various aspects of the browser window are either turned off or disabled in pop-up windows. To better understand the basic characteristics of a pop-up window, it is useful to consider browser windows in general. The following screenshot shows the features of the browser window that you can turn on or off using JavaScript.

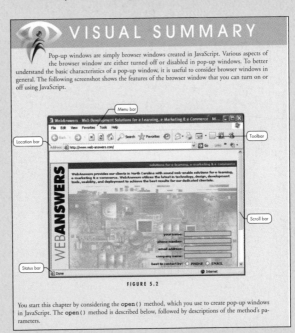

FIGURE 5.2

You start this chapter by considering the `open()` method, which you use to create pop-up windows in JavaScript. The `open()` method is described below, followed by descriptions of the method's parameters.

Step-by-Step Tutorials. ◀ Hands-on tutorials let you learn by doing and include numbered, bold, step-by-step instructions.

If You Have Problems. These short troubleshooting notes help you anticipate or solve common problems quickly and effectively.

CAREERS IN DESIGN

YOUR PROFESSIONAL PORTFOLIO

In today's volatile job market, most professionals find themselves in need of new jobs at one time or another during their careers. To make a job search as quick and painless as possible, Web designers and Web developers must prepare strong portfolios, as well as post a Web site that showcases their accomplishments. Every designer and developer — even those who feel secure in their current positions — should maintain strong portfolios and Web sites that highlight their professional achievements.

When you create a professional portfolio, include screenshots of Web pages that showcase your most creative work. Here are a few tips for creating an effective portfolio:

- Before creating screenshots, size your browser for the optimum resolution of the site you are highlighting.
- Avoid using pictures of yourself in either the site or interface.

Careers in Design. These features offer advice, tips, and resources that will help you on your path to a successful career.

To Extend Your Knowledge. These features provide extra tips, alternative ways to complete a process, and special hints about using the software.

To Extend Your Knowledge . . .

CONSTRUCTOR METHODS

Most constructor methods use the keyword new followed by a space and the type of object being created. A constructor function typically works in the following fashion:

```
myBirthdate=new Date();
```

In this example, a variable named **myBirthdate** represents a Date object. The keyword new indicates that a new object is being created, based on the Date class of objects. The word "Date" is capitalized because it represents a class of objects.

Create a Date Object with a Specific Day and Time

1. In the open constructor.html in your text editor, find the following line of code.

```
currentTime=new Date();
```

This code creates a variable named **currentTime** with the current date stored as the value.

End-of-Chapter Exercises. Extensive end-of-chapter exercises emphasize hands-on skill development. You'll find two levels of reinforcement: Skill Drill and Challenge. ▼

Chapter 4   Working with Variables   **155**

3. You are designing an online test that will ask three questions and then tell the user how many questions he answered correctly. Approximately how many variables do you need to accomplish this task? Name each variable you need and describe its purpose.

4. How are Boolean values different from string values? In what circumstances would Boolean values be useful?

SKILL DRILL

Skill Drill exercises reinforce chapter skills. Each skill reinforced is the same, or nearly the same, as a skill presented in the chapter. Detailed instructions are provided in a step-by-step format. You should work through the exercises in the order provided.

1. Declare Variables

In this Skill Drill, you practice declaring variables and assigning values to the variables. The exercise also asks you to output the value of a variable using the **var** keyword or simply assign values to the variables. You may declare the variables using the **var** keyword or simply assign values to the variables. The exercise also asks you to output the value of a variable in a user-friendly fashion.

1. In your text editor, open skilldeclare.html from the WIP_04 folder.

   A script was started for you.

2. In the script, directly above the **</script>** tag, create a variable named **"theNumber"** and set it equal to **"50"**.

3. Create a variable named **percentAmount** and set the variable equal to **"0.20"**.

4. Create a variable named **calcTotal** and set it equal to **theNumber** multiplied by the variable named **percentAmount**.

5. Create a **document.write()** statement to output the value of the **calcTotal** variable. Make sure you format the output from the **document.write()** statement in a user-friendly fashion.

6. Save the changes in your text editor.

7. Open the file in your browser. You should receive 10 as the result.

The calculation is equal to 10

FIGURE 4.25

8. Close the file in your text editor and browser.

32   Chapter 1   Using JavaScript

CHALLENGE

Challenge exercises expand on, or are somewhat related to, skills presented in the lessons. Each exercise provides a brief introduction, followed by instructions presented in a numbered-step format that are not as detailed as those in the Skill Drill exercises. You should work through these exercises in the order provided.

1. React to Customer Choices

You are a Web developer designing an ordering system for users who book ocean cruises online. On the ordering page, the user can choose the package she wants to book. Based on the user's choice, a script will process certain price details and perform other actions. In this exercise, you develop the functions that will be applied when the user makes a choice.

1. Open Chapter_01>challengecruise.html in your browser. Save it in your WIP_01 folder using the same name.

   This is a basic version of the ordering page you create in this exercise. When you click a link, a function processes the order.

FIGURE 1.26

2. Open the file in your text editor. In the head of the document, create the first function by inserting the following code.

```
<script language="JavaScript" type="text/javascript">
function pickBahamas () {
}
</script>
```

3. Place an alert command in the function that says, "You have picked the Bahamas package".

   This tells the user which package she chose. It also allows you to make sure the function works properly.

4. In the function you created in Step 2, add a comment to explain the purpose of the function. Find the <a> tag for the Bahamas Cruise. Add inline code to trigger the function when the user clicks the link.

Portfolio Builder. At the end of every chapter, these exercises require creative solutions to problems that reinforce the topic of the chapter. ▶

Chapter 5   Using Pop-Up Windows   **205**

PORTFOLIO BUILDER

Build an Interactive Online Gallery

An online image gallery is an effective use of Web interactivity: a user simply clicks a small image (a thumbnail) in a list, and a full-sized version of the image displays. An inexperienced developer building this type of gallery might link the thumbnail to a full-sized image in a normal browser window (not a pop-up). Doing so offers full control of browser toolbars and features — but also offers users an easy way to leave the gallery at any time. A better plan is to integrate JavaScript into the site's code, which allows the developer to control a user's expected behavior.

To prepare for this Portfolio Builder, open the gallery.html page in your browser and review the page. Click the first image; the browser replaces the thumbnail image with a full-size image. Click the Back button; the content of the browser is replaced several times. When you use pop-up windows, you can control the user's experience of the gallery.

To complete this Portfolio Builder, open the gallery.html page from your WIP_05>Portfolio_Builder_05 folder and review the page. Click the first image; the browser replaces the thumbnail image with a full-size image. Click the Back button; the content of the browser is replaced several times. When you use pop-up windows, you can control the user's experience of the gallery.

To complete this Portfolio Builder, enhance the functionality of the gallery.html page in the following ways.

- Create a pop-up window when the user clicks a thumbnail image. The pop-up should contain the full-size image. (The HTML pages and links for each image were created for you.)
- Control the features of the browser window.
- Resize the pop-up window according to the full-size image. Leave the "close window" link visible in the pop-up window.
- Insert the following code into the `<body>` tag.

```
onblur="window.close();"
```

This code checks the focus status (focus or blur) of the window and applies a `window.close()` method. When one of the pop-up windows loses focus (or becomes an inactive window), it automatically closes. This method allows you to avoid a series of pop-up windows that litter the screen when the main browser window closes. (Users will appreciate this thoughtful site design.)

543

INTEGRATING PROJECT

As a junior Web developer for a small marketing firm, you have been asked to use frames and JavaScript commands to finish and enhance a Web site that has been partially completed. The site you will create is a simplified version of Optometric Eye Care Centers actual site, which is located at www.EyeCareCenter.com.

The site is designed to be viewed in a frameset design. This allows several advantages, including ease of maintenance and the ability to keep branding and navigation structures visible at all times. For purposes of this project, assume that you are part of the design team that is building the site. The site structure and site design has been approved by the client. Content has been gathered and many of the components of the site have been built.

HTML pages have been built for the top and left navigation structures. Content pages have also been built. Every content page has been built using a standard template to ensure consistency and professionalism. In addition to the creation of the content pages, members of the project team have used JavaScript to create image rollovers for the navigation buttons, created artwork for a pop-up ad, and designed a Flash animation to show the steps involved in laser vision surgery.

As a Web developer, it will be your job to create the frameset that will bind the pages together in the browser window. Additionally, you will create the code to open a pop-up ad when the frameset is loaded and the code to create a pop-up window to display the Lasik animation. Lastly, you will use JavaScript to improve the usability of the site by adding links to close the ad pop-up window and to create "back" links on several pages.

Setting up the site

1. Copy the RF_JavaScript_L1>IP folder to your Work_In_Progress>WIP_IP folder.
2. Begin to explore the completed components of the site by opening WIP_IP>menu.html in your Web browser.
   This is the page that will form the left navigation structure. From this point forward, when asked to open a file, it is assumed the file will be located within the Work_In_Progress>WIP_IP folder.
3. Repeat step 2 with top.html and main.html to see the top navigation structure and main content page of the site.

Integrating Project. Integrating project are designed to reflect real-world graphic-design jobs, drawing on the skills you have learned throughout this book. ◀

556

ECMASCRIPT REFERENCE

Operations

Operator	Description
ARITHMETIC	
+	Adds 2 numbers.
++	Increments a number.
–	As a unary operator, negates the value of its argument. As a binary operator, subtracts 2 numbers.
--	Decrements a number.
*	Multiplies 2 numbers.
/	Divides 2 numbers.
%	Computes the integer remainder of dividing 2 numbers.
STRING	
+	Concatenates 2 strings.
+=	Concatenates 2 strings and assigns the result to the first operand.
LOGICAL OPERATORS	
&&	(Logical AND) Returns true if both logical operands are true. Otherwise, returns false.
||	(Logical OR) Returns true if either logical expression is true. If both are false, returns false.
!	(Logical negation) If its single operand is true, returns false; otherwise, returns true.
BITWISE OPERATORS	
&	(Bitwise AND) Returns a one in each bit position if bits of both operands are ones.
^	(Bitwise XOR) Returns a one in a bit position if bits of one but not both operands are one.
|	(Bitwise OR) Returns a one in a bit if bits of either operand is one.
~	(Bitwise NOT) Flips the bits of its operand.
<<	(Left shift) Shifts its first operand in binary representation the number of bits to the left specified in the second operand, shifting in zeros from the right.
>>	(Sign-propagating right shift) Shifts the first operand in binary representation the number of bits to the right specified in the second operand, discarding bits shifted off.
>>>	(Zero-fill right shift) Shifts the first operand in binary representation the number of bits to the right specified in the second operand, discarding bits shifted off, and shifting in zeros from the left.

Task Guides. These charts, found at the end of each book, list alternative ways to complete common procedures and provide a handy reference tool. ▶

STUDENT INFORMATION AND RESOURCES

Companion Web Site (www.prenhall.com/essentials).   This text-specific Web site provides students with additional information and exercises to reinforce their learning. Features include: additional end-of-chapter reinforcement material, online Study Guide, easy access to *all* resource files, and much, much more!

Before completing most chapters within this text, you will need to download the Resource files from the Student CD or from Prentice Hall's Companion Web site for the *Essentials for Design* Series. Check with your instructor for the best way to gain access to these files or simply follow these instructions:

If you are going to save these files to an external disk, make sure it is inserted into the appropriate drive before continuing.

1. Start your Web browser and go to http://www.prenhall.com/essentials

2. Select your textbook or series to access the Companion Web site. We suggest you bookmark this page, as it has links to additional Prentice Hall resources that you may use in class.

3. Click the Student Resources link.

4. Locate the files you need from the list of available resources and then click the link to download.

   Moving forward the process will vary depending upon which operating system (OS) you are using. Please select your OS and follow the instructions below:

   Windows OS:

5. Locate the files you need from the list of available resources and click the link to download.

6. When the File Download box displays, click the **Save** button.

7. In the Save As dialog box, select the location to which you wish to save the file. We recommend you saving the file to the Windows desktop or TEMP folder so it is easy to locate, but if you are working in a lab environment this may not be possible. To save to an external disk, simply type in or select your disk's corresponding drive. Example: a:\ where "a" designates an external disk drive.

8. Click the **Save** button to begin the downloading process.

9. Once the download is complete, navigate to the file using Windows Explorer.

10. Double-click on the file to begin the self extraction process and follow the step-by-step prompts.

Mac OS with Stuffit Expander 8.0.2 or greater:

5. Locate the files you need from the list of available resources and click the link to download.

6. With default settings the file will be downloaded to your desktop.

7. Once Download Manager shows status as "complete", double-click on the file to expand file.

NOTE: Stuffit Expander can be downloaded free at <http://www.stuffit.com/>

Mac OS with Stuffit Expander 8:

5. Locate the files you need from the list of available resources and click the link to download.

6. With default settings the file will be downloaded to your desktop.

7. Once Download Manager shows status as "complete", double-click on the file and choose Stuffit Expander as the application to expand file.

NOTE: Stuffit Expander can be downloaded free at <http://www.stuffit.com/>

Need help? Contact Tech Support Online at <http://247.prenhall.com>

Resource CD.   If you are using a Resource CD, all the files you need are provided on the CD. Resource files are organized in chapter-specific folders (e.g., Chapter_01, Chapter_02, etc.), which are contained in the RF_JavaScript_L1 folder. You can either work directly from the CD, or copy the files onto your hard drive before beginning the exercises.

Before you begin working on the chapters or lessons in this book, you should copy the Work_In_Progress folder from the Resource CD onto your hard drive or a removable disk/drive.

Resource Files.   Resource files are organized in chapter-specific folders, and are named to facilitate cross-platform compatibility. Words are separated by an underscore, and all file names include a lowercase three-letter extension. For example, if you are directed to open the file "graphics.eps" in Chapter 2, the file can be found in the RF_JavaScript_L1>Chapter_02 folder. We repeat these directions frequently in the early chapters.

The Work In Progress Folder.   This folder contains individual folders for each chapter in the book (e.g., WIP_01, WIP_02, etc.). When an exercise directs you to save a file, you should save it to the appropriate folder for the chapter in which you are working.

The exercises in this book frequently build upon work that you have already completed. At the end of each exercise, you will be directed to save your work and either close the file or continue to the next exercise. If you are directed to continue but your time is limited, you can stop at a logical point, save the file, and later return to the point at which you stopped. In this case, you will need to open the file from the appropriate WIP folder and continue working on the same file.

Typeface Conventions.   Computer programming code appears in a monospace font that `looks like this`. In many cases, you only need to change or enter specific pieces of code; in these instances, the code you need to type or change appears in a second color and `looks like this`.

INSTRUCTOR'S RESOURCES

Instructor's Resource Center.   This CD-ROM includes the entire Instructor's Manual for each application in Microsoft Word format. Student data files and completed solutions files are also on this CD-ROM. The Instructor's Manual contains a reference guide of these files for the instructor's convenience. PowerPoint slides with more information about each project are also available for classroom use. All instructor resources are also available online via the Companion Web site at www.prenhall.com/essentials.

TestGen Software.   TestGen is a test generator program that lets you view and easily edit test bank questions, transfer them to tests, and print the tests in a variety of formats suitable to your teaching situation. The program also offers many options for organizing and displaying test banks and tests. A built-in random number and text generator makes it ideal for creating multiple versions of tests. Powerful search and sort functions let you easily locate questions and arrange them in the order you prefer.

QuizMaster, also included in this package, enables students to take tests created with TestGen on a local area network. The QuizMaster utility built into TestGen lets instructors view student records and print a variety of reports. Building tests is easy with TestGen, and exams can be easily uploaded into WebCT, Blackboard, and CourseCompass.

Prentice Hall has formed close alliances with each of the leading online platform providers: WebCT, Blackboard, and our own Pearson CourseCompass.

INTRODUCTION

The incredible growth and widespread acceptance of the Internet often obscures the technology that lies behind all of the useful, entertaining, compelling, and (in some cases) disturbing Web pages. One fact, however, is certain: today's site visitor expects visual quality, navigational integrity, and — to an increasingly greater degree — interactivity.

The real world of designing, building, populating, publishing, and maintaining world-class Web sites is far more complex than most people might imagine. Rather than a single process, many smaller procedures and tasks form a workflow, which is usually divided between two distinct groups. The first group includes designers, copywriters, artists, illustrators, photographers, videographers, and other individuals responsible for the creative side of the equation. The other group is technical in nature — those who take care of the coding, testing, database setup, and ongoing site management. While there are certainly some individuals who can design compelling sites and write/test code, that group is relatively small. Generally, the creative side of the house determines how a site should look, and the technical side turns the design into a working reality — which is where JavaScript comes into play.

JavaScript is a universally accepted scripting language responsible for much of the active and interactive technology you encounter on the Web. Before you can use Macromedia Dreamweaver, Microsoft FrontPage, or Adobe GoLive to apply JavaScript code to a page design, you must understand the language itself. Familiarity with JavaScript is critical for those who need to exercise total control over the functionality of their sites.

As this is an introductory book, we assume you have no prior knowledge of JavaScript. If you have basic knowledge of both HTML and Web site construction, you will find the lessons in this book easy to follow and understand.

Despite widespread standardization of the JavaScript language, cross-platform incompatibilities remain. While writing completely compatible code that works correctly on every available browser is an admirable goal, it is currently impossible to attain. We worked diligently to provide code compliant across the widest possible selection of browsers, but some users will undoubtedly encounter compatibility problems. We apologize in advance for this inconvenience. To ensure the best results, we recommend you use Windows XP Professional and Internet Explorer 6.0, the platform we used when writing this book.

CHAPTER 1

Using JavaScript

OBJECTIVES

In this chapter, you learn how to:

- Integrate JavaScript into HTML documents

- Use inline JavaScript within HTML tags

- Create simple functions

- Insert programmer's comments into JavaScript source code

- Hide JavaScript code from incompatible browsers

- Display alternate content in noncompatible browsers

Why Would I Do This?

The JavaScript language was created to overcome the limitations of ***HTML***, which, as you probably know, is a simple markup language that tells a Web browser how to display a Web page. As HTML evolved, Web developers wanted increasing control over the user experience. In particular, developers wanted their pages to react to decisions made by the Web surfer and change accordingly. The framework of HTML did not lend itself to these types of enhancements. This led to the development of new scripting languages — based on more traditional computer programming principles — that would allow for an interactive user experience.

Netscape developed the LiveScript language for use in its Netscape Navigator Web browser. LiveScript's name was changed to JavaScript with the release of Navigator 2.0. The use of the name "JavaScript" was meant to capitalize on the popularity of Sun Microsystems' Java programming language. Even though they have many common characteristics, Java and JavaScript are distinct languages and should not be confused.

Microsoft developed its own version of JavaScript in Internet Explorer 4.0 called JScript. Although similar, the differences between JScript and JavaScript created problems for Web developers. In response to these issues, the European Computer Manufacturers Association (ECMA) developed a standardized version of JavaScript, which became known as ***ECMAScript***. Both Netscape and Microsoft now ensure that their browsers adhere to the ECMAScript standards, although both manufacturers have included additional features in their browsers that extend beyond these standards. The content of this book conforms to the ECMAScript standards.

HTML has recently evolved into XHTML. ***XHTML*** is very similar to traditional HTML, but contains new standards that will make the language more compatible with new technologies such as XML and Cascading Style Sheets (CSS). These standards, in turn, will make Web sites more compatible with mobile devices and new software applications. Minor changes are needed to allow existing JavaScript code to coexist within the XHTML standards.

Strict adherence to XHTML standards cannot be easily accomplished in most browsers. For this reason, the content of this book is written to conform to the transitional form of XHTML. ***Transitional XHTML*** allows most XHTML syntax rules to be implemented without requiring rules that would cause incompatibilities in common browsers. Transitional XHTML also allows developers to keep using HTML presentation elements, such as the <table> tag, which will be eventually removed from the language.

JavaScript allows users to interact with Web pages. It also allows developers to create content based on user choices and take greater control over the Web browser. You can use JavaScript in a number of common applications including:

- Creating a rollover, such as a button graphic, that changes when the user rolls the mouse over it.

- Validating the content of a field in a form, such as ensuring the user entered his e-mail address correctly.

- Computing a calculation, such as the amount of tax on a purchase order.

- Creating a pop-up window to display an advertisement. The ad displays in a separate window from the Web page that triggered it.

- Creating animation using a combination of JavaScript and other technologies, such as Cascading Style Sheets (CSS).

These applications include many of the most common uses of JavaScript. Since JavaScript contains much of the same functionality as traditional programming languages, many additional possibilities also exist.

In this chapter, you insert basic JavaScript commands into an HTML document, as well as learn how to use JavaScript functions. You include programmer's comments in your code. You also explore browser incompatibility issues and discover how to overcome them.

VISUAL SUMMARY

On a basic level, JavaScript is simply text that the browser interprets. JavaScript was designed to enhance HTML, not to replace it. JavaScript is often added to XHTML documents simply by inserting the `<script>` tag, which allows developers to incorporate other scripting languages within HTML pages.

Take a moment to examine the following XHTML code written in Notepad. This simple program tells the browser to display two messages to the user: the first message is "Hello"; the second message is "How are you?"

- You find the *file name* at the top of the window in the main Menu bar.

- The *<script> tag* allows you to insert JavaScript into an HTML document.

- The *language attribute* specifies the scripting language that appears within the HTML. Browsers often support a variety of scripting languages, with JavaScript being the most popular.

- The *type attribute* specifies the type of information included in the script.

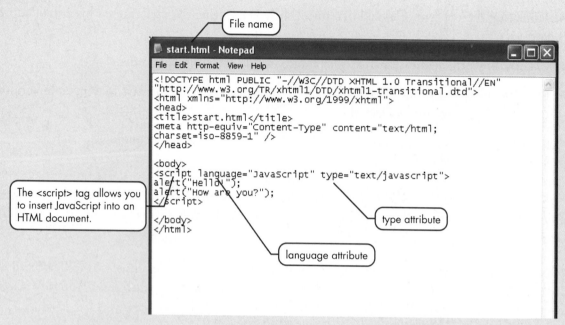

FIGURE 1.1

The following image shows how the above HTML code (with JavaScript) displays in a browser window.

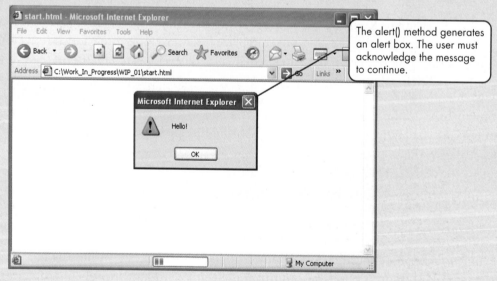

FIGURE 1.2

LESSON 1 Incorporating JavaScript into an HTML Document

JavaScript is a ***scripting language***, which is similar to a traditional programming language, but usually less powerful and often designed for a specific function. In JavaScript's case, the specific function is creating interactive Web pages. When you view a Web page in a browser, an interpreter decides how to display the HTML or JavaScript code and then returns information to the screen. This process is known as ***parsing***.

Most developers use JavaScript for ***client-side scripting***, which means the user's Web browser interprets JavaScript code. In ***server-side scripting***, the Web server processes the script instead of the user's computer. Server-side scripting requires more computer resources than client-side scripting, but is often necessary for tasks that include secure information, such as processing a credit card transaction. Common languages used for server-side scripting include ASP, Java, Visual Basic, and PHP.

You can use JavaScript in several ways:

- Embedding code between the HTML `<script>` and `</script>` tags. In this method, the `<script>` command tells the browser to use the JavaScript interpreter to interpret code until it finds the `</script>` tag.

- Using inline code within HTML code. ***Inline code*** usually means that a single JavaScript command appears inside an HTML tag. Typically, this command is associated with an event, such as when a user clicks a hyperlink.

- Defining code within the `<head>` section of an HTML document as a function that can be called upon within the body of the HTML document. Placing the JavaScript code at the top of the HTML document allows developers to keep track of the code and to reuse code several times without having to rewrite it.

- Storing JavaScript code in an external file that can be linked to the HTML document. This method offers a powerful way to share JavaScript code between multiple documents.

- Entering JavaScript directly into fields normally reserved for URLs. For example, typing `javascript:resizeTo(320,240);` into the address bar of a browser will cause the browser window to resize to 320 pixels wide and 240 pixels tall.

As you learned earlier, you can use the `<script>` tag to incorporate a scripting language into an HTML document. For example, you can use the statement `<script language="VBScript" type="text/VBScript">` to insert a script written in VBScript, which is a scripting language based loosely on Microsoft's Visual Basic programming language. Most browsers have the ability to interpret a variety of scripting languages. The list of available scripting languages varies with each browser.

If you use the `<script>` tag without specifying a language attribute, most browsers assume you mean JavaScript — since it is the most popular scripting language for browsers. We recommend that you always specify a language attribute, however, because most professional Web designers consider it sloppy programming to overlook that important element. The type element has a similar function and should be specified to avoid errors with XHTML compliance.

Methods

JavaScript commands follow a specific syntax — much stricter than the syntax used in XHTML. Included in that syntax are commands that perform actions, better known as *methods*. Think of a method as an action verb. For example, the **alert()** method generates an alert box that the user must acknowledge before he can proceed.

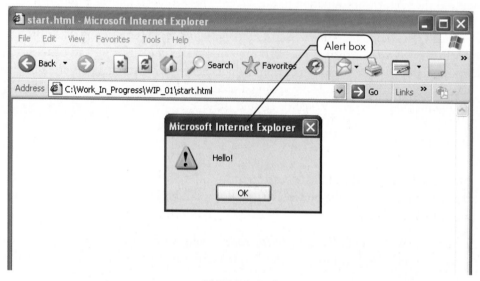

FIGURE 1.3

A method is always written with parentheses, such as **alert()**. Methods may require additional information to perform a specific action. You place that additional information within the parentheses. For example, the statement **document.write("hi");** sends the word "hi" to the screen. When sending information, such as a text message, use quotation marks to signal the beginning and ending of the text.

Use the <script> Tag

In this exercise, you use the **<script>** tag to insert basic JavaScript code into an HTML document. You also use the **alert()** method, a simple JavaScript command, to create a message box that the user must acknowledge before he can proceed.

1   **Open a simple text editor, such as TextEdit (Macintosh) or Notepad (Windows).**

JavaScript code is composed of plain text, the same as HTML. You use a text editor to enter much of the code in this book.

2   **Choose File>New.**

This creates a new document.

3   **Type the following code in your text editor.**

```
<!DOCTYPE html PUBLIC "-//W3C//DTD XHTML 1.0 Transitional//EN"
"http://www.w3.org/TR/xhtml1/DTD/xhtml1-transitional.dtd">
<html xmlns="http://www.w3.org/1999/xhtml">
<head>
<title></title>
</head>
<body>

</body>
</html>
```

These are the basic tags of a transitional XHTML document. The first two lines shown here must be typed as a single line of text (without hitting the Enter/Return key).

4   **Type the following code between the `<body>` and `</body>` tags.**

```
<!DOCTYPE html PUBLIC "-//W3C//DTD XHTML 1.0 Transitional//EN"
"http://www.w3.org/TR/xhtml1/DTD/xhtml1-transitional.dtd">
<html xmlns="http://www.w3.org/1999/xhtml">
<head>
<title></title>
</head>
<body>
<script language="JavaScript" type="text/javascript">
alert("Hello");
alert("How are you?");
</script>
</body>
</html>
```

The `<script>` tag allows you to insert JavaScript code into an HTML document. You can use the `<script>` tag in the head or body section of an HTML document. Notice how semicolons are used at the end of JavaScript statements. Semicolons help the interpreter to understand the JavaScript code.

5 Save the document as "start.html" in the Work_In_Progress>WIP_01 folder.

FIGURE 1.4

Your document should match the screenshot shown above.

6 **Launch your browser.**

We used Internet Explorer (IE) version 6 for the illustrations in this book. Your screen may look slightly different, depending on the browser you use and its configuration.

7 **Choose File>Open (or Open File).**

8 **Choose Browse>Work_In_Progress>WIP_01>start.html (or Locate File>Work_In_Progress>WIP_01> start.html).**

9 **Double-click the file.**

An alert box appears.

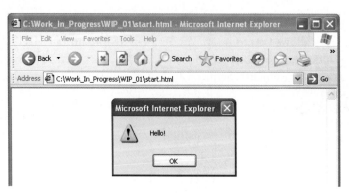

FIGURE 1.5

The alert box appears as soon as the interpreter encounters the **alert()** statement in the JavaScript code. The alert box draws focus from the main browser window and forces the user to acknowledge the message.

10 **Click OK.**

A second alert box appears.

FIGURE 1.6

Again, the user must acknowledge the message. The purpose of the **alert()** method is to create a message the user cannot ignore. Designers should use **alert()** messages sparingly, because some users find them annoying or distracting.

11 **Click OK to close the second alert box.**

12 **Close the file in your browser and text editor.**

To Extend Your Knowledge . . .

PROGRAMMING VS. SCRIPTING LANGUAGES

Traditional programming languages are platform specific, which means they convert to "machine code" that only the intended type of machine can read (UNIX or Windows or Macintosh). Scripting languages, on the other hand, are interpreted (parsed) by the software that reads them. Even though scripting languages usually run slower than programming languages, you can often use scripting languages on multiple hardware platforms — which is a significant benefit. Scripting languages also have built-in security features that stop developers from building harmful or malicious code that could harm a Web surfer's computer.

LESSON 2   Using Inline JavaScript

Inline JavaScript refers to JavaScript code used within an HTML tag. Inline JavaScript appears within quotes, the same as HTML tag attributes. With inline JavaScript, you do not use the **<script>** tag.

Inline JavaScript is triggered by an ***event***, which is an action the user performs, such as clicking an image or a button. An ***event handler*** is a ***keyword*** (a word that has a meaning in the language used) that allows the computer to detect an event. For instance, all event handlers, methods, and other JavaScript commands are keywords in the JavaScript language. JavaScript event handlers can appear as HTML tag attributes or properties.

The event handler tells JavaScript when to carry out a command. In the example below, the **alert()** command activates when the user clicks the mouse (onclick is the event handler).

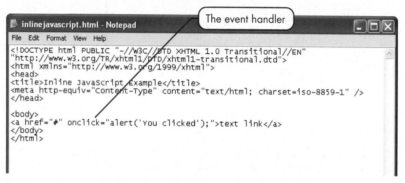

FIGURE 1.7

Use Inline JavaScript in an HTML Tag

In this exercise, you use inline JavaScript within a single HTML tag.

1   **Copy the content of the RF_JavaScript_L1>Chapter_01 folder into your Work_In_Progress>WIP_01 folder.**

Make sure to turn off read-only attributes for these files. You use these files throughout this chapter.

From now on, we refer to the RF_JavaScript_L1>Chapter_01 folder simply as the Chapter_01 folder, and the Work_In_Progress>WIP_01 folder simply as the WIP_01 folder.

2   **Navigate to the WIP_01 folder. Open event.html in your text editor.**

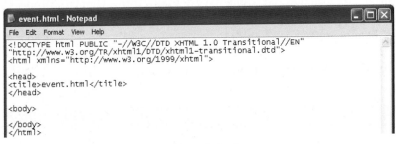

FIGURE 1.8

The page is a very simple XHTML document.

3   **Change the `<body>` tag to read as follows.**

```
<head>
<title>event.html</title>
</head>
<body onload="alert('Welcome to my Web site!');">
</body>
</html>
```

You attached an event handler to the **`<body>`** tag as inline JavaScript.

4   **Between the `<body>` and `</body>` tags, enter the following.**

```
<title>event.html</title>
</head>
<body onload="alert('Welcome to my Web site!');">
<p>Once the page is loaded, you will see a welcome message!</p>
</body>
</html>
```

FIGURE 1.9

These text instructions create a user-friendly page.

5   **Save the file in your WIP_01 folder.**

Some versions of Notepad add .txt to the file extension. If this happens, simply change the file extension to ".html". TextEdit in Macintosh also asks if we want to append the "txt" extension. Student should click "Do not append".

6   **Open the file in your Web browser and view the result.**

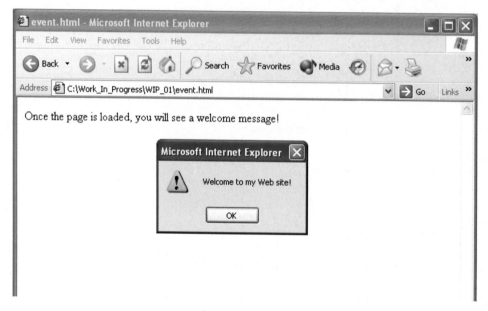

FIGURE 1.10

7   **Close the file in your text editor and browser.**

To Extend Your Knowledge . . .

EVENT HANDLERS AND INLINE JAVASCRIPT

Most practical uses of JavaScript involve event handlers used inline in HTML. Usually, developers want to trigger chunks of scripting code when a specific event occurs in HTML, such as the submission of a form or the user rolling over an image.

LESSON 3   Understanding Functions

Functions are named, reusable sections of code that exist in the head or body section of an HTML document, or in an external file. Functions allow developers to reuse code without having to retype it every time they use it. For instance, when you place a function in an external file, all the documents in a Web site can access (share) the function. In addition, information can be sent to a function and a function can send information back to other scripts or other functions. (We examine functions in detail later in this book.)

The keyword **function** creates a named, reusable section of code. Functions are typically triggered by event handlers that appear as HTML tag attributes. In the example shown below, the function triggers when the user clicks the image.

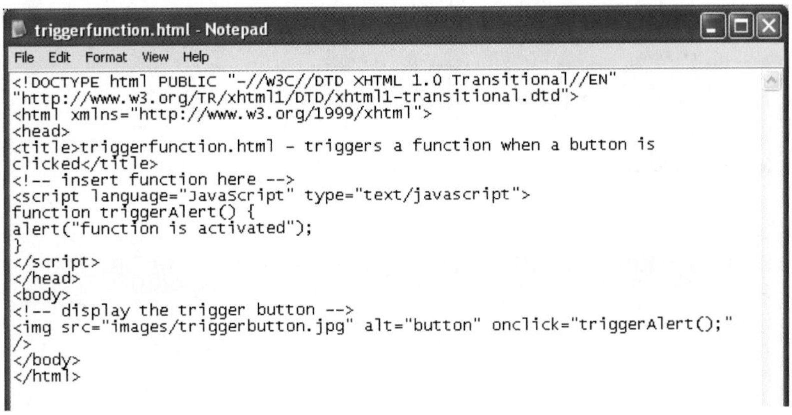

```
triggerfunction.html - Notepad
File  Edit  Format  View  Help
<!DOCTYPE html PUBLIC "-//W3C//DTD XHTML 1.0 Transitional//EN"
"http://www.w3.org/TR/xhtml1/DTD/xhtml1-transitional.dtd">
<html xmlns="http://www.w3.org/1999/xhtml">
<head>
<title>triggerfunction.html - triggers a function when a button is
clicked</title>
<!-- insert function here -->
<script language="JavaScript" type="text/javascript">
function triggerAlert() {
alert("function is activated");
}
</script>
</head>
<body>
<!-- display the trigger button -->
<img src="images/triggerbutton.jpg" alt="button" onclick="triggerAlert();"
/>
</body>
</html>
```

FIGURE 1.11

In the example above, the double slash marks (**/ /**) denote a single-line comment. Developers often insert comments directly into their source code to explain how the code was written or the purpose of a line of code. When an interpreter encounters double slash marks, it ignores all the text that follows the marks and automatically advances to the start of the next line.

Use a Simple Function

In this exercise, you create a simple function in the head of the HTML document.

1   **Navigate to your WIP_01 folder. Open triggerfunction.html in your text editor.**

```
triggerfunction.html - Notepad
File  Edit  Format  View  Help
<!DOCTYPE html PUBLIC "-//W3C//DTD XHTML 1.0 Transitional//EN"
"http://www.w3.org/TR/xhtml1/DTD/xhtml1-transitional.dtd">
<html xmlns="http://www.w3.org/1999/xhtml">
<head>
<title>triggerfunction.html - triggers a function when a button is
clicked</title>
<!-- insert function here -->
</head>
<body>
<!-- display the trigger button -->
<img src="images/triggerbutton.jpg" alt="button" />
</body>
</html>
```

FIGURE 1.12

This simple HTML page displays an image. You use the image as a button.

2   **Open the file in your browser.**

```
triggerfunction.html - triggers a function when a button is clicked - Microsoft Intern...
File  Edit  View  Favorites  Tools  Help
Back  ·        ·        Search   Favorites   Media
Address   C:\Work_In_Progress\WIP_01\triggerfunction.html          Go   Links

trigger
function
```

FIGURE 1.13

The button hasn't yet been programmed to do anything.

3   **Return to your text editor. Find the following code in the head section of the document between the <head> and </head> tags.**

```
<!--insert function here-->
```

4   **Insert the following code before the </head> tag.**

```
<head>
<title>triggerfunction.html—triggers a function when a button is
    clicked</title>
<!--insert function here-->
<script language="JavaScript" type="text/javascript">
```

```
function triggerAlert() {
alert("function is activated");
}
</script>
</head>
<body>
```

This code contains a basic function that triggers an alert box when activated. Next, you add the code to trigger the function.

5 | **Find the following code in your text editor.**

```
<!--display the trigger button-->
<img src="images/triggerbutton.jpg" alt="button"/>
```

6 | **Change the <img> tag to read as follows.**

```
<body>
<!--display the trigger button -->
<img src="images/triggerbutton.jpg" alt="button"
    onclick="triggerAlert();"/>
</body>
</html>
```

Adding an event handler to the **<img>** tag triggers a JavaScript function when the user clicks the object.

7 | **Save the file in your text editor. Refresh the file in your browser.**

8 | **Click the button image.**

The alert box displays on the screen. You may also notice that the mouse pointer does not change to a hand to indicate you can click the image (which happens when the content appears within an **<a>** tag).

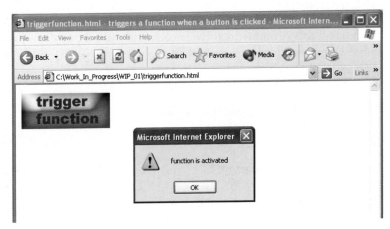

FIGURE 1.14

9 Click OK to close the alert box.

10 Close the file in your Web browser and text editor.

To Extend Your Knowledge . . .

FUNCTIONS AND EVENT HANDLERS

Inline JavaScript can contain multiple code statements, which can quickly lead to cumbersome code that becomes difficult to read. It is much more common to use inline JavaScript to trigger a single function. This allows the code statements to be placed in the function instead of within the inline JavaScript code.

LESSON 4 Programmer's Comments

In the first three lessons, you discovered how to incorporate JavaScript into HTML documents — but you have not yet examined the specifics of how JavaScript works. To understand how the language operates, you must learn the basic rules of writing effective code.

One such rule is including programmer's comments in your code. ***Programmer's comments*** are messages that programmers insert directly into their source code to explain how the code was written. (You used HTML comments in the previous exercise.) Think of a programmer's comment as an electronic post-it note that is only visible to someone who views the source code. End users who view the page in the browser cannot see programmer's comments, and the JavaScript interpreter ignores them.

Using JavaScript Comments

In this exercise, you add programmer's comments to your code and view the results in your browser. You use single-line (**//**) and multiple-line JavaScript comments (**/*** and ***/**). You can use these types of comments in other languages besides JavaScript.

1 Open WIP_01>comments.html in your text editor.

2 Insert a blank line after the following code statement.

```
<script language="JavaScript" type="text/javascript">
```

3 Insert the following line of code.

```
</head>
<body>
<script language="JavaScript" type="text/javascript">
```

```
//this page outputs text to the window
document.write("Hello");
document.write("How are you?");
</script>
```

This statement creates a single-line programmer's comment in the source code. The interpreter ignores any text after the "//" until the start of the next line.

4   **Open the file in your browser.**

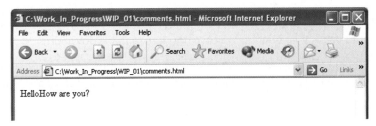

FIGURE 1.15

The **document.write()** statements output information to the screen. Notice how the content of the **document.write()** statements appears on the same line. The browser ignores the comment you created in Step 3 (it does not display in the browser window).

5   **Add /* before the second document.write() statement. Add */ after the semicolon in the same line. Your code should now match the following.**

```
<!DOCTYPE html PUBLIC "-//W3C//DTD XHTML 1.0 Transitional//EN"
"http://www.w3.org/TR/xhtml1/DTD/xhtml1-transitional.dtd">
<html xmlns="http://www.w3.org/1999/xhtml">
<head>
<title>Comments.html</title>
</head>
<body>
<script language="JavaScript" type="text/javascript">
//this page outputs text to the window
document.write("Hello");
/* document.write("How are you?"); */
</script>
</body>
</html>
```

The "/*" and "*/" symbols are designed to create multiple-line comments. If you prefer, you can place them on the same line (a single-line comment), as we did in this step.

6   **Save the changes to your text file.**

7 **Click the Refresh button in the browser.**

FIGURE 1.16

The browser does not display any information contained within a JavaScript comment. The second `document.write()` command is now within a comment, so it does not appear in the browser window.

8 **Keep the file open in both programs for the next exercise.**

To Extend Your Knowledge...

COMMENTS

Use comments to leave notes to yourself or other programmers about the purpose of code statements. Comments are particularly useful when viewing complex code.

LESSON 5 Hiding JavaScript Code from Incompatible Browsers

Inserting programmer's comments into code is an excellent way to provide information to other developers. These comments are invaluable to developers who are trying to understand and often improvise code written by others. Since programmer's comments are ignored by browsers, they can sometimes also be used to hide scripting code that is incompatible with older browsers.

Consider JavaScript as an example. When the language was incorporated into browsers, many older browser versions were still being used that could not interpret JavaScript code. This created serious compatibility issues, with many browsers attempting to display the JavaScript code to the user as if it were text entered into an HTML document.

All modern-day browsers can interpret JavaScript code. Older versions of IE, Navigator, and other browsers, however, cannot interpret JavaScript code. Many times, inability to interpret script code results in the comments displaying in the browser window; this, of course, negatively impacts the viewer's experience.

The work-around for this problem is simple: combine programmer's comments with HTML comment tags. This method hides JavaScript code from browsers that cannot interpret the **<script>** tag or the scripting language contained between the **<script>** and **</script>** tags. For example:

```
<script language="JavaScript" type="text/javascript">
<!-- this line starts an HTML comment to hide JavaScript code-->
document.writeln("Hello");
// this line ends the HTML comment block-->
</script>
</body>
</html>
```

The <noscript> Tag

The above work-around works well with browsers that do not support the **<script>** tag or the JavaScript language. Notice that the **<script>** tag itself is not included within the HTML comment tag. If it were included, the HTML interpreter would ignore the tag completely. Browsers are designed to display problematic or newer code whenever possible. For this reason, browsers ignore HTML tags they do not understand. For example, older browsers will ignore the **<script>** tag.

The **<noscript>** tag allows you to create content that only displays in browsers that do not support the **<script>** tag. Even though most modern browsers support the **<script>** tag, it is considered good form among Web developers to be prepared for the rare circumstance when a particular browser does not support the feature. We recommended that you always include the **<noscript>** tag within your JavaScript code.

Hide Code from Incompatible Browsers

In the following exercises, you use a combination of HTML and JavaScript to ensure that noncompatible browsers display code correctly.

1 **Open WIP_01>comments.html in your text editor. Change the code to match the following.**

```
</head>
<body>
<script language="JavaScript" type="text/javascript">
<!-- this line starts an HTML comment to hide JavaScript code
document.write("Hello");
/* document.write("How are you?"); */
// this line ends the HTML comment block -->
</script>
</body>
</html>
```

2 **Save the changes to the file.**

3 **With the file open in your Web browser, click the Refresh button.**

The comments in this code are hidden from browsers that cannot interpret JavaScript. Since most current Web browsers can interpret JavaScript code, you probably do not see a change in the content that displays on your screen.

4   **Keep the file open in your text editor and browser for the next exercise.**

Add a <noscript> Tag to a Web Page

1   **With comments.html open in your text editor, insert a blank line below the `</script>` tag.**

2   **Insert the following code.**

```
document.write("How are you?");
// this line ends the HTML comment block -->
</script>
<noscript>
Your browser doesn't support JavaScript or JavaScript is disabled.
JavaScript is required to view this page correctly.
</noscript>
</body>
</html>
```

The new content you added only displays in browsers that cannot interpret the **`<script>`** tag. Your file should match the following illustration.

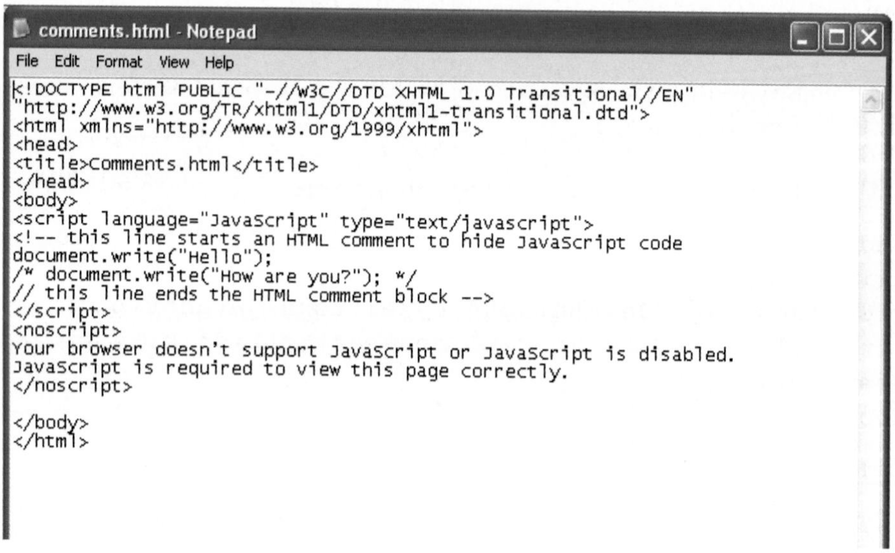

```
comments.html - Notepad
File  Edit  Format  View  Help
<!DOCTYPE html PUBLIC "-//W3C//DTD XHTML 1.0 Transitional//EN"
"http://www.w3.org/TR/xhtml1/DTD/xhtml1-transitional.dtd">
<html xmlns="http://www.w3.org/1999/xhtml">
<head>
<title>Comments.html</title>
</head>
<body>
<script language="JavaScript" type="text/javascript">
<!-- this line starts an HTML comment to hide JavaScript code
document.write("Hello");
/* document.write("How are you?"); */
// this line ends the HTML comment block -->
</script>
<noscript>
Your browser doesn't support JavaScript or JavaScript is disabled.
JavaScript is required to view this page correctly.
</noscript>

</body>
</html>
```

FIGURE 1.17

3   **Save the changes to the file.**

4   **Refresh the file in your browser.**

Since most browsers support the `<script>` tag, it is unlikely that you see the content generated by the `<noscript>` tag. Users whose browsers don't support JavaScript see a message that says they need JavaScript to view the page correctly.

5   **Close the file in your text editor and browser.**

To Extend Your Knowledge . . .

TURNING ON SCRIPT ERROR NOTIFICATIONS

By default, most browsers ignore errors generated by scripting languages, including those generated by JavaScript. This follows HTML's tradition of allowing non-perfect code to display as accurately as possible to shield the end user from minor problems.

To view errors generated by scripting languages, you can turn on the error notifications feature. In newer versions of Internet Explorer, choose Tools>Internet Options>Advanced, and then check the box marked "Display a Notification About Every Script Error." Users may be surprised at the number of errors generated by popular Web sites, many of which result from minor differences in how browsers interpret the JavaScript code.

LESSON 6   Case Sensitivity

Case sensitivity refers to a language's ability to distinguish between uppercase (capital) and lowercase (small) letters. Languages that distinguish between uppercase and lowercase letters are ***case sensitive***. A case-sensitive program that expects you to enter all commands in uppercase does not respond correctly if you enter one or more characters in lowercase. For example, the word "Document" is viewed differently than the word "document." Programs that do not distinguish between uppercase and lowercase letters are ***case insensitive***.

JavaScript is a case-sensitive language. It is different than HTML, which ignores differences between upper- and lowercase letters. For this reason, users must be aware of the proper spelling of JavaScript commands. Errors in case often cause difficult-to-find problems in JavaScript code.

Add Errors to Your Code

In this exercise, you purposely introduce script errors by changing the capitalization of a JavaScript keyword. Depending on your browser and its configuration, this may create an error, the browser may ignore it, or it may display correctly — despite the capitalization error. To ensure the best results in real-world situations, follow the JavaScript standard guidelines for capitalization.

1   **In your text editor and browser, open errors.html from your WIP_01 folder.**

2   Change the "d" in the `document.write()` command to "D". Your code should resemble the following.

```
...
<body>
<script language="JavaScript" type="text/javascript">
<!-- this line starts an HTML comment to hide JavaScript code
Document.write("Hello");
// this line ends the HTML comment block -->
</script>
...
```

3   Save the change to the file.

4   Make sure the file is open in your browser. Click the Refresh button to reload the page.

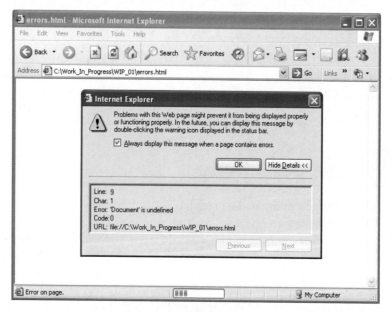

FIGURE 1.18

Most browsers ignore the **Document.writeln()** statement. Depending on which browser you use and how it is configured, the JavaScript interpreter may display an error message. Let's correct the capitalization error.

5   Return to the text editor and change the uppercase "D" to a lowercase "d".

Your statement should now read **document.write("Hello");**.

6   Save the document in your text editor. Refresh the file in the browser.

You should no longer see the error.

7   Close the file in your text editor and browser.

To Extend Your Knowledge...

MORE ABOUT CASE SENSITIVITY

In older browsers event handlers used in HTML commands aren't case sensitive because they appear as HTML attributes — and as you know, HTML is not case sensitive. In many older pages, for example, `onclick` is spelled as `onClick`. XHTML compliance now requires that all HTML attributes be written in lower case, including JavaScript event handlers.

To complicate matters, some browsers ignore some case mistakes in JavaScript code or even require case errors. For example, older versions of Internet Explorer for the Mac require the `onclick` event to be written as `onClick`. This often creates problems, since the developer doesn't notice the error until the code is tested in another browser. For best results, always consult a reference book (such as this one) to confirm your use of upper or lower case.

CAREERS IN DESIGN

YOUR PROFESSIONAL PORTFOLIO

In today's volatile job market, most professionals find themselves in need of new jobs at one time or another during their careers. To make a job search as quick and painless as possible, Web designers and Web developers must prepare strong portfolios, as well as post a Web site that showcases their accomplishments. Every designer and developer — even those who feel secure in their current positions — should maintain strong portfolios and Web sites that highlight their professional achievements.

When you create a professional portfolio, include screenshots of Web pages that showcase your most creative work. Here are a few tips for creating an effective portfolio:

- Before creating screenshots, size your browser for the optimum resolution of the site you are highlighting.
- Avoid using pictures of yourself in either the site or interface.
- Clearly state how you contributed to the project. Avoid the temptation to make it appear as though you were a one-person show; give credit where credit is due.
- List the tools you used to complete the project. Avoid mentioning the version numbers of software, however, because they change frequently and may cause your skill set to appear outdated.
- Ask someone to proofread your copy, which is best when concise and to the point.

SUMMARY

In this chapter, you explored the various ways that JavaScript code can be integrated into HTML pages. It is important to remember that JavaScript was created to extend the capabilities of HTML, not to replace it. When you understand this basic philosophy, you will know how and when to use JavaScript.

You learned that you can use the `<script>` tag to integrate JavaScript into an HTML page. You also learned that Web designers can create named, reusable blocks of code called functions. You discovered how to include programmer's comments, which provide useful information to anyone viewing your source code. You discovered that JavaScript code can be triggered by event handlers that usually appear as attributes of HTML tags. Finally, you explored many browser compatibility issues and learned how to use HTML and the `<noscript>` tag to work around those problems.

KEY TERMS

Case insensitive	Function	Programmer's comment
Case sensitive	HTML	<script> tag
Client-side scripting	Inline code	Scripting language
ECMAScript	Keyword	Server-side scripting
Event	Language attribute	Transitional XHTML
Event handler	Method	Type attribute
File name	Parsing	XHTML

CHECKING CONCEPTS AND TERMS

MULTIPLE CHOICE

Circle the letter of the correct answer for each of the following questions.

1. JavaScript and Java are the same language.
   a. True
   b. False

2. JavaScript is primarily used for _____.
   a. client-side scripting
   b. server-side scripting
   c. creating machine-code files
   d. creating vector graphics

3. ECMAScript _____.
   a. is completely different than JavaScript
   b. is the standardized version of JavaScript

   c. is an old-English font style
   d. is a combination of CSS and JavaScript

4. Inline code refers to code that _____.
   a. is typed without unnecessary white space
   b. is standardized for all browsers
   c. performs an action
   d. appears within an HTML tag

5. A function _____.
   a. is a named, easily reusable piece of code
   b. refers to an occurrence that can be detected by the computer

c. refers to an aspect of an object in JavaScript

d. is part of a programmer's comment

6. The alert() method in JavaScript _____.

a. sends a message to a Web server

b. validates a form

c. requires the end user to acknowledge a message

d. creates a rollover effect for an image

7. The statement Document.write("hi"); will not work in most browsers because _____.

a. the document.write() method requires a Netscape browser

b. the "D" in document is capitalized, and JavaScript requires lowercase letters (it is case sensitive)

c. script error notifications may be turned off in the browser

d. the statement should not have a period between the keyword "document" and the "write()" method

8. The <noscript> tag is used _____.

a. to create content that can be seen by browsers that cannot read the <script> tag

b. to force the browser to ignore any scripts used in the Web page

c. to turn off script error notifications

d. as a JavaScript method

9. The <script> tag _____.

a. must appear within the <head> and </head>tags of an HTML document

b. must appear within the <body> and </body> tags of an HTML document

c. must appear within the <p> and </p> tags in an HTML document

d. can appear within the head or body section of an HTML document

10. You can use the <script> tag _____.

a. to insert JavaScript into an HTML document

b. to insert other scripting languages, such as VBScript, into an HTML document

c. to specify the language attribute when using JavaScript

d. All of the above.

DISCUSSION QUESTIONS

1. Name four ways to insert JavaScript code into an HTML document. Name three common uses for JavaScript code placed into an HTML document.

2. What is the purpose of an event handler? What is inline JavaScript code? Why do you use event handlers in HTML tags?

3. What is a function? Why are functions often placed in an external document?

SKILL DRILL

Skill Drills reinforce lesson skills. Each skill reinforced is the same, or nearly the same, as a skill presented in the lessons. Detailed instructions are provided in a step-by-step format. You can work through one or more exercise(s) in any order.

1. Ask a User to Acknowledge an Alert Message

You are a Web designer. Last month, your client asked you to create a Web page that allows customers to choose options for customized binders. Certain options are only allowed when other options are also chosen. For example, if the user chooses a three-ring binder, he must also choose a glossy finish for the binder.

Currently, the page generates an alert box when the user chooses incompatible options. After the user clicks OK to acknowledge the alert box, the user's choices change automatically. Your client wants to modify this system to allow the user to confirm that he accepts the required changes or cancel the change.

You can use the **confirm()** method to make these changes. This method is similar to the **alert()** method, which is currently used on the page. The client asked you to create a test page to demonstrate the changes. In this exercise, you create the mock-up test page.

1. In your text editor, open skillcurrent.html from your WIP_01 folder.

2. Add a descriptive title between the **<title>** and **</title>** tags.

3. Insert the code necessary to create an alert box. When the box displays, it should say, "You must choose a glossy finish with a 3-ring binder. Your choice will be changed."

4. Save your file and open it in your browser.

5. Your page should match the following screenshot.

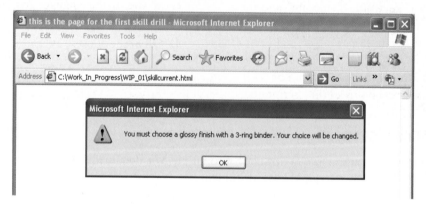

FIGURE 1.19

6. Choose OK to acknowledge the alert message.

7. Close the file in your browser and text editor.

2. Use the confirm() Method

In the previous drill, you created an alert to notify a user that a change had been made in their order. Assume this can create a bad user experience and it would work better to allow users to decide whether they wanted to accept the proposed change. In the following drill, you create a file to confirm the change.

1. In your text editor and browser, open skillconfirm.html.

   This is essentially the same file you created in the previous drill.

2. Change the text of the alert message to, "You must choose a glossy finish with a 3-ring binder. Would you like to change to a glossy finish?"

3. In the code, change the word "**alert**" to "**confirm**" to change to the new method.

4. Save the file and refresh it in your browser.

   The file should now ask a question the user can confirm by clicking OK or cancel by clicking Cancel, as shown below.

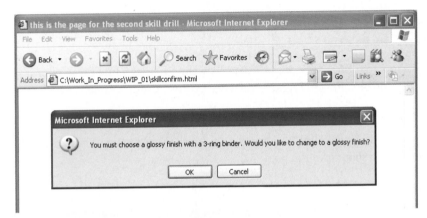

FIGURE 1.20

5. Choose Cancel to deny the confirmation.

6. Close the file in your browser and text editor.

3. Write Information to the Screen

In this drill, you take a closer look at the **document.write()** and **document.writeln()** methods. You discover how you can use these methods to write information to the screen.

1. In your browser and text editor, open skillwrite.html from your WIP_01 folder.

2. Create a script in the body section of the document.

3. Create two different **document.write()** statements that output messages to the screen. In the first statement, enter your name. In the second statement, enter a few hobbies that you enjoy.

4. Save the file and refresh it in your browser.

   In the following illustration, the first **document.write()** statement is "Joe Smith," and the second is "Golf, darts". Notice how all the text appears on the same line.

FIGURE 1.21

5. Return to your document and change the **document.write()** statements to "**document.writeln()**". Make sure to use a lowercase "L" in **writeln()**.

The "ln" is short for "line." The **writeln()** method inserts a line break after it writes text to the screen. Most browsers, however, ignore carriage returns in source code.

6. Save the file and refresh it in the browser.

Older browsers may show a line break at the end of the **writeln()** statement. Newer browsers may insert a single space into the text.

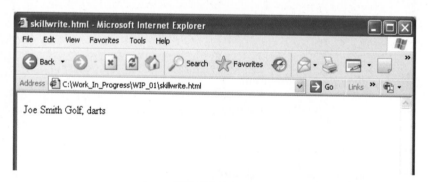

FIGURE 1.22

It appears that JavaScript, similar to HTML, ignores line breaks when writing text to the browser window.

7. Return to your code. Place the **<pre>** tag before the **<script>** tag, and place the **</pre>** tag after the **</script>** tag.

The **<pre>** tag causes the text to render exactly as it was typed, including all spaces and line breaks.

8. Save the file and refresh it in the browser.

The text appears on separate lines because the browser acknowledges the carriage return.

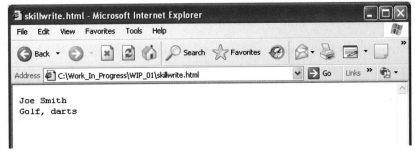

FIGURE 1.23

9. Remove the **<pre>** and **</pre>** tags from your document. Save the file and refresh it in your browser.

    The browser again ignores the carriage returns. This exercise reveals another aspect of the **document.write()** and **document.writeln()** statements: text sent to the screen is interpreted the same way as text in an HTML document.

10. Change the first **document.writeln()** statement to include the **<p>** and **</p>** tags. For example, if your name were Joe Smith, your first line of code would appear as **document.writeln("<p>Joe Smith</p>");**.

11. Save the file and refresh it in the browser.

    Notice that the browser interprets the **<p>** tag as HTML code. In other words, text placed in a **document.write()** or **document.writeln()** statement is sent to the HTML interpreter before it displays on the screen. This is very useful for formatting text created with these methods.

FIGURE 1.24

12. Close the file in your browser and text editor.

4. Add <noscript> Content to an Existing Page

In this exercise, you create content for viewers whose browsers cannot process JavaScript code.

1.   In your text editor and browser, open "skillnoscript.html" from your WIP_01 folder.

2.   Create a script in the body section of your document.

3.   Insert code to create two alert boxes. The first box should say, "Welcome to My Site". The second box should say, "Goodbye!"

4.   Save the file and test it in your Web browser.

5.   Return to your text editor. Use comments to hide the script from incompatible browsers.

6.   Save the file in your text editor and refresh your browser to ensure that you entered the comments correctly.

7.   Return to your text editor. After the **</script>** tag, add the **<noscript>** tag to create content for browsers that cannot interpret the **<script>** tag.

8.   Insert text for the **<noscript>** tag. The text should say, "You need a JavaScript-capable browser."

9.   Add a **</noscript>** tag.

10.   Save the file and refresh it in your browser.

   Since you probably have a JavaScript-capable browser, you most likely won't see a change in your script.

11.   Close the file in the text editor and browser.

5. Use a Mouse Event

In this exercise, you use an event handler and create inline JavaScript. The event handler triggers JavaScript code when the user chooses a text link in an HTML page.

1.   In your text editor and browser, open skillmouse.html from your WIP_01 folder.

2.   Create a hyperlink by placing the following code in the body section of your document.

```
<title>skillmouse.html</title>
</head>
<body>
<a href="#">link text</a>
</body>
</html>
```

Notice the link uses a placeholder (#) instead of an actual URL. When you use a placeholder, your link does not go anywhere when clicked, but appears and acts as any other hyperlink.

3. Add inline JavaScript to the hyperlink to create an alert box when the user clicks the hyperlink text. Use the **onclick** event handler to accomplish this task. The alert box should say, "You clicked".

4. Save the file in your WIP_01 folder. Refresh the file in your browser.

   An alert box should appear when you click the text.

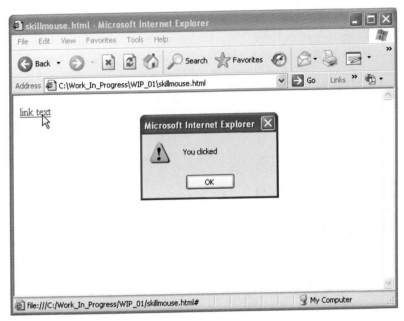

FIGURE 1.25

5. Return to the document in your text editor. Change the **onclick** event handler to "**onmouseover**".

6. Save the file and refresh it in the browser.

   The message should now appear when you move the mouse over the hyperlink text.

7. Change the placeholder (#) in the **href** attribute of the **<a>** tag to the following URL.

   `http://www.prenhall.com/essentials/`

8. Save the file and refresh it in the browser. Roll your mouse over the hyperlink. Does the action still work?

9. Change the event handler back to **onclick**. Click the link.

   Does the page change to the new URL? Does the alert box appear? Do both actions take place when you click the text?

10. Close the file in your browser and text editor.

CHALLENGE

Challenge exercises expand on, or are somewhat related to, skills presented in the lessons. Each exercise provides a brief introduction, followed by instructions presented in a numbered-step format that are not as detailed as those in the Skill Drill exercises. You should work through these exercises in the order provided.

1. React to Customer Choices

You are a Web developer designing an ordering system for users who book cruises online. On the ordering page, the user can choose the package she wants to book. Based on the user's choice, a script will process certain price details and perform other actions. In this exercise, you develop the functions that will be applied when the user makes a choice.

1. Open Chapter_01>challengecruise.html in your browser. Save it in your WIP_01 folder using the same name.

   This is a basic version of the ordering page you create in this exercise. When you click a link, a function processes the order.

FIGURE 1.26

2. Open the file in your text editor. In the head of the document, create the first function by inserting the following code.

```
<script language="JavaScript" type="text/javascript">
function pickBahamas () {
}
</script>
```

3. Place an alert command in the function that says, "You have picked the Bahamas package".

   This tells the user which package she chose. It also allows you to make sure the function works properly.

4. In the function you created in Step 2, add a comment to explain the purpose of the function.

5. Find the <a> tag for the Bahamas Cruise. Add inline code to trigger the function when the user clicks the link.

```
<a href="#" onclick="pickBahamas()">Bahamas Cruise</a>
| <a href="#">Alaska Cruise</a>
| <a href="#">Caribbean Cruise </a>
```

6. Save the file and test it in your browser.

    Assuming you completed the steps correctly, the alert box appears when you click the Bahamas Cruise link.

7. Return to your text editor. Create a function named "pickAlaska" and another named "pickCaribbean". Place a comment in each function to explain its purpose. Place an alert command in each function to tell the user which package he chose.

8. Insert inline code to trigger the pickAlaska function when a user clicks the Alaska Cruise link.

9. Insert inline code to trigger the pickCaribbean function when a user clicks the Caribbean Cruise link.

10. Save and test your file.

11. Keep the file open for the next exercise.

2. Safeguard the File Against NonCompatible Browsers

Even though most of today's Web browsers can interpret JavaScript code, you should write code that accommodates the small percentage of users who use non-JavaScript-compatible browsers. In this exercise, you add safeguards to ensure the page displays correctly in browsers that cannot interpret JavaScript code.

1. In the open file, add HTML and JavaScript comments to hide scripting code from non-compatible browsers.

2. Insert content for browsers that cannot interpret the **`<script>`** tag. Make sure you use the **`<noscript>`** tag.

3. In the **`<noscript>`** content area, copy and paste the code for the three links. Remove any inline JavaScript code from the three hyperlinks that appear in this section.

    This allows end users to see the same information, even if their browsers do not support JavaScript.

4. In the **`<noscript>`** area, change the URL for the first link to "pickBahamas.html".

    Let's assume that users whose browsers do not support JavaScript will be directed to another URL that does not require client-side code.

5. Change the URL for the second link to "pickAlaska.html".

6. Change the URL for the third link to "pickCaribbean.html".

    Since these pages have not been created, the links do not work correctly.

7. Save the file and refresh it in your browser.

    If you had a noncompatible browser, you would not see any JavaScript code or be reliant on any JavaScript code to process the order.

8. Close the file in your browser and text editor.

PORTFOLIO BUILDER

Using JavaScript to Improve Site Functionality

The Travel Agency hired you to enhance the functionality of its corporate Web site. Currently, a travel agent sends an e-mail to a customer after the customer books his travel arrangements online. This thank-you note includes a confirmation number. Instead of this manual method, the client wants each customer to receive an automated e-mail that contains a link to the customer's confirmation number. As an added incentive, each customer will receive a complimentary tropical shirt when he books a cruise online.

The files you need to complete this exercise are in the RF_JavaScript_L1>Chapter_01>Portfolio_Builder_01 folder. If you have not already done so, copy the content of this folder to your WIP_01 folder. The pages were already designed, and the HTML page (confirmation.html) is ready for additional JavaScript functionality. As you enhance the pages, incorporate the following features.

- When a customer receives an e-mail from The Travel Agency, he should click a link to retrieve his confirmation number. The confirmation page will then load in the customer's browser.

- The confirmation number is important. Use an alert box to tell the customer to "Print this page for your records."

- After the customer clicks OK, he sees the confirmation number and the special gift offer — a tropical shirt. To claim this gift, a customer must click a link to choose a shirt size. An alert box should say, "Your <size> shirt will be waiting for you in your cabin on the ship." Replace <size> with the stated size of that particular link.

- While you add client-side scripting, think about any other improvements you could suggest to the lead developer on the project.

CHAPTER 2

Introduction to Object-Based Languages

OBJECTIVES

In this chapter, you learn how to:

- Create objects and classes

- Use basic methods

- Manipulate properties

- Use common properties

- Incorporate events

- Apply correct syntax

Why Would I Do This?

JavaScript is an object-based language. ***Object-based language (OBL)*** refers to a style of programming that relies on reusing objects in multiple computer programs. It is relatively easy to write code in an OBL language because the language imitates how you talk and think in everyday life. As a simple analogy, think of ***objects*** as nouns that you can use in the JavaScript language. You can use other aspects of JavaScript to describe the characteristics of the object (the equivalent of adjectives), as well as describe what the object does (comparable to verbs).

Earlier programming languages used a strict sequence of commands that were usually numbered in the order they were executed. This worked well for simple tasks, but quickly became cumbersome as applications grew in complexity. An OBL language is loosely organized, since you define an object once, and then use it anywhere you choose — without having to rewrite the code you used to define the object.

A ***class*** represents the definition of an object. A class doesn't actually exist in physical form; rather, it simply describes an object. For example, Joe Smith is an object that belongs to the human class. Objects in the human class have two arms and two legs, among other characteristics, and walk upright. Therefore, the class describes basic characteristics of the object, as well as describes any actions the object can perform.

As you learned in Chapter 1, methods represent actions that an object can perform. For instance, a browser window is represented by a window object and can generate an alert box through the `alert()` method. Methods can accomplish a variety of tasks, depending on the object. Each type of object performs tasks specific to its type.

Properties represent characteristics of an object, such as its color. It is often useful to change the property of an object to suit a specific purpose or to discover the value of a specific property. For example, you might want to identify the background color of the current page or change the background color of the current page.

Designers who learn one OBL language can easily adapt to other OBL environments. In this chapter, you learn about and use the JavaScript OBL language.

VISUAL SUMMARY

All OBL languages and environments include common characteristics in grammar, syntax, and construction, as well as contain classes, objects, methods, properties, and events. JavaScript uses ***dot syntax***, which is a special kind of ***syntax*** (the set of rules that dictates how the language is written), to show the relationship of the items in the code. Dot syntax simply means that periods are used within the code to note how items relate to one another. Dot syntax is the preferred method of writing code, and you should use it whenever possible. Let's take a moment to examine code created using dot syntax.

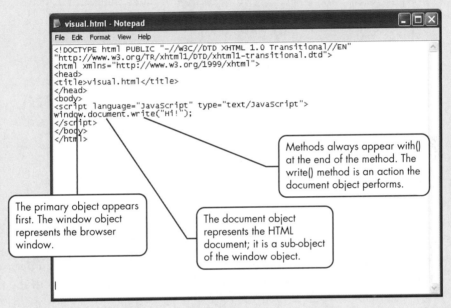

FIGURE 2.1

Dot syntax uses a "top-down" method of writing code. For instance, if you want to call on the **value** property of an element in a form, you can write the statement in the following fashion

```
form.element.value;
```

Periods (dots) are placed between the words to denote the hierarchy of the objects from the generic to the specific. You can use dot syntax to write an address

```
USA.FL.FortJackson.MainStreet.Apt321
```

Dot syntax is one part of the overall JavaScript syntax. JavaScript's syntax rules are more complex than those in the HTML scripting language, but simpler than those in most programming languages. Examples of JavaScript syntax rules include the following.

- Case sensitivity, which means that a program distinguishes between upper- and lowercase letters.

- You must use a semicolon to denote the end of a line of code.

- When you use text strings in methods, you must enclose the text strings within matching quotes.

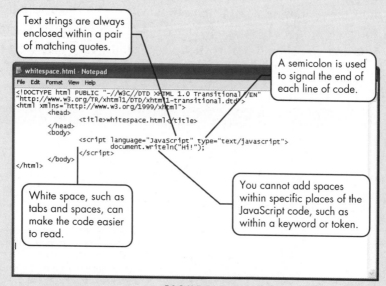

FIGURE 2.2

Unlike many programming languages, JavaScript allows you to insert white space into the code. *White space* includes tabs and spaces and is often used to make the code easier to read. You cannot insert space into *tokens*, which are keywords or other items that have significance to the *interpreter* (the program that executes instructions). Inserting space into tokens creates syntax errors in the code.

LESSON 1   Objects and Classes

In an object-based environment, code is organized into objects. Using objects, you can group commands according to how humans categorize information. Let's use a theoretical object to illustrate the OBL language.

- You have a car object, which is called myCar. It represents an automobile.

- The definition of a car states that it must have four tires and a steering wheel, among other common characteristics.

- In programming terms, the definition of the car is known as the class. A class is simply the definition of the object, similar to the definition included in a traditional dictionary. A class defines basic information about the object. For instance, every car belongs to the car class, but each car is slightly different from every other car. The myCar object is an occurrence of the car class.

It's important to remember that classes are theoretical; they don't actually exist as tangible objects. For instance, the definition of a car is something that you understand, but you will never see outside the pages of a book or dictionary. An *occurrence* of the car class, however, is what you see in the street in the form of a physical automobile.

Class	Object
A type of bank account	Joe's checking account
A car	Sue's 2003 Honda Accord
A person	Bill Jones
A sphere	A baseball

Objects can include sub-objects, or subcategories. A *sub-object* is one part of another object. For instance, a car has a steering wheel, which is a separate object, but exists as part of the greater whole (the car). In OBL languages, you can create sub-objects so they describe the relationship of the objects, such as:

```
myCar.steeringWheel
```

Objects can assume many forms in JavaScript. For example:

- The *window object* represents the browser window.

- The *document object* represents the HTML document loaded into the browser window.

- A *form object* represents a form in the HTML document.

Use the Window Object

1 **Copy the content of your RF_JavaScript_L1>Chapter_02 folder to your Work_In_Progress>WIP_02 folder.**

From this point forward, we refer to the RF_JavaScript_L1>Chapter_02 folder simply as the Chapter_02 folder, and the Work_In_Progress>WIP_02 folder as the WIP_02 folder. You open most resource files from the WIP_02 folder. Make sure to turn off read-only attributes for these files.

2 In your browser, open windowfocus.html from your WIP_02 folder.

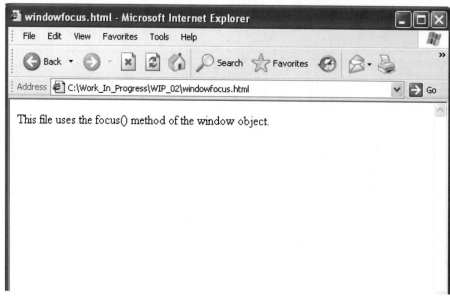

FIGURE 2.3

This is a standard HTML file.

3 Open windowfocus.html in your text editor.

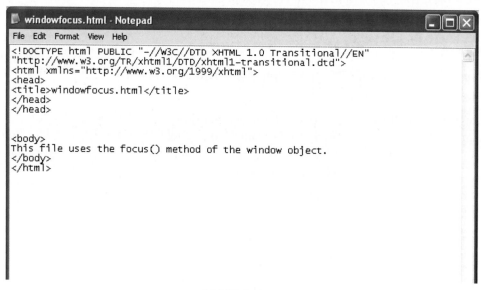

FIGURE 2.4

4   **Change the `<body>` tag to the following.**

```
<body onblur="window.focus();">
```

When an event occurs, programmers say that it "fires." In this instance, the **onblur** event fires when the user chooses a different window by clicking a different program or another browser window. This causes the browser to blur the current window and focus on the new window. The word **window** in JavaScript always means the current browser window.

5   **Save the changes to the .html file. Refresh the file in the browser.**

?   If you have problems . . .

Some versions of Notepad in Windows operating systems append the .txt file extension to the file name when you save the document. If this happens, simply change the file name back to the .html file extension.

---

6   **Click your text editor window.**

The browser window blurs, and the text editor window comes into focus.

FIGURE 2.5

On Windows XP systems, the window blinks in orange to indicate the requested focus. In many operating systems, the window appears in front of the other windows.

7   **Close the file in your text editor and browser.**

In this exercise, you used the **focus()** method of the window object to draw focus back to the window when you choose another window. The window object allows you to manipulate the browser window in a number of important ways. Remember, the document object is part of the window object; the document object represents the HTML code that displays in the browser window.

Use the Document Object

1   **In your text editor and browser, open links_href.html from your WIP_02 folder.**

2   **Insert the following HTML code in your document.**

```
<title>links_href.html</title>
</head>
<body>
<a href="http://vig.prenhall.com">Prentice-Hall</a><br />
```

```
<body>
</html>
```

The document object represents the HTML code shown in the browser window. Sub-objects of the document object represent various HTML elements in the page. Therefore, the **<a>** tag you just created will be a subordinate object of the document object.

3   **Add the following code before the </body> tag to demonstrate the properties of the link object.**

```
</head>
<body>
<a href="http://vig.prenhall.com">Prentice-Hall</a><br />
<script language="JavaScript" type="text/javascript">
document.write("Link object href:"+ document.links[0].href);
</script>
</body>
```

The link object represents the **<a>** tags in the document. The **link.href** property contains the full address specified within the **href** attribute parentheses in the **<a>** tag. The number **0** means the first link in the HTML page. Notice that we placed a space between the colon (:) and the end quote in the string to improve the code's formatting.

4   **Save the document in your text editor. Refresh the document in your Web browser.**

You should see the result of the **href** property.

As you can see, the **href** property contains the full text specified in the href attribute of the **<a>** tag.

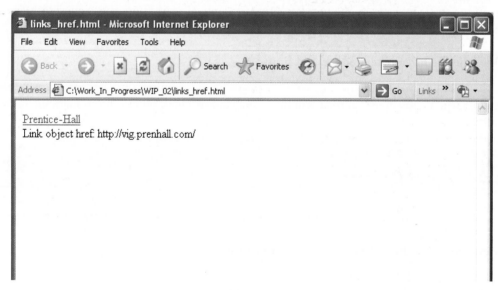

FIGURE 2.6

5   **Close the file in your browser and text editor.**

The document object is extremely useful, since the document object represents the HTML code in the document. Remember, the document object is a sub-object of the window object.

Use the Math Object

In this exercise, you explore the *Math object*, which is used to complete various calculations.

1   **In your text editor, open mathobject.html from your WIP_02 folder.**

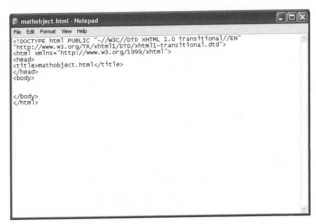

FIGURE 2.7

2   **Insert the following code between the `<body>` and `</body>` tags.**

```
<body>
<script language="JavaScript" type="text/javascript">
</script>
</body>
```

3   **Insert the following code directly before the `</script>` tag.**

```
<script language="JavaScript" type="text/javascript">
document.write(Math.random());
</script>
```

The Math object allows you to complete various calculations. The **random()** method is used to generate random numbers. Notice how the Math object is always capitalized, unlike most other objects, which are lowercased.

4   **Save the changes to the .html file. Open the document in your Web browser.**

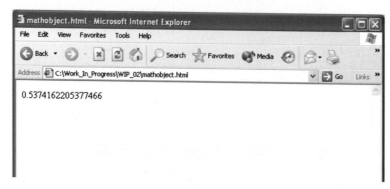

FIGURE 2.8

The number on your screen is probably different than what you see above, because the **random()** method generates a random number between 0 and 1.

5   **Click the refresh button on your browser.**

A different random number appears every time the page reloads.

6   **Close the file in your browser and text editor.**

To Extend Your Knowledge...

FOCUS AND BLUR

The idea behind focus and blur is quite prevalent in modern operating systems. If an element has *focus,* any key that you press is directed to that element. In a previous exercise, you used the focus() method of the window object to draw focus to the browser window. You can use other objects to draw focus to other elements, such as a field in a form. When you draw focus to an element, another element is automatically blurred; only one element can be in focus at any given time. The term *blur* means that you redirect keystrokes to another object.

LESSON 2 Using Basic Methods

Aside from describing objects, you can use dot syntax to write other aspects of JavaScript, including methods. As you know, methods represent actions that objects can perform; they are the "verbs" of the object-based language. As an example, consider that you have a dog, which you refer to as myDog. The myDog object has several methods, including **bark()** and **growl()**. In programming terms, you can write the following statements to tell the myDog object to bark or growl.

```
myDog.bark();
myDog.growl();
```

Methods are always written in the form **methodName()**. The parentheses indicate that this is a method. If information appears within the parentheses, such as a number or text, it indicates that the information is being passed to the method. For some methods, no information is required; for other methods, however, specific information is required to achieve the desired action. A code statement that uses a method is often referred to as a **method call**. For instance, we might tell the myDog object to bark three times by sending the number 3 to the **bark()** method.

```
myDog.bark(3);
```

As an actual coding example, consider the **alert()** method that you used in Chapter 1. The purpose of the **alert()** method is to create an alert box. This command is a method of the browser window. In other words, the browser window can create an alert box. As an example, you can generate an alert box that displays the word "hello" using either of the following statements.

```
alert("hello");
window.alert("hello");
```

As you can see, the object name (window) is optional in some cases. In the case of the **alert()** method, you pass a message to it, and the message displays to the user. The message is simple text — it is not the name of an object. For this reason, you place the text within quotes. Plain text is referred to as a **text string** or **string**.

Use the prompt () Method

1 **In the text editor, open prompt.html from your WIP_02 folder.**

FIGURE 2.9

2 **Insert the following code into your script.**

```
<script language="JavaScript" type="text/javascript">
prompt("What's your favorite color?");
</script>
```

You use the **prompt()** method to ask a question.

3   Save the file in your text editor, and then open the file in your browser.

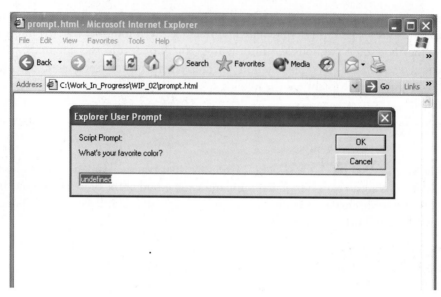

FIGURE 2.10

The **prompt()** method is similar to the **alert()** method, but the **prompt()** method allows the user to type in a response to the question in the prompt box. The term "undefined" simply means that you haven't yet placed a default answer in the answer box.

4   Type in your favorite color and click OK.

The prompt box disappears.

5   Return to the text editor. Change the **prompt()** statement to the following.

```
prompt("What's your favorite color?","");
```

Placing a comma after the text string and typing a set of double quotes sends an empty text string to the **prompt()** method.

6 Save the file. Click the Refresh button in the browser.

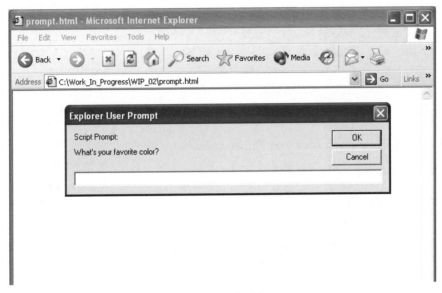

FIGURE 2.11

The term "undefined" doesn't appear in the response area.

7 Click OK.

8 Keep the file open in both applications for the next exercise.

In this exercise, you used the **prompt()** method, which is part of the window object. The primary purpose of the **prompt()** method is to ask the user a question. Unlike the methods you used earlier, the **prompt()** method can pass two values: one value is the message that appears in the prompt window, and the second value is the default message that appears in the answer field.

Return Information from a Method

In this exercise, you use the **prompt()** method to return information to the script.

1 Return to the open prompt.html in your text editor.

2 Examine your script. It should match the code shown below.

```
<script language="JavaScript" type="text/javascript">
prompt("What's your favorite color?","");
</script>
```

3 Change the **prompt** statement to match the following.

```
answer=prompt("What's your favorite color?","");
```

This change in the code creates a temporary storage space for the information that will return from the method. The storage space is named **answer**.

4   **Add the following statement before the `</script>` tag.**

```
<script language="JavaScript" type"text/javascript">
answer=prompt("What's your favorite color?","");
document.write("You said "+answer);
</script>
```

This statement returns the stored color.

5   **Save the .html file and refresh it in your browser.**

A prompt box appears.

6   **Enter a color and click OK.**

FIGURE 2.12

The color value returns to you.

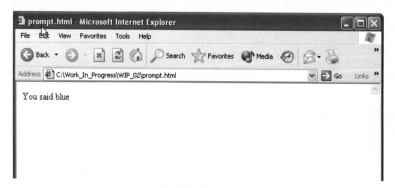

FIGURE 2.13

7   **Close the file in your text editor and browser.**

In this exercise, you returned and used information generated by a method. This is a valuable function, since many methods gather information or transform information in one way or another.

Use Methods within Methods

1 **In your text editor, open math.html from your WIP_02 folder. Examine the code shown below.**

This program computes and displays the square root of 1600 using the **sqrt()** method of the Math object and the **write()** method of the document object.

```
<script language="JavaScript" type="text/javascript">
document.write("The square root of 1600 is" + Math.sqrt(1600));
</script>
```

Notice how the script uses the **Math.sqrt()** method within the **document.write()** method. Notice how the plus sign (+) combines a text string with the **Math.sqrt()** method within the **document.write()** statement.

2 **Open the file in your Web browser and examine the result.**

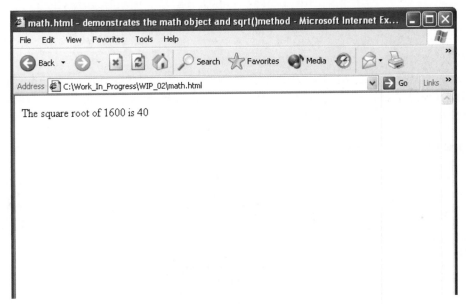

FIGURE 2.14

3 **Change the document.write() line of code to read as follows.**

```
</head>
<body>
<script language="JavaScript" type="text/javascript">
window.alert("The square root of 1600 is" + Math.sqrt(1600));
</script>
</body>
</html>
```

This change allows you to practice using other methods.

4   **Save the .html file and refresh the Web browser.**

FIGURE 2.15

5   **Change the `window.alert()` statement to the following.**

```
<body>
<script language="JavaScript" type="text/javascript">
window.alert ("3 to the power of 2 is " + Math.pow(3,2));
</script>
</body>
</html>
```

The code calculates the number 3 raised to the power of 2. For this calculation, you need the **`Math.pow()`** method. The **`Math.pow()`** method requires two arguments — the number to use and the power to which it is raised.

6   **Save the file and refresh the browser window.**

FIGURE 2.16

7   **Close the file in the text editor and browser.**

LESSON 3   Manipulating Properties

Properties are characteristics of an object. Using the theoretical myCar object as an example, the object may include properties such as color, make, model, and mileage. If you want to access a property of an object, you can do so using dot syntax. For example, you could use the following statement to refer to the color property of the myCar object.

```
myCar.color;
```

Each property stores one piece of information about an object. In the statement above, the word "color" might refer to the value of red. If you want to change the color of the car to green, you would type the following statement.

```
myCar.color="green";
```

This statement sets the value of the color property of the myCar object to green. You can also determine the value of a property by referring to it in JavaScript. For instance, if you want to output the current color of the myCar object, you would type the following statement.

```
document.write(myCar.color);
```

Change Properties of Objects

1   **From your WIP_02>links folder, open main.html in your browser. Examine the links in the document.**

This mock site contains three simple pages that link to one another. Each page consists of a title and links to the other pages. In most browsers, the link color changes from blue to purple to indicate a link you already clicked.

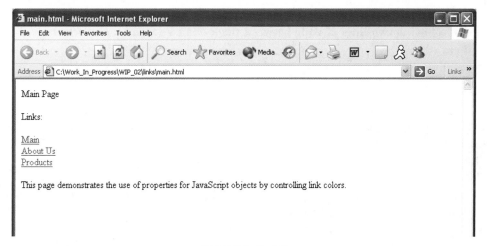

FIGURE 2.17

2   **Open main.html in your text editor.**

```
main.html - Notepad
File  Edit  Format  View  Help
<!DOCTYPE html PUBLIC "-//W3C//DTD XHTML 1.0 Transitional//EN"
"http://www.w3.org/TR/xhtml1/DTD/xhtml1-transitional.dtd">
<html xmlns="http://www.w3.org/1999/xhtml">
<head>
<title>main.html</title>

</head>
<body bgcolor="#FFFFFF">
<p>Main Page</p>
<p>
Links:</p>
<p><a href="main.html">Main</a> <br />
<a href="aboutus.html">About Us</a> <br />
<a href="products.html">Products</a> <br />
</p>
<p>This page demonstrates the use of properties for JavaScript objects by
controlling link colors.</p>
</body>
</html>
```

FIGURE 2.18

3   **Add the following two lines of code between the </title> and </head> tags of the document.**

```
<html xmlns="http://www.w3.org/1999/xhtml">
<head>
<title>main.html</title>
<script language="JavaScript" type="text/javascript">
</script>
</head>
```

4   **Add the following commands between the <script> and </script> tags to change the default link colors in the Web browser.**

```
<head>
<title>main.html</title>
<script language="JavaScript" type="text/javascript">
// change default link colors
document.alinkColor="#CC0000";
document.vlinkColor="#666666";
</script>
</head>
```

This code makes active links appear in dark red (#CC0000), and previously visited links appear in dark gray (#666666). Those students who know HTML will recognize the hexadecimal numbers used to identify the colors.

5 | Save the changes to the document. Refresh main.html in your Web browser.

At this point, it is likely that most of the links on the main page appear in dark gray, since you recently visited these pages.

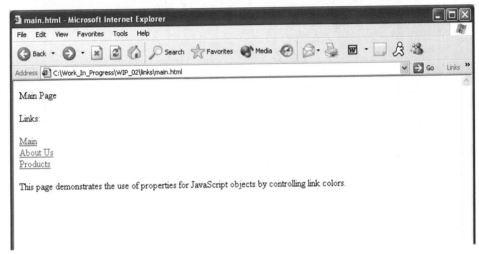

FIGURE 2.19

6 | Repeat Steps 3–5 for aboutus.html and products.html to apply the same styles to those documents.

You can find both of these files in the WIP_02>links folder.

7 | View the pages in your browser, and then click the Refresh button.

The link colors should change on each page.

In most browsers, you can press the Tab key to make each link active.

8 | Leave these files open in your browser and text editor.

In this exercise, you changed properties of the document object — you changed the default link colors of the HTML page.

Display Properties of Objects

In this exercise, you discover how to ask JavaScript to output the value of a property — to display the `vlinkColor` and `alinkColor` properties.

1   **Ensure that main.html is open in your text editor and browser.**

2   **Add a blank line between the </p> and </body> tags, as shown in Figure 2.20.**

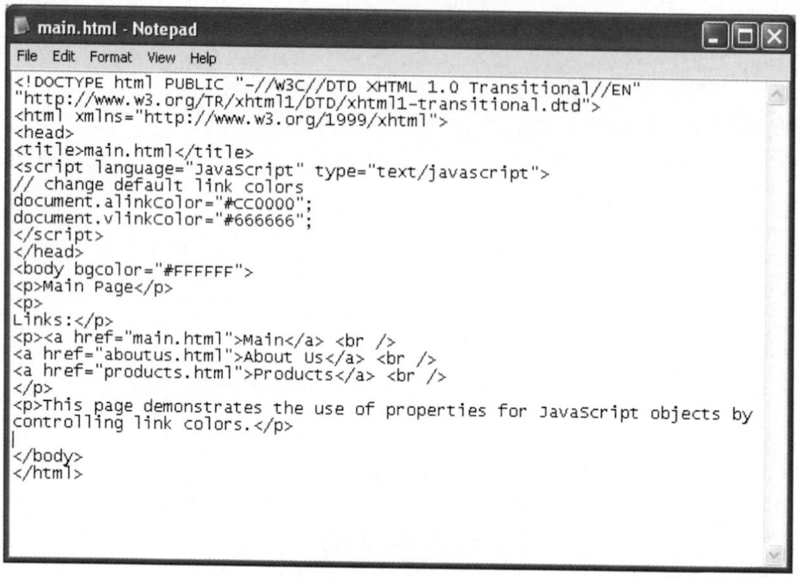

```
main.html - Notepad
File  Edit  Format  View  Help
<!DOCTYPE html PUBLIC "-//W3C//DTD XHTML 1.0 Transitional//EN"
"http://www.w3.org/TR/xhtml1/DTD/xhtml1-transitional.dtd">
<html xmlns="http://www.w3.org/1999/xhtml">
<head>
<title>main.html</title>
<script language="JavaScript" type="text/javascript">
// change default link colors
document.alinkColor="#CC0000";
document.vlinkColor="#666666";
</script>
</head>
<body bgcolor="#FFFFFF">
<p>Main Page</p>
<p>
Links:</p>
<p><a href="main.html">Main</a> <br />
<a href="aboutus.html">About Us</a> <br />
<a href="products.html">Products</a> <br />
</p>
<p>This page demonstrates the use of properties for JavaScript objects by
controlling link colors.</p>

</body>
</html>
```

FIGURE 2.20

This creates an empty space where you can add code.

3   **Type the following code in the empty space.**

```
</p>
<p>This page demonstrates the use of properties for JavaScript
objects by controlling link colors.</p>
<script language="JavaScript" type="text/javascript">
</script>
</body>
</html>
```

4   **To display the active links color to the end user, insert a blank line after the last <script> tag, and then insert the following code.**

```
</p>
<p>This page demonstrates the use of properties for JavaScript
objects by controlling link colors.</p>
<script language="JavaScript" type="text/javascript">
//the next line shows the active links color
document.write("The Active links color
is"+document.alinkColor+"<br />");
</script>
</body>
</html>
```

The **alinkColor** property represents the default color of active hyperlinks in the document.

FIGURE 2.21

5   **To display the visited links color to the end user, insert the following lines into the script after the code you created in Step 4.**

```
</p>
<p>This page demonstrates the use of properties for JavaScript
objects by controlling link colors.</p>
<script language="JavaScript" type="text/javascript">
//the next line shows the active links color
document.write("The Active links color
is"+document.alinkColor+"<br />");
//the next line shows the visited links color
document.write("The Visited links color is"+document.vlinkColor);
</script>
</body>
</html>
```

The **vlinkColor** property represents the default color of previously visited links. The browser's internal history list determines whether a link has been previously visited.

6   Examine your code. At this point, it should match the code in Figure 2.22.

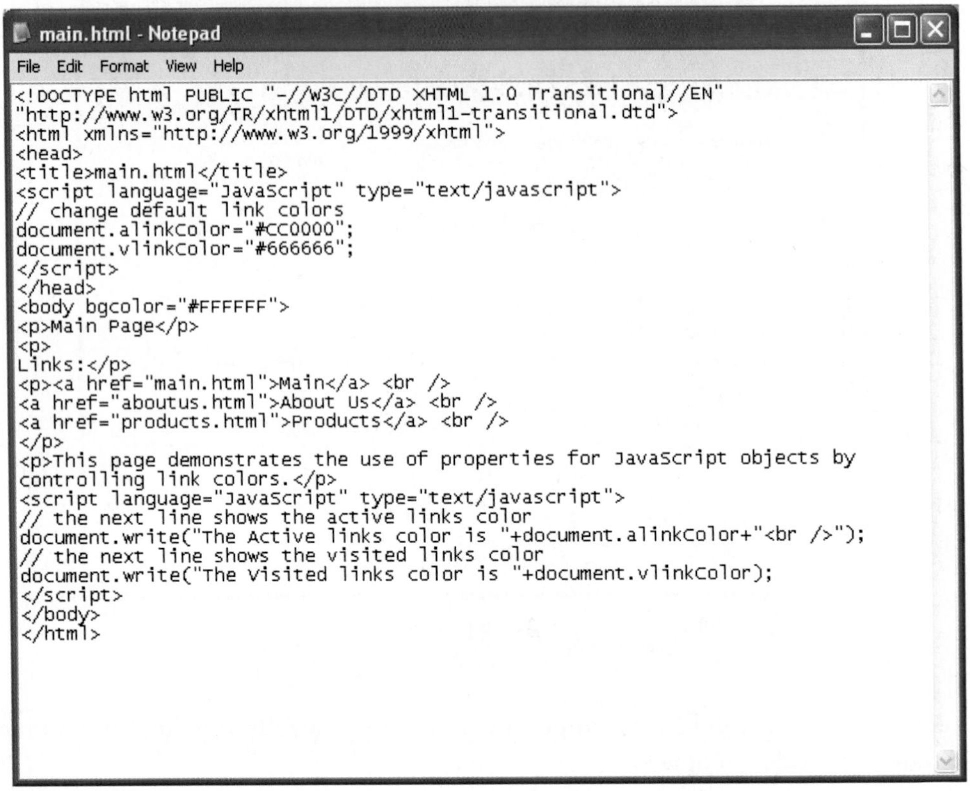

```
main.html - Notepad
File  Edit  Format  View  Help
<!DOCTYPE html PUBLIC "-//W3C//DTD XHTML 1.0 Transitional//EN"
"http://www.w3.org/TR/xhtml1/DTD/xhtml1-transitional.dtd">
<html xmlns="http://www.w3.org/1999/xhtml">
<head>
<title>main.html</title>
<script language="JavaScript" type="text/javascript">
// change default link colors
document.alinkColor="#CC0000";
document.vlinkColor="#666666";
</script>
</head>
<body bgcolor="#FFFFFF">
<p>Main Page</p>
<p>
Links:</p>
<p><a href="main.html">Main</a> <br />
<a href="aboutus.html">About Us</a> <br />
<a href="products.html">Products</a> <br />
</p>
<p>This page demonstrates the use of properties for JavaScript objects by
controlling link colors.</p>
<script language="JavaScript" type="text/javascript">
// the next line shows the active links color
document.write("The Active links color is "+document.alinkColor+"<br />");
// the next line shows the visited links color
document.write("The Visited links color is "+document.vlinkColor);
</script>
</body>
</html>
```

FIGURE 2.22

7   Save the changes you made to the document.

8   **Load the document into your Web browser. Examine the result.**

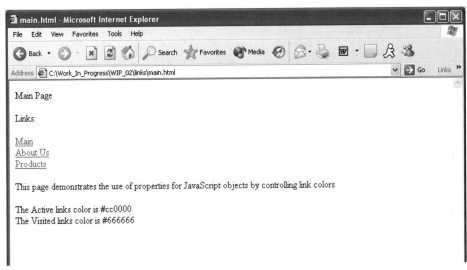

FIGURE 2.23

The color values stored in the **alinkColor** and **vlinkColor** properties should output at the bottom of the browser window.

9   **Close the file in your text editor and browser.**

Delete the Browser's History List

When you view a Web page, your browser uses an internal history list to determine whether the page was recently viewed and if it should display links as visited. In this exercise, you learn how to delete the browser's history list and return all links to their original state.

1   In Internet Explorer 6.0, choose Tools>Internet Options. In Mozilla Firefox, choose Tools>Options.

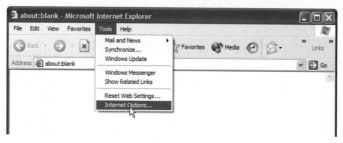

FIGURE 2.24

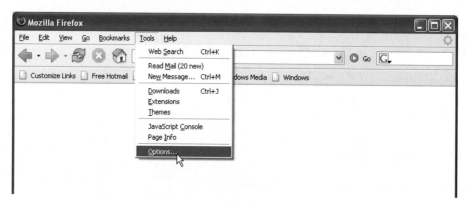

FIGURE 2.25

2   IE 6.0 users should choose Clear History in the Internet Options dialog box.

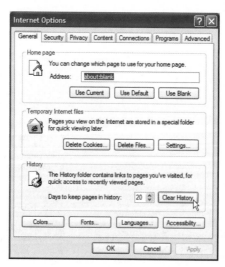

FIGURE 2.26

3 Firefox users should choose Privacy under the Category list, and then click the Clear button in the History section.

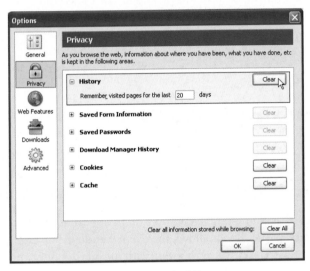

FIGURE 2.27

4 In your browser, open main.html from your WIP_02 folder.

The links now appear in the default link color, since the browser no longer considers these as recently visited locations.

5 Click various links to look around the site.

The colors of the links change as the browser adds the links to the history list.

6 Close the file in the text editor.

Resetting the browser's history list is often useful when developing Web sites that use properties related to the history list, such as the link color properties you used in previous exercises.

To Extend Your Knowledge...

COMMON PROPERTIES

Those who know HTML will probably realize that the `vlinkColor`, `alinkColor`, and `linkColor` properties control the same settings as the `link`, `alink`, and `vlink` HTML attributes of the `<body>` tag. These similarities are common between HTML and JavaScript. HTML tags are represented by matching objects in JavaScript. Attributes of HTML tags are usually represented by properties of the matching objects in JavaScript.

This relationship provides added flexibility in many areas. For instance, you could set the default link colors in the HTML <body> tag; later, you could change the colors using JavaScript. With this flexibility, you can create a page that allows users to pick their own link colors without loading a new Web page.

LESSON 4 Incorporating Events

As you remember from Chapter 1, events are occurrences that the programming environment detects. Event handlers are JavaScript keywords that detect events. For example, the **onclick** event handler detects when the user clicks the mouse button while the mouse pointer hovers over an object.

Event handlers are usually used as inline JavaScript; they often appear as attributes of an HTML tag. You can use event handlers if the class of the object allows the event handler. For example, image objects represent images in JavaScript. You can use the **onclick** event with an image object, but you cannot use it with the Math object, since the Math object has no visual representation.

Use an Inline JavaScript Event

In this exercise, you discover how event handlers detect events.

1 In your text editor, open event.html from the WIP_02 folder.

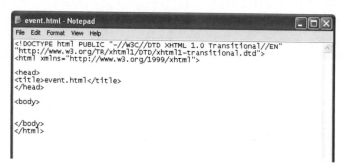

FIGURE 2.28

2 To attach an event handler to the <body> tag as inline JavaScript, change the <body> tag to read as follows.

```
<head>
<title>event.html</title>
</head>
<body onload="alert('Welcome to my Web site!');">
</body>
```

In this example, the **alert()** method uses single quotes, since double quotes would end the text field you are creating for the **onload** event handler.

3   **Type the following code between the <body> and </body> tags.**

```
</head>
<body onload="alert('Welcome to my Web site!');">
<p>Once the page is loaded, you will see a welcome message!</p>
</body>
```

This text creates a user-friendly page.

FIGURE 2.29

4   **Save the changes to the file. Open the file in your Web browser to see the result.**

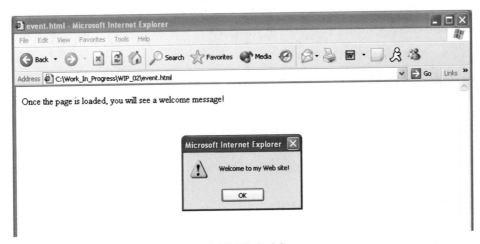

FIGURE 2.30

5   **Click OK to close the alert window.**

6   **Close the file in your text editor and browser.**

In this exercise, you used an event handler to trigger an alert box. Events are usually attached to HTML tags as attributes of the tag. The **onload** event occurs when the page has finished loading.

To Extend Your Knowledge . . .

UNDERSTANDING CASE SENSITIVITY

XHTML rules require inline event handlers to be lower case. In rare situations, older browsers may be case sensitive to an inline event handler. For best results, always use the correct capitalization when using JavaScript.

LESSON 5   Understanding Syntax Requirements

Each language (whether human- or computer-readable) has its own set of syntax requirements. For example, when writing sentences in the English language, you must capitalize the first word and place ending punctuation after the last word. In some cases, you can break syntax rules, but this often creates problems in the reader's ability to interpret the language.

Computer languages typically include strict syntax requirements based on the language used. These rules exist for two reasons. First, the interpreter for the language is typically quite limited; interpreters become "confused" by code that doesn't follow established syntax rules. Second, following syntax rules ensures that others do not confuse the intent of your statements. For example, imagine that you received the following written instruction from your manager.

"Order twenty eight year old blocks of Romano cheese."

In an effort to follow orders, you ordered twenty blocks of eight-year-old cheese. What your manager actually wanted you to do, however, was order twenty-eight (28) year-old blocks whenever you place an order for Romano cheese. Your manager could have avoided this miscommunication if he had followed the established rules of grammar and syntax. In the following exercises, you learn the basic syntax rules for JavaScript.

Use SemiColons to End Statements

1   **In your text editor, open syntax.html from the WIP_02 folder.**

The following code generates two successive alert boxes.

```
alert("Hi!"); alert("What's up?");
```

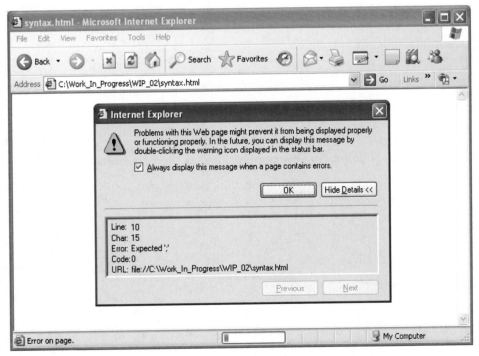

```
syntax.html - Notepad
File Edit Format View Help
<!DOCTYPE html PUBLIC "-//W3C//DTD XHTML 1.0 Transitional//EN"
"http://www.w3.org/TR/xhtml1/DTD/xhtml1-transitional.dtd">
<html xmlns="http://www.w3.org/1999/xhtml">

<head>
<title>syntax.html</title>
</head>

<body>
<script language="JavaScript" type="text/javascript">
alert("Hi!");  alert("what's up?");
</script>

</body>
</html>
```

FIGURE 2.31

2 **Open the file in your Web browser to see the result.**

3 **Return to the text editor. Remove the semicolons (;) from the alert statements. The line should now read as follows.**

```
alert("Hi!") alert("What's up?")
```

4 **Save the .html file and refresh the browser.**

Depending on the browser used and whether error suppression is turned off or on, the commands are ignored or you receive an error message.

```
syntax.html - Microsoft Internet Explorer
File Edit View Favorites Tools Help
Back          Search   Favorites
Address  C:\Work_In_Progress\WIP_02\syntax.html          Go  Links

    Internet Explorer
        Problems with this Web page might prevent it from being displayed properly
        or functioning properly. In the future, you can display this message by
        double-clicking the warning icon displayed in the status bar.

        ☑ Always display this message when a page contains errors.

                                    OK        Hide Details <<

        Line: 10
        Char: 15
        Error: Expected ';'
        Code: 0
        URL: file://C:\Work_In_Progress\WIP_02\syntax.html

                                    Previous       Next

Error on page.                                          My Computer
```

FIGURE 2.32

5   **Return to the text editor. Place your cursor after** `alert("Hi!")`, **and press Enter/Return to move the second alert statement to a separate line.**

```
alert("Hi!")
alert("What's up?")
```

6   **Save the file and refresh the browser.**

Since you no longer have two commands on the same line without a semicolon to separate them, the code works correctly.

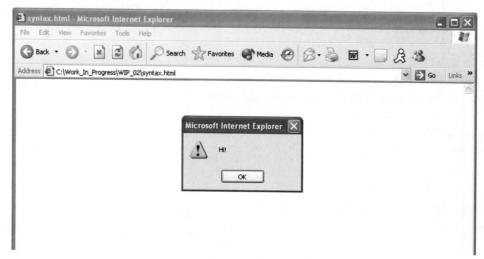

FIGURE 2.33

7   **Click OK to close the alert boxes.**

8   **Return to the code in your text editor. Insert a semicolon at the end of each alert statement.**

```
alert("Hi!");
alert("What's up?");
```

9   **Save the file and keep it open in both applications for the next exercise.**

Although not technically required in this situation, inserting semicolons at the ends of statements is good programming practice; it prevents errors in some situations.

Correct Text String Quote Errors

In this exercise, you mix single and double quotes to introduce another kind of syntax error.

1 | **In the alert statements in the open .html file, change the ending double quote marks to single quotes.**

Leave the opening quotes as double quotes.

```
alert("Hi!');
alert("What's up?');
```

This introduces another syntax error into the code. The editor cannot correctly determine where the text strings begin and end.

2 | **Save the document in the text editor and refresh the browser.**

The browser either ignores the code or generates an error message, depending on whether error suppression is turned on or off.

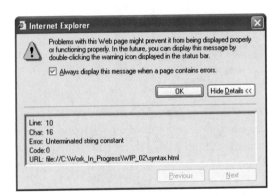

FIGURE 2.34

3 | **Return to the text editor. Edit the code so the first alert statement has single quotes, and the second alert statement has double quotes.**

```
alert('Hi!');
alert("What's up?");
```

You can use either single or double quotes, but you must use them in matching pairs.

4 | **Save the document in the text editor and refresh the browser.**

The code works correctly.

5 | **Return to the text editor. Remove the quotes from the alert statements.**

```
alert(Hi!);
alert(What's up?);
```

6   **Save the document in the text editor and refresh the browser.**

The code does not work properly without the quote marks. Quotes are required in JavaScript; they tell JavaScript not to interpret the text in the alert statement.

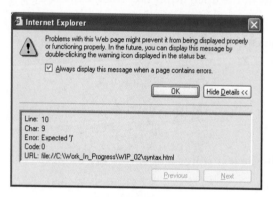

FIGURE 2.35

7   **Correct the quotes in the text editor and refresh the browser.**

If the alert boxes appear, you can confirm that your changes are correct.

8   **Close the file in the text editor and browser.**

In this exercise, you created and then corrected various errors associated with quotes. JavaScript uses pairs of quotes to note the beginning and end of a text string. Remember, you can use either single or double quotes, but you must use them in matching pairs.

Use White Space for Code Formatting

1 In your text editor, open whitespace.html from your WIP_02 folder.

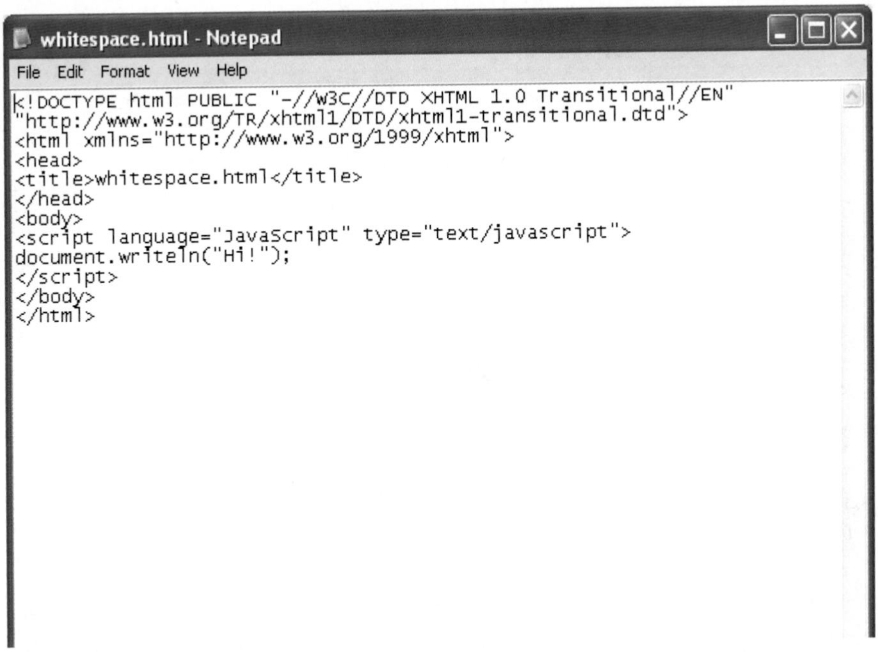
whitespace.html - Notepad

File Edit Format View Help

```
<!DOCTYPE html PUBLIC "-//W3C//DTD XHTML 1.0 Transitional//EN"
"http://www.w3.org/TR/xhtml1/DTD/xhtml1-transitional.dtd">
<html xmlns="http://www.w3.org/1999/xhtml">
<head>
<title>whitespace.html</title>
</head>
<body>
<script language="JavaScript" type="text/javascript">
document.writeln("Hi!");
</script>
</body>
</html>
```

FIGURE 2.36

2 Click the mouse pointer at the beginning of each line and insert tabs to show nested commands, as shown in Figure 2.37.

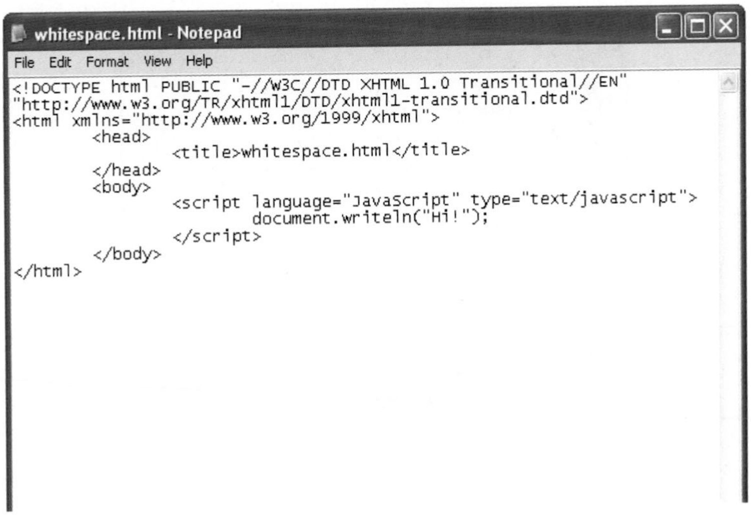
whitespace.html - Notepad

File Edit Format View Help

```
<!DOCTYPE html PUBLIC "-//W3C//DTD XHTML 1.0 Transitional//EN"
"http://www.w3.org/TR/xhtml1/DTD/xhtml1-transitional.dtd">
<html xmlns="http://www.w3.org/1999/xhtml">
		<head>
				<title>whitespace.html</title>
		</head>
		<body>
				<script language="JavaScript" type="text/javascript">
						document.writeln("Hi!");
				</script>
		</body>
</html>
```

FIGURE 2.37

3   **Save the document in your text editor, and then open it in your browser.**

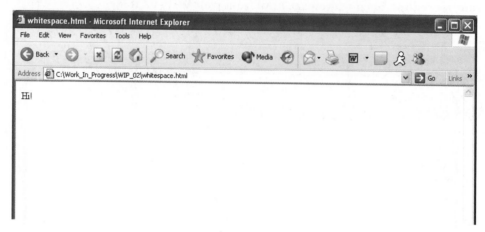

FIGURE 2.38

4   **Insert a space between `write` and `ln`.**

```
document.write ln("Hi!");
```

Inserting white space into a token (**`document.writeln`**) creates a syntax error in your code. Remember that a token is a keyword or other text element that has meaning to the interpreter. You must not divide tokens with spaces or tabs.

5   **Save the document and refresh your browser.**

The code no longer works. If your browser is configured to show errors, you may receive an error message.

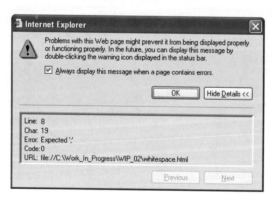

FIGURE 2.39

6   **Return to the document in your text editor. Remove the space you inserted in Step 4. Save the file and refresh the browser.**

The problem is resolved.

7   **Close the file in the text editor.**

In this exercise, you used white space to increase the readability of your code and to show how elements are nested in the code. JavaScript ignores most white space, unlike many other languages. The exception to this rule is when a user accidentally places a space within a token, which confuses the JavaScript interpreter.

SUMMARY

In Chapter 2, you learned the basic aspects of an object-based programming (OBL) environment. You incorporated many aspects of OBL environments into your sample code, including objects, properties, methods, and events. You learned that objects, similar to nouns in traditional languages, are the cornerstones of an OBL language. You learned that objects are based on classes, which represent the definitions of objects.

You also learned that dot syntax is a method of writing code statements using periods to represent hierarchy and the relationship of the elements in the statement. You discovered that events are occurrences that the programming environment can detect and that event handlers are keywords that allow JavaScript to detect and react to events.

In Chapter 2, you used a number of common objects, including the window object, the document object, and the Math object. Each object has its own set of methods, properties, and events, determined by the class to which it belongs.

KEY TERMS

Blur	Math object	Sub-object
Class	Method call	Syntax
Document object	Object	Text string
Dot syntax	Object-based language (OBL)	Token
Focus	Occurrence	White space
Form object	Properties	Window object
Interpreter	String	

CHECKING CONCEPTS AND TERMS

MULTIPLE CHOICE

Circle the letter that matches the correct answer for each of the following questions.

1. A class is _____.
   a. a theoretical definition that doesn't exist in the real world
   b. an action an object can perform
   c. a characteristic of an object
   d. an occurrence you can detect
   e. None of the above.

2. A property is _____.
   a. a theoretical definition that doesn't exist in the real world
   b. an action an object can perform
   c. a characteristic of an object
   d. an occurrence you can detect
   e. None of the above.

3. An event is _____.
   a. a theoretical definition that doesn't exist in the real world
   b. an action an object can perform
   c. a characteristic of an object
   d. an occurrence you can detect
   e. None of the above.

4. A method is _____.
   a. a theoretical definition that doesn't exist in the real world
   b. an action an object can perform
   c. a characteristic of an object
   d. an occurrence you can detect
   e. None of the above.

5. A method _____.
   a. may not require information
   b. may receive one item of information
   c. may receive two or more pieces of information
   d. All of the above.

6. A string is _____.
   a. a piece of plain text
   b. a code block of statements
   c. the same thing as a property
   d. a command written using dot syntax

7. A token cannot include white space.
   a. True
   b. False

8. If you draw focus to an object, _____.
   a. the object closes
   b. keystrokes are directed to the object
   c. Both of the above.
   d. None of the above.

9. A semicolon is used in JavaScript to _____.
   a. create inline JavaScript
   b. separate values sent to a method
   c. denote the end of a line of code or code statement
   d. None of the above.

10. When you use quotes to enclose text strings, _____.
   a. you must use matching pairs of quotes
   b. you can use a pair of single quotes
   c. you can use a pair of double quotes
   d. All of the above.

DISCUSSION QUESTIONS

1. How are OBL environments similar? Would learning JavaScript make it easier to learn another OBL language? Why or why not?

2. How is the Math object different from other objects, such as the document object or the window object?

3. Why do event handlers often appear outside the **<script>** tags? Why do JavaScript keywords, such as **onclick**, seem to belong to both HTML and JavaScript?

4. Many designers consider the document object as the most important element of the JavaScript language. What does the document object represent? Why would that make the document object so important?

SKILL DRILL

Skill Drills reinforce lesson skills. Each skill reinforced is the same, or nearly the same, as a skill presented in the lessons. Detailed instructions are provided in a step-by-step format. You can work through one or more exercises in any order.

1. Create an Alert Box with a Random Number

In this Skill Drill, you use a method within a method. When you create complex statements, it is often best to start simple, test the code, and then add complexity.

In the following exercise, you create an alert box that displays a random number. Create a simple alert box first, and then add the code to create the random number.

1. In your text editor, open the alertrandom.html from your WIP_02 folder.

    This is a simple XHTML document.

2. Create a script in the body of the document.

    You insert additional code between the **<script>** and **</script>** tags in the steps that follow.

3. To create code that generates an alert box with a random number in the alert box, you must insert a method into a method. The random number should be a decimal number between 0 and 1. Hint: **Math.random()** will generate the proper number.

FIGURE 2.40

4. Test your code in the browser to make sure it works correctly.

5. Close the file in the text editor and browser.

2. Use the prompt() Method

In this exercise, you use a method that can pass multiple pieces of information. You use the **prompt()** method to generate a question box for the user. Then, you pass a second piece of information to the method to generate a default answer.

1. In your text editor, open the promptskill.html from your WIP_02 folder.

2. Create a script in the head of the HTML document.

   You insert additional code between the **<script>** and **</script>** tags in the steps that follow.

3. Create code to generate a prompt box between your **<script>** and **</script>** tags. The prompt box should ask the user if he wants fries with his order, as shown in Figure 2.41.

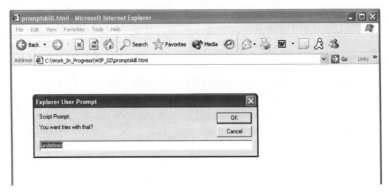

FIGURE 2.41

4. Test your code in the browser to make sure it works correctly.

5. Change the code so the word "Yes" appears as the default value to the question.

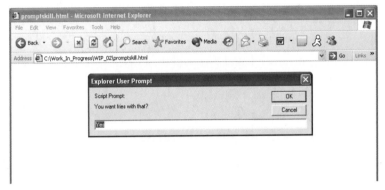

FIGURE 2.42

6. Save the file and test the result in your browser.

7. Close the file in your browser and text editor.

3. Correct Syntax Errors

Students learning HTML are often confused by the different syntax rules associated with JavaScript. During the first two chapters in this book, you learned several of the basic JavaScript syntax requirements/rules. In this exercise, you use those rules to correct a script that contains errors.

1. In your text editor, open errors.html from your WIP_02 folder.

FIGURE 2.43

2. Find and correct the four errors in the source code of this page.

3. Save the file and test it in your browser.

    Once corrected, the file generates an alert box, and then writes text to the screen.

4. Close the file in the browser and text editor.

4. Use an Event Handler with a Visual Element

Event handlers detect a number of events. Many events, such as **onclick**, are used with visual elements placed on the screen. In this exercise, you attach an event to an image and cause a prompt box to appear when the user clicks the image.

1. In your Web browser, open inlineskill.html from the WIP_02 folder.

FIGURE 2.44

2. Open the file in your text editor.

3. Use inline JavaScript to create a **prompt()** box when the **onclick** event is detected on the image. The prompt box should ask, "What color?" when the user clicks her mouse on the image.

    Hint: start with **onclick="prompt(' ')"** and then fill in the information needed in the **prompt()** method call.

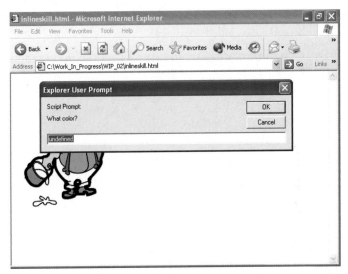

FIGURE 2.45

4. Save the file and test it in your browser.

5. Close the file in your browser and text editor.

CHALLENGE

Challenge exercises expand on, or are somewhat related to, skills presented in the lessons. Each exercise provides a brief introduction, followed by instructions presented in a numbered-step format that are not as detailed as those in the Skill Drill exercises. You should work through these exercises in the order provided.

1. Return a Number from a Method

Your instructor asked you to write a script that calculates the circumference of a circle. You can use the following formula to determine the circumference of a circle:

Circumference = diameter * pi

In this exercise, you write a script that asks the user for the diameter of the circle. Then, you design a calculation and return the correct answer to the user.

1. In your text editor, open circumference.html from the WIP_02 folder.

    Numerous programmer's comments were placed in the code to indicate the steps you need to take.

2. Find the first comment, which says:

    ```
    // ask the user for a diameter
    ```

3. Below this comment, create a **prompt()** statement that asks the user to enter the diameter of a circle.

4. Change the **prompt()** statement so the information is returned from the **prompt()** method and stored in a temporary storage space called "diameter".

   Hint: start with **diameter=prompt();**, and then fill in the information needed in the prompt() statement.

5. Find the comment that reads:

   ```
   //output the information to the user
   ```

6. Below this line, enter the following code statement.

   ```
   document.write(diameter);
   ```

   This allows you to test the code you entered.

7. Save the file and test it in your browser.

   A prompt box should appear. After the user enters a diameter, the diameter should write to the screen.

8. Keep the file open in your text editor for the next exercise.

9. Close your browser.

2. Use Math Properties to Complete a Calculation

In this Challenge, you start with the file from the previous exercise. You add code to complete the mathematical calculation. To achieve the best result, you use a property of the Math object.

1. With circumference.html open in your text editor, save the file as "circumference2.html" in your WIP_02 folder.

2. Find the following comment in your code.

   ```
   //calculate circumference=diameter multiplied by pi
   ```

3. After this statement, insert the following code to calculate the circumference.

   ```
   circumference = diameter * 3.14;
   ```

   Pi is equal to 3.14 — when rounded to two decimal places.

4. Change your **document.write()** statement to output the circumference instead of the diameter.

5. Save the file and test it in your browser.

   Using the number 5 as the diameter should generate 15.700000000000001 as the circumference.

6. In your calculation, you used the number 3.14 to approximate the value of pi. Including additional decimal places would allow you to calculate pi more accurately. Replace the number 3.14 with the **PI** property of the Math object (**Math.PI**).

   This property makes your script more accurate.

7. Save the file in your text editor and refresh the browser.

Using the number 5 for the diameter should generate 15.707963267948965 as the circumference. Your results may be slightly different, due to rounding differences with different hardware and operating system configurations.

8. Close the file in the browser and text editor.

3. Use the resizeTo() Method

In this chapter, you learned several basic methods and properties of the window object. A window object represents a browser window in JavaScript. The word **window** always represents the current browser window in JavaScript. In this Challenge, you use the **resizeTo()** method of the window object to resize a browser window.

1. In your text editor, open resizeto.html from your WIP_02 folder.

2. Create a script in the body of the document.

3. Write a line of code to resize the current browser window to 300 pixels wide and 240 pixels high.

    You use the **resizeTo()** method to resize the current browser window. The **resizeTo()** method requires two pieces of information: the width of the window and the height of the window. Both pieces of information are sent to the method as numbers, not text.

4. Save the file in the text editor.

5. Load the file in your browser.

    The window automatically resizes to 300 × 240 pixels.

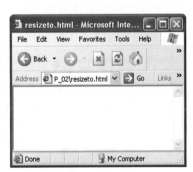

FIGURE 2.46

6. Return to your text editor. Change the **resizeTo()** width dimension to 390 pixels.

7. Save the file in the text editor. Keep the file open in the text editor for the next challenge.

8. Close the file in the browser.

4. Event Actions with Form Elements

In the previous Challenge, you used the **resizeTo()** method to automatically resize the browser window. In this exercise, you use event handlers to resize the browser window when a specific event occurs. You use form elements to create a button and then use inline JavaScript to trigger actions during specific events.

1. In the open resizeto.html in your text editor, insert a blank line after the **<body>** tag. Insert the following code to create a button within a form.

    ```
    <title>resizeto.html</title>
    </head>
    <body>
    <form name="form1" method="post" action="">
      <input type="button" name="Resize" value="Resize"/>
    </form>
    </body>
    </html>
    ```

2. Add the **onclick** event handler as an attribute of the tag that creates the button.

3. Program the **onclick** event to resize the browser window when the user clicks the button shown on the page. The window should resize to 400 pixels wide and 250 pixels high.

4. Remove the script that already exists in the page.

5. Save the file and test it in your browser.

    The window should open at one size and then resize after the user clicks the button.

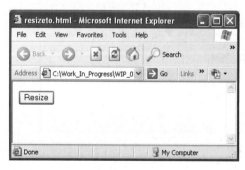

FIGURE 2.47

6. Close the file in your browser and text editor.

PORTFOLIO BUILDER

Customizing Screen Size

Client-side scripting allows sophisticated interaction between users and their Web browsers. For example, users can input information and it automatically appears on screen, and users can accomplish mathematical calculations with or without direct input.

A typical use for JavaScript is to allow users to customize certain aspects of their Web-browsing experience. Due to the myriad possible screen resolutions, designers cannot anticipate every possible setting and preference. Knowing this, Web designers allow users limited control over their displays. Use your knowledge of the material covered in the first two chapters of this book to write code that allows a user to select a browser size that suits his individual preferences.

1. Make sure script error message notifications are turned on in your browser.

2. Open resizer.html from your WIP_02 folder.

3. Load the file in your browser.

   Your browser generates an error. Look closely at the error dialog box; it tells you what the browser expects. A number of errors exist in the JavaScript code.

4. Correct the syntax error in the following statement.

   ```
   <body onload="alert('Please choose a browser resolution for
   your viewing pleasure")">
   ```

   The error you corrected was causing the browser to ignore the **alert()** statement. Another error is preventing the instructional text from writing to the browser window. The text should say, "Please click a button to change the size of the browser window."

5. Correct the scripting error to allow the text to write to the browser window.

   The window shows a row of buttons that correspond to different browser sizes. When a user clicks one of the buttons in the window, her browser window should resize according to the dimensions of the button text. Currently, the first button is the only one that works correctly.

6. Using the first button as a guide, create event handlers for the rest of the buttons to resize the browser window to the specified resolutions.

CHAPTER 3

Understanding the JavaScript Object Model

OBJECTIVES

In this chapter, you learn how to:

- Use dot syntax

- Use the JavaScript Object Model

- Manipulate the document object

- Interact with HTML dynamically

- Incorporate the form object

- Use nontraditional objects

Why Would I Do This?

Now that you are familiar with objects and object-based language (OBL) environments, the next step is to examine object models. An ***object model*** is a map of the organizational structure of an OBL environment. The JavaScript Object Model defines the classes of JavaScript objects. Understanding the object model of a particular language allows you to know what an object is, what it can do, and other characteristics of that object. In this chapter, you consider the JavaScript Object Model from a conceptual point of view, as well as explore some common JavaScript objects.

As you learned in Chapter 2, code is organized into objects in OBL environments. Objects allow you to group information and commands based on how humans categorize information. Let's continue to use the hypothetical `myCar` object from Chapter 2, which has four tires, a steering wheel, and other characteristics in common with all other car objects. You can have subcategories of the car object, such as `car.Dodge` and `car.Volkswagen`, which are both car objects, even though they are slightly different from each other.

In JavaScript, you use dot syntax to separate object names, subcategories, characteristics, and other aspects of an object. The following are some examples of objects in JavaScript.

- Programmers create ***user-defined objects*** to bring consistent structure to specific programming tasks.

- The JavaScript language includes ***built-in objects***. Examples of built-in objects include the Date and Math objects, which allow developers to manipulate dates and perform complex mathematical calculations.

- ***Browser objects*** control specific aspects of the Web browser. An example of a browser object is the window object, which allows developers to open and manipulate new browser windows.

- ***Document objects*** allow the developer to control aspects of HTML and cascading style sheet (CSS) code. Various document objects allow you to interact with information in forms and other aspects of HTML documents.

The ***JavaScript Object Model*** is a map of how objects are categorized in JavaScript. It starts with objects at the highest level of the language and then describes subcategories of the objects and their related characteristics. Think of the object model as a chart of the organizational structure of the JavaScript language. For instance, the window object can contain subordinate objects, such as the document object. The document object has its own associated properties, subordinate objects, and events.

Every version of the JavaScript language has a slightly different object model — which explains why many compatibility issues exist. In addition, every browser typically includes a set of objects designed for use with that particular browser — another reason for compatibility problems.

Variables are important foundational elements in every programming and scripting language. A ***variable*** is a named temporary storage area for a piece of information or an object. Variables are also objects. In JavaScript, when you create a variable, the information assigned to the variable name determines the type of object.

As you might remember from Chapters 1 and 2, you can create a variable with a statement, such as `myName="Jack";`. This sample code creates a variable named `myName,` which stores the string "`Jack`." Since the variable stores a text string, the variable is also a *string object*, and you can use *string methods* to control this variable.

In this chapter, you explore the basic aspects of the object model, learn about variables, and discover several methods used to control variables. You find out how these important elements are used in the JavaScript OBL environment.

VISUAL SUMMARY

The JavaScript Object Model is the entire scripting language organized into categories. The *Browser Object Model* is the JavaScript language adapted for Web browsers. Since individual browsers (such as IE and Navigator) often include JavaScript commands unavailable to other browsers, slightly different object models are assigned to each of the Web browsers; however, most of these differences have been eliminated since ECMA began to standardize the language. Take a moment to examine the diagram of the Browser Object Model shown below.

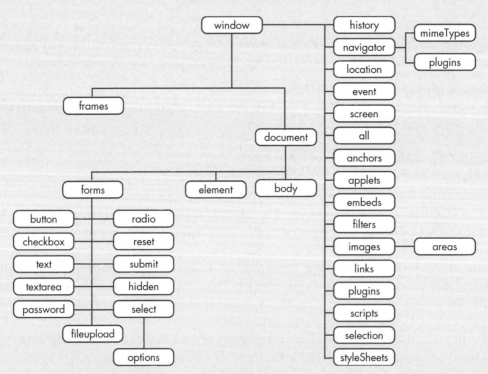

FIGURE 3.1

A comprehensive diagram of the Browser Object Model would include the properties and methods of each object. To display such a diagram in its entirety would require a large poster, which is outside the confines of this book. The most useful part of the complete object model is the *Document Object Model (DOM)*, because it provides direct control over HTML and CSS coding.

Objects in the DOM represent HTML code. When JavaScript encounters an HTML tag, JavaScript often creates a matching object to represent the HTML tag. The following table shows several HTML tags, their matching JavaScript objects, and how JavaScript references the objects.

HTML Tag	JavaScript Object	Reference
<a>	Link	links[object number]
<form>	Form	forms[object number]
<img>	Image	images[object number]

TABLE 3.1

For example, the `<img>` tag displays an image in HTML. This tag also creates a matching object in JavaScript known as an image object. In JavaScript, you can use the following notation to refer to an image.

```
window.document.images[0]
```

This code refers to the first image in the HTML document. JavaScript always refers to the first object as [**0**]. The second object in the HTML file is referred to as [**1**], the third object is [**2**], and so forth. In many programming and scripting languages, the number [**0**] is often used to refer to the first object in a series of objects.

Outside the Browser Object Model, JavaScript also contains several built-in objects that are useful for a variety of purposes. Examples of built-in objects include the Math object, which you can use to complete complex mathematical operations, and the Date object, which makes it easy to manipulate dates and times.

LESSON 1 Using Dot Syntax

As you know from your work in Chapter 2, many objects exist within other objects. For example, the document object (which represents HTML code) is part of the window object (which represents the browser window). In some cases, you must note the relationship between objects in your code.

Dot syntax is the primary method for noting the relationship between objects and their associated methods and properties. Using dot syntax to illustrate these relationships, you could write the following pseudocode.

```
object.subobject.method();
```

If the **myCar** object had a horn, you could write the following statement to call for the **honk()** method.

```
myCar.horn.honk();
```

Using an actual JavaScript method, you could write the following statement using dot syntax.

```
window.document.write("hello");
```

The document object is a subordinate object of the window object. The **write()** method belongs to the document object.

Use Dot Syntax

1 | **Copy the content of the Chapter_03 folder to the WIP_03 folder.**

You use these files for the exercises in this chapter.

2 | **Open WIP_03>scenic.html in your browser and text editor.**

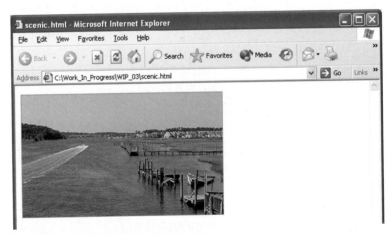

FIGURE 3.2

This simple HTML file displays a photo.

3 | **Find the following code in the HTML file.**
```
<img src="scenic.jpg" alt="Little River, SC" name="LittleRiver"
width="350" height="206" id="LittleRiver"/>
```

You should recognize this as the source of the image on your screen. When you use an **<img>** tag in HTML, an image object is also created in JavaScript.

4 | **Before the </body> tag, insert the following code to start a script.**
```
. . .
</head>
<body>
```

```
<img src="scenic.jpg" alt="Little River, SC" name="LittleRiver"
width="350" height="206" id="LittleRiver"/>
<script language="JavaScript" type="text/javascript">
</script>
</body>
</html>
```

5 **Insert the following code.**

```
...
<body>
<img src="scenic.jpg" alt="Little River, SC" name="LittleRiver"
width="350" height="206" id="LittleRiver"/>
<script language="JavaScript" type="text/javascript">
//display a property of the image object
alert();
</script>
</body>
</html>
```

Next, insert code in the **alert()** method to display a property of this object.

6 **Change the alert() statement to the following.**

```
alert(window.document.images[0].src);
```

The word "**window**" represents the browser window. The word "**document**" represents the HTML document. The code **images[0]** refers to the first **<img>** tag found in the HTML document. The **src** property holds the value created by the **src** attribute of the **<img>** tag.

7 **Save the file in your text editor and refresh your browser.**

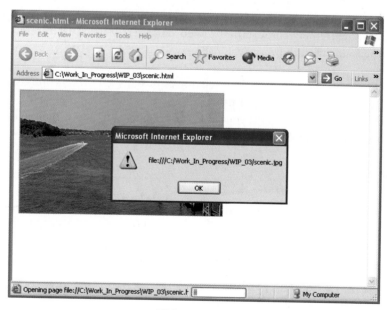

FIGURE 3.3

The value stored in the **href** property of the first image object displays in the alert box.

8 **Keep the file open in your text editor for the next exercise. Close the file in your Web browser.**

In the previous exercise, you used dot syntax to specify a property of the first image object (the first **<img>** tag), which was part of the document object (the HTML code), which was part of the window object (the browser window). At this point, you should understand how the object model structures JavaScript.

To Extend Your Knowledge . . .

USING DOT SYNTAX TO WRITE CODE

Many languages offer multiple ways to write statements (code). When using dot syntax, you write the object name first, followed by the name of a sub-object, a property, or a method. Dot syntax is the standardized method of writing code; you should use it whenever possible.

LESSON 2 Using the JavaScript Object Model

The JavaScript Object Model is the organizational chart for the entire language. Each browser has its own object model, which varies slightly from every other browser's object model. In addition, subordinate objects have their own object models. If you were to draw a diagram of the Document Object Model, it would show every characteristic, every event, and every subordinate object available to the document object.

Recall from previous chapters that the document object represents the HTML document (HTML code) loaded into the browser. Understanding the DOM allows you to interact with and change existing HTML code. For this reason, the DOM is extremely important to Web designers who must interact with HTML code, because— HTML is the foundation of every Web page.

In the following exercises, you learn how to note relationships between objects and assign specific names to objects. You also use JavaScript to address and control these objects. As you complete these exercises, you receive a broad exposure to JavaScript. Don't worry if you have specific questions about the methods or objects used in the exercises; we discuss them in detail in other chapters in this book.

Name an Object

1 **In the open scenic.html in your text editor, save the file as "nameobject.html" in your WIP_03 folder.**

2 **Find the following code in your document.**

```
alert(window.document.images[0].href);
```

3   **Change the code to the following.**

```
alert(window.document.images[0].name);
```

The **alert()** method returns the **name** property of the image object.

4   **Save the file to your text editor and open it in your browser.**

FIGURE 3.4

The **name** property appears. This is the same information created by the **name** attribute in the **<img>** tag.

5   **Return to your code in your text editor. Change the alert() statement to the following.**

```
alert(window.document.LittleRiver.height);
```

Aside from being a property of the image object, the **name** attribute is also used to name the object (as you might have guessed). You can use the name stored in the **name** attribute to refer to the property.

6   **Save the file in your text editor and refresh your browser.**

FIGURE 3.5

The value stored in the **height** property returns to the user.

7   **Close the file in the browser and text editor.**

Various aspects of the document object and its subordinate objects often represent objects that have already been created in HTML. You can include a **name** attribute in most HTML tags to create an object name, which you can then use in JavaScript.

To Extend Your Knowledge . . .

NAMING OBJECTS

When you name an object in JavaScript, you do not need to use the full path to address the object. This makes the code easier to read. The usefulness of this feature often depends on the application. For instance, if you want to use the same object repeatedly, it may be easier to assign an easy-to-remember name. If you always want to use a specific object, such as the third image, it may be better to address the object generically.

Create a New Window Object

1   **In your text editor open openwindow.html from your WIP_03 folder.**

2   **Insert the following code in the body section of the document.**

```
. . .
</head>
<body>
<script language="JavaScript" type="text/javascript">
</script>
</body>
</html>
```

You inserted a script into the body section of the HTML document. Omitting the **</script>** tag causes many browsers to ignore the commands that follow the **<script>** tag.

3   **Type the following statement within the <script> and </script> tags.**

```
. . .
<body>
<script language="JavaScript" type="text/javascript">
adWindow=open("","mywin","height=300,width=300");
</script>
</body>
</html>
```

You created a new window object by naming and opening a new window. In this example, you named the window object "adWindow", and set the dimensions to a smaller size than a standard window. The smaller size allows you to see both windows at the same time.

4   **Save your file. Open the file in your browser.**

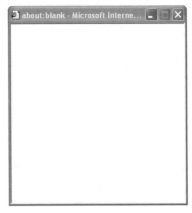

FIGURE 3.6

A second window opens. A matching window object is also created in JavaScript.

| **5** | **Close the smaller window.** |

| **6** | **Keep openwindow.html open in your text editor and browser for the next exercise.** |

In this exercise, you used a method of the window object to create an object. You can now use JavaScript to manipulate the object the same way that you can manipulate existing objects.

To Extend Your Knowledge . . .

PARAMETERS OF THE OPEN() METHOD

In the previous exercise, the two double quote characters in the `open()` method indicate that the first parameter is blank. Double quotes are also used on both sides of the other parameters. The `height` and `width` attributes are part of the third parameter (the screen properties parameter), so you should not use double quotes between them. Don't mistake the double quote characters for two single quotes—and always remember that quote characters must be used in matching pairs.

The second parameter of the `open()` method is a name property that you can reference through JavaScript. You can name the window object by typing a name and the equal (=) sign before the `window.open()` method. This may seem confusing, since the `open()` method allows two different ways to name the window object; however, each of the two ways to name the object has a slightly different purpose in the code.

Manipulate a Second Window Object

| **1** | **In the open openwindow.html in your text editor, find the following line of code.** |

```
adWindow=open("","mywin","height=300,width=300");
```

2 Insert a blank line after the `open()` statement and add the following line of code.

```
. . .
<script language="JavaScript" type="text/javascript">
adWindow=open("","mywin","height=300,width=300");
adWindow.document.write("Free fish with dog purchase!");
</script>
</body>
</html>
```

Content displays in your new window. This occurs because you entered the object's name (adWindow) and used dot syntax to access the **write()** method of the document object.

3 Add the following lines of code after the existing `document.write` statement.

```
. . .
<script language="JavaScript" type="text/javascript">
adWindow=open("","mywin","height=300,width=300");
adWindow.document.write("Free fish with dog purchase!");
//the next statement sends content to the original window
window.document.write("This is the original window");
</script>
</body>
</html>
```

Content displays in the original window because you used another **document.write** statement.

4 Save the file in your text editor and refresh your browser.

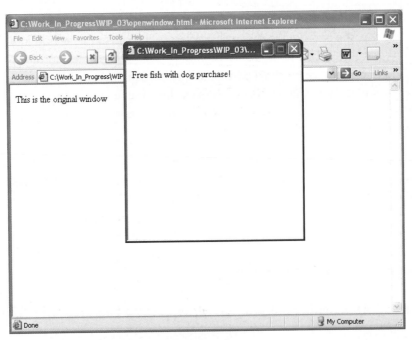

FIGURE 3.7

In most browsers, the pop-up window appears in the upper-left corner. In Figure 3.7 we moved the original window so you could see the text.

Now that you have created a second window object, let's find out what happens if you don't specify a window in the **document.write()** statement.

5 | **Delete the word "window" and the first period from the beginning of the following statement.**

```
window.document.write("This is the original window");
```

The statement should now read:

```
document.write("This is the original window");
```

6 | **Save the document in your text editor and refresh your browser.**

The result is the same as before. JavaScript assumes you mean the original window (where the code exists) if you don't specify the window's name.

7 | **Close the document in your text editor and browser.**

In the previous exercises, you discovered how to use JavaScript to create and manipulate objects. You learned that HTML tags have matching objects within the document object in JavaScript. You found that when you manipulate various aspects of the document object, you change aspects of the HTML code when the script is interpreted.

To Extend Your Knowledge...

FUNCTIONS

As you know, you use methods to manipulate objects. You can also create your own methods by creating functions. Functions are similar to methods, except that the user creates functions, whereas methods are built into the JavaScript language. You can use functions to create custom objects. Don't worry if this seems overwhelming — you explore functions in detail later in this book.

LESSON 3 | Manipulating the Document Object

The document object represents the XHTML or CSS code used in the browser. The document object is the strength behind JavaScript because it allows you to combine the full power of a programming language with the simplicity of HTML. For this reason, the Document Object Model is the most important part of JavaScript, and the document object is the most revered object in JavaScript.

You can use the various parts of the DOM to complete many different tasks. For example, you may want an image that you created in HTML to display a rollover effect when the user moves her mouse over the image. As another example, you may want to validate the content of a form you created in HTML to verify that the user entered his email address correctly.

When you create HTML tags, matching objects are created in JavaScript. The JavaScript objects represent the HTML tags. You can use methods or properties of the objects to manipulate the HTML when the browser interprets the script. With JavaScript, many additional functions are available to you — functions not available in HTML.

Manipulate a Link Object

In the following exercises, you learn how to access an object that is part of the document object. First, you manipulate an object created by an HTML tag. Then, you discover how to create HTML from within JavaScript.

1   **Open WIP_03>links.html in your text editor and browser.**

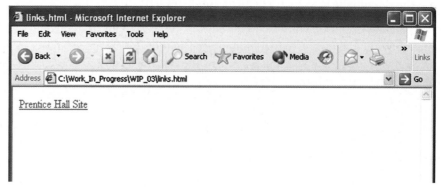

FIGURE 3.8

This simple HTML file contains a hyperlink to the Prentice Hall publishing Web site.

2   **Find the following code in your text editor.**

```
<script language="JavaScript" type="text/javascript">
</script>
```

4   **Insert the following line of code.**

```
<script language="JavaScript" type="text/javascript">
alert(window.document.links[0].href);
</script>
```

The link object represents **<a>** tags in the HTML document. The link object is, of course, a part of the document object. The keyword "**links**" is used to denote all links in the HTML document. The first object found in a category is always noted as **[0]**. The second link object is noted as **links[1]**, and so forth.

4   **Save the file in your text editor and refresh your browser.**

FIGURE 3.9

The value stored in the **href** property appears in the alert box.

5   **Click OK. Return to your text editor. Change the alert() statement to the following.**

```
alert(window.document.links[0].target);
```

The **target** property represents the **target** attribute of the **link** object or **<a>** tag.

6   **Save the file in your text editor and refresh your browser.**

FIGURE 3.10

The value stored in the **target** attribute displays in the alert box.

7   **Click OK.**

8   **Close the file in your browser and text editor.**

To Extend Your Knowledge . . .

LINK AND ANCHOR OBJECTS

Link objects represent <a> tags in the HTML document. Anchor objects also represent <a> tags in the HTML document. In theory, the link object is designed for use when the <a> tag links to a URL, such as index.html or http://www.web-answers.com.

The anchor object is designed for use when the <a> tag links to another point or anchor within the HTML page. In reality, the objects represent the same information and can be used interchangeably.

Create an Image Object in JavaScript

1   **In your text editor, open imageobject.html from your WIP_03 folder.**

2   **Insert the following line of code.**

```
. . .
<title>imageobject.html</title>
<script language="JavaScript" type="text/javascript">
//create an image object
myImage=new Image();
</script>
</head>
<body>
. . .
```

This code creates a new image object called **myImage**.

3   **Insert the following line of code into the script in the head section of the document.**

```
. . .
<script language="JavaScript" type="text/javascript">
//create an image object
myImage=new Image();
myImage.src="scenic.jpg";
</script>
</head>
<body>
. . .
```

A URL is assigned as the **src** (source) property of the image object. This code causes the image to load into the browser's cache.

4   **Save the file in your text editor and open it in your browser.**

The browser loads the file into the browser's cache, but does not display the image.

5 Insert the following line of code into the script in the body section of the document.

```
. . .
<body>
<script language="JavaScript" type="text/javascript">
//manipulate the image object
document.write(myImage.height);
</script>
</body>
</html>
```

6 Save the file in your text editor and refresh your browser.

FIGURE 3.11

The height of the loaded image (206) displays.

7 Close the file in your browser and text editor.

In this exercise, you learned to create an image object from within JavaScript. This is in contrast to previous exercises, where you manipulated an image object that was created with HTML. This brings up an interesting aspect of JavaScript — you can use it to create and change elements of HTML while the script is being interpreted. You explore this feature in detail in the next lesson.

To Extend Your Knowledge . . .

PRELOADING IMAGES

The ability to create image objects in JavaScript and assign the `src` property allows an image to pre-load into the browser's cache before the image is used. This is a valuable feature when you create rollover effects and slide shows. Without this feature, the user must wait for the image to load when an event occurs, such as when the user rolls her mouse over a button. With this feature, the image loads in the background before the event occurs.

LESSON 4 Interacting with HTML Dynamically

In previous lessons, you learned that JavaScript creates objects to represent various aspects of the HTML code loaded into the browser. Since the DOM represents the HTML code in the document, you can use a variety of the DOM features to change the existing HTML code.

It is also possible to create new HTML code from within JavaScript. This is usually done using the **write()** or **writeln()** methods of the document object. Consider the following code as an example.

```
document.write("<i>Hello</i>");
```

HTML code is embedded into the text string being passed to the method. This code is interpreted by the HTML interpreter after being interpreted by the JavaScript interpreter. Consider the result of this code, shown below.

FIGURE 3.12

In the following exercises, you learn how to change the content of an HTML tag. In many cases, you can accomplish this with the **innerHTML** property of the object that represents the HTML tag.

Use the InnerHTML Property

1   **From your WIP_03 folder, open innerHTML.html in your text editor and find the following line of code.**

```
alert(window.document.links[0].target);
```

This code simply displays the **target** property of the first **<a>** tag in the HTML document. This is essentially the same file you modified in a previous exercise.

2   **Change the code to the following.**

```
alert(window.document.links[0].innerHTML);
```

The **innerHTML** property represents the text between the **<a>** and **</a>** tags.

3   Save the file in your text editor and open it in your browser.

FIGURE 3.13

The text between the `<a>` and `</a>` tags displays in the alert window.

4   Click OK, and then return to your text editor.

5   Directly before the `</script>` tag, add the following line of code.

```
...
<script language="JavaScript" type="text/javascript">
alert(window.document.links[0].innerHTML);
window.document.links[0].innerHTML="Essentials Series";
</script>
</body>
</html>
```

6   Save the file in your text editor and refresh your browser.

7   Click OK to acknowledge the alert box.

FIGURE 3.14

As soon as you acknowledge the alert box, the text of the hyperlink changes.

8   Close the file in your browser and text editor.

In this exercise, you used the **innerHTML** property to change the text that appears between a starting HTML tag (such as an `<a>` tag) and an ending tag (such as an `<a/>` tag).

To Extend Your Knowledge...

CHANGING THE CONTENT OF AN HTML TAG

The `innerHTML` property is useful when you want to change the content of an HTML tag as the result of a user action. This property works with many HTML tags that display text, including the `<td>` tag.

Write HTML Dynamically

In this exercise, you learn how to create HTML code dynamically as the script executes. This is usually done with the `write()` method of the document object.

1   **In your text editor, open writehtml.html from your WIP_03 folder.**

2   **Insert the following line of code.**

```
...
</head>
<body>
<script language="JavaScript" type="text/javascript">
document.write("some text");
</script>
</body>
</html>
```

3   **Save the document in your text editor and open it in your browser.**

FIGURE 3.15

The text writes to the screen.

4   **Return to your text editor and modify the `document.write()` statement as follows.**

```
document.write("<strong>some <i>text</i> </strong>");
```

This code inserts HTML formatting into the text string sent to the **document.write()** method.

5   **Save the file in your text editor and refresh your browser.**

FIGURE 3.16

This code applies bold and italic styles to the HTML code.

6   **Keep the file open for the next exercise.**

In this exercise, you created HTML code using the **write()** method of the document object. This brings up an interesting question: Does JavaScript create objects to represent HTML code created within JavaScript? You explore this topic in the next exercise.

To Extend Your Knowledge...

CREATING HTML IN JAVASCRIPT

The ability to create HTML code from within JavaScript is useful for a number of reasons. Since HTML is specifically designed to format text, it is often used to format the output of a script to create professional-looking results. This is virtually impossible to do with JavaScript, since the language offers few formatting options.

Interact with Dynamically Written HTML

1   **In the open writehtml.html in your text editor, find the following line of code.**

```
document.write("<strong>some <i>text</i></strong>");
```

2   **Replace this line with the following code.**

```
document.write("<a href='http://www.web-answers.com'>
link</a><br />");
```

3   **Save the file in your text editor and refresh your browser.**

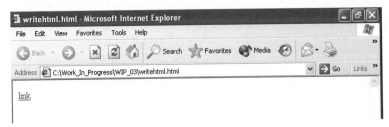

FIGURE 3.17

The JavaScript code creates the hyperlink.

4   **Return to your text editor. Add the following line of code after the code you modified in Step 2.**

```
document.write(document.links[0].href);
```

This code returns the **href** property of the first hyperlink in the document.

5   **Save the file in your text editor and refresh your browser.**

FIGURE 3.18

The **href** property of the object displays, even though JavaScript created this object dynamically.

6   **Close the file in your browser and text editor.**

In this exercise, you learned that JavaScript objects also represent HTML code that JavaScript creates. This feature is especially useful in advanced scripts.

To Extend Your Knowledge . . .

WRITING HTML DYNAMICALLY

Information sent to the **write()** method of the document object is interpreted by the HTML interpreter before being output to the screen.

LESSON 5 Using the Form Object

When you insert a `<form>` tag into an XHTML document, a form object is created. Traditionally, HTML forms allowed users to insert information that was sent to the server for processing. The server verified that the user entered the information correctly.

Using server-side scripting to process the information on a form is often a waste of resources. For example, let's say that a user enters an invalid e-mail address on a form. He doesn't realize his error and submits the form. The information travels over the Internet to the server. The server devotes processing time to determine if the user entered correct information. When the server determines that the information is incorrect, the server responds to the end user and prompts him to fix the error. The end user corrects his error, resubmits the form, and the process starts all over again.

A simpler method allows the client machine to check for errors before transmitting the information to the server. Using this method (called client-side scripting), JavaScript can interact with the information entered into the form and check for errors. The form object and its methods and properties are useful in this situation. The *element object* represents individual fields in the form. Each element in a form is represented by a matching element object in JavaScript. The `value` property represents the information stored in a form field.

Interact with an HTML Form

1 **Open WIP_03>form1.html in your text editor and browser.**

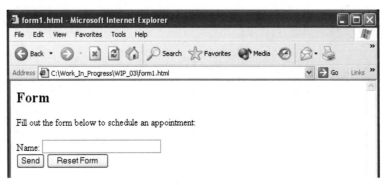

FIGURE 3.19

This simple form was created with the HTML `<form>` tag.

2 **In your text editor, insert a blank line between the `</form>` and `</body>` tags.**

3 Add the following code.

```
. . .
</form>
<script language="JavaScript" type="text/javascript">
</script>
</body>
. . .
```

The **<form>** tag creates a matching form object in JavaScript. You use this script to interact with the form.

4 Insert the following code into your script.

```
. . .
</form>
<script language="JavaScript" type="text/javascript">
document.write(window.document.forms[0].id);
</script>
</body>
. . .
```

This script displays the **id** property of the first form object in the HTML document. The first **<form>** tag in the document creates the first form object.

5 Save the file in your text editor and refresh your browser.

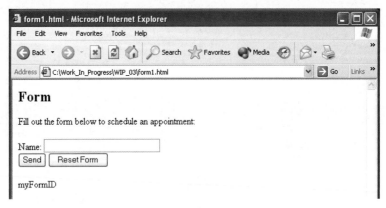

FIGURE 3.20

The **id** property of the form displays below the form. This property was established within the **<form>** tag.

6 Keep the file open in your text editor and browser for the next exercise.

In this exercise, you successfully interacted with a form object in JavaScript. Similar to many other objects, a form object results when you insert an HTML **<form>** tag in your code.

Write Object Paths

In this exercise, you interact with an element within a form.

1 **In the open form1.html in your text editor, find the following line of code.**

```
document.write(window.document.forms[0].id);
```

This code displays the value stored in the **name** property of the first form in the HTML document within the current browser window.

2 **Modify the code as follows.**

```
document.write(forms[0].id);
```

This statement simply refers to the first form without noting that it belongs to the current browser window or to the document object.

3 **Save the file in your text editor and refresh your browser.**

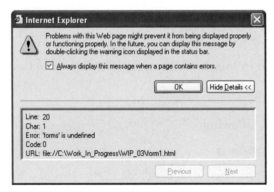

FIGURE 3.21

Most browsers generate errors, if error notifications are enabled. The code statement is not executed, and the browser fails to recognize the form object.

4 **Click OK to close the error message box (if it displayed).**

5 **Return to your text editor and change the line of code as follows.**

```
document.write(document.forms[0].id);
```

6 **Save the file in your text editor and refresh your browser.**

The code works correctly.

7 **Return to your text editor and change the code statement to the following.**

```
document.write(myForm.id);
```

8   **Save the file in your text editor and refresh your browser.**

The code works correctly. Notice that it wasn't necessary to specify that the form belonged to the document object when you used the name specified in the **name** property.

9   **Keep the file open in your text editor and browser for the next exercise.**

In this exercise, you learned some of the common ways to write pathways to objects.

To Extend Your Knowledge . . .

OBJECT PATHWAYS

Some objects, such as the form object, require you to specify the word document so JavaScript knows that the object exists within the document object. In many cases, you can refer to the object by the name assigned in the **name** property. This isn't consistent within JavaScript, however, and can prove confusing for novice programmers.

Access an Element of a Form Tag

1   **In the open form1.html in your text editor, find the following line of code.**

```
document.write(myForm.id);
```

2   **Change the code to the following.**

```
document.write(myForm.elements[0].name);
```

The keyword "**elements**" refers to the individual elements of a form. As with other objects, **[0]** means the first element found.

3   **Save the file in your text editor and refresh your browser.**

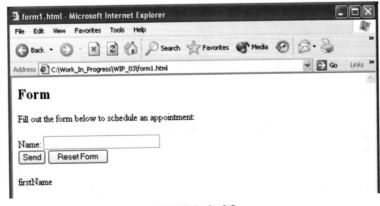

FIGURE 3.22

The name of the form element displays in the browser window below the form.

4   **Return to your text editor and change your code to the following.**

```
document.write(myForm.firstName.name);
```

This code allows the name specified in the **name** attribute of the HTML tag to be accessed through the element object.

5   **Save the file in your text editor and refresh your browser.**

The name of the object displays.

6   **Close the file in your text editor and browser.**

In this exercise, you used dot syntax and the object model to refer to a form element. Remember, the form element is an object that represents the individual parts of a form. The form exists within the document object, which exists within the window object.

Return the Value Stored in a Form Field

1   **Open WIP_03>form2.html in your text editor and browser.**

This is essentially the same form you used in the previous exercises.

2   **In your text editor, find the following code in the body of the document.**

```
<form action="" method="post" name="myForm"id="myForm">
```

3   **Change the code to the following.**

```
<form action="" method="post" name="myForm" id="myForm"
onsubmit="checkValue()">
```

This code triggers a function called **checkValue()** when the user submits the form. The function hasn't yet been created.

4   **Insert the following code in the head of the document.**

```
...
<head>
<title>form2.html</title>
<script language="JavaScript" type="text/javascript">
function checkValue(){
alert(myForm.firstName.value);
}
</script>
</head>
<body>
...
```

This code creates the function **checkValue()**, which triggers when the user clicks the submit button. The function returns the value stored in the form element called **firstName**.

5 | Save the file in your text editor and refresh your browser.

6 | Enter your first name in the First Name field, and then click the Send button.

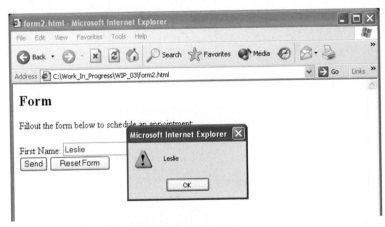

FIGURE 3.23

Your name returns to the alert box when you click the Send button.

7 | Click OK to acknowledge the alert box.

8 | Close the file in your browser and text editor.

In this exercise, you learned how to extract the value stored within a form element. This commonly used JavaScript feature allows you to test form information before you send it to the server for processing.

To Extend Your Knowledge . . .

USING VALUES FROM FORMS

When you extract information from an HTML form, always remember to include the **value** property when referring to a form element; otherwise, your code will generate an error.

LESSON 6   Using Nontraditional Objects

You know that you can use HTML code to create objects. You can also use a ***constructor method*** to generate a new object. Earlier in the chapter, you used the **open()** method of the window object to create a new browser window, which also created a second window object. The **open()** method is a constructor method, because it creates new objects.

A number of built-in objects exist in JavaScript — ones not typically considered "objects" — including the Date object, Math object, and String object. The Date object is different from most of the objects you have created; you create the ***Date object*** specifically to hold date or time information and to make this information easy to manipulate.

In the following exercises, you use constructor methods to create new objects. You also consider several nontraditional types of objects and learn some of the basic ways they are used. These exercises provide a clear overview of the object model and allow you to plainly see how objects are used in JavaScript.

Use a Constructor Method to Create an Object

1   **Open WIP_03>constructor.html in your text editor.**

2   **Insert the following lines of code into the script in the head of the document.**

```
. . .
<script language="JavaScript" type="text/javascript">
//this code creates a new date object
currentTime=new Date();
</script>
. . .
```

This code uses a constructor method to create a new Date object named **currentTime**. You must insert a space between the keyword **new** and the keyword **Date()**.

3   **Insert the following code in the body of the document.**

```
. . .
</script>
</head>
<body>
<script language="JavaScript" type="text/javascript">
document.write(currentTime);
</script>
</body>
</html>
```

4   Save the file in your text editor. Open the file in your browser.

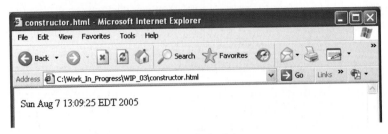

FIGURE 3.24

The current date and time display.

5   Keep the file open in your text editor and browser for the next exercise.

To Extend Your Knowledge...

CONSTRUCTOR METHODS

Most constructor methods use the keyword **new** followed by a space and the type of object being created. A constructor function typically works in the following fashion.

```
myBirthdate=new Date();
```

In this example, a variable named **myBirthdate** represents a Date object. The keyword **new** indicates that a new object is being created, based on the Date class of objects. The word "Date" is capitalized because it represents a class of objects.

Create a Date Object with a Specific Day and Time

1   In the open constructor.html in your text editor, find the following line of code.

```
currentTime=new Date();
```

This code creates a variable named **currentTime** with the current date stored as the value.

2   Change this line of code to the following.

```
specificDate=new Date("October 18, 1969 15:40:00");
```

This code inserts a new Date object called **specificDate** as well as stores October 18, 1969, as the date and 3:40 P.M. as the time.

3   Find the following statement in your code.

```
document.write(currentTime);
```

4   Change this statement to the following.

```
document.write(specificDate);
```

The statement uses the new object name you entered in Step 2.

5   Save the file in your text editor and refresh your browser.

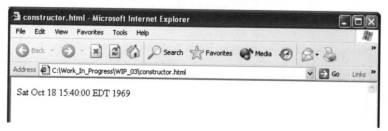

FIGURE 3.25

The date you entered appears.

6   Close the file in your browser and text editor.

In this exercise, you created a Date object by creating a variable and using a constructor function. Remember, variables serve as named storage areas for information; they are also objects you can manipulate.

To Extend Your Knowledge . . .

THE DATE OBJECT

The Date object was designed to make it easier to work with dates and times. You can manipulate the Date object in time periods as small as milliseconds. The Date object is extremely useful when determining the amount of time elapsed since an event or until an event.

Use a Variable as an Object

1   Open WIP_03>variable.html in your text editor.

2   Insert the following code in the head section of the document.

```
. . .
<title>variable.html</title>
<head>
<script language="JavaScript" type="text/javascript">
//this code creates a variable
myName="Michael";
</script>
</head>
<body>
. . .
```

This code creates a variable called **myName**. The variable is a string object, because it stores a text string.

3   **Insert the following line of code into the body section of the document.**

```
. . .
</head>
<body>
<script language="JavaScript" type="text/javascript">
document.write(myName.toUpperCase());
</script>
</body>
</html>
```

The **toUpperCase()** method is a string method you can apply to a string object.

4   **Save the file in your text editor. Open the file in your browser.**

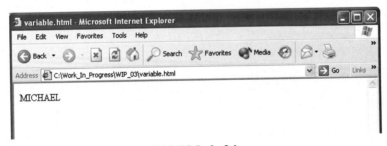

FIGURE 3.26

The value stored in the string object converts to uppercase letters because of the **toUpperCase()** method.

5   **Close the file in your browser and text editor.**

In this exercise, you learned that a variable is actually an object and can use object methods. The type of information stored within the variable determines the type of object.

To Extend Your Knowledge . . .

THE STRING OBJECT

You can use string methods to manipulate string objects. For example, string methods allow a programmer to search through a string for a particular character or string of characters. As another example, the `parseInt()` method allows you to convert a text string to a number so you can use it in mathematical calculations.

Use the History Object

1   **Open WIP_03>historyobject1.html in your browser.**

FIGURE 3.27

This simple HTML file contains a link to another HTML file.

2   **Click the hyperlink in your browser window.**

FIGURE 3.28

The historyobject2.html page loads into your browser and becomes the current entry in the browser's history list.

3   Open WIP_03>historyobject2.html in your text editor.

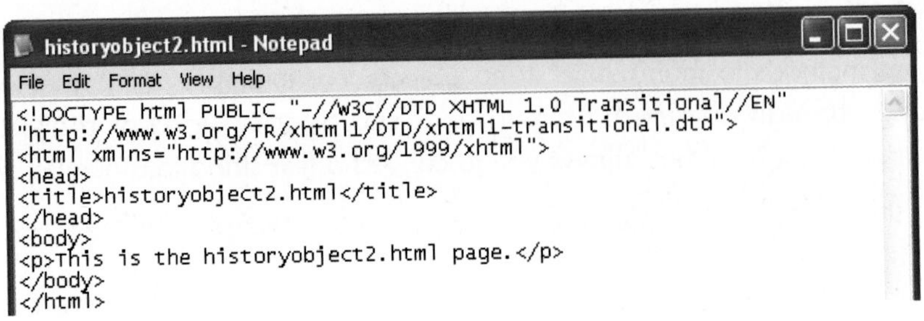

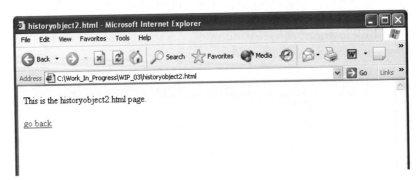

FIGURE 3.29

4   Immediately before the **</body>** tag, insert the following code.

```
...
</head>
<body>
<p>This is the historyobject2.html page.</p>
<a href="javascript:window.history.back();">go back</a>
</body>
</html>
```

You can use the keyword **javascript** in URLs to trigger inline JavaScript commands.

5   Save the file in your text editor and refresh your browser.

FIGURE 3.30

6   Click the "go back" link.

Your browser loads the file recorded in the browser's history list.

7   Close the file in your browser and text editor.

To Extend Your Knowledge . . .

THE HISTORY OBJECT

The **history object** represents the browser's history list. The history methods allow you to manipulate the history list. In recent years, the methods that allowed scripts to identify visited URLs were removed from the Browser Object Model. Older browsers (with older Browser Object Models) may still allow scripts to identify visited URLs (using history methods) and transmit this information.

Use the String Object

1 Open WIP_03>stringobject.html in your text editor. Examine the JavaScript code in the body section of the document.

```
<script language="JavaScript" type="text/javascript">
firstName="mike";
document.write(firstName+"<br />");
</script>
```

This simple file creates a variable called **firstName**, assigns the text string "**mike**" to the variable, and then displays the content of the variable on the screen.

2 Open the file in your browser.

FIGURE 3.31

3 Return to your text editor. Insert the following line of code directly before the `</script>` tag.

```
. . .
<script language="JavaScript" type="text/javascript">
firstName="mike";
document.write(firstName+"<br />");
document.write(firstName.toUpperCase());
</script>
. . .
```

4   Save the file in your text editor and refresh your browser.

FIGURE 3.32

5   Close the file in your text editor and browser.

CAREERS IN DESIGN

YOUR PORTFOLIO

Getting a job as a Web developer or Web designer requires you to have a strong portfolio Web site to show potential employers. Start by identifying projects that will represent the scope of your work. A good portfolio site has a bare minimum of five projects shown.

If you have significant experience, you may have a large number of projects that can be shown. If this is the case, break your portfolio down into sections such as Web Design, Animation, and Photography. Keep each section to a reasonable length. Five to eight portfolio pieces in each section are usually plenty. In each section, always start by showing your best piece of work in that category.

Many designers have older pieces that seem a bit outdated. Your skills have probably improved dramatically since your first piece of work. Ask your friends, professors, or others for honest feedback on how individual pieces can be improved. Don't be afraid to redo older projects from scratch, if necessary. You will probably be amazed at how much your productivity and skill level has improved since you initially completed the project.

SUMMARY

In Chapter 3, you learned that JavaScript is organized into a hierarchy known as the object model. You learned that the object model for an individual browser is known as the Browser Object Model, which can differ from one browser to the next. This inconsistency can result in browsers having different objects, methods, or properties, as well as slightly different organizations of the JavaScript language—which can lead to compatibility issues.

You discovered that the window object exists at the top of the Browser Object Model; it represents the browser window. You learned that the document object represents the HTML document and the associated HTML code. When you interact with parts of the object model, you interact with various aspects of the HTML page, such as forms and hyperlinks.

You learned that when an **`<img>`** tag is encountered in HTML code, a matching image object is created in JavaScript. When you manipulate properties of the object, you can also change various aspects of the HTML tag.

In this chapter, you learned how to use dot syntax to address various objects and properties within the JavaScript Object Model. You also learned how to name an object and refer to it by name. In various exercises, you learned how to access form elements and extract values from the form fields. You used the **`window.open()`** method to create an object, and you used the **`innerHTML`** property to dynamically change the text that appeared within an HTML tag.

You discovered how to create objects in a number of ways: the browser creates some objects, including the history object; HTML code generates other objects, including the link object. You also created objects with the constructor methods, which are specifically designed to create new objects.

KEY TERMS

Browser object	Document object	Object model
Browser Object Model	Document Object Model (DOM)	String method
Built-in object	Element object	String object
Constructor method	History object	User-defined object
Date object	JavaScript Object Model	Variable

CHECKING CONCEPTS AND TERMS

MULTIPLE CHOICE

Circle the letter that matches the correct answer for each of the following questions.

1. In many cases, when an HTML tag is encountered, _____.

   a. a matching object is created in JavaScript

   b. JavaScript cannot interact with the HTML tag

   c. an error is generated in JavaScript

   d. All of the above.

   e. None of the above.

2. The document object is extremely important to JavaScript developers because it allows interaction with _____.

a. the browser's history list

b. the HTML document

c. a pop-up window

d. the user's printer

3. Why is it useful to dynamically create HTML in JavaScript?

  a. It is the only way you can use HTML with JavaScript.

  b. It is more efficient than writing HTML code.

  c. It makes it easy to format output from a script.

  d. None of the above.

4. The form object is useful because _____.

  a. you can interact with form data without using a server

  b. it represents an HTML <element> tag

  c. Both of the above.

  d. None of the above.

5. When dealing with an object that represents an HTML tag, [0] means _____.

  a. the object does not exist

  b. the object is a variable

  c. it is the first HTML tag of that type found in the document

  d. None of the above.

6. HTML created dynamically by JavaScript _____.

  a. can be manipulated through JavaScript

  b. also represents JavaScript objects

  c. Both of the above.

d. None of the above.

7. Date and Math objects are examples of _____.

  a. user-defined objects

  b. built-in objects

  c. browser objects

  d. None of the above.

8. When you give an object a name in JavaScript or HTML, _____.

  a. you typically have to write the full path to the object using the object model

  b. you can simply refer to the object by name

  c. the name is entered in the browser's history list

  d. None of the above.

9. The ability to create image objects in JavaScript is useful because _____.

  a. you can preload images into the browser's cache before the image is used

  b. you can draw an image on the screen using image methods

  c. you can load a sound through this object

  d. All of the above.

  e. None of the above.

10. The innerHTML method is useful because it allows you to change the _____.

  a. text within the HTML starting and ending tags

  b. width or height of an object

  c. source URL of an object

  d. low-resolution source of an image

DISCUSSION QUESTIONS

1. What does the JavaScript Object Model represent? How would you describe the object model?

2. Why is the document object so important to developers?

3.   Why does JavaScript create objects to represent HTML tags?

4.   Why is it useful to write HTML dynamically?

SKILL DRILL

Skill Drill exercises reinforce chapter skills. Each skill reinforced is the same, or nearly the same, as a skill presented in the chapter. Detailed instructions are provided in a step-by-step format. You can work through one or more exercises in any order.

1. Use the Link Object

1.   Open skill_link.html from your WIP_03 folder.

2.   Create hyperlinks in the body of the document that link to your two favorite Web sites.

FIGURE 3.33

3.   Directly before the **</body>** tag, create a script in the body of the document.

4.   In the script, create code to write the **href** property of the second link object back to the screen.

Hint: the second link object is referred to as [**1**].

5.   View your file in the browser. The URL of the second link should be visible at the bottom of the screen.

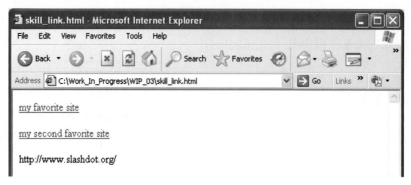

FIGURE 3.34

6. Close the file in the browser and text editor.

2. Create a Date Object

In the following exercise, you use a constructor method to create a Date object.

1. In your text editor, open the file named dateskill.html from the WIP_03 folder.

2. Find the following line of code.

    ```
    <script language="JavaScript" type="text/javascript">
    ```

3. Directly before this statement, insert the following code.

    ```
    <p>The date stored is
    ```

4. After the **</script>** tag, insert the following code.

    ```
    </p>
    ```

5. Create a statement to generate a Date object named "**theDate**". Insert the date "June 14, 1973" into the Date object.

6. Create a second statement that uses a **document.write()** statement to output the date to the screen.

7. Save the file in your text editor and view it in your browser. It should match the following illustration.

FIGURE 3.35

8. Close the file in your browser and text editor.

3. Extract Information from a Form Element

In this exercise, you use JavaScript to retrieve information from an HTML form. We created the form for you; we also created a function, which you eventually use to display information retrieved from the form. Your task is to complete the necessary code to display the information.

1. In your text editor, open the file named formskill.html from the WIP_03 folder.

    This page contains a form. When you submit the form, the **checkValue()** function activates.

2. In the function located in the head of the document, insert an **alert()** statement that says "function activated".

    This allows you to test your function and make sure it works correctly.

3. Save the file in your text editor and open it in your browser.

4. Test the function by clicking the Send button.

    An alert box appears.

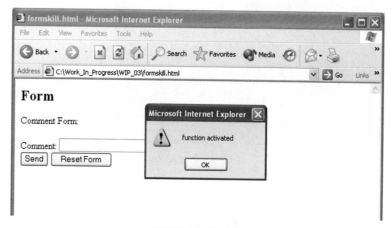

FIGURE 3.36

5. Click OK to acknowledge the alert box.

6. Return to your text editor. Change the alert to output the value of the comment field when the form is submitted.

7. Save and test your file.

8. Close the file in your browser and text editor.

4. Manipulate an Image Object

1. In your text editor, open the file named imageskill.html from the Chapter_03 folder. Save the file in your WIP_03 folder using the same file name.

2. Make sure truck.jpg has been copied from your Chapter_03 folder to your WIP_03 folder. You use this file in this exercise.

3. In the **<img>** tag, use the **name** attribute to name the image "**truck**".

4. In the script provided, use the object name "**truck**" to write an **alert** statement to output the width of the truck object.

5. Save and test your file.

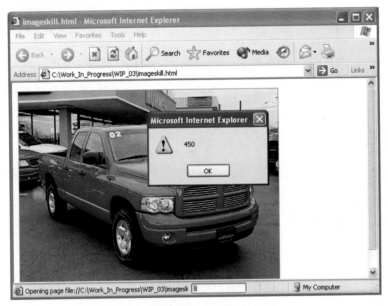

FIGURE 3.37

6. Close the file in your browser and text editor.

CHALLENGE

Challenge exercises expand on, or are somewhat related to, skills presented in the lessons. Each exercise provides a brief introduction, followed by instructions presented in a numbered-step format that are not as detailed as those in the Skill Drill exercises. You should work through these exercises in the order provided.

1. Resize an Image Object

You are developing a system that allows users to sell their cars online. In your system, a user uploads a picture of his vehicle to a Web site. The picture is usually quite large when uploaded, but you want the picture to initially appear at a smaller size on the first page shown to a potential buyer. In this Challenge, you create JavaScript code to resize the image to a specific size.

1. In your text editor, open the file named imagechallenge.html from the WIP_03 folder.

2. Open the file in your browser.

   This simple file displays an image.

3. Insert the following code after the <**img**> tag.

```
<script language="JavaScript" type="text/javascript">
</script>
```

4. In the script, use only JavaScript code to set the **height** property of the image object to "**200**".

   Hint: you can refer to the image as **window.document.images[0]** in JavaScript.

5. In the script, use only JavaScript code to set the **width** property of the image object to "**150**".

6. Save and test your file.

   The image is much smaller than before, because you reset the properties through JavaScript.

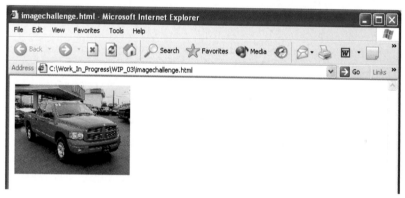

FIGURE 3.38

7. Close your browser. Keep the file open in your text editor for the next exercise.

2. Change an Image Object Source

In the previous challenge, you created a Web page with an image that displays at a specific size. In this exercise, you use JavaScript to dynamically change the image after the user acknowledges an alert box. You convert the image object to reference a different image by changing the src property of the image object.

1. In the open imagechallenge.html in your text editor, save the file as "imagechallenge2.html" in your WIP_03 folder.

2. The imagechallenge2.html file contains a script that resizes the image — the script you created in the previous challenge. After the code that resizes the image object, enter code that creates an alert box that says, "Welcome to my Web site".

3. Save the file and test it in your browser.

   The page and an alert box appear.

4. Return to your text editor.

5. After the code that creates the alert box, change the **src** property of the image object to "**scenic.jpg**". Be sure to place the file name within quotes.

6. Save and test your file. Acknowledge the alert box.

   The picture changes, but remains at the same size.

7. Close the file in your browser and text editor.

3. Manipulate a String Object

In the previous challenge, you manipulated the **src** property of an image object to change the image. In this challenge, you manipulate a string object to output a string value in all uppercase letters.

1. Open stringchallenge.html from your Chapter_03 folder. Save it in your WIP_03 folder using the same file name.

2. Open the file in your browser.

   This file simply displays a text string from a variable.

3. Use a string method to change the **document.write()** statement to output the variable in uppercase letters.

4. Save and test your file to ensure it works correctly.

5. Change the string method to the **toLowerCase()** method.

   This method displays the text in lowercase letters.

6. Save and test your file.

7. Retrieve the character in the fifth position within the string object. Change the string method to the **charAt()** method.

   Hint: If you were trying to retrieve the character in the third position, you would use **charAt(2)**.

8. Save and test your file.

   You should notice that the first position is noted as position [**0**], so specifying the character at position [**5**] should return the sixth character in the string.

9. Change the **charAt()** method to retrieve the character at position [**12**].

10. Save and test your file.

11. Close the file in your browser and text editor.

4. Write Text to Window Objects

In this exercise, you create and manipulate new objects. The provided file creates a second browser window and a second window object. You enter additional code to create another window object and then write text to each of the open windows.

1. In your text editor, open windowchallenge.html from your WIP_03 folder.

2. Test the file in your browser.

   The script contains a statement that creates a second window object.

3. Create another window object named "**secondWindow**".

   This window object should be identical to the **firstWindow** object.

4. Save and test your file.

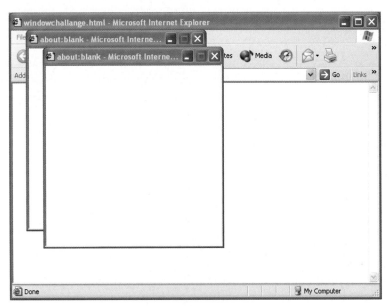

FIGURE 3.39

5. Write a different text message to each of the three windows.

6. Save and test your file.

7. Close the file in the browser and text editor.

PORTFOLIO BUILDER

User Profiles and Interactivity

In this Portfolio Builder, you profile a Web user and discover ways to use client-side scripting to enhance his experience. Before you create your own user profile, consider the following profile of a fictional user whose name is Eva.

Every day, Eva uses a Web browser to check her e-mail. She enters her username and password and then clicks the Submit button. A pop-up window appears with an advertisement that she immediately dismisses. The main window shows her mailboxes and her newest e-mail messages. When Eva replies to an e-mail message, she clicks Submit to send the message. An alert box warns her that she has left the Subject field blank. She quickly types in the Subject field and submits the e-mail. Junk mail filters often delete messages with the empty Subject fields. Thanks to a form validation script, Eva's e-mail is delivered to the intended recipient.

To complete this Portfolio Builder:

- Create a user profile for someone you know. Outline the entire user experience.

- Identify the primary URL's of Web sites they visit in a typical day.

- Browse these sites and write down ways that client-side scripting enhances the user experience, such as image rollovers, form validation, pop-up windows, and other interactive elements created with JavaScript.

- After you examine these sites, use search engines to look for JavaScript code examples. In particular, find at least three Web sites that contain JavaScript code repositories.

- Visit these sites and read about the purpose of various JavaScript code examples that you can download.

- Write down how the JavaScript code examples on these sites could further enhance the browsing experience of the user you profiled.

CHAPTER 4

Working with Variables

OBJECTIVES

In this chapter, you learn how to:

- Declare a variable

- Manipulate a variable numerically

- Use a string variable

- Understand data typing in JavaScript

- Recognize variable name limitations

- Make a Boolean comparison

Why Would I Do This?

As you learned in Chapter 3, variables are named storage areas that hold information. Variables are fundamental in any programming or scripting language; their true power lies in their ability to keep track of changing values during the course of a computer program or script. For example, every time you play a video game, you see variables in action — your score is stored in a variable, and the value (your score) changes according to your actions.

In Chapters 1–3, you used several properties of JavaScript objects. As you remember, properties are simply variables that exist inside objects. Object properties usually have an initial value. For example, the background color of a Web page is usually set to a default property of white. Using JavaScript, you can change the default property values to suit your specific needs.

In this chapter, you learn how to create variables as well as discover several basic methods for manipulating variable values. During this process, you learn about the basic types of data that can be stored within a variable, including (but not limited to) the following.

- Numbers

- The result of a mathematical calculation

- A true or false value

- The result of a comparison between two values

- A value entered by a user

- Text

- Array values

The type of information stored in a variable determines how you can manipulate the variable. For example, a variable that holds a number can be raised to the power of another number; if a variable holds a sentence of text, you can extract the first word of the sentence by manipulating the variable.

VISUAL SUMMARY

Variables are temporary storage areas for information. Each variable has an assigned name and value. For instance, if you need to identify the number of items in a sales transaction and then store that information, you could use an assignment statement such as **numberItems=8;**. Using pseudocode, the statement says, "Assign the number **8** to the variable **numberItems**." This is one of the simplest statements in JavaScript.

You must declare the variable name before using the variable. You can do this with the keyword **var**, such as **var a;**. The act of assigning a value to a variable name "declares the variable," as in **a=23**. In either case, you must declare the variable name before you can use the variable in your code. The statement **document.write(a);** is an invalid statement until you declare the variable **(a)**.

You can assign numbers, text strings, or calculations to variables. For example, you can assign two numbers to two variables (**price** and **taxRate**) with the following statements.

```
price=100;
taxRate=0.04;
```

Once you know the price and the tax rate, you can create a third variable (**taxAmount**) to hold the amount of tax created when the tax rate is applied to the price.

```
taxAmount=price * taxRate;
```

Using a simple statement, you can tell the user the amount of tax he will pay on the item.

```
document.write("You will pay" + taxAmount + "in taxes on this item.");
```

The following script demonstrates the creation and basic manipulation of variables.

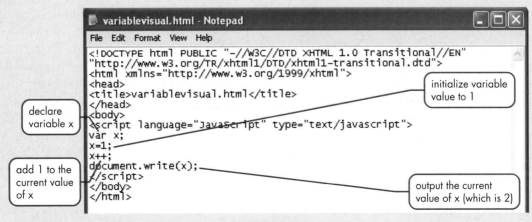

FIGURE 4.1

This code yields the following results.

FIGURE 4.2

A variable can also include a string value. Remember that strings are always enclosed within quotes; in JavaScript, this can mean double or single quotes, as long as you use matching pairs of quotes. For instance, if you want to use a variable to hold someone's last name, you could use the following statement.

```
lastName="Smith";
```

Revisiting JavaScript's syntax rules, you can also use the following statements, all of which are valid.

```
lastName='Yamamoto';
fullName="Jack O'Malley";
line1="Jack said, 'save yourself', then left";
```

The following statements are invalid, because they violate JavaScript syntax rules.

```
lastName='Smith";
fullName="Jack O"Malley";
line1="Jack said, "save yourself', then left"";
```

There are ways to get around the limitations imposed by JavaScript's syntax rules, which become valuable in situations where you must include quotes within text strings. You explore these options later in the book.

The idea of the variable's scope is also worth noting. A variable can have a local scope or a global scope. In general, a variable with a *local scope* only exists within a function; a variable created within a function is only available within the function and is considered a *local variable*. Variables declared outside functions can be used anywhere (they have *global scope*) and are considered *global variables*.

You can use the keyword **var** to declare a variable. The term "declaring a variable" simply means you create a variable and assign a name to it. If you want to create a variable named "**a**", you can use the following statement.

```
var a;
```

The **var** keyword is important because JavaScript requires you to declare a variable before you use it. For instance, you've already seen that the following lines of code can create variables and assign initial values.

```
a=10;
b=23;
```

These statements assign initial values, which automatically declare the variables. If you *initialize* a variable, you assign a beginning value to the variable. The statements shown above can also be expressed as the following.

```
var a=10;
var b=23;
```

You can also combine the statements using the **var** keyword.

```
var a=10, b=23;
```

JavaScript does not require you to initialize variables when you create them; however, it is good practice to initialize variables by assigning a beginning value. This holds true for any programming or scripting language.

LESSON 1　Declaring a Variable

Variable rule number one: you must declare a variable *before* you can use it. The translation of this rule is that when you write JavaScript code, you must place the statement that declares a variable before a statement that includes the variable. To declare a variable, you can use the **var** statement or you can assign an initial value to the variable.

For example, until you declare the variable named **angle**, the statement **document.write(angle)** is considered invalid. If you first create a variable named **angle** using the **var** keyword (**var angle;**), however, the statement **document.write(angle)** is considered valid.

In the example above, the variable would have a value of **undefined** if it were declared without assigning an initial value. To declare a variable that has an assigned value, you can write the following code.

```
var angle=90;
```

The **var** keyword is optional in most circumstances. If you assign a value to the variable, you can declare the variable without using the **var** keyword, as in **angle=90**. JavaScript allows you to declare the variable and assign a value at the same time.

Data Types

Many programming languages require you to declare the variable name and the data type of the variable before you can use the variable. The ***data type*** of the variable determines the kind of information the variable can hold. Traditional programming languages invoke this requirement for two reasons — to use the smallest amount of memory possible for that type of variable, and to ensure that programmers do not accidentally assign the wrong kind of data to the variable. This requirement can make programming tedious, however, because you must always declare the variable type before you can use the variable. The requirement also makes it difficult to convert a variable from one type (such as a number) to another type (such as a string).

In contrast, JavaScript does not require you to declare the data type before using the variable. JavaScript determines the variable's data type when you assign information to the variable. The type of data assigned to the variable determines how the variable is used in JavaScript. For instance, in the statement `city="Cleveland";`, JavaScript treats the variable as a string variable, because you assigned a string value to the variable.

If you decide to change the variable to use a numeric code for the city, you could include a second assignment statement, such as `city=10`. This statement converts the variable to a numeric variable. If the statement were written with quotes around the number, `city="10";`, the variable would still be considered a string variable.

Use the var Keyword

1   **Copy the contents of the Chapter_04 folder into your WIP_04 folder.**

You use these files in this chapter.

2   **Open WIP_04>var.html in your text editor.**

FIGURE 4.3

A script was started for you in the body of the document.

3   **Insert the following code into your script.**

```
...
</head>
<body>
<script language="JavaScript" type="text/javascript">
```

```
//create two variables
var number;
var name;
</script>
</body>
</html>
```

This code creates two variables.

4 **Insert the following code below the code you inserted in the previous step.**

```
...
//create two variables
var number;
var name;
//output the value of the variables
document.write(number);
document.write("<br />");
document.write(name);
</script>
</body>
</html>
```

These statements output the values stored in the variables.

5 **Save the file in your text editor and open it in your browser.**

FIGURE 4.4

A value of **undefined** returns for these variables because no value was assigned.

6 **Keep the file open for the next exercise.**

In this exercise, you used the **var** keyword to create variables. At this point, JavaScript simply reports a value of **undefined**, because no value or data type has been determined.

To Extend Your Knowledge . . .

IDENTIFYING THE PURPOSE OF A VARIABLE

When programmers create new variables, most add comment statements to their code to identify the exact purpose of each variable. Being able to identify the purpose of each variable is useful when you review or use code that you did not write.

LESSON 2   Writing Assignment Statements

You already learned that an equal sign (=) assigns a value to a variable. In a statement such as **variableName="value"**, the equal sign is the *assignment operator*, which is a character or characters that assign a value to a variable. This is the simplest assignment statement in JavaScript. You learn more about simple assignment operators while you complete the following exercises.

Declare by Assigning Values

1 Make sure var.html is open in your browser and text editor.

2 In your text editor, find and delete the following code.

```
var number;
var name;
```

3 Replace the code you just deleted with the following.

```
number=30;
name="Michael";
```

You can declare the variables without using the **var** keyword, if you assign values to the variables.

4 Save the file in your text editor and refresh your browser.

FIGURE 4.5

The values stored in the variables return to the user.

5   Keep the file open in your browser and text editor for the next exercise.

In this exercise, you created variables by assigning data to them. It is not necessary to use the **var** key-word to create the variables before assigning data to them; the act of assigning a value is sufficient to declare the variable.

Variations of Variable Assignments

1   Make sure var.html is open in your browser and text editor.

2   In your text editor, find the following code.

```
number=30;
name="Michael";
```

3   Insert the keyword **var** at the beginning of these code statements.

```
var number=30;
var name="Michael";
```

You can use the **var** keyword in assignment statements.

4   Save the file in your text editor and refresh your browser.

The values appear the same as before.

5   Return to your text editor and find the following code.

```
var number=30;
var name="Michael";
```

6   Replace these two lines of code with the following line of code.

```
<body>
<script language="JavaScript" type="text/javascript">
//create two variables
var number=30, name="Michael";
//output the value of the variables
document.write(number);
document.write("<br />");
```

7   Save the file in your text editor and refresh your browser.

FIGURE 4.6

The code appears the same as before.

8   **Close the file in your browser and text editor.**

The **var** keyword allows you to use a single statement to create multiple variables. It also allows you to assign multiple values to the variables.

Use a Method to Assign a Variable

1   **In your text editor and browser, open methodassign.html from your WIP_04 folder.**

2   **Insert the following line of code.**

```
. . .
<body>
<script language="JavaScript" type="text/javascript">
//ask the user for information
name=prompt("What is your name?","");
//output the value of the variable
</script>
. . .
```

The variable **name** will hold the information returned from the user.

3   **Insert the following line of code.**

```
. . .
//ask the user for information
name=prompt("What is your name?","");
//output the value of the variable
document.write(name);
</script>
</body>
</html>
. . .
```

This code writes the value of the variable named **name**.

4   **Save the file in your text editor and refresh your browser.**

FIGURE 4.7

A prompt box appears.

5 Enter the name "Michael" in the value field and click OK.

FIGURE 4.8

The name you typed appears on the Web page.

6 Close the file in your browser and text editor.

In this exercise, you used a method to declare a variable. This is a common way to declare a variable; it is also a common way to assign values to variables, because many methods return information.

To Extend Your Knowledge . . .

THE IMPORTANCE OF VARIABLES

Much of the power behind programming languages is due to variables and decision statements. They allow you to gather information and then make decisions based on that information. Variables and decision statements allow you to add interactivity to your Web sites and create the critical distinction between noninteractive technologies (HTML) and technologies such as JavaScript.

LESSON 3   Manipulating a Variable Numerically

You can manipulate variables that hold mathematical values in a number of ways. For example, programmers often need to add a certain amount to the current value of a variable. They can accomplish the task with the following statement.

```
total=total+1;
```

In programming, it is common to increase the value of a variable by 1 to create a new value for a variable (**total=total+1**). In fact, this type of calculation is so commonplace in programming statements that the following shorthand was developed to make writing the statement easier.

```
total++;
```

In the first example, `total=total+1`, the equal sign (=) is the assignment operator. In the second example, `total++;`, the characters "`++`" are the assignment operator. These assignment operators are virtually identical in every programming language.

Whenever you increase the value of a variable by 1, you *increment* the variable. In the statement above, the assignment operator "`++`" means "take the current value of the variable on the left and add 1." If you decrease the value of a variable by 1, you *decrement* the variable. You use two minus signs (– –) to decrement a variable.

```
total--;
```

When viewing source code created by other developers, you are more likely to see a statement written as `total++;` than `total=total+1`. In this lesson, you explore the basics of these and other ways of manipulating variables mathematically. You examine these methods in greater depth later in this book.

Basic Mathematical Manipulation

1   **Open WIP_04>variablemath.html in your text editor.**

2   **Find the following line of code.**

```
// **** insert code here ****
```

Next, you create two variables to hold numbers and initialize the variables by assigning values to them.

3   **Type the following statements below the comment.**

```
// **** insert code here ****
numberOne=56;
numberTwo=2;
```

4   **Insert another statement to multiply the two variables.**

```
// **** insert code here ****
numberOne=56;
numberTwo=2;
total=numberOne*numberTwo;
```

This statement multiplies the two variables and stores the result in a third variable named `total`.

5   **Add the following line of code to output the result to the user.**

```
// **** insert code here ****
numberOne=56;
numberTwo=2;
total=numberOne*numberTwo;
document.write(total);
```

6   **Save the file in your text editor and open it in your browser.**

The result of the calculation returns to the user.

FIGURE 4.9

7 To make the file more user friendly, change the `document.write()` statement to the following.

```
// **** insert code here ****
numberOne=56;
numberTwo=2;
total=numberOne*numberTwo;
document.write(numberOne+" multiplied by "+numberTwo+"
    equals "+total);
```

8 Save the file in your text editor and refresh your browser.

FIGURE 4.10

9 Close the file in the browser and text editor.

In this exercise, you used basic mathematical manipulations to assign a variable value. One of the primary purposes of a computer program is to adjust to current values when completing calculations, which makes variables especially useful.

Increment Variables

1 Open WIP_04>incrementing.html in your text editor.

A script was started for you.

2 Insert the following code into the script.

```
...
</head>
<body>
<script language="JavaScript" type="text/javascript">
number=1;
number=number+1;
document.write(number);
</script>
</body>
</html>
```

3   Save the file in your text editor and open it in your browser.

FIGURE 4.11

The number 2 returns in the browser window.

4   Find the following code statement in your text editor.

```
number=number+1;
```

5   Change the statement to the following.

```
number++;
```

6   Save the file in your text editor and refresh your browser.

The same result returns to the browser.

7   Keep the file open in your text editor. Close the file in your browser.

In this exercise, you incremented a variable by adding 1 to the current value. The process of incrementing a variable is common in many programming situations; you can accomplish the task using shorthand notation.

Decrement Variables

1   In the open incrementing.html in your text editor, change the `<title>` tag to the following.

```
<title>decrementing.html</title>
```

2   Save the file as "decrementing.html" in your WIP_04 folder.

3   Find the following line of code.

```
number=1;
```

4   Change this line of code to the following.

```
number=10;
```

5   Find the following line of code.

```
number++;
```

This statement currently indicates that JavaScript should add one to the current value of the variable.

6   Change this code to the following.

```
number--;
```

This statement is the functional equivalent of **number=number-1**. Note: you must not put a space between the two dashes.

7   Save the file in your text editor and open it in your browser.

FIGURE 4.12

8   Close the file in your browser and text editor.

In this exercise, you decremented a variable by subtracting the number 1 from the current value of the variable.

To Extend Your Knowledge . . .

MULTIPLICATION

In most computer applications and languages, an asterisk (*) denotes multiplication. An "x" cannot be used for this purpose.

LESSON 4   Using String Variables

As you learned in Chapter 2, a text string is simply text within your code. Variables that possess string values are referred to as *string variables*. String variables are useful for holding any type of textual information, such as an address, name, or description.

String variables are also string objects. You can use string methods to manipulate string variables. For example, the following lines of code create a variable named **password** and then use a string method to convert the variable to uppercase letters.

```
password="mary1";
password=password.toUpperCase();
```

Assign Strings to Variables

In the following exercises, you explore text strings in variable values, assign text string values to variables, and use the variables in a simple script.

1   **Open WIP_04>assignstrings.html in your text editor.**

Use this simple HTML script as the beginning of your code.

2   **In the script, insert the following code.**

```
...
</head>
<body>
<script language="JavaScript" type="text/javascript">
//create first name
firstName="Joe";
</script>
</body>
</html>
```

This creates a variable named **firstName** and assigns a text string with the value of **Joe**.

3   **Below this code, insert the following.**

```
...
//create first name
firstName="Joe";
//create last name
lastName="Smith";
</script>
</body>
</html>
```

This code creates a second variable to hold the last name.

4   Insert the following code below the code you inserted in Step 3.

```
//create first name
firstName="Joe";
//create last name
lastName="Smith";
//display information
document.write(firstName);
document.write("<br />");
document.write(lastName);
</script>
</body>
</html>
```

This code displays the information to the end user.

5   Save the file in your text editor and open the file in your browser.

FIGURE 4.13

6   Keep the file open in your text editor for the next exercise. Close your browser.

In this exercise, you assigned text string values to variables and used the values in a simple script. Remember, you must always enclose text strings within matching quotes; otherwise, JavaScript assumes you are using a variable name and tries to insert a value stored in the variable.

To Extend Your Knowledge . . .

STRING VARIABLES

String variables are useful in any coding situation where you need to include text. This may sound simple, but you can use string variables to create powerful results. For example, you could create a file name within JavaScript by **concatenating** (combining) a variable name with a period and a file extension.

Concatenate Variables

In this exercise, you explore the benefits of concatenating (combining) text strings.

1 In the open assignstrings.html in your text editor, save the file as "concatenate.html" in your WIP_04 folder.

2 Change the `<title>` tag to the following.

```
<title>concatenate.html</title>
```

3 Find the following code.

```
lastName="Smith";
```

4 Create a blank line after this line of code and insert the following statement.

```
lastName="Smith";
fullName=firstName+lastName;
```

This code concatenates the strings saved in the two variables you previously created.

5 Delete the following lines of code.

```
document.write(firstName);
document.write("<br />");
document.write(lastName);
```

6 Replace the code you deleted in Step 5 with the following line of code.

```
document.write(fullName);
```

7 Save the file in your text editor and open the file in your browser.

FIGURE 4.14

The name looks strange, because the first and last names are not separated by a space.

8 Return to your text editor. Change the statement that creates the `fullName` variable to the following.

```
fullName=firstName+" "+lastName;
```

You inserted a third text string (a space) between the other two text strings.

9   **Save the file in your text editor and refresh your browser.**

FIGURE 4.15

A space now separates the first and last names.

10   **Close the file in both applications.**

In this exercise, you combined two text string values into a single text string value and then stored the value in a single variable. Remember, a text string is simply one possible data type you can store in variable.

To Extend Your Knowledge...

VARIABLE CONCATENATION

The term "concatenate" simply means you combine two or more text string values into a single text string. Concatenation is an important part of every scripting language.

LESSON 5   Understanding JavaScript Data Typing

In JavaScript, variables behave differently according to the type of data stored in the variable. In many other programming languages, a variable can only hold a specific type of data, which must be declared when you create the variable. Since JavaScript does not require you to declare the data type when you create the variable, the JavaScript language is described as a *loosely typed language*.

Working with a loosely typed language is simpler than working with a strictly typed language. *Strictly typed languages* require you to specify the data type used with a specific variable when you create the variable. In strictly typed languages, it is difficult (sometimes impossible) to convert a variable to a different data type. It is easier to write code in a loosely typed language than it is in a strictly typed language — it is also easier to make mistakes.

You can store several different data types within variables. For example, you can store string values, numeric values, or Boolean values in a variable (more on Boolean values later). The variable can have a variety of methods available, depending on the type of data stored within the variable. In this lesson, you explore several types of data typing and discover how mistakes in data typing can create script errors. Let's start by creating a file that allows users to enter variable values when they view the page.

Enter Values Dynamically

1   **Open WIP_04>datatyping.html in your text editor and examine the source code.**

This code uses the **prompt()** method to create two variables and then creates a third variable to hold the number derived by multiplying the two numbers.

2   **Open the file in your browser.**

FIGURE 4.16

A prompt box appears.

3   **Enter a number (any number you prefer) and then click OK.**

A second prompt box appears.

4   **Enter a second number (any number you prefer) and then click OK.**

The Web page displays the result of the calculation.

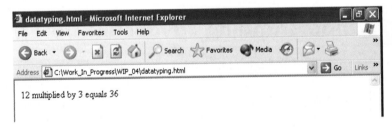

FIGURE 4.17

5   **Keep the file open in your text editor and browser for the next exercise.**

In this exercise, you used **prompt()** methods in variable assignments to declare the variables. Then, you multiplied the values and stored the result in a third variable. In this situation, JavaScript assumed the results were numeric values, because you multiplied the values together.

To Extend Your Knowledge . . .

DATA TYPING

Remember that JavaScript knows the data type based on the type of value entered and how the value is used. For example, if you place a variable value within quotes, JavaScript assumes the value is a text string. If you enter a number or calculation, JavaScript assumes the value is an integer.

Data Typing Errors

In this exercise, you consider a situation where JavaScript is unsure of whether to use an integer data type or a text string data type to manipulate the variable.

1 In the open datatyping.html in your text editor, find the following line of code.

```
total=number1*number2;
```

2 Change this code to the following.

```
total=number1+number2;
```

3 Delete the following line of code.

```
document.write(number1+" multiplied by "+number2+"
equals "+total);
```

4 Replace the `document.write()` statement you deleted with the following.

```
document.write(number1+" plus "+number2+" equals "+total);
```

5 Save the file in your text editor and refresh your browser.

6 Enter a first number (any number you prefer) and then click OK.

7 Enter a second number (any number you prefer) and then click OK.

The result of the calculation appears in the browser window.

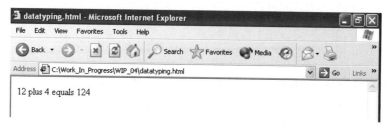

FIGURE 4.18

The script concatenates the values of the variables instead of adding them together. In this case, JavaScript assumes the values are strings instead of numbers and treats them accordingly. This is an example of a data type error.

8   **Keep the file open in your text editor and browser for the next exercise.**

In this exercise, you purposely created a data type error that caused JavaScript to interpret the data as a text string, even though you wanted numerical information.

To Extend Your Knowledge...

DATA TYPE ERRORS

Errors involving data types are common problems in JavaScript; they are referred to as **data type errors**. The same holds true in many scripting languages, because the languages are often designed to make code writing simple. Full-blown programming languages often include strict rules regarding data typing. These rules make code writing more difficult, but also make data type errors more difficult to produce.

Use parseInt ()

In this exercise, you learn how to use a method to change the data from a text string to an integer.

1   **In the open datatyping.html in your text editor, find the following statement.**

```
total=number1+number2;
```

This statement concatenates the values of the two variables and stores the result in the variable named **total**.

2   **Directly before this line of code, insert the following statements.**

```
//convert strings to integers
number1=parseInt(number1);
number2=parseInt(number2);
total=number1+number2;
```

This code converts the strings into numbers for use in the calculation.

3   **Save the file in your text editor and refresh your browser.**

The first prompt box appears.

4 **Enter the same numbers from the previous exercise and then click OK.**

The result appears in the browser window.

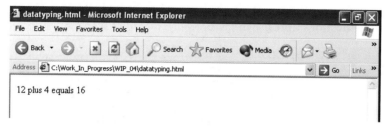

FIGURE 4.19

The numbers are added instead of concatenated.

5 **Close the file in your browser and text editor.**

In this exercise, you used the **parseInt()** method to convert the data type from a text string to an integer. This resolves the data type error from the previous exercise.

To Extend Your Knowledge...

THE PROMPT() METHOD

JavaScript assumes the `prompt()` method returns a string value when you use the plus sign (+) with variables, but assumes the values are integers if you use another operator, such as the asterisk (*) for multiplication.

LESSON 6 | Recognizing Variable Name Limitations

JavaScript includes simple rules concerning variable names. Similar to other aspects of JavaScript, variable names are case sensitive. For this reason, if you create a variable named **lastName**, you cannot reference it as **LastName** or **LASTNAME** without causing errors.

Variable names must start with an alphabetic character, an underscore (_), or a dollar sign ($). Variable names can contain alphabetic characters, numeric digits, dollar signs, or underscore characters. Variable names cannot contain special characters such as asterisks (*), slashes (/, \), colons, semicolons, or spaces.

JavaScript allows you to assign long variable names, but it is usually best to keep them relatively short. Older programming environments required short variable names, which made reading the code difficult, because cryptic acronyms were often used. Variable names are often used repeatedly in complex programs, so it is best to choose names that are short enough to type easily, yet long enough to be descriptive and easily identifiable.

You cannot assign any of the JavaScript-reserved words as variable names. **Reserved words** are names of commands used in the programming language. JavaScript's reserved words include words currently used in the language as well as words planned for future use in JavaScript. JavaScript's reserved words include the following.

abstract	boolean	break	byte	case	catch	char
class	const	continue	debugger	default	delete	do
double	else	enum	export	extends	false	final
finally	float	for	function	goto	if	implements
import	in	instanceof	int	interface	long	native
new	null	package	private	protected	public	return
short	static	super	switch	synchronized	this	throw
throws	transient	true	try	typeof	var	void
volatile	while	with				

TABLE 4.1

Correct Capitalization Errors

1 Open WIP_04>cap.html in your text editor.

2 Insert the following code.

```
. . .
<body>
<script language="JavaScript" type="text/javascript">
//create a variable
myPick="item3";
//use a variable
</script>
. . .
```

This code declares a variable named **myPick** and assigns the text string **item3**. Make sure you capitalize the "**P**" in "**Pick**."

3 Insert the following code.

```
. . .
//create a variable
myPick="item3";
//use a variable
alert(mypick);
```

```
</script>
</body>
</html>
```

Make sure you use a lowercase "**p**" in this line. You are purposely creating an error in the code.

4 **Save the file in your text editor and open the file in your browser.**

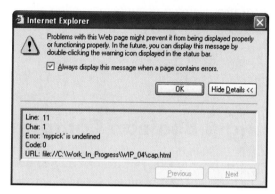

FIGURE 4.20

If error notifications are enabled, you see a message that says, "'mypick' is undefined". The capitalization in your code does not match, so JavaScript sees **mypick** and **myPick** as different variables. In this case, the variable is considered undeclared because it hasn't previously appeared in the code.

5 **Click OK to close the error notification box. Return to your text editor.**

6 **Correct the variable name in the alert() statement (capitalize the "P" in "Pick").**

```
alert(myPick);
```

7 **Save the file in your text editor and refresh your browser.**

FIGURE 4.21

The file works correctly.

8 **Close the file in both applications.**

To Extend Your Knowledge . . .

NAMING CONVENTIONS

In this exercise, you deliberately introduced an error by changing the case in a variable name. To avoid making similar mistakes, choose a standard way to create variable names (a ***naming convention***) and stick with it. For instance, if you create a variable named `firstName`, don't create a second variable named `last_Name`. Using a naming convention allows you to consistently name all of your variables as well as remember the names once assigned.

LESSON 7 Making a Boolean Comparison

Boolean values refer to a data type that is set to either **true** or **false**. Boolean values are not string values; rather, Booleans refer to variables or questions that require a yes or no answer. To illustrate the importance of using Boolean values, let's consider the following example.

Assume that you are building an online test. The design of the test should allow users to answer a question once. After the user answers the question, you need to update the score on the test. You can accomplish this task by creating a variable that tells you whether the user has answered the current question. If they have answered the question, you can make an assignment similar to the following statement

```
questionAnswered=true;
```

A Boolean variable that determines whether an event has occurred is usually referred to as a ***flag***. Most software packages contain hundreds (sometimes thousands) of flags. For example, if you turn off script error notifications in your browser, it is likely that a statement such as the following is created.

```
scriptNotifications=false;
```

Boolean variables often hold the answer to a yes or no question. For example, the following statement asks JavaScript whether a variable named **amount** is greater than a variable named **limit**.

```
overLimit=amount>limit;
```

Boolean values represent a different kind of data type than string or integer values. For this reason, variables assigned Boolean values are used in a slightly different manner than other data types. In this lesson, you consider Boolean values as a different data type for a variable.

Assign Boolean Values to a Variable

1   Open WIP_04>boolean.html in your text editor.

2   Insert the following code into the script.

```
...
</head>
<body>
<script language="JavaScript" type="text/javascript">
answer=true;
document.write(answer);
</script>
</body>
</html>
```

This code creates a variable with a Boolean data type. Notice the word **true** isn't enclosed within quotes, because it isn't a text string.

3 **Save the file in your text editor and open it in your browser.**

The word "true" returns to the browser.

4 **Keep the file open in your browser and text editor for the next exercise.**

FIGURE 4.22

In this exercise, you assigned a Boolean value to a variable and used it in a simple script. By assigning a Boolean value, the variable is treated as a Boolean variable and used as a Boolean data type.

To Extend Your Knowledge . . .

TRUE AND FALSE VALUES

The words **true** and **false** are JavaScript reserved words. For this reason, they can't be used as variable names, and JavaScript knows they aren't variables when you use them without quotes in code statements.

Use Boolean Operators

1 **In the open boolean.html in your text editor, find the following line of code.**

```
answer=true;
```

2   **Change this line of code to the following.**

```
answer=17<3;
```

This line of code asks JavaScript if 17 is less than 3. JavaScript returns an answer of true or false.

3   **Save the file in your text editor and refresh your browser.**

FIGURE 4.23

A Boolean value of **false** returns, because 17 is not less than 3.

4   **Return to your text editor. Change the variable assignment statement to the following.**

```
answer=3<10;
```

This statement asks JavaScript whether 3 is less than 10.

5   **Save the file in your text editor and refresh your browser.**

FIGURE 4.24

A value of true returns, because 3 is less than 10.

6   **Close the file in both applications.**

To Extend Your Knowledge . . .

BOOLEAN COMPARISONS

Using Boolean values, you can create **decision statements**, which are questions the interpreter must answer based on the relationship of the variables. For example, the code in a video game may need to determine whether the user has reached 10,000 points and, if so, allow the user to progress to the next level. The program bases its decision on the number of points the user has received.

SUMMARY

In Chapter 4, you learned that variables are temporary storage containers for information. Variables can consist of various data types, including integers, text strings, and Boolean values. You assigned values to variables through calculations, methods, and other assignment statements.

You learned that you can assign values to a variable using the equal sign, which is an assignment operator that tells JavaScript to assign a value to a variable. Other assignment operators exist, such as **++** and **--**, which respectively increment and decrement a variable value by one.

You discovered that in JavaScript, it isn't necessary to state the data type when you create the variable. JavaScript automatically determines the data type depending on the value assigned to the variable or how the variable is used in the script. You learned that JavaScript is a loosely typed language — you do not have to declare variable types, and you can convert variable values from one data type to another.

You also learned that you must declare a variable before you can use it in your JavaScript code. You can declare variables using the **var** keyword, or simply assigning a value to the variable. Finally, you explored variable names and found that they can consist of letters, numbers, underscore characters, and dollar signs; variable names cannot contain spaces or special characters (including parentheses, brackets, braces, or the asterisk), nor can they contain JavaScript keywords or reserved words.

KEY TERMS

Assignment operator	Flag	Loosely typed language
Boolean value	Global scope	Naming convention
Concatenate	Global variable	Reserved words
Data type	Increment	Strictly typed language
Data type error	Initialize	String variable
Decision statement	Local scope	
Decrement	Local variable	

CHECKING CONCEPTS AND TERMS

MULTIPLE CHOICE

Circle the letter that matches the correct answer for each of the following questions.

1. In JavaScript, a variable must be declared or created before you can use it.

   a. True

   b. False

2. How can you create a variable in JavaScript?

   a. Using the var keyword to declare the variable.

   b. Assigning a value to the variable.

   c. Either of the above.

   d. None of the above.

3. Information stored in a variable can include _____.

   a. text

   b. numbers or results of calculations

   c. information returned from a method

   d. All of the above.

4. A Boolean value _____.

   a. can be a number or text string

   b. is always true or false

   c. consists of a string method

   d. None of the above.

5. In JavaScript, variable names _____.

   a. are case sensitive

   b. are case insensitive

   c. are limited to letters with no numbers

   d. cannot include underscores

6. When naming variables, it is best to _____.

   a. use variations, such as midterm_grade and finalGrade

   b. be consistent, such as midtermGrade and finalGrade

   c. include special characters, such as %, @, and #

   d. None of the above.

7. An assignment operator _____.

   a. is a letter or letters that assigns a value to a variable

   b. compares two values to see how they relate

   c. removes the assignment from a variable

   d. None of the above.

8. Variables created inside functions have a _____.

   a. global scope

   b. local scope

   c. file extension of .var

   d. None of the above.

9. Variables created outside functions _____.

   a. have a global scope

   b. have a local scope

   c. reference an array value

   d. None of the above.

10. Which of the following can you use to start a variable name?

    a. An underscore character (_).

    b. An alphabetic character, such as a, b, or c.

    c. A dollar sign ($).

    d. Any of the above.

DISCUSSION QUESTIONS

1. List at least three ways to create variables in JavaScript.

2. List the kinds of data you can store in a variable.

3. You are designing an online test that will ask three questions and then tell the user how many questions he answered correctly. Approximately how many variables do you need to accomplish this task? Name each variable you need and describe its purpose.

4. How are Boolean values different from string values? In what circumstances would Boolean values be useful?

SKILL DRILL

Skill Drill exercises reinforce chapter skills. Each skill reinforced is the same, or nearly the same, as a skill presented in the chapter. Detailed instructions are provided in a step-by-step format. You should work through the exercises in the order provided.

1. Declare Variables

In this Skill Drill, you practice declaring variables and assigning values. You may declare the variables using the **var** keyword or simply assign values to the variables. The exercise also asks you to output the value of a variable in a user-friendly fashion.

1. In your text editor, open skilldeclare.html from the WIP_04 folder.

   A script was started for you.

2. In the script, directly above the **</script>** tag, create a variable named "**theNumber**" and set it equal to "**50**".

3. Create a variable named "**percentAmount**" and set the variable equal to "**0.20**".

4. Create a variable named "**calcTotal**" and set it equal to **theNumber** multiplied by the variable named **percentAmount**.

5. Create a **document.write()** statement to output the value of the **calcTotal** variable. Make sure you format the output from the **document.write()** statement in a user-friendly fashion.

6. Save the changes in your text editor.

7. Open the file in your browser. You should receive 10 as the result.

FIGURE 4.25

8. Close the file in your text editor and browser.

2. Use an Assignment Operator

In this Skill Drill, you create a script to calculate the total amount of a purchase transaction after a discount amount is applied. You use an assignment operator to accomplish the task.

1. In your text editor, open skillassign.html from the WIP_04 folder.

    This file creates two variables: one for the **total** and one for the **discountRate**. The **discountRate** variable is the amount someone would pay after a special promotional discount is applied (in this case, 85% of the total amount).

2. Find the following code.

    ```
    // compute the total after discount rate is applied
    ```

3. After this code, insert a code statement to set the variable total to be equal to its current value multiplied by the discount rate. In other words "total equals current value * **discountRate**".

4. Find the following code.

    ```
    //output results
    ```

5. After this comment, insert a **document.write()** statement to output the total back to the user after the discount rate is applied.

    Format your **document.write()** statement so your output is user-friendly.

6. Save the file in your text editor and open the file in your browser. You should receive a result similar to the following illustration.

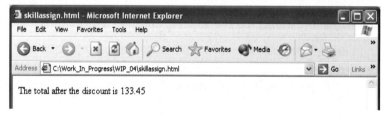

FIGURE 4.26

7. Return to your text editor. Find the statement you wrote that assigns a new value to the variable **total** by multiplying it by the discount rate. Change the code to the following.

    ```
    total*=discountRate;
    ```

    The statement now uses the assignment operator for multiplication.

8. Save the file in your text editor and refresh your browser.

    The answer is the same as before.

9. Close the file in your text editor and browser.

3. Use a Method to Assign a Variable Value

In this Skill Drill, you practice assigning values to a variable using object methods. You use the **prompt()** and **Math.pow()** methods to assign values to variables.

1. In your text editor, open skillmethod.html from the WIP_04 folder.

    A variable named **myNumber** was created for you.

2. After this variable, create another variable named "**power**". Assign the result of a **prompt()** method to the **power** variable. The prompt should ask the question, "To what power would you like to raise the number?"

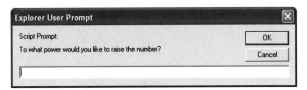

FIGURE 4.27

3. After the **power** variable, create another variable named "**result**" by inserting the following code.

    ```
    result=Math.pow(myNumber, power);
    ```

4. Write a **document.write()** statement to output the result to the user. Format the output in a user-friendly fashion.

5. Save the file in your text editor and open the file in your browser.

6. In your browser, enter "10" for the number and click OK.

7. Enter "2" for the power and click OK.

    You should receive 100 as the result. Due to rounding differences, some browsers may return a slightly different result (such as 99.9999999999998).

FIGURE 4.28

8. Close the file in your text editor and browser.

4. Use a Boolean Data Type

In this Skill Drill, you use Boolean data types in variables. This exercise also offers a glimpse of decision statements.

1.   In your text editor, open skillboolean.html from the WIP_04 folder.

2.   Insert the following code directly above the **</script>** tag.

```
result=32<46;
```

This statement assigns a true-or-false Boolean value to the variable named **result**.

3.   Below the code you just entered, insert the following code.

```
if (result==true) {
alert("The answer is true");
}
```

This code creates a decision statement that performs additional actions if the variable is true.

4.   Save the file in your text editor and open it in your browser.

The code should generate an answer of true, because 32 is less than 46.

FIGURE 4.29

5.   Click OK to close the alert box.

6.   Return to your code in your text editor. Change the number 46 to any number that is less than 32.

7.   Save the file in your text editor and refresh your browser.

The alert box should not appear, because false is the variable value.

8.   Close the file in your browser and text editor.

CHALLENGE

Challenge exercises expand on, or are somewhat related to, skills presented in the lessons. Each exercise provides a brief introduction, followed by instructions presented in a numbered-step format that are not as detailed as those in the Skill Drill exercises. You should complete the exercises in the order provided.

1. Compute Sales Tax

In this Challenge, you write a computer program to compute sales taxes on a transaction. In this scenario, the user enters a subtotal amount, the script computes the amount of tax on the transaction and then outputs the subtotal, tax rate, amount paid in tax, and the total amount to be paid.

1. In your text editor, open challengetax.html from the WIP_04 folder.

2. Create a `prompt()` box that asks for the subtotal of a sales transaction. Place the result in a variable named "`subTotal`".

3. Create a variable named "`taxRate`" and set the variable equal to "`5.75%`" (`0.0575`).

4. Create a variable named "`taxAmount`" and make it equal to the amount of tax the user has to pay on the subtotal amount (the subtotal multiplied by the tax rate).

5. Create a variable named "`total`" and set it equal to the total amount of subtotal and tax amount added together.

6. Create single-line comments to explain the purpose of each variable assignment statement. For example, you could create the following comment for the variable known as "`subTotal`".

    ```
    // subTotal is the total amount before taxes are added
    ```

7. Create `document.write()` statements that display the amount of each variable in a simple, easy-to-read fashion.

8. Save the file in your text editor and open it in your browser.

9. Test the file by entering "100" as the subtotal amount.

    Your result should resemble the following. Hint: you may need to change the data type of a variable using `parseInt()` to receive the correct answer.

FIGURE 4.30

10. Close the file in your browser and text editor.

2. Correct Data Type Errors

In the previous exercise, you dynamically assigned a value to a variable using the `prompt()` method. You also assigned values to variables by completing various calculations. In this exercise, you solve a data type error.

1. In your text editor, open challengeavg.html from the WIP_04 folder. Examine the source code.

   This script asks an end user for three numbers, adds them together, and then arrives at the average of the three numbers. Problems exist in the script, and it is incomplete.

2. Open the file in your browser.

FIGURE 4.31

3. Enter "1" for the first number, and then click OK. Enter "2" for the second number, and enter "3" for the third number.

   The script should output 6 as the total amount; instead, it returns an incorrect amount of 123.

FIGURE 4.32

4. Return to your text editor. Convert the three variables to integer values.

5. Save and test your file.

   The script should return 6 as the result.

FIGURE 4.33

6. Return to your editor. Insert a line of code to create a variable named "**average**". Divide the total by 3 and assign this value to the variable named **average**.

   Hint: average equals total/3.

7. Create a **document.write()** statement to output the value of the variable named **average** to the user.

8. Save and test your file by entering the same numbers again.

FIGURE 4.34

9. Close the file in your browser and text editor.

3. Correct Variable Names

In the previous exercise, you corrected data type errors and completed variable calculations. In this Challenge, you correct errors in variable names in a financial calculation. Bond traders use this calculation to determine the quoted rate for a bond issue.

1. In your text editor, open challengenames.html from the WIP_04 folder. Examine the source code.

   A financial analyst started this script that adds three variables together to determine a variable named **quotedRate**.

2. Open the file in your browser.

   An error returns. The analyst suspects the error is related to the name of the variable **k***, which represents a variable known as the "risk-free rate" in certain financial equations.

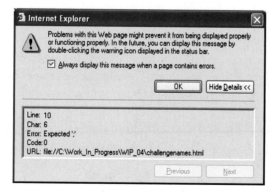

FIGURE 4.35

3. Change the variable name for the risk-free rate to a name that does not generate errors. Make sure you change the name throughout the script.

4. Save and test your file.

Two other errors exist in the statement that generates the **quotedRate** calculation.

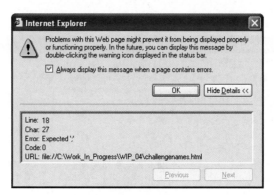

FIGURE 4.36

5. Acknowledge the error message. Return to your text editor and correct the two other errors in the **quotedRate** assignment statement. A result of 8 should return to the end user.

FIGURE 4.37

6. Close the file in your browser and text editor.

4. Correct Errors in Variable String Assignments

In the previous Challenge, you corrected errors in variable names. In this exercise, you correct errors in variable string assignments. You create three string variables to represent three sentences. You create a fourth variable to create a paragraph. The fourth variable is the result of the concatenated values of the sentence variables.

1. In your text editor, open challengestrings.html from the WIP_04 folder. Examine the source code.

The code was written for you, but it contains errors in the assignment statements of the variables.

2. Open the page in your browser.

An error message appears.

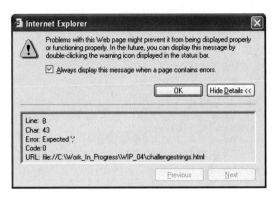

FIGURE 4.38

3. Acknowledge the error. Return to your text editor and find the following line of code.

   ```
   sentence1='Joe once met a man named Jim O'Brien.';
   ```

4. Correct this assignment statement without removing the single quote between the "**O**" and the "**B**" in "**Brien**".

5. Correct the second assignment statement shown below without removing the double quote marks around the quote, "**is that your car?**"

   ```
   sentence2="Jim said "is that your car?"";
   ```

   Remember that you can enclose text strings within pairs of single quotes.

6. Correct the error in the following assignment statement.

   ```
   sentence3="Joe doesn't own a car.;
   ```

7. Save the file in your text editor and refresh your browser.

   Your output should match the following.

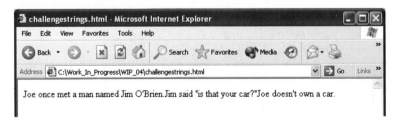

FIGURE 4.39

8. Return to your text editor. Change the assignment statement for the **paragraph** variable to insert a single space between each sentence in the paragraph.

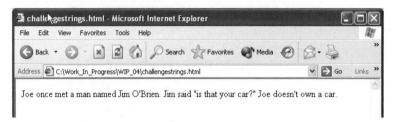

FIGURE 4.40

9.   Close the file in your browser and text editor.

PORTFOLIO BUILDER

Add Variables to a Shopping Cart Page

Thousands of people use the Web to make online purchases. To cultivate customer trust, the online-ordering process must be secure, and the forms must be easy to follow and easy to complete. Rather than forcing customers to proofread every bit of data they enter on their order forms, your e-commerce pages should include pages that perform the necessary calculations to check the data.

You will use the file shopping_cart.html, located in the WIP_04>Portfolio_Builder_04 folder.

In this Portfolio Builder, we created the shopping cart page for you, as well as created the **item1**, **item2**, **item3**, and **item4** variables. Your task is to create additional variables to process a transaction. Follow the following steps as you create your variables.

1.   Create a variable named "**taxRate**" and assign the results of a prompt box that asks "What is the tax rate where you live?" Be sure to use the **parseInt()** method to convert the prompt response to an integer.

2.   Divide the current value in the **taxRate** variable by 100. This converts the value from a percentage (such as 4 for 4 percent) to a decimal (such as 0.04). When performing calculations, decimals are easier to use than percentages.

3.   Create a variable named "**subTotal**" and assign the sum of **item1**, **item2**, **item3**, and **item4** to this variable.

4.   Create a variable named "**salesTax**" to hold the amount generated by multiplying **subTotal** times **taxRate**.

5.   Create a variable named "**shipping**" and set its value equal to 8 to create a shipping cost of $8.00.

6.   Create a variable named "**total**" to represent the total amount calculated by adding the **subTotal**, **salesTax**, and **shipping** amounts.

7.   Code was already written to create formatted headings. Insert statements to output the value of each variable as necessary.

CHAPTER 5

Using Pop-Up Windows

OBJECTIVES

In this chapter, you learn how to:

- Create window objects with JavaScript

- Control features of the browser window

- Use the window.close() method

- Use focus() and blur()

- Manipulate window properties

Why Would I Do This?

HTML allows programmers to link to other documents as well as open new browser windows using the **_blank** option of the **target** attribute of an **<a>** tag — not a very impressive variety of features from which to choose. JavaScript, however, offers extensive control over various aspects of browser windows. In fact, manipulating windows is one of the most common uses of JavaScript.

Windows created in JavaScript are commonly referred to as ***pop-up windows***. Pop-up windows are widely used in Web development, most commonly as online advertisements. It is important to remember that a pop-up window is simply another browser window that can show any URL.

Consider the following pop-up window, which was taken from a Web site on laser vision correction. The pop-up window demonstrates the various steps in the laser-vision-correction process. Several features of the browser were turned off in the pop-up window, and the window was sized to the proper width and height.

FIGURE 5.1

When a pop-up window appears on the screen, it draws focus away from the main window. This is often undesirable for Web site designers who use pop-up windows to display advertisements but do not want users to lose interest in the main page. Using various JavaScript techniques, designers often create pop-up windows that display *behind* the main browser window — which are aptly called ***pop-under windows***.

Many users find pop-up windows annoying because they get in the way of normal computer usage. For this reason, numerous users install ***pop-up blockers***, which are software packages designed to stop scripts from generating pop-up windows without the user's permission. For this reason, designers often choose to keep essential content out of pop-up windows.

You know that you can create new window objects (browser windows) using the **open()** method of the window object. Using the **open()** method and turning various features of the browser window on or off, you can create pop-up windows for virtually any purpose. In this chapter, you learn how to create and use pop-up windows. As you read the lessons, you discover how to use numerous methods and properties of the window object related to using pop-up windows.

VISUAL SUMMARY

Pop-up windows are simply browser windows created in JavaScript. Various aspects of the browser window are either turned off or disabled in pop-up windows. To better understand the basic characteristics of a pop-up window, it is useful to consider browser windows in general. The following screenshot shows the features of the browser window that you can turn on or off using JavaScript.

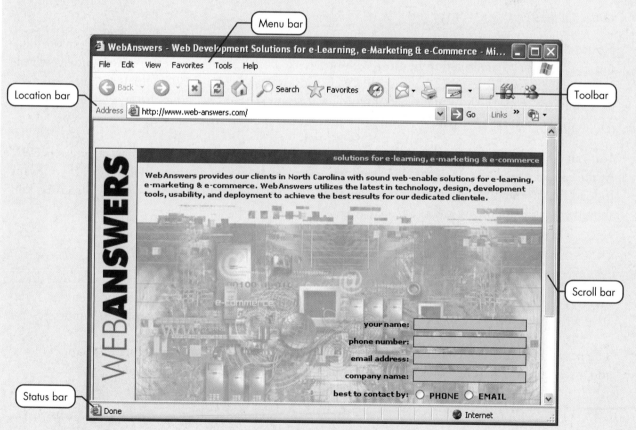

FIGURE 5.2

You start this chapter by considering the **open()** method, which you use to create pop-up windows in JavaScript. The **open()** method is described below, followed by descriptions of the method's parameters.

open()

The **open()** method generates a new window and creates a new window object. The following statement opens a blank browser window.

```
open();
```

The **open()** method also includes several optional parameters that you can set. Within the parenthesis, you separate the parameters with commas, and you must list the parameters in a specific order. Using pseudocode, the **open()** method takes the general form of

```
open(url,name,features,replace);
```

For instance, if you want to open a new window and load the Web Answers Web site into the window, you should use the following command.

```
open("http://www.web-answers.com");
```

Notice that you indicate the protocol (http:) as part of the Web site address. Leaving off the protocol causes the script to malfunction in most Web browsers. This is a common error among novice developers. The protocol is required because this Web address is an ***external URL***, which simply means the page resides outside the local Web site. Not only is this an external URL, it is also an ***absolute reference***, which means you are specifying the complete path of the file you want to open.

You can also use the name of a local file as a URL. A link to a local file is known as an ***internal URL***. In the case of a local file (internal URL), you do not need to specify a protocol or a path. If you want to load the products.html file into a new window, and the file is stored in the current directory, you should enter the following code.

```
open("products.html");
```

The internal URL is also a ***relative reference*** because the path to the file is relative to the current document. A relative reference tells JavaScript to look in the same directory as the currently open file. A relative reference usually consists of the name of the file or a simple path, such as images/banner.gif.

The **name** attribute sets the name of the window object. Assuming you want to open a blank window and assign a **name** attribute of **myWindow**, you should use the following command.

```
open("","myWindow");
```

Features refer to attributes of the browser window; they occupy the third parameter of the **open()** method. Using JavaScript, you can control whether the new window includes scroll bars and toolbars, as well as state the height and width of the browser window. You explore these features in the following section on creating pop-up windows.

The **replace** attribute allows you to specify whether the URL of the pop-up window replaces the current entry in the browser's history list. The **replace** attribute is a Boolean variable, which means its value is either true or false. For example, you can use the following command to create a new window to load the products.html page and place products.html as the current entry in the browser's history list.

```
open("products.html","","","true");
```

close()

The **close()** method closes the associated browser window. Security measures in modern browsers only allow you to close windows you have created. Windows created by the operating system display a warning message when a Web page tries to close the window. Windows created by the operating system include the window that opens when you launch your Web browser, as well as windows that trigger when you choose a Web page by opening a file without first opening the browser. Consider the following code as an example.

```
var myWindow = window.open();
myWindow.close();
window.close();
```

The term "**window**" always means the current window object. When you view this code within a Web page, the browser closes the window you created in the code but generates a confirmation window before closing the primary window. This is a security feature built into the browser.

FIGURE 5.3

The closed Property

This **closed** property tells you if a window object represents an open browser window. If the window is open, the **closed** property is false; if the window is closed, the **closed** property is true. If you want to know whether **adWindow** is open or closed, you can include a statement such as:

```
document.write("The status of the closed window property is
"+adWindow.closed);
```

In this chapter, you explore these aspects of the window object through many hands-on exercises. In Lesson 1, you start by exploring the basics of the **open()** method.

LESSON 1   Creating Window Objects with JavaScript

In JavaScript, window objects represent the browser window and appear at the top of the object model. You can use simple JavaScript or HTML statements to create window objects. For example, the following HTML code creates a new browser window (a window object) when the user clicks a link on the page.

```
<a href="products.html" target="_blank">link</a>
```

You can create a similar statement in JavaScript using the following code.

```
onclick="window.open('products.html');"
```

The JavaScript **open()** method allows you to create pop-up windows. Manipulating various attributes of this method allows you to create and control browser windows with more flexibility than HTML allows. For example, the following statement creates a window that displays a page called products.html at a height of 200 pixels, width of 400 pixels, no scroll bars, no menu bar, and no location bar.

```
window.open("products.html","","height=200,width=400,scrollbars=no,
menubar=no,location=no");
```

You can use the **open()** method to create a simple browser window or a complex pop-up window that contains a number of controlled features. In the following exercise, you learn how to create a pop-up window with an external URL using an absolute reference.

Create a Window Object with an External URL

1   **Copy the content of the Chapter_05 folder to the WIP_05 folder.**

You use these files throughout this chapter. As with other chapters, you will open files from your WIP folder (WIP_05) and save them back to the same folder as you complete the exercises.

2   **Open WIP_05>openexternal.html in your text editor.**

We started this script for you.

3   **Insert the following line of code.**

```
...
<head>
<title>openexternal.html</title>
<script language="JavaScript" type="text/javascript">
```

```
window.open("http://www.web-answers.com");
</script>
</head>
<body>
. . .
```

4   **Save the file in your text editor and open it in your browser.**

A second browser window opens.

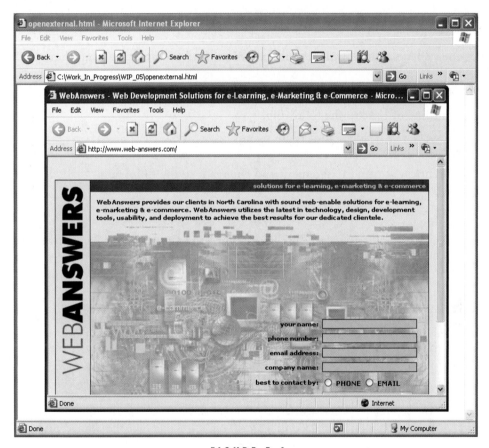

FIGURE 5.4

5   **Close both browser windows. Keep the file open in the text editor for the next exercise.**

In this exercise, you created a window object and loaded an external URL. You use a similar process to load a relative URL. In the next exercise, you load a local file into the pop-up window using a relative URL.

To Extend Your Knowledge . . .

REMEMBER THE PROTOCOLS

In most programming environments, you must specify the protocol (http:) before linking to external Web sites. It's a common mistake for novice developers to type a Web site address as "www.web-answers.com" instead of "http://www.web-answers.com".

Create a Window with a Relative URL

1   In the open openexternal.html in your text editor, find the `<title>` tag shown below.

```
<title>openexternal.html</title>
```

2   Change this line of code to the following.

```
<title>openinternal.html</title>
```

3   Find the `window.open()` statement and change it to the following.

```
window.open("products.html");
```

4   Save the file as "openinternal.html" in your text editor. Open the file in your browser.

A second browser window opens and displays the products.html page.

FIGURE 5.5

5   Close both browser windows.

6   Keep the file open in the text editor for the next exercise.

In this exercise, you created a pop-up window to display a local file. You can also use the `open()` method to open a blank Web page in a browser window, which you practice in the following exercise.

To Extend Your Knowledge . . .

DEFAULT FILE NAMES

When you specify a domain name, such as http://www.web-answers.com, you don't specify the name of a file to load. The Web server automatically sends the default home page for the Web site, which is usually named index.htm, index.html, or possibly default.asp. Developers who need assistance setting the default file name (or knowing the default file name) should speak with their hosting provider or network administrator.

Create a Blank Window

1 In the open openinternal.html in your text editor, find the `<title>` tag shown below.

```
<title>openinternal.html</title>
```

2 Change this line of code to the following.

```
<title>openblank.html</title>
```

3 Find the `window.open()` statement and change the URL to the following.

```
window.open("about:blank");
```

If you use **about:blank** in a URL field, the browser generates a blank window.

4 Save the file as "openblank.html" in your text editor. Open the file in your browser.

A blank browser window appears.

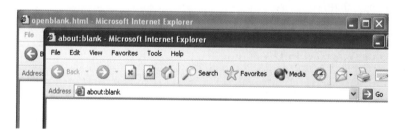

FIGURE 5.6

5 Close both browser windows.

6 Keep the file open in the text editor for the next exercise.

To Extend Your Knowledge . . .

CREATING BLANK WINDOWS

You can use the URL about:blank to generate a blank browser window. When you use the `open()` method, the statements `window.open("")`, `window.open()`, or `window.open("about:blank")` all open a blank browser window.

Name a Window Object

In this exercise, you learn how to name a window object so you can further manipulate the object in JavaScript.

1 | **In the open openblank.html in your text editor, find the `<title>` tag shown below.**

```
<title>openblank.html</title>
```

2 | **Change this line of code to the following.**

```
<title>openname.html</title>
```

3 | **Find the `window.open()` statement and change it to the following.**

```
myPopup=window.open("about:blank","myPopup");
```

You can name the object **myPopup** because you created the object as a variable. The **name** attribute is also set to **myPopup**. Since they have slightly different uses in the code, the two names do not have to be identical — but it is less confusing if you use the same name in both instances.

4 | **Insert the following line of code.**

```
<title>openname.html</title>
<script language="JavaScript" type="text/javascript">
myPopup=window.open("about:blank","myPopup");
myPopup.moveTo(300,200);
</script>
</head>
<body>
```

You can now control the window object using the object name and dot syntax. The **moveTo()** method moves the browser window after it appears.

5 | **Save the file as "openname.html" in your text editor. Open the file in your browser.**

FIGURE 5.7

The window object named **myPopup** appears and moves to the X and Y position specified in the code.

6   Close the file in your browser windows and text editor.

To Extend Your Knowledge . . .

NAMING BROWSER WINDOWS

It is usually best to use a variable name to name a pop-up window and use the **name** attribute of the **open()** method to name the object, as in the following statement where the name is **myWindow**:

```
myWindow=window.open("about:blank","myWindow");
```

LESSON 2   Controlling Features of the Browser Window

The primary reason to use pop-up windows is to control various features of the browser window. To accomplish this, you manipulate the features parameter of the **open()** method. The *features parameter* allows developers to turn on menu bars, toolbars, and scroll bars, as well as control the width and height aspects of the pop-up window.

The features parameter always appears as the third option in the **open()** method; any options you specify appear within the quotes of this parameter, separated by commas. You turn on features of the window object with the keyword **yes** and turn them off with the keyword **no**, such as **scrollbars=no**. Let's take a few moments to review the various options of the features parameter of the **open()** method.

■ *Directories option*. The **directories** option of the **open()** method allows the directory buttons to appear. It is rarely a good idea to turn on the directories option. In addition, older browsers do not contain a directories bar and ignore this parameter. The `open("","","directories=yes");` command turns on the directories option.

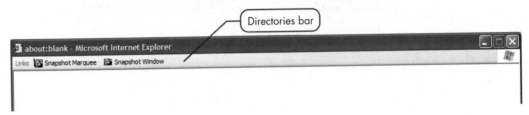

FIGURE 5.8

- *Location option*. The `location` option includes the URL location box. To activate the location box, type `open("","","location=yes");`. It is usually best to turn off the location option, because you don't want Web surfers to type in a new URL in the pop-up window.

To avoid confusing users, it is best to either turn on the toolbar, menu bar, and location bar, or turn off all these options. It is not good practice to turn on one or two and leave the other option/s turned off.

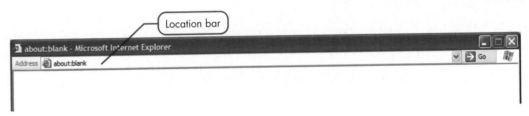

FIGURE 5.9

- *Menubar option*. As you might expect, the `menubar` option turns on the browser's menu bar. The `open("","","menubar=yes");` command turns on the `menubar` option.

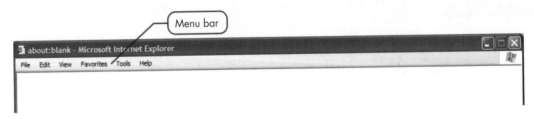

FIGURE 5.10

- *Resizable option*. If a particular window is best viewed at a specific size, you might opt to restrict the user from resizing the open window. The `resizable` option determines whether the user is allowed to resize the window once it opens. The `open("","","resizable=yes");` command allows the user to resize an open window.

- **Scrollbars option.** The `scrollbars` option determines whether the scroll bars appear. If you do not specify this option, scroll bars do not appear on most browsers. To activate the `scrollbars` option, type `open("","","scrollbars=yes");`.

- **Status option.** The `status` option turns on the browser's status bar, which appears at the bottom of the window in most browsers. The status bar displays URLs when the user rolls over links; you can also use it to deliver messages to the user. The `open("","","status=yes");` command opens a window with the status bar enabled.

- **Toolbar option.** When creating a pop-up window, you can specify whether the window displays toolbars by entering `toolbar=yes` in the features parameter of the `open()` method. The `open("","","toolbar=yes");` command opens a window with the toolbar enabled.

FIGURE 5.11

You can turn off the toolbar by typing `open("","","toolbar=no");`.

FIGURE 5.12

- **Height option.** Unlike the other options of the features parameter, you must specify a value for height and width, instead of simply specifying "yes" or "no," which is the case with the other options. The `open("","","height=200");` command opens a blank window with a height of 200 pixels.

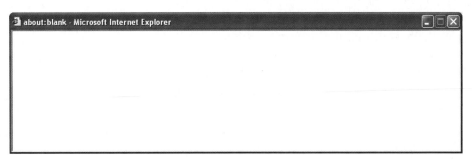

FIGURE 5.13

■ *Width option*. You can also specify the width of the browser window in the features parameter of the **open()** method. The **open=("","","width=200");** command opens a blank window with a width of 200 pixels.

FIGURE 5.14

Change a Window's Width and Height

In the following exercises, you explore each aspect of the features parameter of the **open()** method. You start by manipulating the width and height of a pop-up window.

1 Open WIP_05>width.html in your text editor.

2 Insert the following line of code.

```
...
<body>
<script language="JavaScript" type="text/javascript">
//insert code here
window.open("","","width=200");
</script>
</body>
</html>
```

3   Save the file in your text editor and open it in your browser.

FIGURE 5.15

A second browser window opens at the specified width. Newer browsers automatically turn off most features (toolbars, menu bars, directories, etc.) if you specify a width or height.

4   Return to your text editor. Change the `window.open()` command to the following.

```
window.open("","","height=200");
```

5   Save the file in your text editor and refresh your browser.

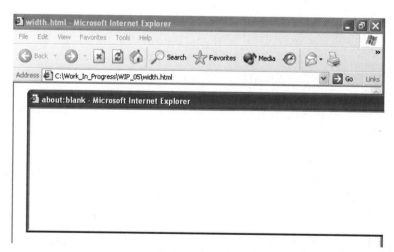

FIGURE 5.16

The height of the window is now 200 pixels.

6   Return to your text editor. Change the `window.open()` command to the following.

```
window.open("","","width=200,height=200");
```

Notice how the **width** and **height** settings both appear within the third set of quotes (the features parameter), separated by commas.

7   Save the file in your text editor and refresh your browser.

FIGURE 5.17

Both the **width** and **height** parameters are 200 pixels.

8   Close the file in your browser and text editor.

Control the Toolbar and Menu Bar

1   Open WIP_05>toolbar.html in your text editor.

2   Insert the following line of code.

```
...
<body>
<script language="JavaScript" type="text/javascript">
//insert code here
window.open("http://www.web-answers.com","","toolbar=no");
</script>
</body>
</html>
```

3   Save the file in your text editor and open it in your browser.

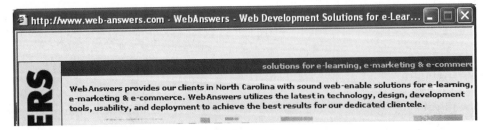

FIGURE 5.18

The page appears without the toolbar. By default, most browsers turn off other toolbars when a single toolbar is disabled.

4   **Close the pop-up window.**

5   **Return to your text editor. Change the `window.open()` command to the following.**

```
window.open("http://www.web-answers.com","","toolbar=no,
menubar=yes");
```

This code turns on the browser's menu bar when the window opens.

6   **Save the file in your text editor and refresh your browser.**

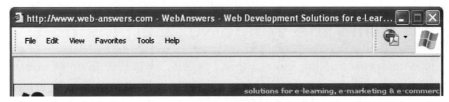

FIGURE 5.19

The browser's menu bar appears.

7   **Close the pop-up window.**

8   **Return to your text editor. Change the `window.open()` command to the following.**

```
window.open("http://www.web-answers.com","","toolbar=yes,
    menubar=yes");
```

9   **Save the file in your text editor and refresh your browser.**

FIGURE 5.20

Both the menu bar and toolbar appear in the pop-up window.

10   **Close the file in your browser and text editor.**

11   **Close the pop-up window.**

In this lesson, you learned how to control various attributes of pop-up windows by manipulating the features parameter of the **open()** method. In the next lesson, you learn how to use JavaScript to close pop-up windows.

To Extend Your Knowledge . . .

BROWSER FEATURES

The ability to control the width and height of a window is the most common reason to use JavaScript to create pop-up windows.

LESSON 3   Using the window.close() Method

Along with the ability to open a window, it is also useful to close a window. To do so, you use the JavaScript `close()` method. Developers can instruct JavaScript to close pop-up windows in different ways, including clicking a button on the page or triggering the `close()` method from a script in another file.

Consider the following pop-up window, which contains a form used to schedule a car service appointment. A user can close the window by clicking the close button in the upper-right corner of the page.

FIGURE 5.21

In this example, the close button is a graphic created with the following statement.

```
<img src="closebutton.jpg" onclick="window.close()">
```

In this example, inline JavaScript programs the button to close when clicked. (Remember, the word "**window**" refers to the current browser window.) In addition, the window automatically closes when the form is submitted. After the form is submitted, the following code executes.

```
window.close();
```

A third option allows you to close a window object from a script in another open browser window. Assuming the window object's name is **servicePopup**, you can close the object by referring to it as follows.

```
servicePopup.close();
```

Close the Current Browser Window

1 Open WIP_05>closecurrent.html in your text editor.

2 Insert the following line of code.

```
...
<title>closecurrent.html</title>
<script language="JavaScript" type="text/javascript">
// insert code here
window.close();
</script>
</head>
<body>
...
```

This code closes the current browser window when the new window opens.

3 Save the file in your text editor and open the file in your browser.

A message box asks you to confirm if you want to allow a Web page script to close the open window. Older browsers may simply close the window.

FIGURE 5.22

4 Click Yes to close the page.

5 Close the file in the text editor.

In this exercise, you attempted to use the **close()** method to close the current browser window. In most browsers, this method triggers an alert message that asks you to confirm that you want to close the window.

Use an Inline Event to Close a Window

1 Open WIP_05>inlineclose.html in your text editor and browser.

This file opens a blank browser window as a pop-up window.

2 In your text editor, find the following code.

```
window.open("about:blank");
```

3   **Change this code to the following.**

```
myPopup=window.open("about:blank","myPopup");
```

This code assigns **myPopup** as the name of the pop-up window.

4   **Insert the following line of code after the `<body>` tag.**

```
...
<title>inlineclose.html</title>
</head>
<body>
<a href="#" onclick="myPopup.close()">close the pop-up</a>
<script language="JavaScript" type="text/javascript">
myPopup=window.open("about:blank","myPopup");
</script>
...
```

5   **Save the file in your text editor and refresh your browser.**

FIGURE 5.23

Two browser windows appear. If necessary, move the pop-up window out of the way so you can see the original window.

6   **Click the hyperlink.**

The pop-up window closes, and the original window remains open.

FIGURE 5.24

| 7 | **Close the file in your browser and text editor.** |

In this exercise, you used inline JavaScript to close a pop-up window. To do so, the object (the pop-up window) must be a named variable.

To Extend Your Knowledge . . .

WINDOW.CLOSE()

Newer browsers contain security precautions that do not allow scripts to close the primary browser window. This rule only applies to windows created by the operating system — it does not apply to windows created with JavaScript.

LESSON 4   Using focus() and blur() Methods

You can use the **focus()** and **blur()** methods to control the focus of window objects. As you learned in Chapter 2, when a window has focus, it receives notification of keys pressed on the user's keyboard. When a window is blurred, it is not selected and does not receive notification of keys pressed on the user's keyboard. All commands are directed to the window that is "in focus."

blur()

The **blur()** method removes focus from a specified window. A blurred window no longer receives keystrokes from the user's keyboard. When one window is blurred, another window comes into focus; the blurred window moves behind the open window currently in focus. You typically use the **blur()** command to create pop-under advertisements — a new window opens and moves to the back of the open browser window. The end user discovers the pop-under when he finishes browsing. To blur a window, you can use a statement such as:

```
var myWindow=window.open();
myWindow.blur();
```

focus()

The **focus()** method changes focus to the specified window object. The **focus()** method has the same effect as a user clicking in or on a window to make it the active window. Once a window is in focus, it appears in front of the other windows and keystrokes are directed to that window. Assuming you opened a window called **adWindow**, you could use the following command to change the focus to **adWindow**:

```
adWindow.focus();
```

The ability to control focus and blur offers new possibilities for controlling pop-up windows. You explore these possibilities in the following exercises.

Create a Pop-Under Ad

1   **Open WIP_05>popunder.html in your browser.**

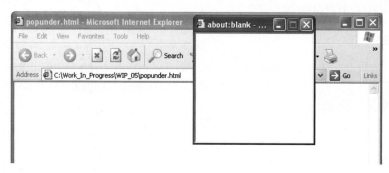

FIGURE 5.25

A simple pop-up window with a blank page displays.

2   **Close the pop-up window. Open WIP_05>popunder.html in your text editor.**

3   **Find the following line of code.**

```
myPopup=window.open("about:blank","myPopup","width=200,
height=180");
```

This statement creates the pop-up window you just saw in your browser.

4   **Add the following lines of code below the open() statement.**

```
...
<title>popunder.html</title>
<script language="JavaScript" type="text/javascript">
myPopup=window.open("about:blank","myPopup","width=200,
    height=180");
// blur the window to make it pop under the main browser window
    myPopup.blur();
</script>
</head>
<body>
...
```

This statement places the pop-up window behind the main browser window. Remember to type the name of the window object exactly as written in the **open()** statement — including the capital "**P**."

5 | **Save the file in your text editor and refresh your browser.**

You may see the pop-up appear and then disappear as it blurs.

6 | **Close the main browser window.**

The pop-up appears behind the window you just closed.

7 | **Keep the file open in your text editor for the next exercise. Close the pop-up window.**

In this exercise, you created a pop-under window by first creating a pop-up window and then blurring the window to make it appear behind the main browser window.

When you blur a pop-up, you automatically draw focus to the remaining browser window. You can achieve the same effect using the **focus()** method on the main browser window, as you see in the next exercise.

To Extend Your Knowledge . . .

FOCUS AND BLUR

Browser windows are normally sized at 100% of the available screen size, which completely obscures blurred windows from view. If the user resizes the browser window to take up a smaller portion of the screen, however, part of a blurred window may become visible.

Draw Focus to a Window

1 | **In the open popunder.html in your text editor, find and delete the following lines of code.**

```
// blur the window to make it pop under the main browser window
    myPopup.blur();
```

2 | **Insert the following lines of code in place of the code you just deleted.**

```
...
<title>popunder.html</title>
<script language="JavaScript" type="text/javascript">
myPopup=window.open("about:blank","myPopup","width=200,
    height=180");
// draw focus to the main window
window.focus();
</script>
</head>
<body>
...
```

| 3 | **Save the file in your text editor and open it in your browser.** |

The pop-up window moves behind the main browser window (in most browsers). Keystroke control returns to the main window.

| 4 | **Close the file in the browser and text editor.** |

| 5 | **Close the pop-up window.** |

In this exercise, you used the **focus()** method to draw focus back to the main window after a pop-up window was created. This method often keeps users from becoming distracted by the pop-up window. You can use either **blur()** or **focus()** to create pop-under windows in JavaScript.

To Extend Your Knowledge . . .

FOCUS() AND POP-UNDER WINDOWS

The focus() method is often used in conjunction with pop-up ads. Web designers often want to display pop-up ads to generate revenue, but they don't want the user's focus to stray from the main site. When the pop-up window displays, it takes keyboard and mouse focus away from the main window. Developers often use the focus() method to return focus to the main window.

LESSON 5   Manipulating Window Properties

Window objects have specific properties you can access and use. For example, the **closed** property tells you if a particular window object is currently open or closed. If you want to know if a window is closed, you can write a statement to output the value stored in the **closed** property. Assuming you have a window called **thePopup**, you could write the following statement.

```
document.write(thePopup.closed);
```

The statement outputs **true** if the window object is closed; the statement outputs **false** if the window object is still open. Developers often use this property to determine whether a window is closed and, if so, perform a specific set of actions.

The defaultStatus Property

In this exercise, you use the **defaultStatus** property of the window object to place a message in the status bar of a pop-up window. This message appears by default unless overridden by temporary messages.

| 1 | **Open WIP_05>defaultstatus.html in your text editor.** |

2   **Insert the following code.**

```
. . .
<title>defaultstatus.html</title>
<script language="JavaScript" type="text/javascript">
// insert code here
myWindow=window.open("about:blank","myWindow","height=210,
    width=600,status=yes");
</script>
</head>
<body>
. . .
```

This code creates a pop-up window named **myWindow** with the status bar feature turned on.

3   **Save the file in your text editor and open it in your browser.**

FIGURE 5.26

4   **Close the pop-up window and return to your text editor.**

5   **Add the following line of code before the </script> tag.**

```
. . .
<script language="JavaScript" type="text/javascript">
// insert code here
myWindow=window.open("about:blank","myWindow","height=210,
    width=600,status=yes");
myWindow.defaultStatus="Welcome to my Web site!";
</script>
</head>
<body>
. . .
```

6   **Save the file in your text editor. Refresh the document in the main browser window.**

FIGURE 5.27

A message appears in the status bar of the pop-up window. Please note: this method is not supported in most Mac browsers.

7   **Close the file in the browser and text editor.**

To Extend Your Knowledge . . .

MANIPULATING THE STATUS BAR

You can use the `defaultStatus` property or the `status` property to place a message in the status bar. Messages created by the `status` property are only visible for a short time. When you use the `defaultStatus` property to insert a message, the message remains visible unless a status message displays temporarily.

Use the closed Property

In this exercise, you use the **closed** property of the window object to instruct JavaScript to tell you if a window is currently open or closed.

1 | **Open WIP_05>closedproperty.html in your text editor. Examine the code.**

This simple script generates a blank pop-up browser window.

2 | **Leave the file open in your text editor and open it in your browser.**

In the illustration shown below, we moved the pop-up window to allow you to see the main page.

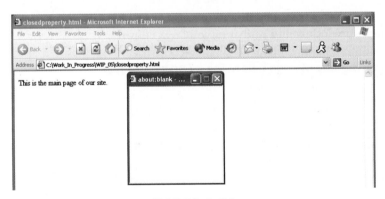

FIGURE 5.28

3 | **Find the following comment statement.**

```
//***** Insert your code below this statement *****
```

4 | **Directly below this statement, add the following code.**

```
. . .
<script language="JavaScript" type="text/javascript">
adWindow=open("about:blank","adWindow","status=no, toolbar=no,
    resizable=no, width=200,height=200, scrollbars=no, menubar=no,
    location=no");
```

```
document.write("<p>");
//***** Insert your code below this statement *****
document.write("The closed property for the adWindow is
    "+adWindow.closed);
document.write("</p>");
</script>
</body>
. . .
```

This statement shows the status of the **closed** property for the pop-up window.

5   **Save the file in your text editor and refresh your browser.**

Since the window is open, the **closed** property is false.

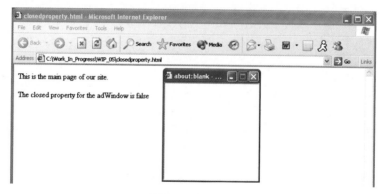

FIGURE 5.29

6   **Directly before the `</script>` tag, insert a blank line and insert the following code.**

```
. . .
//***** Insert your code below this statement *****
document.write("The closed property for the adWindow is
    "+adWindow.closed);
document.write("</p>");
adWindow.close();
</script>
</body>
</html>
```

This code closes the pop-up window.

7   **Highlight the following statement in your code.**

```
document.write("The closed property for the adWindow is
    "+adWindow.closed);
```

8   **Choose Edit>Copy to copy the code to the clipboard.**

Now that you have inserted a statement to close the window, you check the **closed** property of the window a second time.

9 | **Create a blank line directly before the </script> command. Choose Edit>Paste in your text editor to paste the code from the clipboard.**

Your code should match the following.

```
<!DOCTYPE html PUBLIC "-//W3C//DTD XHTML 1.0 Transitional//EN"
"http://www.w3.org/TR/xhtml1/DTD/xhtml1-transitional.dtd">
<html xmlns="http://www.w3.org/1999/xhtml">
<head>
<title>closedproperty.html</title>
</head>
<body>
This is the main page of our site.
<script language="JavaScript" type="text/javascript">
adWindow=open("about:blank","adWindow","status=no, toolbar=no,
    resizable=no, width=200,height=200, scrollbars=no, menubar=no,
    location=no");
document.write("<p>");
//***** Insert your code below this statement *****
document.write("The closed property for the adWindow is
    "+adWindow.closed);
document.write("</p>");
adWindow.close();
document.write("The closed property for the adWindow is
    "+adWindow.closed);
</script>
</body>
</html>
```

When you make changes to your code, get in the habit of making two or three changes at a time, scanning for mistakes, and then checking the code in the browser to ensure you made the changes correctly. This is tedious work, but usually less time consuming and frustrating than looking for a simple error in a large block of code.

10 | **Review your code to make sure it matches the example in Step 9. Save the code in your text editor and refresh your browser.**

Note the sequence of commands in the source code. The **closed** property is considered false until the window closes.

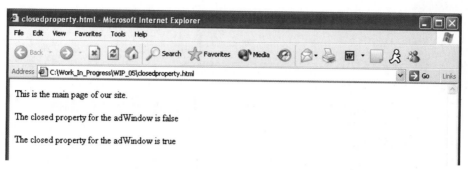

FIGURE 5.30

11 **Close the file in your text editor and browser.**

In this exercise, you used the **closed** property to determine whether a window is currently open or closed. If the window is closed, the **closed** property is true; if the window is open, the **closed** property is false.

To Extend Your Knowledge . . .

CLOSED AND CLOSE()

Novice programmers commonly confuse the **close()** method (which closes a window) with the **closed** property (which tells you if a window is currently closed).

CAREERS IN DESIGN

Pop-Up Windows in Your Portfolio

Pop-up windows offer a nice touch on portfolio Web sites. This is particularly true for Web designers and developers whose portfolio sites primarily consist of other Web sites. Using pop-up windows, you can show the sites in your portfolio at the optimum browser size.

Using pop-up windows also allows you to open projects in another window without forcing the user to leave the main portfolio interface. Here are a few tips for using pop-up windows in your portfolio.

- Avoid opening more than one pop-up window at a time. They clutter an interface when overused.

- Use pop-up windows in a consistent manner. For example, you could use them anytime the user chooses a View Site link on a project description page.

- Use pop-up windows when you need to display large images or animations that do not fit into your standard interface. For example, if you want to link to an image file that has a resolution of 640 by 480, place the image in an HTML file and display it in a pop-up window, rather than simply creating a hyperlink to the image (which requires the user to leave your interface).

SUMMARY

In Chapter 5, you learned that pop-up windows offer excellent advantages to the JavaScript programmer — they allow you to open a new browser window, keep your current content visible, and control the Web surfer's navigation possibilities. Many users find pop-up windows annoying, however, so you should use them sparingly.

Numerous Web surfers choose to use pop-up-blocking software to keep Web page scripts from generating pop-up windows. This trend is likely to become more popular as pop-up ads proliferate. As a general rule, use pop-up windows for nonessential information.

In this chapter, you learned how to create new window objects and assign names to the objects. You discovered how to use the **URL** property of the **open()** method to specify which file should open in a pop-up window. You also discovered the difference between relative URLs (local) and external URLs (remote).

You learned that the features parameter of the **open()** method controls the appearance of the pop-up window. Using various attributes of this parameter, designers can control the width and the height of the window. This important feature allows developers to set the optimal resolution (size) for viewing a Web page, which avoids the difficulty of creating pages that must adapt to various screen resolutions to be viewed as intended. Using the features parameters, designers can control many other features, such as allowing the user to resize the window or if the window has scroll bars.

You learned how to use the **defaultStatus** property to place a message in the status bar of the pop-up window. You also used the **closed** property to determine if a specific window is closed or open. You discovered how to apply the **close()** method to close a pop-up window as well as use the **focus()** and **blur()** methods to direct keystrokes to a particular window.

KEY TERMS

Absolute reference	Internal URL	Relative reference
Directories option	Location option	Resizable option
External URL	Menubar option	Scrollbars option
Feature	Pop-under window	Status option
Features parameter	Pop-up blocker	Toolbar option
Height option	Pop-up window	Width option

CHECKING CONCEPTS AND TERMS

MULTIPLE CHOICE

Circle the letter that matches the correct answer for each of the following questions.

1. You use the _____ method to create pop-up windows.
   a. resize()
   b. moveTo()
   c. open()
   d. create()
   e. None of the above.

2. The URL parameter of the open() method can contain _____ .
   a. an internal link
   b. a relative reference
   c. an external link
   d. an absolute reference
   e. Any of the above.

3. A window that receives keystrokes from the keyboard _____ .
   a. has focus
   b. is blurred
   c. is closed
   d. None of the above.

4. The replace attribute of the open() method _____ .
   a. is true if the pop-up window replaces the current Web page in the browser's history list
   b. is false if the pop-up window replaces the current Web page in the browser's history list
   c. closes the main browser window when the pop-up window is created
   d. None of the above.

5. The features parameter of the open() method _____ .

   a. sets the width of a pop-up window

   b. sets the height of a pop-up window

   c. allows the user to resize a pop-up window

   d. All of the above.

   e. None of the above.

6. You can create blank browser windows by placing _____ in the URL parameter of the open() method.

   a. about:blank

   b. " "

   c. Both of the above.

   d. None of the above.

7. The directories option of the features parameter _____ .

   a. is available on most browsers

   b. brings up a directory on the users computer

   c. is not available on most Web browsers

   d. changes the way users view folders on their computer

8. You can use the close() method to _____ .

   a. close pop-up windows

   b. close the main browser window with the user's permission

   c. Both of the above.

   d. None of the above.

9. You can use inline events to close windows.

   a. True

   b. False

10. You can create pop-under windows by _____ .

   a. blurring a pop-up window

   b. focusing the main browser window

   c. Both of the above.

DISCUSSION QUESTIONS

1. What advantages do pop-up windows offer over windows created with HTML `<a>` tags?

2. Why would developers want to avoid using pop-up windows? Under what circumstances would pop-up windows be most appropriate?

3. Why would you want to blur a pop-up window?

4. In JavaScript, how is `close()` different from `closed`?

SKILL DRILL

Skill Drill exercises reinforce chapter skills. Each skill reinforced is the same, or nearly the same, as a skill presented in the chapter. Detailed instructions are provided in a step-by-step format. You should work through these exercises in the order provided.

1. Control Scroll Bars

In this Skill Drill, you use the **scrollbar** feature of window object. This feature controls whether scroll bars appear in a pop-up window.

1. In your text editor and browser, open skillscroll.html from the WIP_05 folder.

    This file creates a simple pop-up window that displays the Web Answers Web site.

2. In your text editor, examine the code that creates the pop-up window.

    The code creates a pop-up window that is 800 pixels wide and 600 pixels tall. The site looks best at this resolution (size).

3. In the code, change both the height and width of the pop-up window to 400 pixels.

4. Save the file in your text editor. Close the pop-up window in the browser, and then refresh the browser.

    A much smaller pop-up window appears. In most browsers, scroll bars do not appear, even though they are needed.

5. Close the pop-up window in your browser and return to your text editor.

6. Add the **scrollbars=yes** option to the features parameter of the **open()** method.

7. Save the file in your text editor and refresh your browser.

Scroll bars appear on the page.

FIGURE 5.31

8. Close the open browser windows and close the file in your text editor.

2. Make Pop-Up Windows Resizable

In the previous exercise, you used the **scrollbars** attribute to turn on scroll bars in a pop-up window. The **resizable** attribute allows developers to make pop-up windows resizable. You explore the **resizable** feature in this Skill Drill.

1. In your text editor and browser, open skillresize.html from the WIP_05 folder.

This file creates a simple pop-up window.

2. Place your cursor on the lower-right corner of the browser window and try to change the size of the pop-up window.

In IE 6.0, the ability to resize most pop-up windows is turned off by default; therefore, the mouse pointer does not change to indicate you can resize the window. Other browsers may change the mouse pointer to indicate you can resize the window.

3. Close the pop-up window.

4. Return to your code in the text editor. In the **window.open()** statement, turn on the **resizable** feature of the pop-up window by adding **resizable=yes** to the features parameter of the **open()** method.

5. Save the file in your text editor and refresh your browser.

You can now drag the window's lower-right corner to resize the window.

FIGURE 5.32

6. Close the file in your browser and text editor.

3. Use the Location Bar Feature

In the previous Skill Drill, you used the **resizable** parameter of the **open()** method. In this exercise, you use the **location** attribute to turn on the location bar.

1. In your text editor, open skilllocation.html from the WIP_05 folder.

    We started a script for you.

2. Write a line of code that opens a blank window and turns off the menu bar.

3. Save the file in your text editor and open the file in your browser.

    A blank browser window appears when the file opens.

4. Return to your text editor. Add a location bar to the pop-up window by adding the **location=yes** option to the features parameter of the **window.open()** statement.

5. Save and test your file.

    The location bar appears on the page.

FIGURE 5.33

6. Close the file in your browser and text editor.

4. Use an Inline Event to Open a Pop-Up

In this Skill Drill, you open a window in response to a user event, such as when the user clicks an object on the screen.

1. In your browser, open skillinlineopen.html from the WIP_05 folder.

   This file creates a simple hyperlink.

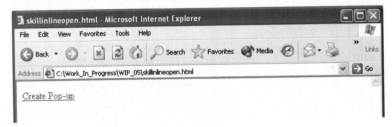

FIGURE 5.34

2. Open the file in your text editor. Find the following inline JavaScript code contained in the **<a>** tag.

   ```
   onclick="//insert code here"
   ```

3. Replace the JavaScript comment with a **window.open()** statement. The statement should create a blank browser window with a height of 250 pixels and a width of 300 pixels.

   Hint: Use single quotes in the **window.open()** statement to avoid a syntax error with the double quotes in the **onclick** statement.

4. Save the file in your text editor and refresh your browser.

5. Click the hyperlink.

   A pop-up window appears.

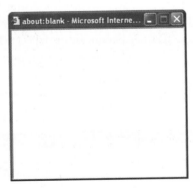

FIGURE 5.35

6. Close the file in your browser and text editor.

CHALLENGE

Challenge exercises expand on, or are somewhat related to, skills presented in the lessons. Each exercise provides a brief introduction, followed by instructions presented in a numbered-step format that are not as detailed as those in the Skill Drill exercises. You should work through the exercises in the order provided.

1. Create a Pop-Up Window in a Function

In previous exercises, you wrote code to generate pop-up windows. In this Challenge, you create a pop-up window by writing code within a function. Using a function is desirable because you can easily adapt the function for a number of uses.

1. In your browser, open challengepopup.html from the WIP_05 folder.

    This simple page includes a link that triggers a JavaScript function. The function is incomplete.

FIGURE 5.36

2. Click the hyperlink.

    An alert box appears.

FIGURE 5.37

3. Open the file in your text editor and examine the code. The following statement triggers the function when the user clicks the hyperlink.

    ```
    <a href="javascript:createPopup();">open pop-up window </a>
    ```

    Another option for creating this link is to use the **onclick** event handler instead of placing the function call within the **href** property. Note: the **javascript** keyword may not work in Mac versions of Internet Explorer.

4. Find the following statement in the code.

```
alert("function has been triggered");
```

This statement ensures the function triggers correctly.

5. Replace this statement with the following statement.

```
thePopup=window.open("charlotte.html","thePopup");
```

6. Save the file in your text editor and refresh your browser. Click the hyperlink.

A pop-up window appears with the charlotte.html page. This is a location page for the regional office of a mortgage company.

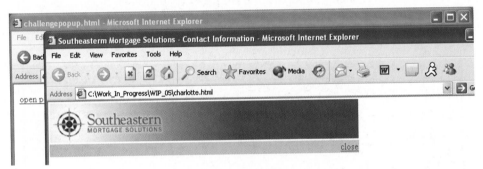

FIGURE 5.38

7. Close the pop-up window. Keep challengepopup.html open in your browser and text editor for the next exercise.

2. Create Complex Pop-Up Windows

In this Challenge, you create complex pop-up statements to create a pop-up window that includes a status bar.

1. Return to challengepopup.html in your text editor.

2. Add the following features to the **open()** method: set the pop-up window width to 430 pixels, set the height to 450 pixels, make sure the window is not resizable, and turn off the scroll bars, menu bar, and toolbar.

3. Save the file in your text editor and test it in your browser.

The pop-up window resizes to an optimum setting.

4. Close the pop-up window.

5. Return to your text editor.

6. The features parameter includes an option to turn on the browser's status bar. Turn on this option by including the **status=yes** parameter.

7. Save the file in your text editor and refresh your browser.

The pop-up includes a status bar at the bottom of the window.

FIGURE 5.39

8. Roll your cursor over the hyperlink that says "Email Us."

Information about the hyperlink appears in the status bar.

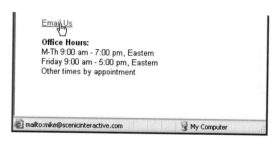

FIGURE 5.40

9. Keep the pop-up window and challengepopup.html open in your browser for the next exercise.

10. Close the file in the text editor.

3. Create a Close Link

In this Challenge, you create a link to close an open pop-up window. As an alternative, you can just as easily place the link on an image — but that's for another exercise.

1. In the open pop-up window from the previous exercise, find the "close window" link near the top of the window.

FIGURE 5.41

2. Click the link.

An alert box appears, indicating the function was triggered.

FIGURE 5.42

3. Acknowledge the alert box.

4. Open charlotte.html in your text editor and find the following line of code.

```
<a href="#" onclick="closePopup();">close window </a>
```

This code triggers the function in the head of the document that eventually closes the window.

5. Find the following code in the head of the document.

```
alert("function has been triggered");
```

6. Replace the code you found in step 5 with a line of code that closes the current browser window.

7. Save the file in your text editor and test it in your browser.

Assuming you completed the steps correctly, the pop-up window closes when you click the "close window" button.

8. Keep challengepopup.html open in the browser for the next exercise. Close charlotte.html in your text editor.

4. Create a Pop-Under Window

In this Challenge, you practice your pop-up window skills by creating a pop-under window.

1. With challengepopup.html open in your browser, open the file in your text editor.

2. Find the **createPopup()** function in the head of the document. Find the "**}**" character that ends the function. Directly before this character, insert a line of code to blur the window object, which is named **thePopup()**.

3. Save the file in your text editor.

4. Refresh the file in your browser.

The code effectively makes the object appear behind the main browser window to create a pop-under window.

5. Remove the line of code you added in Step 2, and then save the file.

6. Close challengepopup.html in your text editor. Load charlotte.html into your text editor.

7. Find the **<body>** tag in charlotte.html.

8. Insert the following code into the **<body>** tag of charlotte.html to make the window blur as soon as the file finishes loading.

```
onload="blur();"
```

9. Save the file.

10. Close the pop-up window, which should be located behind your main browser window.

11. Refresh challengepopup.html in your browser. Click the link to open the pop-up file.

The file blurs as soon as the last character of the page loads into the browser.

12. Close both browser windows and close the file in your text editor.

PORTFOLIO BUILDER

Build an Interactive Online Gallery

An online image gallery is an effective use of Web interactivity: a user simply clicks a small image (a thumbnail) in a list, and a full-sized version of the image displays. An inexperienced developer building this type of gallery might link the thumbnail to a full-sized image in a normal browser window (not a pop-up). Doing so offers full control of browser toolbars and features — but also offers users an easy way to leave the gallery at any time. A better plan is to integrate JavaScript into the site's code, which allows the developer to control a user's expected behavior.

To prepare for this Portfolio Builder, open the gallery.html page in your browser and review the page. Click the first image; the browser replaces the thumbnail image with a full-size image. Click the Back button; the content of the browser is replaced several times. When you use pop-up windows, you can control the user's experience of the gallery.

To complete this Portfolio Builder, open the gallery.html page from your WIP_05>Portfolio_Builder_05 folder and review the page. Click the first image; the browser replaces the thumbnail image with a full-size image. Click the Back button; the content of the browser is replaced several times. When you use pop-up windows, you can control the user's experience of the gallery.

To complete this Portfolio Builder, enhance the functionality of the gallery.html page in the following ways.

- Create a pop-up window when the user clicks a thumbnail image. The pop-up should contain the full-size image. (The HTML pages and links for each image were created for you.)

- Control the features of the browser window.

- Resize the pop-up window according to the full-size image. Leave the "close window" link visible in the pop-up window.

- Insert the following code into the **<body>** tag.

```
onblur="window.close();"
```

This code checks the focus status (focus or blur) of the window and applies a **window.close()** method. When one of the pop-up windows loses focus (or becomes an inactive window), it automatically closes. This method allows you to avoid a series of pop-up windows that litter the screen when the main browser window closes. (Users will appreciate this thoughtful site design.)

CHAPTER 6

Working with If Statements

OBJECTIVES

In this chapter, you learn how to:

- Add Boolean values

- Use if statements

- Compare mathematical values

- Contrast string values

- React to user choices

- Work with logical operators

- Create complex decision statements

Why Would I Do This?

In many situations, you must evaluate a condition before taking action. For instance, imagine that you operate a cash register in a department store. After you enter the prices of the individual items into the cash register, you receive the total amount of the purchase, which you present to the customer. When the customer gives you money to pay for the items, you must evaluate the situation. There are three likely outcomes.

- If the total is greater than the amount offered by the customer, you ask for more money.

- If the total is less than the amount offered, you give the customer the appropriate amount of change.

- If the total is equal to the amount offered, you do nothing, and the transaction is complete.

In this simple example, you must compare the total cost of the items with the amount of money the customer gives to you. To successfully complete this transaction, you must perform comparisons between variables. In computer languages, specific characters or phrases (called *comparison operators*) make comparisons among/between values. Comparison operators are easy to understand. In an elementary school math class, you might have made a comparison similar to the following.

```
28 > 59
```

Most readers understand that the translation of this mathematical equation is "The number 28 is greater than the number 59." This statement is false because 28 is certainly not greater than 59. In this example, the greater-than symbol is the comparison operator.

As you learned in Chapter 4, a decision statement evaluates a condition — one set of actions occurs if the statement is true, and a different set of actions occurs if the statement is false. Decision statements are also known as *flow-of-control statements.* You can write decision statements in various ways, but all decision statements perform (basically) the same function. Using pseudocode, you could describe a decision statement in the following manner.

```
if (a condition is true) then perform a set of actions, else (if the
condition is false) do nothing
```

You could also write the statement using pseudocode in this fashion.

```
if (a condition is true) then perform a set of actions, else (if the
condition is false) perform a different set of actions
```

Comparison operators and decision statements are useful whenever you need to make decisions based on changing information. In this chapter, you explore comparison operators and decision/flow-of-control statements while you consider how these statements are written in JavaScript.

VISUAL SUMMARY

Decision statements allow JavaScript code to branch off in a number of directions, depending on the variables in the script. When faced with complex programming problems that involve numerous decision statements, many developers prefer to map out the solution in the form of a flowchart. A *flowchart* is simply a diagram that shows how a script progresses during execution. For example, if you were designing a script for an online test, your flowchart might resemble the following diagram.

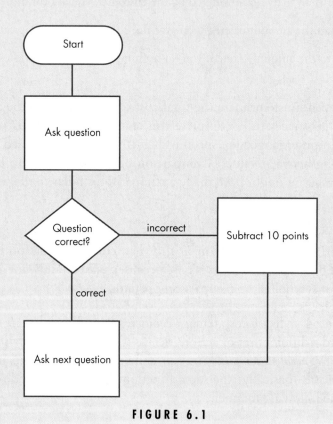

FIGURE 6.1

After you complete the flowchart, it is usually an easy task to convert the script to actual code. Many programmers use slightly different shapes and conventions for diagramming programming problems and apply advanced diagramming schemes to complex problems.

In the above flowchart, a simple scheme uses an oval to show the beginning of the program, rectangles to show the processing steps, and diamonds to show decision (`if`) statements. This diagram contains everything you need to create your JavaScript code.

Comparison Operators

Comparison operators are characters or phrases that allow you to compare two values and then receive a true or false answer. The less than or greater than operators are the easiest to understand — you use them to determine if one value is greater than or less than another value.

Assume that you assign numbers to the following variables.

```
var x=50;
var y=88;
var z=3;
```

You can use the comparison operators shown below to compare the values.

Operator	Operation	Code	Result
<	Less than	x<y	True
>	Greater than	z>y	False
<=	Less than or equal to	y<=z	False
>=	Greater than or equal to	x>=y	True
==	The values are equal	x==y	False
!=	The values are not equal	x!=z	True

TABLE 6.1

The == operator is known as the *equality operator*; it means "the values are equal." The != operator is known as the *inequality operator*; it means "the values are not equal." Even though this may seem counterintuitive, the inequality operator evaluates a value of **true** if the values are not equal, and a value of **false** if the values are equal.

Logical Operators

In complex comparisons, it is often necessary to evaluate more than one Boolean value to make a decision. As an example, let's consider a class registration system at a college. To receive permission to register for a class, a student must have an account in good standing (he paid his tuition fees), and the student must have completed the prerequisites for the class. You can create variables that tell you this information. Assuming a student has both paid his fees and completed the prerequisites, you might write statements such as the following.

```
var preReqs=true;
var goodStanding=true;
```

Next, you need to make a comparison to decide if the student has permission to register for a class. Using pseudocode, you can write the basic meaning of the statements.

```
if preReqs==true and goodStanding==true then set the variable
permission=true, otherwise, set permission=false;
```

In other words, if both **preReqs** and **goodStanding** evaluate to **true**, then you can set a third variable named **permission** to **true**. If **permission** is set to **true**, the system allows the student to register for the class.

This type of comparison is common in many programming tasks. It is so common, in fact, that JavaScript includes special operators (called logical operators) to simplify the task. *Logical operators* are designed to compare two **true** or **false** values. Using a logical operator, you can create the following comparison statement.

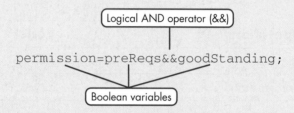

The "**&&**" is called a *logical AND operator*; it evaluates whether both variables are set to **true**. The logical AND operator returns **true** if (and only if) both variables are set to **true**.

As another example, assume that you decide a student can register for a class if she passed the prerequisite classes or her account is in good standing. In this case, you should assign the value of **true** to the **permissions** variable if either of the other two variables is equal to **true**. You can accomplish this using the logical OR operator (| |) shown in the following statement.

```
permission=preReqs||goodStanding;
```

The *logical OR operator* returns a value of **true** if any of the variables compared is equal to **true**. It only returns a value of **false** if all of the variables compared are equal to **false**. The *exclusive OR operator* (^) is a bit trickier; it returns a value of **true** if (and only if) one of the values is **true**. If both values are **false**, the exclusive OR statement returns a value of **false**. If both values are **true**, the exclusive OR statement is also **false**. Assuming both variables are set to **true**, the following statement would return a value of **false**.

```
permission=preReqs^goodStanding;
```

| **LESSON 1** | # Understanding Boolean Values and Expressions |

In programming languages, it is often useful to include a variable that has a **true** or **false** value. As you learned in Chapter 4, the term "Boolean" describes a variable that has one of two possible values, (**true** or **false**), which are often represented as yes or no, on or off, or 0 or 1. You can assign a Boolean value to a variable, just as you can assign a string or number. To assign a Boolean value in JavaScript, you can write statements such as the following.

```
var testComplete=false;
var waiverSigned=true;
```

Since these Boolean values are not "strings" in the strict definition of the term, the words **true** and **false** are not placed within quotes. Boolean values are actually another category of data type you can use as variables, similar to strings or numbers. The terms **true** and **false** are keywords in the JavaScript language; they have special meaning to the JavaScript interpreter, which means you cannot use them as variable names.

When you make a decision, you usually use a Boolean comparison of one sort or another. In the previous example of the department store, you were forced to consider true or false questions to decide on the proper course of action. Consider the first question you had to answer.

```
Is the total greater than the amount offered by the customer?
```

You answer these types of questions numerous times every day, often without consciously thinking about the question. If the answer to the question is true, you perform a specific action; if the answer is false, you might perform a different action, make another comparison, or do nothing. This is essentially how flow-of-control statements work in JavaScript or other languages: a question is evaluated to produce a true or false answer, which dictates the next action — or no action, as the case may be.

Assign Boolean Values

1   **Copy the content of your Chapter_06 folder into your WIP_06 folder.**

You use these files throughout this chapter.

2   **In your text editor, open boolean.html from your WIP_06 folder.**

3   **Insert the following line of code to create a variable with a Boolean value.**

```
...
<body>
<script language="JavaScript" type="text/javascript">
// insert code here
flag=false;
</script>
</body>
</html>
```

Notice the keyword **false** is not contained in quotes since it is not a text string.

4   **Insert the following decision statement.**

```
...
<script language="JavaScript" type="text/javascript">
// insert code here
flag=false;
if (flag==true)
alert("The variable is true!");
</script>
</body>
</html>
```

5   **Save the file in your text editor and open it in your browser.**

FIGURE 6.2

The alert statement is not executed because the value of the variable is **false**.

6   **Find the assignment statement shown below.**

```
flag=false;
```

7   **Modify the assignment statement to set the variable value to true.**

```
flag=true;
```

8   **Save the file in your text editor and refresh your browser.**

FIGURE 6.3

9   **Click OK to acknowledge the alert box.**

10   **Close the file in your browser and text editor.**

To Extend Your Knowledge . . .

BOOLEAN VALUES

You can assign the number 0 (for `false`) or the number 1 (for `true`) to variables to represent Boolean values. (Actually, you can use any number other than 0 to represent `true`.) JavaScript and most computer languages evaluate these values as if they were `true` or `false`.

LESSON 2 If Statements and Mathematical Values

The `if` statement is the simplest flow-of-control statement in JavaScript. Using pseudocode to describe the structure of the `if` statement, you might write the following.

```
if (a condition is true) then
complete an action;
```

For instance, suppose you are building a video game that involves driving at high speed. When the user gets three or more tickets, he receives a message that his license has been suspended. The code statement for such a situation would resemble the following.

```
if (tickets>=3)
document.write("Your license is suspended!");
```

The structure of the statement is simple: JavaScript evaluates the expression in the parentheses, and if the expression evaluates to **true**, the **document.write()** statement executes. Assuming you want to execute more than one statement if the condition is **true**, you can use braces to denote a code block, as illustrated in the following example.

```
if (tickets>=3)
  {
  document.write("Your license is suspended!");
  document.write("You have to go to driving school!");
}
```

You can use the keyword `else` to note an alternative statement or segment of statements to perform if the condition evaluates to `false`. Consider the following code.

```
if (tickets>=3)
{
document.write("Your license is suspended!");
document.write("You have to go to driving school!");
}
```

```
else
  {
  document.write("If you get 3 tickets, your license will be suspended");
  }
```

In this example, the condition is evaluated (whether the variable **tickets** is greater than or equal to 3). If the condition is **true**, JavaScript outputs the following text.

```
Your license is suspended!
You have to go to driving school!
```

If the condition evaluates to **false**, JavaScript executes the statement(s) attached to the **else** keyword. Assuming the tickets variable is currently equal to 2, the user receives the following output.

```
If you get 3 tickets, your license will be suspended
```

If Statements and Mathematical Comparisons

If statements that involve mathematical manipulation are probably the easiest decision statements to understand. For example, assume you are giving the user an online math test. You want to know if the user's answer is correct. If the answer is correct, you could tell the user that his answer is correct. Otherwise, you might want to tell the user he answered incorrectly and then decrease his score by 10 points. The JavaScript code for the preceding scenario might resemble the following.

```
if (answerGiven==correctAnswer) {
  alert("Your answer is correct!");
}
else {
  alert("Your answer is incorrect!");
  score=score-10;
}
```

If statements that make mathematical comparisons use comparison operators, including greater than (**>**), less than (**<**), less than or equal to (**<=**), and greater than or equal to (**>=**). Comparison operators also include the equality operator (**==**) and the inequality operator (**!=**).

Assume that you want to alter your online test. You no longer want the user notified if he misses a question or answers a question correctly, but you still want to deduct 10 points from his score when he answers incorrectly. You could use the inequality operator to rewrite the above code example, as shown below.

```
if (answerGiven!=correctAnswer) {
  score=score-10;
}
```

It is easy to confuse assignment operators (such as **=**) with comparison operators (such as **==**); be careful that you use these operators appropriately. Remember:

- Assignment operators always set a variable equal to a value.

- Comparison operators compare two values to yield a **true** or **false** value.

The **if** and **else** statements are the most common types of decision statements; they appear (in some form) in virtually every computer language. JavaScript also includes a number of other useful flow-of-control statements that you evaluate in future projects.

Use the Equality Operator

In the following exercises, you explore various ways to use comparison operators in decision statements.

1 **Open WIP_06>equality.html in your text editor.**

2 **Insert the following code into the script.**

```
. . .
</head>
<body>
<script language="JavaScript" type="text/javascript">
// create two variables
number1=3;
number2=4;
</script>
</body>
</html>
```

This code creates two variables and stores two numbers.

3 **Insert the following code below the code you inserted in Step 2.**

```
. . .
// create two variables
number1=3;
number2=4;
// compare two variables
if (number1==number2) {
        alert("The numbers are equal!");
}
</script>
</body>
</html>
```

4 **Save the file in your text editor and open it in your browser.**

Nothing happens because the condition is **false**.

5 **Return to your text editor and find the following statement.**

```
number2=4;
```

6   Change this statement to the following.

```
number2=3;
```

Both numbers are now equal to 3.

7   Save the file in your text editor and refresh your browser.

An alert box appears because the condition is now **true**.

FIGURE 6.4

8   Click OK to acknowledge the alert box.

9   Close the file in your browser and text editor.

In this exercise, you used the equality operator to make a comparison. You compared two mathematical values to check if they were equal.

To Extend Your Knowledge . . .

EQUALITY COMPARISONS VS ASSIGNMENTS

It is a common mistake to confuse the assignment operator "=" with the comparison operator "==." Remember that "=" means "set the value on the left equal to the value on the right." The "==" operator asks, "is the value on the left equal to the value on the right?"

Use Greater Than Comparisons

1   Open WIP_06>greaterthan.html in your text editor.

2   Insert the following code.

```
. . .
<script language="JavaScript" type="text/javascript">
numberOne=5;
numberTwo=7;
//insert code here
```

```
if (numberOne>numberTwo) {
    alert(numberOne+" is greater than "+numberTwo);
}
else {
    alert(numberOne+" is not greater than "+numberTwo);
}
</script>
</body>
</html>
```

This code compares the two numbers to test whether the first number is greater than the second number.

3 | **Save the file in your text editor and open it in your browser.**

FIGURE 6.5

This alert appears because the first number was not greater than the second number (causing the else code was executed).

4 | **Click OK to acknowledge the alert box.**

5 | **Close your browser. Keep the file open in your text editor for the next exercise.**

In this exercise, you used the greater than operator in a comparison. This comparison is commonly used in programming applications to determine whether a variable has reached a specific limit.

To Extend Your Knowledge . . .

GREATER THAN COMPARISONS

You can use the greater than or equal to (>=) comparison operator when you want to know if the value on the left is greater than or the same as the value on right.

Make Less Than Comparisons

1 | **Save the open greaterthan.html as "lessthan.html" in your WIP_06 folder.**

2 | **Change the `<title>` tag to the following.**

```
<title>lessthan.html</title>
```

3   **Find the `if` statement, and then change the first line to the following.**

```
numberOne=5;
numberTwo=7;
//insert code here
if (numberOne<numberTwo) {
  alert(numberOne+" is greater than "+numberTwo);
}
else {
  alert(numberOne+" is not greater than "+numberTwo);
}
```

The "**<**" character is the less than operator.

4   **Replace the word "greater" with the word "less" in both `alert` statements.**

5   **Save the file in your text editor and open it in your browser.**

FIGURE 6.6

The alert appears because the first number is less than the second number (and the condition in the if statement evaluates to true).

6   **Click OK to acknowledge the alert box.**

7   **Close the file in your browser and text editor.**

In this exercise, you used the less than comparison operator. The not equal to operator is useful for making comparisons when you want to ensure a particular value is not present.

Add Not Equal To

1   **Open WIP_06>notequalto.html in your text editor.**

2   **Insert the following code.**

```
...
<script language="JavaScript" type="text/javascript">
document.write("The number must not be 5 to be accepted<br />");
//create variable
numberOne=5;
document.write("The number is "+numberOne+"<br />");
</script>
</body>
</html>
```

This code creates the variable and outputs the value stored in the variable.

3 | **Insert the following code to create the decision statement.**

```
...
//create variable
numberOne=5;
document.write("The number is "+numberOne+"<br />");
// check to see if number is 5
if (numberOne!=5) {
        document.write("The number is not 5");
}
</script>
</body>
</html>
```

The **if** statement only outputs text if the number is not 5.

4 | **Save the file in your text editor and open it in your browser.**

FIGURE 6.7

The message in the **if** statement does not display because the number is equal to 5.

5 | **Return to your text editor. Change the variable assignment to make the value 7.**

```
numberOne=7;
```

6 | **Save the file in your text editor and refresh your browser.**

FIGURE 6.8

The final message displays because the condition is **true**. The condition is **true** because the value stored in the variable is not equal to 5.

7   **Close the file in your browser and text editor.**

In this exercise, you used the not equal to comparison operator in a decision statement. Throughout this lesson, you used a variety of comparison operators to compare mathematical operators. In the next lesson, you make comparisons using string values.

To Extend Your Knowledge . . .

LESS THAN COMPARISONS

You can use the less than or equal to (<=) comparison operator when you want to know if the value on the left is less than or the same as the value on right.

LESSON 3   Comparing String Values

Many decision statements involve the comparison of string values. When you fill out a form, most of the information you enter consists of string values. Imagine that you need to write an e-commerce application that calculates the tax on a sales transaction. Different states have different sales tax rates, so you must write a decision statement to set the proper tax rate, depending on which state the user entered on the form. If the tax rate in North Carolina is 7.5%, you might write the following simple JavaScript statement.

```
if (state=="NC") {
  taxRate=0.075;
}
```

Comparing string values offers powerful flexibility, as well as new challenges, which you can usually meet by adding string methods to your code. As an example, you might use a string method to search for a specific word in a long section of text, use an **if** statement to find out if the keyword was located, and then return a positive result to the user.

Since JavaScript is case sensitive, it is somewhat difficult to compare strings of differing case. In JavaScript, the string "Joe" and the string "joe" are considered different text strings. Using various text string methods allows you to work around this restriction, as you see in the following exercises.

Check for Equality

1   **Open WIP_06>stringequality.html in your text editor.**

2   **Insert the following code.**

```
. . .
nameOne="Joe";
nameTwo="Joe";
// insert code here
if (nameOne==nameTwo) {
  alert("names are equal");
}
</script>
</body>
</html>
```

3   Save the file in your text editor and open it in your browser.

FIGURE 6.9

The alert appears because the variables have the same value and the condition in the if statement evaluates to true.

4   Click OK to acknowledge the alert box.

5   Keep the file open for the next exercise.

In this exercise, you completed a simple script to test whether two string values were equal. You used the equality operator (==) for this purpose, just as you use it in mathematical computations.

To Extend Your Knowledge . . .

COMPARING STRINGS

Remember that you can use double or single quotes to denote text strings, as long as you use them in matching pairs. You can write comparisons as `name1=="Sue"` or `name1=='Sue'`.

Consider Case Sensitivity

1   In the open stringequality.html in your text editor, change the capital "J" in the following statement to a lowercase "j".

```
nameTwo="joe";
```

2   Insert the following code after the ending brace (}) in your if statement.

```
...
if (nameOne==nameTwo) {
  alert("names are equal");
}
else {
  alert("names are not equal");
}
</script>
</body>
</html>
```

This alert statement displays if the condition is **false**.

3   **Save the file in your text editor and refresh your browser.**

FIGURE 6.10

The condition evaluates to **false** because case was not matched in the string values.

4   **Click OK to acknowledge the alert message.**

5   **Keep the file open in your browser and text editor for the next exercise.**

In this exercise, you observed the effect of case sensitivity on comparisons used in decision statements. In the next exercise, you learn how to work around this problem by converting the case of the characters before you make a comparison.

To Extend Your Knowledge . . .

CASE SENSITIVITY

Case-sensitivity issues can create significant problems in decision statements (if statements). Many users leave their Caps Lock keys turned on, or often type in all upper- or all lowercase letters.

Ignore Case in Comparisons

1   **In the open stringequality.html in your text editor, find the following line of code.**

```
if (nameOne==nameTwo) {
```

2 | Change this line of code to read as follows.

```
if (nameOne.toUpperCase()==nameTwo.toUpperCase()) {
```

3 | Save the file in your text editor and refresh your browser.

The values are now both compared in uppercase letters.

FIGURE 6.11

4 | Click OK to acknowledge the alert box.

5 | Close the file in your text editor and browser.

In this exercise, you used string methods in a comparison. You used the methods to avoid creating case-sensitivity issues.

To Extend Your Knowledge . . .

AVOID CASE SENSITIVITY

Use `toUpperCase()` or `toLowerCase()` to avoid situations where users may inadvertently make case-sensitivity errors.

LESSON 4   Reacting to User Choices

The primary reason to use decision statements is to react to changing conditions as the script is interpreted. This often involves the user's choices, which guide the decision-making process. A user can make choices in a number of different ways.

- A user can click an area on an image to make a choice.

- A user can click radio buttons or check boxes on a form to make one or multiple choices.

- A user can enter a value into a prompt box/value field.

In this lesson, you consider the various ways users can make choices, and then use decision statements to respond to those choices. You start with a confirmation box that you create with the **confirm()** method. This method returns a **true** or **false** Boolean value stored in a variable.

Confirm a User Choice

1   Open WIP_06>confirm.html in your text editor.

2   Insert the following code to ask the user to confirm if she wants to go to another site.

```
...
</head>
<body>
<script language="JavaScript" type="text/javascript">
ask=confirm("Want to go to another site?");
// check response
</script>
...
```

3   Insert the following code.

```
...
// ask the user to confirm
ask=confirm("Want to go to another site?");
// check response
if (ask==true) {
window.location.href="http://www.web-answers.com";
}
</script>
</body>
</html>
```

This **if** statement redirects the user to another Web page if the user clicks OK.

4   Save the file in your text editor and open it in your browser.

FIGURE 6.12

5   Click OK.

The browser redirects to the Web Answers Web site.

6 Click the Back button in your browser. Click Cancel when the confirm box appears.

Nothing happens because the condition is now **false**.

7 Keep the file open in your browser and text editor for the next exercise.

In this exercise, you used the **confirm()** method to allow the user to confirm his choice: if the user clicks OK, the **confirm()** method returns a value of **true**; if the user clicks Cancel, the **confirm()** method returns a value of **false**. You explore other ways to evaluate Boolean variables in the following exercise.

Evaluate a Boolean Variable

1 In the open confirm.html in your text editor, find the following line of code.

```
if (ask==true) {
```

2 Change this line of code to the following.

```
if (ask) {
```

Since the variable is storing a Boolean value, it is equivalent to asking if the variable is equal to **true**.

3 Save the file in your text editor and refresh your browser.

FIGURE 6.13

4 Click Cancel.

The page does not redirect because the variable is set to **false**.

5 Refresh the file and click OK.

The page redirects to the Web Answers Web site.

6 Close the file in your browser and text editor.

You can evaluate a variable with Boolean values simply by placing the variable name in the parentheses of the **if** statement. In this lesson, you used some basic techniques to allow the user to make a choice and then evaluated the user's choice in the decision (**if**) statement.

To Extend Your Knowledge . . .

PROMPTING USERS FOR INFORMATION

In the previous exercises, you used the `confirm()` method to gather information from end users. The design of the `confirm()` method allows users to confirm their choices. You can use the `prompt()` method to allow users to enter information when prompted with a question. In addition, advanced techniques often use form elements to require users to enter information. In either case, you can use decision statements to evaluate the users' choices.

LESSON 5 Working with Logical Operators

Logical operators are comparison operators that compare Boolean values. For example, let's say you run a business that rents cars to customers. Before you provide a car to a customer, you must answer two questions.

- Did the customer provide proof of insurance?

- Did the customer pay for the rental car?

In this case, the answer to both questions must be true. Using pseudocode, you might write the statement as follows.

```
if (customer provides insurance AND customer paid) {
  provide car to customer;
}
```

If you convert this pseudocode to a workable form of JavaScript, the statement might read as follows.

```
if (insuranceProvided && customerPaid) {
  provideCar();
}
```

In this example, **insuranceProvided** and **customerPaid** must both be variables with Boolean values set to **true**; otherwise, the condition evaluates to **false** and the code block for the **if** statement does not execute. This code is an example of the logical AND (**&&**) operator.

Other examples might require you to evaluate whether one of two conditions is **true**. For example, to pick up an airline ticket, you may need to present a passport or a driver's license. Your decision statement might resemble the following.

```
if (identification=="passport"||identification=="drivers license") {
  issueTicket();
}
```

This example uses the logical OR (||) operator. The logical OR operator allows the condition to evaluate to **true** if either comparison evaluates to **true**. In the following exercises, you work with a variety of logical operators to complete various decision statements.

Use Logical AND (&&)

1   **Open WIP_06>logicalstart.html in your text editor.**

2   **Change the `<title>` tag to the following.**

```
<title>logicaland.html</title>
```

3   **Insert the following lines of code.**

```
...
<body>
<script language="JavaScript" type="text/javascript">
// assign Boolean variables
boolOne=true;
boolTwo=true;
</script>
</body>
</html>
```

This code creates two variables with Boolean values.

4   **Insert the following code, directly below the code you inserted in Step 4.**

```
...
boolOne=true;
boolTwo=true;
// compare to see if both are true
if (boolOne==true && boolTwo==true) {
  document.write("Both variables are true");
} // end if
else {
  document.write("One or both variables are false");
} // end else
</script>
</body>
</html>
```

Notice how single-line comments make code blocks easier to distinguish.

5   **Save the file as "logicaland.html" in your text editor. Open the file in your browser.**

FIGURE 6.14

Both variables are **true**, so the condition is **true**.

6   **Return to your text editor. Change the assignment of the boolTwo variable to be equal to false.**

```
boolTwo=false;
```

7   **Save the file in your text editor and refresh your browser.**

FIGURE 6.15

8   **Return to your text editor. Change the if statement to the following.**

```
if (boolOne && boolTwo) {
```

This is essentially the same code as before. Both variables are evaluated to find out if they are **true**. Using the logical and operator (&&), both variables must be true for the condition of the if statement to evaluate to true.

9   **Save the file in your text editor and refresh your browser.**

The code works as before.

10   **Keep the file open in your browser and text editor for the next exercise.**

Use Logical OR (||)

1   **In the open logicaland.html in your text editor, change the <title> tag to the following.**

```
<title>logicalor.html</title>
```

2   **Find the following comment in the code.**

```
// compare to see if both are true
```

3   **Change the comment to the following.**

```
// compare to see if either value is true
```

4   **Change the if statement to the following.**

```
...
if (boolOne || boolTwo) {
  document.write("One OR both variables are true");
} // end if
else {
  document.write("Both variables are false");
} // end else
...
```

5   **Save the file as "logicalor.html". Open the file in your browser.**

FIGURE 6.16

The code block for the **if** statement executes because one of the variables is equal to **true**.

6   **Return to your text editor and make both variables equal to false.**

```
boolOne=false;
boolTwo=false;
```

You set the boolTwo variable to **false** in the previous exercise.

7   **Save the file in your text editor and refresh your browser.**

FIGURE 6.17

8   Return to your text editor and make both variables equal to `true`.

```
boolOne=true;
boolTwo=true;
```

9   Save the file in your text editor and refresh your browser.

The condition is **true** because both variables are **true**.

FIGURE 6.18

10   Keep the file open in your text editor for the next exercise. Close the file in your browser.

In this exercise, you used the logical OR operator to make a comparison. The logical OR operator is useful when you want to know if either condition evaluates to **true**.

To Extend Your Knowledge . . .

LOGICAL VS. EXCLUSIVE OR

Don't confuse the logical OR (||) and exclusive OR (^) operators — they function differently. The exclusive OR (^) only returns a value of **true** if one (and only one) operator is true. If both values are **true**, the condition evaluates to **false**.

Use Exclusive OR (^)

1   In the open logicalor.html in your text editor, change the `<title>` tag to the following.

```
<title>exclusiveor.html</title>
```

2   Change the `if` statement to the following.

```
...
if (boolOne ^ boolTwo) {
     document.write("One OR the other variable is true");
} // end if
else {
```

```
        document.write("Both variables are false or both are true");
} // end else
...
```

3 Save the file as "exclusiveor.html" in your text editor. Open the file in your browser.

FIGURE 6.19

4 Return to your text editor. Change the variable assignment statements to make one of the variables `false` and one of the variables `true`.

```
boolOne=false;
boolTwo=true;
```

5 Save the file in your text editor and refresh your browser.

FIGURE 6.20

6 Close the file in your browser and text editor.

In this exercise, you used the exclusive OR logical operator. The exclusive OR operator returns a value of **true** if one (and only one) of the values is **true**. In the next exercise, you use the logical NOT (!) operator to reverse the Boolean value.

To Extend Your Knowledge . . .

XOR

The exclusive OR operator appears in virtually every programming language, but may look slightly different from one language to the next. Programmers typically refer to this operator as *XOR*, which is pronounced "ex or."

Use Logical NOT (!)

1   **Open WIP_06>logicalnot.html in your text editor.**

2   **Insert the following line of code.**

```
. . .
<body>
<script language="JavaScript" type="text/javascript">
// assign Boolean variables
boolOne=false;
</script>
</body>
</html>
```

This code creates a variable with a Boolean value.

3   **Insert the following code.**

```
. . .
<script language="JavaScript" type="text/javascript">
// assign Boolean variables
boolOne=false;
// negate the value in a comparison
if (!boolOne) {
    document.write("The variable is false");
} // end if
</script>
</body>
</html>
```

The comparison is based on the *negated* (opposite) value of the variable. In this case, the condition evaluates to **true** because the logical NOT (!) operator is used in the comparison.

4   **Save the file in your text editor and open it in your browser.**

FIGURE 6.21

5   **Return to your text editor. Change the variable value to `true`.**

```
boolOne=true;
```

6   **Save the file in your text editor and refresh your browser.**

FIGURE 6.22

The page appears blank because the condition evaluates to **false** because the opposite of true is false. The code block does not execute.

7   **Close the file in your browser and text editor.**

In this exercise, you used the logical NOT operator. The ***logical NOT operator*** negates a Boolean value. Throughout this lesson, you used a variety of logical operators to complete various complex comparisons.

To Extend Your Knowledge . . .

LOGICAL NOT

The logical NOT operator takes the opposite of the value normally returned by the comparison. This operator is often useful for dealing with a situation where something wrong occurred in the sequence of the script. For example, if the user makes an incorrect choice in a game, the `if` statement would evaluate as "if the choice made is not the correct choice."

LESSON 6   Creating Complex Decision Statements

In the simplest form, the **if** statement is easy to understand and apply. In reality, however, many programming problems require complex, complicated decision structures that you cannot complete with simple **if** statements. You can add the power and flexibility of logical operators, which are useful when you want to evaluate multiple Boolean values; but sometimes your programming problems involve an even greater level of complexity.

Decision statements often require complex trees of interrelated variables. If one variable is **true**, you may want to evaluate a second condition and then perform a specific action if the second condition is also **true**. In this situation, it is useful to *nest* **if** statements within other **if** statements. In this lesson, you consider situations where the code becomes increasingly complicated and, therefore, difficult to read.

Use Comments to Enhance Visibility

1   **Open WIP_06>nested.html in your browser.**

The page asks if you want a lollipop.

FIGURE 6.23

2   **Click Cancel.**

Nothing happens, because you clicked Cancel, and the variable was set to **false**.

3   **Refresh the page and click OK.**

FIGURE 6.24

An alert box appears.

4   **Click OK to acknowledge the alert.**

5   **Keep the file open in your browser and open it in your text editor.**

6 **Find the following code.**

```
if (question) {
  alert("The user chose OK");
}
```

This is the **if** statement that creates the alert if the user clicks OK.

7 **Change the last line of the if statement to the following.**

```
if (question) {
  alert("The user chose OK");
} // end if question
```

As you add complexity to the code, this minor change makes the code easier to read.

8 **Below this line, insert the following code.**

```
if (question) {
  alert("The user chose OK");
} // end if question
else {
  alert("You chose no lollipop.");
} // end else
```

The interpreter ignores the words after the two forward slashes (**//**) because they are part of a programmer's comment. The words are only present to make the code blocks easier to see.

9 **Save the file in your text editor. Refresh the file in your browser so you can test the change.**

10 **Click Cancel.**

FIGURE 6.25

11 **Click OK to acknowledge the alert box.**

12 **Keep the file open in your browser and text editor for the next exercise.**

To Extend Your Knowledge . . .

USE WHITE SPACE FOR CODE FORMATTING

Using tabs or spaces in code formatting is especially useful when creating complex nested decision statements.

Use Nested If Statements

In this exercise, you use nested **if** statements to create additional levels of complexity, which allow you to add increasingly complicated decision statements to the code.

1   **In the open nested.html in your text editor, find and delete the following line of code.**

```
alert("The user chose OK");
```

2   **Insert the following code.**

```
. . .
question=confirm("Do you want a lollipop?");
// check response
if (question) {
  isRed=confirm("Is red OK?");
  if (isRed) {
  alert("You chose red.");
} // end if red
} // end if question
else {
  alert("You chose no lollipop.");
. . .
```

This code creates a nested **if** statement.

3   **Check your code against the following screenshot to make sure you entered it correctly.**

You can use tabs to make the nested commands easier to read.

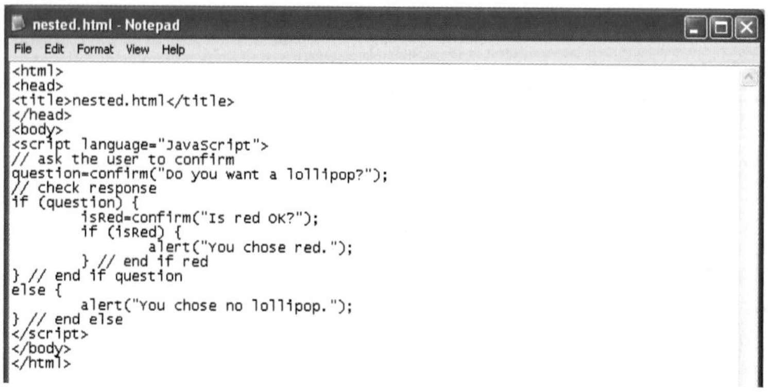

```
nested.html - Notepad
File  Edit  Format  View  Help
<html>
<head>
<title>nested.html</title>
</head>
<body>
<script language="JavaScript">
// ask the user to confirm
question=confirm("Do you want a lollipop?");
// check response
if (question) {
        isRed=confirm("Is red OK?");
        if (isRed) {
                alert("You chose red.");
        } // end if red
} // end if question
else {
        alert("You chose no lollipop.");
} // end else
</script>
</body>
</html>
```

FIGURE 6.26

4 Save the file in your text editor and refresh it in the browser.

FIGURE 6.27

5 Click OK.

FIGURE 6.28

Another confirmation box appears.

6 Click OK.

FIGURE 6.29

7 Click OK.

At this point, the script is finished.

8 Keep the file open in your browser and text editor for the next exercise.

In this exercise, you nested an **if** statement within another **if** statement. ***Nested statements*** are often necessary for complex code solutions.

To Extend Your Knowledge . . .

SINGLE-LINE COMMENTS

Use single-line comments at the end of code blocks to make nested code easier to read. Single-line comments also allow you to ensure code blocks have an equal number of starting and ending code block braces and that the braces are positioned correctly.

Add Additional Complexity

1   In the open nested.html in your text editor, find the following lines of code.

```
    } // end if red
} // end if question
```

2   Insert a blank line between these lines of code and insert the following code.

```
    } // end if red
else {
   alert("Then you must take blue.");
       } // end else
} // end if question
```

Remember to use tabs to make the nesting easier to see.

3   Check your code against the following screenshot.

```
 nested.html - Notepad
File  Edit  Format  View  Help
<!DOCTYPE html PUBLIC "-//W3C//DTD XHTML 1.0 Transitional//EN"
"http://www.w3.org/TR/xhtml1/DTD/xhtml1-transitional.dtd">
<html xmlns="http://www.w3.org/1999/xhtml">
<head>
<title>nested.html</title>
</head>
<body>
<script language="JavaScript" type="text/javascript">
// ask the user to confirm
question=confirm("Do you want a lollipop?");
// check response
if (question) {
        isRed=confirm("Is red OK?");
        if (isRed) {
              alert("You chose red.");
        } // end if red
else {
              alert("Then you must take blue.");
        } // end else

} // end if question
else {
        alert("You chose no lollipop.");
} // end else

</script>
</body>
</html>
```

FIGURE 6.30

4   Save the file in your text editor and refresh your text editor.

5   **Click OK to accept a lollipop.**

The next alert box asks if red is OK.

FIGURE 6.31

6   **Click Cancel.**

FIGURE 6.32

7   **Click OK to acknowledge the alert box.**

8   **Close the file in your browser and text editor.**

Throughout this lesson, you completed various exercises to create complex decision structures. In these exercises, you created a script that leads a user through a complex decision-making process. This process allows you to evaluate user decisions and react accordingly.

To Extend Your Knowledge . . .

MAPPING COMPLEX DECISION STATEMENTS

Programmers often use flowcharts to map complex decision statements. You can use a program such as Microsoft Visio to create complex flowcharts.

SUMMARY

In Chapter 6, you explored basic decision statements using **if** statements. **If** statements evaluate whether a condition is **true** and, if so, perform a specific set of actions. You can add **else** statements as alternative code that executes when a condition evaluates to **false**.

You started the chapter by performing basic mathematical comparisons. You learned how to complete these calculations with a variety of comparison operators that determine whether two values are equal or not equal, or if one value is greater than or less than another value. You discovered that the equality operator (`==`) is the most-used operator; it determines if two values are equal.

You worked with logical operators, which allow you to add complexity in comparison statements. Logical operators enhance comparisons; they allow you to make multiple comparisons and return the result as a simple `true` or `false` value. You learned that the exclusive OR operator (`^`) returns a value of `true` if one (and only one) of the values evaluates to `true`. Finally, you learned how to nest decision statements within one another to provide additional complexity in your code.

KEY TERMS

Comparison operators	Inequality operator	Negated
Equality operator	Logical AND operator	Nest
Exclusive OR operator	Logical NOT operator	Nested statements
Flow-of-control statement	Logical operator	XOR
Flowchart	Logical OR operator	

CHECKING CONCEPTS AND TERMS

MULTIPLE CHOICE

Circle the letter that matches the correct answer for each of the following questions.

1. A comparison operator _____.
 a. compares two values or variables
 b. assigns values to variables
 c. processes an action
 d. None of the above.

2. A flow-of-control statement is the same as a/an _____ .
 a. method
 b. assignment statement
 c. decision statement
 d. None of the above.

3. A logical operator _____.
 a. compares two comparisons or Boolean values
 b. assigns a value to a variable

 c. performs an action
 d. None of the above.

4. You can nest `if` statements within each other.
 a. True
 b. False

5. The `!=` operator is the _____ operator.
 a. logical AND
 b. exclusive OR
 c. not equal to
 d. None of the above.

6. The logical OR operator _____.
 a. returns true if neither value is true
 b. returns true if both values are true

c. returns true if either or both values are true

d. None of the above.

7. The exclusive OR operator _____.

a. returns true if neither value is true

b. returns true if both values are true

c. returns true if and only if either value is true

d. None of the above.

8. Negation refers to the process of using an operator to _____.

a. reverse the result of a comparison

b. add one to a value

c. decrement a value

d. None of the above.

9. The logical and exclusive OR operators are different because _____.

a. logical OR returns true if both values are true

b. exclusive OR does not return true if both values are true

c. Both of the above.

d. None of the above.

10. You can use the equality and inequality operators to compare _____.

a. string values

b. mathematical values

c. Both of the above.

d. None of the above.

DISCUSSION QUESTIONS

1. What are the differences between assignment and comparison operators?

2. Which assignment operator and which comparison operator are often confused? Why?

3. Why are decision statements useful?

4. Why are logical operators useful when writing complex decision statements?

SKILL DRILL

Skill Drill exercises reinforce chapter skills. Each skill reinforced is the same, or nearly the same, as a skill presented in the chapter. Detailed instructions are provided in a step-by-step format. You should work through these exercises in the order provided.

1. Use a Method in a Comparison

In this Skill Drill, you place a method inside a decision statement (a comparison). This is perfectly acceptable in situations where the method returns a **true** or **false** result (such as the **confirm()** method). If this sounds difficult, don't worry — it is simple to implement, as you soon see.

1. In your text editor, open skillmethod.html from your WIP_06 folder.

2. Find the following code.

```
if ( ) {
```

We started an **if** statement for you. You write the condition to be evaluated.

3. Insert the following code.

```
confirm("are you sure?")
```

This method returns a **true** or **false** answer. The code generates a confirm box, which asks the user to choose OK or Cancel.

4. If the user clicks OK, use the **document.write()** method to present a message to the user that says "decision confirmed".

5. Add code that outputs text that says "decision aborted" if the user clicks Cancel.

Hint: use an else statement.

FIGURE 6.33

6. Save your changes and test the file.

7. Close the file in your browser and text editor.

2. Check a Password

In this Skill Drill, you use a decision statement to verify that the correct password was entered.

1. Open WIP_06>skillpassword.html in your browser.

A prompt box appears that asks users to enter their password.

2. Enter a password and then click OK.

The script is incomplete, so nothing happens.

3. Open the file in your text editor and find the following code.

```
. . .
// ask for password
passwordEntered=prompt("What is your password?","");
correctPassword="sneaky";
// see if password entered is correct password
. . .
```

This code creates the prompt box and sets up the default password.

JavaScript is not a particularly secure language; it is easy to see the source code (and the correct password). For this reason, security routines are not usually written in client-side scripting languages (such as JavaScript).

4. Insert an **if** statement that checks if **passwordEntered** is equal to **correctPassword**. If yes, the page should generate a message that the password is correct.

5. Insert additional code to generate the following message if the password entered is not the same as the correct password.

FIGURE 6.34

6. Save and test the file.

7. Close the file in your browser and text editor.

3. Check for Password Length

When creating passwords, many systems require the user to enter a minimum number of characters. In this Skill Drill, you write a script that ensures a password contains at least six characters.

1. Open WIP_06>skilllength.html in your browser.

   A prompt box appears.

2. Click OK to close the prompt box. Open the file in your text editor.

   This script asks the user to enter a proposed password. Next, you write a decision statement to verify that the password is the correct length.

3. Return to your text editor and find the following code.

   ```
   // see if password is at least 6 characters
   ```

   All variables with string values have a **length** property that holds the number of characters stored in the string. For the **password** variable, you can access the **length** property by typing **password.length** in the code.

4. Create an **if** statement to convert the following pseudocode to working JavaScript.

   ```
   If password.length is less than 6, then create an alert box that
   says "password must be at least 6 characters"
   ```

FIGURE 6.35

5. Test the file in your browser to ensure the alert box appears if the user enters a password with less than six characters.

6. Close the file in your browser and text editor.

4. Use Logical AND

You are developing a grading system for a class you are going to teach next semester. The grading system will not accept assignments that are late or incomplete. Write the code to decide if the conditions for acceptance have been met and whether the assignment is acceptable.

1. Open WIP_06>skilllogical.html in your text editor.

2. Find the following line of code.

```
// assign Boolean variables
```

3. Create a variable to record whether the assignment was returned to you on time. Set the variable value to a Boolean value of **true**.

4. Create a variable to record whether the assignment is complete. Set the variable to a Boolean value of **true**.

5. Create an **if** statement that determines if both variables are set to **true**. If yes, the **if** statement should use a **document.write()** statement to output the message, "Your assignment is accepted."

6. Add to your **if** statement to create an alert box if one of the variables is **false**. The alert box should output the message, "Your assignment cannot be accepted."

7. Save the file in your text editor and test it in your browser. Change both variables to **true** and retest. Set one of the variables to **true** and one to **false** and then retest again.

8. Close the file in your browser and text editor.

CHALLENGE

Challenge exercises expand on, or are somewhat related to, skills presented in the lessons. Each exercise provides a brief introduction, followed by instructions presented in a numbered-step format that are not as detailed as those in the Skill Drill exercises. You should work through these exercises in the order provided.

1. Compare User-Entered Numbers

In this Challenge, you prompt the user to enter values and then use decision statements to compare those values.

1. Open WIP_06>challengegreater.html in your browser.

   The script prompts the user to enter two numbers, and then the numbers convert to integers. This ensures JavaScript doesn't interpret the numbers as strings.

2. Open the file in your text editor and find the following code.

   ```
   // insert code here
   ```

3. Insert code to determine if the first number is greater than or equal to the second number. If yes, output a message that says, "The first number is greater than or equal to the second number."

4. Add additional code so the script outputs the following message if the condition is not **true**: "The first number is not greater than or equal to the second number."

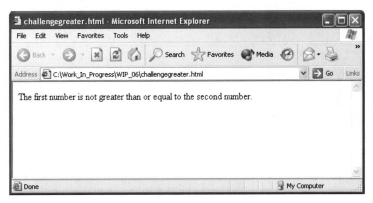

FIGURE 6.36

5. Test the file in your browser to ensure it works in all situations.

6. Close the file in your browser and text editor.

2. Confirm an E-mail Address

In the previous Challenge, you made a comparison and performed actions based on numbers the user entered. In many situations, Web sites often ask users to enter their e-mail addresses. Even though e-mail addresses are important, users have a tendency to type them incorrectly. In this Challenge, you write a script to ensure users enter their e-mail addresses correctly.

1. Open WIP_06>challengeemail.html in your browser.

   The script prompts the user to enter an e-mail address and then reenter the address to make sure the information is correct.

2. Open the file in your text editor and find the following code.

   ```
   // insert code here
   ```

3. Insert code to determine if the first e-mail address entered is the same as the second e-mail address. If not, generate an alert message that says, "The e-mail addresses you entered do not match!"

4. Test the file in your browser to ensure it works in all situations.

5. Close the file in your browser and text editor.

3. Use Form Information in a Decision Statement

In this Challenge, you use a script to check a form field for a blank value to ensure the user entered information into the field. Your task is to write the comparison statement and finish the script. To check for blank values, you can use comparisons that compare variable values to quotes with no spaces (" "). The part of this code that requires knowledge of form interaction was already written for you.

1. Open WIP_06>challengeform.html in your browser.

   This page is a simple form.

FIGURE 6.37

2. Open the file in your text editor and find the following code in the head section of the document.

   ```
   if ( )
   ```

   We wrote most of the code for you, but you need to insert the comparison.

3. Change the **if** statement to compare whether **field.value** is equal to a blank text string (**""**).

4. Find the following code.

   ```
   // insert code here
   ```

5. Insert the following code.

   ```
   alert("You must enter a phone number.");
   ```

6. Save the file in your text editor and open it in your browser.

7. Test the script by leaving the form blank and clicking the Submit button. Then, test your script by entering a value and submitting the form.

8. Close the file in your browser and text editor.

4. Create a Sequence from a Flowchart

In this Challenge, your task is to write a code sequence for an e-commerce project. The company wants to waive shipping fees on orders over $100. They provided you with the following flowchart to use while you write the code.

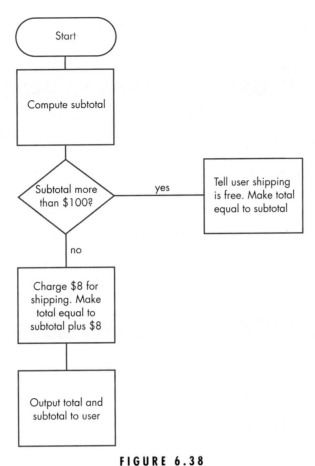

FIGURE 6.38

1. Open WIP_06>challengeflowchart.html in your text editor.

2. Find the following line of code.

    ```
    // insert code here
    ```

3. Insert an **if** statement to determine if the subtotal is greater than or equal to 100.

4. In the **if** statement, insert the following code.

    ```
    document.write("Your shipping is free!");

    total=subtotal;
    ```

5. Write an **else** statement that executes the following code if the subtotal is less than 100.

    ```
    total=subtotal+8;
    ```

6. Write **document.write()** statements that output the subtotal and total to the viewer in a user-friendly way after the **if-then-else** statement is evaluated.

FIGURE 6.39

7. Return to your text editor and change the value of the subtotal variable to a number greater than 100.

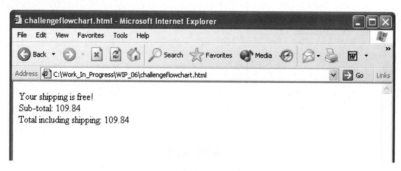

FIGURE 6.40

8. After testing the file, close it in your browser and text editor.

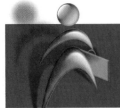

PORTFOLIO BUILDER

Enhance a Form

When you write code, you should always follow standard naming and formatting conventions. This practice allows for increased code portability and productivity. In a Web-development environment, following conventions allows multiple developers to work on the same project cooperatively and simultaneously. This applies not only to code, but to the final Web page, as well. Using standardized methods, you can add common functionality to Web page elements that enhance the user's experience and allow you to collect business data.

In this Portfolio Builder, your task is to enhance the functionality of an existing Web page. The page contains a simple contact form with four fields: Name, E-mail, Phone, and Comments. Even though the file is simple, someone removed a common code-formatting convention from the file: the white space. You need to insert tabs into the code so it adheres to common programming standards. This helps to increase code legibility and allows for easy integration of new code.

As you reformat the code, you will find existing scripts and HTML comments that tell you where to output the script. You will need to add a validation routine to check the information in the form fields. Look at the page named contact.html (located in the WIP_06>Portfolio_Builder_06 folder). The Name and E-mail fields are marked as "required". To process the form data correctly, you need to validate the fields to be certain they contain data (they are not blank).

- The Name field contains an **onblur** event handler calling the **checkName** function to verify that text was entered. If a user fails to enter data in the Name field, an alert box should tell the user he needs to enter his name.

- Create a **checkEmail** function to check the entry in the E-mail field. Use the **onfocus** event handler to call your function by placing the following code in the **<input>** tag for the E-mail field.

  ```
  onblur="checkEmail();"
  ```

- Create a **checkComments** function to verify the Comments field contains data. Use the **onsubmit** event handler in the **<form>** tag to check this field. If the Comment field is blank when a user clicks Submit, create a confirm box to make sure the user wants to send the message with no comments.

CHAPTER 7

Understanding Functions

OBJECTIVES

In this chapter, you learn how to:

- Use a simple function

- Pass information to a function

- Return information from a function

- Use a function in an external file

- Include local- and global-scope variables

- Implement object inheritance and properties

- Create a custom method for a custom object

Why Would I Do This?

In many long programs, you often need to include the same block of code at various intervals. When you do so, you increase the file size substantially, as well as endure the tedium of repeatedly retyping and inserting the same chunks of code. You also create a redundancy problem. For example, imagine that you wrote JavaScript code to create a row of cells that displays a product's name and supporting information in an HTML table. If you have 30 products, that means your table has 30 rows, and therefore you must repeat the code 30 times. Now imagine that your manager decides to change the colors in the table. You have to track every instance of the code block and change every single one. If you miss an instance, the colors in the output would not match, resulting in an unprofessional (and unacceptable) appearance.

Instead of following the above process, using a function would allow you to avoid these problems. As you remember from Chapter 1, a function is simply a block of code that you can name and reuse whenever necessary. Many programmers define a function in the head section of an HTML document. You can also store a function in an external file, which allows multiple Web pages to access (share) the function.

Think of a function as a method you can create. You can call a function by name to invoke it. The term *invoke* simply means you call the function by name to tell the function to perform its designated action. The same syntax you use to invoke methods is also used to invoke functions. Depending on the function's designated action, it can receive information, it can complete an action or actions, and/or it can return information to you. In this chapter, you learn how to create and use functions in your JavaScript code.

VISUAL SUMMARY

To create a function, you first declare it using the `function` keyword followed by a name. Then, you create a code block (similar to the code blocks you created for `if` statements in Chapter 6) that includes instructions for the function to execute. To illustrate functions, let's consider a simple function that converts a variable value to all uppercase letters. Since all uppercase letters create the appearance of shouting, let's name the function `shout`.

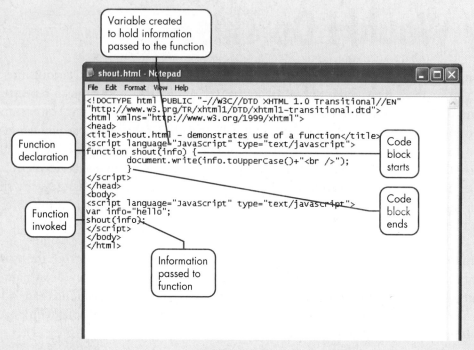

FIGURE 7.1

FIGURE 7.2

As you examine the code more closely, you see the function declared in the head of the HTML document. You are not required to declare a function in the head of an HTML document, but doing so allows you to quickly find the functions used in a page and update them as necessary. Unlike the other code you have examined in this book, a function does not execute until called upon somewhere else in the code — which is why you can place functions in the head of an HTML document, rather than in sequence within the script.

In the example, we created a variable named **info** and passed the variable to the function as a parameter. To invoke the function, simply call it by name, as shown below.

```
shout(info);
```

The function is designed to accept a piece of information named **info**, shown in the statement that starts the function.

```
function shout(info)
```

You could pass any string or variable to the function. For instance, you could add another statement in the main page to call upon the function by passing the string **"whatever."**

```
shout("whatever");
```

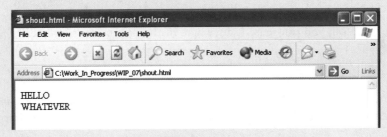

FIGURE 7.3

Similar to methods, functions do not require arguments. For example, assume you want to create a function named **panic()**, which generates an alert when invoked. You could write the function in the following fashion.

```
function panic() {
   alert("RUN FOR YOUR LIFE!");
}
```

To invoke the function, simply call it by name. In this way, you do not pass information to the function, but simply tell JavaScript to execute the code stored in the function (in this case the code simply generates an alert).

```
panic();
```

Functions are an important part of any object-based environment. You can consider functions as methods you create and reuse when necessary — either within the same Web page or on another page. Using advanced techniques, you can even create custom objects using functions. To start the discussion, let's create and use some simple functions.

LESSON 1   Using Simple Functions

As a general rule, you place functions in the head section of an HTML document. This precedence was originally set because older browsers only allowed the use of functions located in the head sections of documents. Today, developers continue to prefer to place functions in the head sections of HTML documents, but they are free to place functions anywhere in the document they prefer — as well as in external files.

A function consists solely of the **function** keyword, followed by the name of the function and a code block of commands to execute when the function is called. For example, consider that you want to create a simple function to add the number 2 to the number 3 and display the result.

```
function addThem() {
   var total=2+3;
   document.write(total);
}
```

Once you create the function, you can reuse it anywhere in the document; simply call the function by name within a script.

```
addThem();
```

A function often performs an action when an event occurs. For example, you can use event handlers and inline JavaScript to trigger a function. Let's assume you want to call the **addThem();** function when a user clicks a hyperlink.

```
<a href="#" onclick="addThem()">Add the numbers</a>
```

Functions allow you to glimpse the true essence of programming power in an object-oriented environment. Using functions, developers can create named reusable chunks of code — which result in increased productivity, decreased development cycles, and controlled file sizes.

Create a Simple Function in the Head of a Document

1   **Copy the contents of your Chapter_07 folder to your WIP_07 folder.**

2   **In your text editor, open WIP_07>simple.html.**

You use these files throughout this chapter.

3   **Insert the following code.**

```
...
<title>simple.html</title>
<script language="JavaScript" type="text/javascript">
// insert code here
function sayHello() {
    alert("Hello");
}
</script>
```

```
</head>
<body>
. . .
```

This creates the function named **sayHello()**.

4   **Insert the following line of code.**

```
. . .
<body>
<script language="JavaScript" type="text/javascript">
// invoke function
sayHello();
</script>
</body>
</html>
```

This invokes the function when the script executes.

5   **Save the file in your text editor and open it in your browser.**

FIGURE 7.4

The function triggers when the page opens and the alert appears.

6   **Click OK to close the alert box.**

7   **Keep the file open in your browser and text editor for the next exercise.**

In this exercise, you created a simple function in the head section of an HTML document. This is the most common place for functions to appear; most Web developers prefer to place functions in the head section of their HTML documents.

Create a Simple Function in the Body of a Document

1   **In the open simple.html in your text editor, find and delete the following code in the head section of the document.**

```
function sayHello() {
    alert("Hello");
}
```

2   **Insert the following code directly before the last </script> tag in the body of the document.**

```
...
<script language="JavaScript" type="text/javascript">
// invoke function
sayHello();
function sayHello() {
    alert("Hello");
}
</script>
</body>
</html>
```

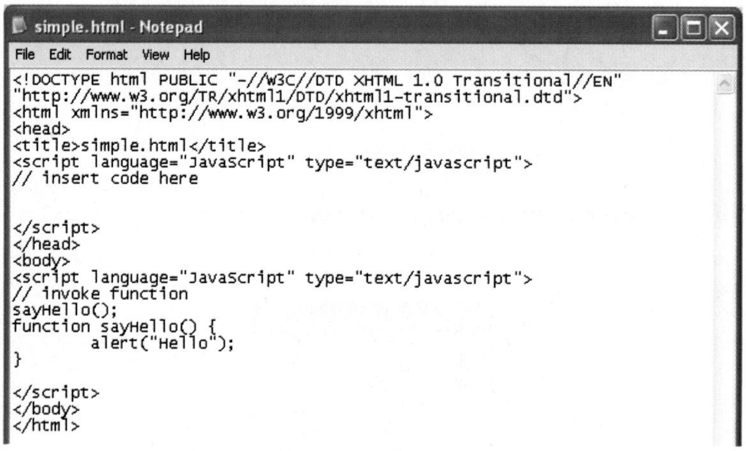

FIGURE 7.5

The statement that invokes the function now comes before the function definition.

3   **Delete the following lines of code in the head section of the document.**

```
<script language="JavaScript" type="text/javascript">
// insert code here

</script>
```

You no longer need this code.

4   **Save the file in your text editor and refresh your browser.**

The function invokes and the alert box appears as before. Older browsers may generate an error.

5   **Click OK to acknowledge the alert box.**

6   **Close the file in your browser and text editor.**

In this exercise, you created a simple function in the body of the document. Although less common than placing functions in the head section of a document, this method is perfectly acceptable under modern ECMAScript standards.

To Extend Your Knowledge . . .

FUNCTION PLACEMENT

In theory, you can place functions in the head section, the body section, another frame (in a frameset), or in an external file. You can even declare functions after they are invoked (the interpreter is supposed to scan every loaded document for functions before interpreting any code). Most developers prefer to place functions in the head section of the document to accommodate older browsers that only allow functions to be placed within the head section of the HTML document.

Invoke a Function Using an Event Handler

1   In your text editor, open WIP_07>event.html.

2   Insert the following code.

```
. . .
<title>event.html</title>
<script language="JavaScript" type="text/javascript">
// create function
function sayHi() {
    document.write("Hi<br />");
}
</script>
</head>
<body>
. . .
```

This code creates a function named **sayHi()**.

3   Within the **<body>** and **</body>** tags, insert the following code.

```
. . .
</script>
</head>
<body>
<a href="#" onclick="sayHi()">click here to say Hi!</a>
</body>
</html>
```

4   **Save the file in your text editor and open the file in your browser.**

FIGURE 7.6

5   **Click the hyperlink.**

FIGURE 7.7

The function performs its action.

6   **Close the file in your browser and text editor.**

In this exercise, you used an event handler to invoke a function. This very common practice is used for a variety of purposes when creating Web pages.

To Extend Your Knowledge . . .

FUNCTIONS AND EVENT HANDLERS

Event handlers normally trigger functions in an HTML document. Most practical examples of useful functions require the user to take action, such as submit a form, roll over an image, or click a hyperlink.

LESSON 2   Passing Information to a Function

It is often necessary (as well as useful) to pass information to a function. For example, you may want to create a function to open a browser window. Assume that you want to open a different window every time the function is invoked. To do so, you could write several similar functions, each of which opens a different URL — but that would negate the primary purpose of functions, which is to avoid writing redundant code.

Instead, it would be much more effective to simply pass information to the function when the function is invoked. You can accomplish this in the same way you pass information to methods. Assuming you created a function named **createWindow()**, you might want to pass the URL **project1.html** to the function as follows.

```
createWindow("project1.html");
```

The function would need a receptacle to store the information, which you can accomplish by creating a variable. You can create a variable named **page** in the following manner.

```
function createWindow(page) {
   window.open(page);
}
```

You can also pass the information to the function using a variable value. Assume you use a variable named **URL** to store the name of the file in a script that appears in the body of the document. You could call the function as follows.

```
URL="http://www.web-answers.com";
createWindow(URL);
```

It may seem confusing, but don't worry about using a variable of one name (**URL**) in the script that invokes the function and a variable of another name (**page**) in the function; the interpreter still passes the information as before. You explore various ways of passing information to functions in the following lesson.

Send a Text String to a Function

1   **In your text editor, open WIP_07>whisper.html.**

2   **Insert the following function.**

```
...
<title>whisper.html</title>
<script language="JavaScript" type="text/javascript">
// create function
function whisper(info) {
    document.write(info.toLowerCase()+"<br />");
}
</script>
</head>
<body>
...
```

This function accepts a text string and displays it in all lowercase letters.

3 Find the second script located in the body section of the document. Insert the following code before the `</script>` tag.

```
...
<body>
<script language="JavaScript" type="text/javascript">
// invoke function
whisper("HELLO CLEVELAND!");
</script>
</body>
</html>
```

4 Save the file in your text editor and open it in your browser.

FIGURE 7.8

5 Keep the file open in your text editor and browser for the next exercise.

In this exercise, you passed a text string to a function. A number could have been sent to the function in the same manner (except a number would not be in quotes). It is often more useful to send information based on changing conditions or user choices, which require variables.

To Extend Your Knowledge . . .

SENDING INFORMATION TO FUNCTIONS

Similar to methods, functions may or may not receive arguments. The function definition determines how many pieces of information are sent to the function.

Send Variable Information to a Function

1 In the open whisper.html in your text editor, find the following line of code.

```
whisper("HELLO CLEVELAND!");
```

2   **Delete this line of code and insert the following lines of code.**

```
...
<body>
<script language="JavaScript" type="text/javascript">
// invoke function
myString="HEY MAN!";
whisper(myString);
</script>
</body>
</html>
```

3   **Save the file in your text editor and refresh your browser.**

FIGURE 7.9

4   **Close the file in your text editor and browser.**

In this exercise, you passed variable information to a function in the form of a string value. It is also acceptable to send Boolean values, numbers, or other types of variable information.

To Extend Your Knowledge . . .

FUNCTIONS RECEIVING INFORMATION

When you write a function to receive information, you actually create a variable in the function declaration. As an example, the statement `function shout(info)` creates a variable named `info` that holds the information being passed to the function. Developers often use the same variable name in the statement calling the function and in the function declaration, but the interpreter does not require you to do so.

Send Multiple Values to a Function

1   **In your text editor, open WIP_07>volume.html.**

You use this file to compute the volume of a rectangular prism.

2 Insert the following code.

```
. . .
<title>volume.html</title>
<script language="JavaScript" type="text/javascript">
// create function
function determineVolume(theLength,width,height)  {
  volume=theLength*width*height;
  document.write("The volume is "+volume);
}
</script>
</head>
<body>
. . .
```

This code creates the function named **determineVolume()**.

3 Insert the following code.

```
. . .
<body>
<script language="JavaScript" type="text/javascript">
// send information to the function
theLength=100;
width=20;
height=5;
determineVolume(theLength,width,height);
</script>
</body>
</html>
```

The word **length** cannot be used for a variable name because it is a reserved word in JavaScript.

4 Save the file in your text editor and open it in your browser.

FIGURE 7.10

5   **Close the file in your browser and text editor.**

In this exercise, you passed multiple pieces of information to a function to complete a calculation. In the following exercises, you further explore sending information to functions. When creating complex functions, it is often useful to create a simple function, test the function to ensure it invokes properly, and then add complexity to the function.

Test a Function Trigger

In this exercise, you create a simple function, and then you use an online event to test the function to ensure it triggers properly.

1   **In your text editor, open WIP_07>tax.html.**

You use this file to create a function to calculate taxes on a purchase.

2   **Insert the following code.**

```
...
<title>tax.html</title>
<script language="JavaScript" type="text/javascript">
// create function
function computeTax() {
  alert("function is triggered!");
} // end function
</script>
</head>
<body>
...
```

This code initially sets up the function and allows you to test the trigger that will invoke the function. Notice that a comment was added to the ending braces; the comment makes the ending braces easier to locate.

3   **Insert the following code.**

```
...
<p>Tax rate is 6.5%</p>
<p>Purchase amount is $1,000</p>
<!—invoke function—>
<a href="#" onclick="computeTax()">Compute tax amount</a>
</body>
</html>
```

4   **Save the file in your text editor and refresh your browser.**

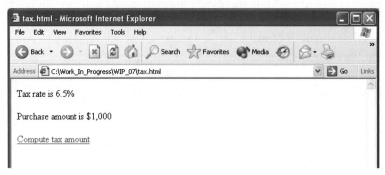

FIGURE 7.11

5   **Click the hyperlink.**

FIGURE 7.12

An alert box tells you the function triggered.

6   **Click OK to acknowledge the alert box.**

7   **Keep the file open in your browser and text editor for the next exercise.**

To Extend Your Knowledge . . .

DATA TYPING

Remember to use the proper data type when sending data to functions. A common mistake is to send data in the wrong format—which generates errors in the code. For instance, if you invoke a function with the code `figurePayment("400","36")`, you could not use those values in calculations without first converting them to integer values (instead of string values). Assuming these were integer values, it makes more sense to invoke the function as `figurePayment(400,36)`.

Send Information from Inline Events

In this exercise, you pass multiple pieces of information to a function when an event is detected.

1   **In the open tax.html in your text editor, delete the following code.**

```
alert("function is triggered!");
```

2   Insert the following code in the place of the code you deleted in Step 1.

```
...
<script language="JavaScript" type="text/javascript">
// create function
function computeTax() {
taxAmount=purchaseAmount*taxRate;
document.write("Tax amount is "+taxAmount);
} // end function
</script>
</head>
...
```

This code computes the amount of tax and outputs the results to the user.

3   Find the following line of code.

```
function computeTax() {
```

This code creates the function.

4   Change the code to the following.

```
function computeTax(purchaseAmount,taxRate) {
```

This code allows the function to accept two pieces of information.

5   Find the following code, which invokes the function when the user clicks a hyperlink.

```
<a href="#" onclick="computeTax()">Compute tax amount</a>
```

6   Change this line of code to the following.

```
<a href="#" onclick="computeTax(1000,0.065)">Compute tax amount</a>
```

This code passes the information to the function. Notice that the data must be listed in the same order as in the function declaration (purchase amount first, tax rate second). The tax rate is in decimal form because it is a percentage.

7   Save the file in your text editor and refresh your browser.

FIGURE 7.13

8   Click the hyperlink.

FIGURE 7.14

The amount of tax returns.

9   Close the file in your browser and text editor.

LESSON 3   Returning Information from a Function

Similar to methods, functions may or may not return values. You can use the keyword **return** to tell JavaScript to return data to the statement that called the function. For example, let's imagine that you want to construct a function to calculate the sales tax on a purchase amount. Assuming the sales tax is 6%, you could write the function as follows.

```
function computeTax(amount) {
var tax=amount*.06;
return tax;
}
```

With the exception of the **return** statement, this is essentially the same type of function that you created previously. The function accepts one piece of information (the amount of the purchase), makes a calculation, and then returns the amount of tax. You explore this example further in the following exercise.

Return Information from a Function

1   In your text editor, open WIP_07>random.html.

2   Insert the following lines of code.

```
...
<title>random.html</title>
<script language="JavaScript" type="text/javascript">
// create function
function makeRandom() {
  randomNumber=Math.random();
  return randomNumber;
} // end function
```

```
</script>
</head>
<body>
. . .
```

3   In the body of the document, insert the following code.

```
. . .
</script>
</head>
<body>
<script language="JavaScript" type="text/javascript">
document.write("<p>"+makeRandom()+"</p>");
</script>
</body>
</html>
```

4   Save the file in your text editor and open it in your browser.

FIGURE 7.15

A random number between 0 and 1 displays on your screen. (Your random number is undoubtedly different than the number shown above.)

5   Refresh the file in your browser several times to generate various random numbers.

6   Keep the file open in your text editor and browser for the next exercise.

Assign Function Results to a Variable

1   In the open random.html in your text editor, insert the following line of code.

```
. . .
</head>
<body>
<script language="JavaScript" type="text/javascript">
myNumber=makeRandom();
document.write("<p>"+makeRandom()+"</p>");
</script>
</body>
. . .
```

2   Change the `document.write()` statement as follows.

```
document.write("<p>"+myNumber+"</p>");
```

3   Save the file in your text editor and refresh your browser.

FIGURE 7.16

4   Close the file in your browser and text editor.

To Extend Your Knowledge . . .

ASSIGNING DATA VIA FUNCTIONS

Data from functions can be assigned to variables in the same way that data from methods can be assigned to variables.

LESSON 4   Using Functions in External Files

In Lessons 1 – 3, you learned how to create functions in the body and head sections of an HTML document. You also learned how to create a function by declaring a variable, which is known as a ***function literal***. In addition, you discovered that you can place functions in external files, which allows the functions to be shared among pages and users. When you place JavaScript functions in external files, you eliminate redundant code; you declare a function on one page, and any other page can then reference the function — without rewriting the code.

Functions are the only type of JavaScript code that you can place in external files. External JavaScript files are simply text files (similar to HTML files) that you create in any text editor. In addition to sharing functions among pages and users, functions in external files can often be shared among different languages — especially if the languages are ECMAScript compliant — including JavaScript-empowered HTML pages and Flash ActionScript code.

As a general rule, most developers use the ".js" file extension to name an external JavaScript file, but this is not required by the interpreter. Any text file with valid functions will work for this purpose, regardless of the file name and extension. You use the **src** attribute of the **<script>** tag to link functions in external files. For example, you could link to an external code file named myFunctions.js using the following code.

```
<script language="JavaScript" src="myFunctions.js">
</script>
```

Once you add this code to a document, any functions located in the myFunctions.js file become available in JavaScript, as if they existed in the same file. Functions in external files work the same as functions created in the document. Information can be passed to the function in the same way, and information can be returned from the function in the same way. In the following exercise, you create a function in an external file. Later, you create a link to the external functions from an HTML file and use the functions in a script.

Create an External JavaScript File

1 **Open a new blank file in your text editor.**

2 **Insert the following code.**

```
// JavaScript functions follow
function panic() {
  alert("Run!!!");
}
```

3 **Save the file as "panic.js" in your WIP_07 folder.**

4 **Close the file in your text editor.**

In this brief exercise, you created an external JavaScript code file. This simple process requires users to insert JavaScript functions into a text file. In the next exercise, you create a link to this document in an HTML file.

Link External Files to HTML Documents

1 **Open WIP_07>external.html in your text editor.**

2 **In the head section of the document, before the </head> tag, insert the following code.**

```
<html>
<head>
<title>external.html</title>
<script language="JavaScript" src="panic.js"
type="text/javascript">
</script>
</head>
<body>
...
```

This code creates the link to the external JavaScript file that you created in the previous exercise.

3   **In the body of the document, insert the following code.**

```
...
</script>
</head>
<body>
<a href="#" onclick="panic();"><img src="panic.jpg" width="154"
height="58" border="0"></a>

</body>
</html>
```

This code creates an image with a hyperlink. The hyperlink does not link to anything, but the function is set to activate when the user clicks her mouse on the hyperlink.

4   **Save the file in your text editor and open the file in your browser.**

FIGURE 7.17

5   **Click the Panic button.**

FIGURE 7.18

The function in the external file activates.

5   **Click OK to acknowledge the alert box.**

| 7 | **Close the file in your browser and text editor.** |

In this lesson, you created JavaScript code that was placed in an external file. You also created a link to an HTML file that makes the functions available in that document. Remember, all the pages in a Web site, as well as other sites, can access (share) functions stored in external files.

LESSON 5 Using Local and Global Scope Variables

The scope of a variable defines where you can use the variable in a script. Variables defined (declared) outside functions have ***global scope***, which means you can use the variables anywhere in the script. Variables with global scope are known as ***global variables***.

Variables declared within a function using the **var** keyword have ***local scope***, which means you can only use the function within the originating document. Variables with local scope are known as ***local variables***.

Even though you can assign the same name to local and global variables, it is considered poor programming practice to do so; it can create confusion and difficulties for even the most brilliant programmers. If a global variable exists with the same name as a local variable, the local variable takes precedence in the function.

Here are a few simple facts to remember regarding local and global variables:

- Variables created outside functions have global scope.

- Variables created inside functions with the **var** keyword have local scope only and are only accessible from inside the function.

- Variables created inside functions without the **var** keyword have global scope.

- Variables with local scope override global scope variables within a function. A local scope variable ceases to exist when the function is complete, and the global variable with the same name then becomes accessible again.

Understanding variable scope is a critical element in learning how to use functions effectively. Developers who do not understand that certain variables are only accessible within functions often make mistakes, which in turn generate errors. To further your understanding of variable scope, you explore the relationship between local and global variables in the following exercises.

Use a Local Scope Variable

| 1 | **In your text editor, open WIP_07>scope.html. Find the following code in the head section of the document.** |

```
function myFunc() {
// create global variable

}
```

This code creates a simple function named **myFunc()**.

2   Insert the following code in your function. Please note: this code must be typed as a single line.

```
...
function myFunc() {
// create global variable
a=32;
document.write("In the function the variable value is
"+a+"<br />");
}
...
```

3   Find the script in the body of the document and insert the following code.

```
...
</head>
<body>
<script language="JavaScript" type="text/javascript">
myFunc();
document.write("Outside the function, the variable value is "+a);
</script>
</body>
</html>
```

4   Save the file in your text editor and open it in your browser.

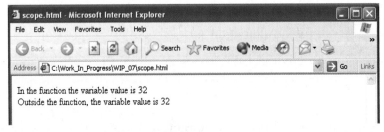

FIGURE 7.19

5   Return to your text editor and change the first two lines of code in the function to the following.

```
...
function myFunc() {
// create local variable
var a=32;
document.write("In the function the variable value is
"+a+"<br />");
}
...
```

6   **Save the file in your text editor and refresh your browser.**

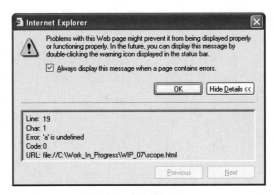

FIGURE 7.20

If error notifications are enabled, an error appears because the variable is inaccessible outside the function. Depending on your browser and its configuration, your error may look slightly different than the error shown above.

7   **Click OK to close the error notification.**

8   **Keep the file open in your browser and text editor for the next exercise.**

In this exercise, you used local and global scope variables. You learned that it is possible to assign the same name to local and global scope variables.

Distinguish Between Local and Global Scope Variables

1   **In the open scope.html in your text editor, find the following code in the body of the document.**

```
<script language="JavaScript" type="text/javascript">
myFunc();
```

2   **Between these lines of code, insert the following code.**

```
...
<script language="JavaScript" type="text/javascript">
// create a global variable
var a=10;
myFunc();
...
```

3   **Save the file in your text editor and refresh your browser.**

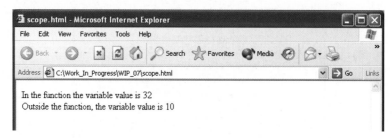

FIGURE 7.21

JavaScript considers the variable **a** to be two separate variables, with one existing inside the function and another existing everywhere else.

4   **Return to your text editor and delete the following code in the function.**

```
var a=32;
```

The **var** keyword causes the variable to exist only within the function.

5   **Save the file in your text editor and refresh your browser.**

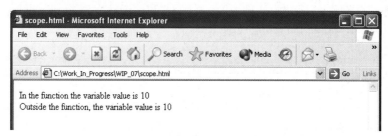

FIGURE 7.22

The script now assumes all references to the variable **a** refer to the variable created in the body of the document.

6   **Close the file in your browser and text editor.**

You now know how to distinguish between local and global scope variables. In the next lesson, you learn how to create new custom objects and manipulate properties of those objects.

To Extend Your Knowledge . . .

LOCAL VARIABLES

Do not use the `var` keyword in a variable declaration inside a function unless you want to ensure the variable is only used within the function. Variables created with the `var` keyword in a function are inaccessible outside the function.

LESSON 6 Using Custom Objects and Properties

As you learned in Chapter 2, a class is the definition of an object that includes the properties, methods, and events available to the object. You usually create classes with **constructor functions**, which are methods or functions that create new objects. A few constructor functions are built into the JavaScript language, including the `Date()` function, the `Array()` function, and the `Object()` function. Consider the following line of code, which creates a date object named `myDate`.

```
myDate=new Date();
```

Objects inherit the properties and methods of the class or constructor function from which they are created. When you create an object from a parent class, the object is **instantiated**—it is an **instance** of the parent class. You can build **custom objects** by first creating a class and then instantiating (creating) an object based on the class.

Developers can also build custom objects by creating their own constructor functions, which consist of properties and methods. A property of a custom object is a variable that exists within the constructor function. A method of a custom object is a function called within the constructor function. Custom object methods can be methods built into JavaScript or other functions.

There are two primary methods for building custom objects. The first method is the `Object()` method, which offers a simple way to build custom objects. Suppose you want to create a one-of-a-kind object named **person**. You might write the following code to create **person**.

```
person=new Object();
person.name="Joe"
person.age=32;
person.weight=160;
```

In this example, the `Object()` function is the constructor method that creates a new object. Using dot syntax, the other statements create properties for the **person** object. For example, if you want to output the **name** property of the **person** object, you could create the following statement.

```
document.write(person.name);
```

The only problem with this method of creating a custom object is that you have not yet created a class (template) you can use to create additional objects; all you did was create a single custom object and then assign properties to the object. To rectify this problem, you can use the **this** keyword to refer to the object that calls a function. With the **this** keyword, you can use a function to create a class. Consider the following constructor function (a class) named **Account**.

```
function Account(type, minimum, fee) {
      // type means the type of account (such as checking or savings)
      this.account_type=type;

      // minimum is the minimum balance
      this.account_minimum=minimum;

      // fee is the monthly fee
      this.account_fee=fee;
}
```

You can use this constructor function to create a bank account object. Objects created from this constructor function will have three properties that represent the type of account, the minimum balance, and the monthly fee for the account. To create a new object based on this class, you only have to call the function as a variable and use the **new** keyword.

```
myAccount=new Account("checking",500,10);
```

In this example, you are creating an account named **myAccount,** which is based on the **Account** class. The account is a checking account with a $500 minimum balance and a $10 monthly fee. The statement that calls the constructor function instantiates a new object and **myAccount** is an instance of the **account** class. Remember, an instance is an occurrence of a particular class.

JavaScript objects inherit all of the variables and statements of the constructor function on which they are based; this is known as *inheritance*. The **this** keyword refers to the current object that is called the constructor function. Using the **this** keyword is one of the primary differences between standard functions and constructor functions. Standard functions do not include the **this** keyword, because standard functions are not used to create objects.

An object created with the **Account** constructor function includes the **account_type**, **account_minimum**, and **account_fee** properties. After you create a new object based on a constructor function, you can add properties to the object by simply inserting a period and then adding the property. For example, the following statements create a new account based on the **Account()** constructor function and add a new property to the **myAccount** object named **balance**.

```
myAccount=new Account("checking",500,6);
myAccount.balance="1000";
```

When you use this method to create a new object from a constructor function and add a new property, the property is only available to the **myAccount** object; the property is not available to the other objects instantiated from the **Account()** constructor function. If you want to make the property available to the constructor function and any function created by the constructor function, you can use the prototype property. The *prototype property* is a built-in property that specifies the constructor from which an object was created and allows the property to extend to all objects created from the constructor. You can use the following code to create and add the **balance** property to the constructor function.

```
Account.prototype.balance=1500;
```

This statement adds the **balance** property to every object based on the **Account** class. You can base a new constructor function on an existing function and then add properties to the new constructor function as necessary. For example, you could use the **Account** object as the basis of a new **CheckingAccount** object. The new **CheckingAccount** object would inherit all of the properties from the **Account** object, and then you could add other properties specific to the **CheckingAccount** object. Take a moment to examine the following code.

```
function CheckingAccount(classification, number) {
    // classification is type of account (personal or business)
    this.account_class=classification;
    // number is account number
    this.account_number=number;
}

CheckingAccount.prototype=new Account();
```

You could create a secondary type of object for savings accounts.

```
function SavingsAccount(classification, number) {
    // classification is type of account (personal or business)
    this.account_class=classification;
    // number is account number
    this.account_number=number;
}

SavingsAccount.prototype=new Account();
```

Using constructor functions to create classes can seem overwhelming to novice programmers; but once you take the time to inspect the code, the process becomes much easier to comprehend. In the following exercises, you explore various ways to create custom objects and custom properties. You begin by using the **Object()** method to create a new object.

Create a Custom Object

1 **In your text editor, open WIP_07>object.html.**

2 **Insert the following code.**

```
...
<title>object.html</title>
<script language="JavaScript" type="text/javascript">
// create rectangle object
var rectangle=new Object();
</script>
</head>
<body>
...
```

This code creates a new object named **rectangle**.

3   **Insert the following code.**

```
. . .
<script language="JavaScript" type="text/javascript">
// create rectangle object
var rectangle=new Object();
//create object properties
rectangle.height=12;
rectangle.width=5;
</script>
</head>
<body>
. . .
```

This code creates two properties for the **rectangle** object.

4   **Insert the following code.**

```
. . .
//create object properties
rectangle.height=12;
rectangle.width=5;
// use the object
area=rectangle.height*rectangle.width;
document.write("Area is "+area);
</script>
</head>
<body>
. . .
```

This code uses the properties of the **rectangle** object in a calculation.

5   **Save the file in your text editor and open it in your browser.**

FIGURE 7.23

The script completes a calculation.

6   **Close the file in your browser and text editor.**

In this exercise, you used the **Object()** method to create a new object. You can also use the **Object()** method with the **new** keyword to create a new object. This is not a particularly useful method, however, because you cannot reuse the code to create additional similar objects.

To Extend Your Knowledge . . .

CONSTRUCTOR FUNCTIONS

In JavaScript, you can use all the built-in functions as constructor functions when you use the **new** keyword. Developers use the new keyword to create objects to represent such things as objects, arrays, and images. For example, **myPic=new Image()** will create a new image object. As you have seen, the new keyword can also be used to create new classes. The **Object()** method is less useful because you cannot use it to create a class.

Create an Object with a User-Defined Function

In this exercise, you use the **this** keyword to create an object using a user-defined function. This method allows you to create multiple objects from the same code.

1   **In your text editor, open WIP_07>constructor.html.**

2   **Insert the following code.**

```
. . .
<title>constructor.html</title>
<script language="JavaScript" type="text/javascript">
// create constructor here
function Vehicle(make,model) {
   this.vehicle_make=make;
   this.vehicle_model=model;
} // end function
</script>
</head>
<body>
. . .
```

This code creates the constructor function named **Vehicle**.

3   **Insert the following code.**

```
. . .
<body>
<script language="JavaScript" type="text/javascript">
// create an object from the constructor
myCar=new Vehicle("Ford","Escort");
</script>
</body>
</html>
```

This code creates an object from the **Vehicle** constructor function. Make sure the word "**myCar**" is one word. This is a variable name (and the name of your object); you must spell it exactly as shown above to avoid errors in your code.

4   **Below this code, insert the following code.**

```
. . .
<script language="JavaScript" type="text/javascript">
// create an object from the constructor
myCar=new Vehicle("Ford","Escort");
document.write(myCar.vehicle_make);
document.write("<br />");
document.write(myCar.vehicle_model);
</script>
</body>
</html>
```

This code displays properties of the object you created from the constructor function.

5   **Save the file in your text editor and open the file in your browser.**

FIGURE 7.24

The properties of the object return to the user.

6   **Close the file in your text editor and browser.**

To Extend Your Knowledge . . .

CLASS NAMES

In traditional computer programming languages, class names are usually initial capped—they start with capital letters. Most JavaScript developers also choose to initial cap constructor function names because constructor functions are basically the same as classes.

CAREERS IN DESIGN

Using Functions in Your Portfolio Site

Every type of site you create — portfolio, personal, corporate, e-commerce — will benefit from clear, consistent formatting. Because functions are reusable named blocks of code, you can use functions to ensure consistency from one page to the next, or one site to the next. In addition, developing reusable functions allows for easier site maintenance.

For example, let's say your portfolio site contains seven sample Web sites. Your home page includes seven thumbnails that represent the seven sites. A user can click a thumbnail image to display the full-size site. If each site were designed to display at an 800 × 600-pixel resolution, it would make sense to use a separate pop-up window to display each site individually. One way to accomplish this is to rewrite the code seven times to generate seven pop-up windows. If you decide to change any aspect of the pop-up windows, however, you would need to change the code in all seven places to ensure consistency on every page.

Instead of applying this time-consuming method, you could write a function that creates a pop-up window and then reuse the function to create all seven of the windows. The function would simply need to accept the file name of the page to display. If you place the function in an external file, updating the entire site becomes quick and easy; all you need to do is modify the external file, and the changes reflect in every page on the site. Using this method, it becomes a simple matter to add new pages to the site as necessary.

SUMMARY

In Chapter 7, you learned how to use functions to create named, reusable chunks of code. You discovered that functions are often created in the head of the document, but you can create functions in the body of a document or in an external text file. To invoke (trigger) a function, you can call it by name or use event handlers placed in HTML tags.

You discovered that information can pass to functions in the same way that information can pass to methods. You also learned that functions can return information using the **return** keyword; information returned from functions is often stored as variable values.

In this chapter, you explored the important topics of local and global scope variables. You discovered that most variables created in JavaScript are global variables, which are available in any script in the page. Local variables created in functions using the **var** keyword, however, are only available inside the function.

During the discussion on constructor functions, you learned how to create new objects. You discovered that when you create a new object, it inherits the properties and methods of the class upon which the new object is based. You also learned how to use the **Object()** keyword to create custom constructor functions. You used dot syntax to added properties to individual objects, and you used the **prototype** keyword to add properties to all the objects based on the same class.

KEY TERMS

Constructor function	Global variables	Invoke
Custom object	Inheritance	Local scope
Function literal	Instance	Local variables
Global scope	Instantiated	Prototype property

CHECKING CONCEPTS AND TERMS

MULTIPLE CHOICE

Circle the letter that matches the correct answer for each of the following questions.

1. Functions may appear _____ .
   a. in the head of an HTML document
   b. in the body of an HTML document
   c. in an external file
   d. All of the above.
   e. None of the above.

2. Functions can _____ .
   a. receive one piece of information
   b. receive multiple pieces of information
   c. return a value
   d. All of the above.
   e. None of the above.

3. A function that creates a new object is known as a _____ .
   a. creator function
   b. constructor function
   c. template function
   d. None of the above.

4. When invoking a function stored in an external file, a developer must _____ .
   a. use the file name as an object name before calling the function

   b. redefine the function within the document
   c. use the src attribute of the <script> tag to link the external file to the current file
   d. All of the above.

5. Variables created in a function using the var keyword _____ .
   a. are only accessible in the function
   b. are accessible from anywhere in the document
   c. Both of the above.
   d. None of the above.

6. Objects created in JavaScript inherit the properties and methods of the class they are based upon.
   a. True
   b. False

7. Using the **this** keyword to refer to the calling object in a function allows developers to effectively _____ .
   a. create a function literal
   b. create a class
   c. return a value from the function
   d. None of the above.

8. When a function name starts with a capital letter, it usually means _____.

   a. the function will be used as a constructor function

   b. the function is a class

   c. Both of the above.

   d. None of the above.

9. Functions are basically custom _____.

   a. methods

   b. events

   c. literals

   d. properties

10. Information can be sent to a function from an inline event.

   a. True

   b. False

DISCUSSION QUESTIONS

1. What is a function? Why are functions useful?

2. How do functions help developers avoid redundancy? Why is it important to avoid redundancy when writing code?

3. Why would it be useful to place functions in an external file?

4. How can users create custom objects in JavaScript?

SKILL DRILL

Skill Drill exercises reinforce chapter skills. Each skill reinforced is the same, or nearly the same, as a skill presented in the chapter. Detailed instructions are provided in a step-by-step format. You should work through these exercises in order.

1. Create a Simple Function

In this Skill Drill you to create a simple function. You use the function to compute the value of a number raised to a specific power.

1. In your browser, open skillsimple.html from your WIP_07 folder.

   The prompt asks you to enter a number.

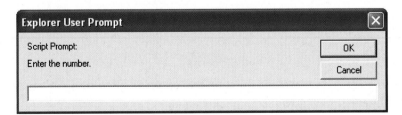

FIGURE 7.25

2. Enter a number and click OK.

   The prompt asks you to enter a power to raise the number to.

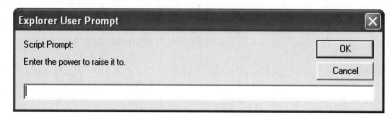

FIGURE 7.26

3. Enter a number to use for the power and click OK.

   Nothing happens at this point because you have not yet written the code that completes the calculation.

4. Open the file in your text editor.

5. In the head of the document, find the following comment.

   ```
   // create function
   ```

6. Create function called **raisePower()**. The function should accept two variables in the function declaration. Name the first variable "**number**" and name the second "**power**."

7. Insert the following line of code in the function to complete the calculation.

   ```
   calculation=Math.pow(number,power);
   ```

8. Create an additional statement in the function that outputs the result of the calculation in an alert box as follows.

FIGURE 7.27

9. Find the following comment.

   ```
   // invoke function
   ```

10. Insert a line of code that invokes the function named **raisePower()**. Pass the **number** and **power** variables to the function.

11. Save and test your file.

    Enter 3 for the number and 2 for the power. The result should be 9.

12.   Keep the file open in your browser and text editor for the next exercise.

2. Trigger the Function from an Inline Event

In the previous exercise, you created a simple function to calculate the value of a number raised to a power. This required you to send two values to the function to complete the calculation. In this exercise, you add complexity to this script by triggering the function from an inline event.

1.   In the open skillsimple.html in your text editor, delete the following line of code from the body section of the document.

```
raisePower(number,power);
```

You created this line of code in Step 10 of the previous exercise.

2.   After the **</script>** tag, insert the following code.

```
...
power=parseInt(prompt("Enter the power to raise it to.",""));
// invoke function
</script>
<input type="button" name="Calculate" value="Calculate">
</body>
</html>
```

This code creates a button.

3.   In the line of code you just created, use the **onclick** event handler to make the button trigger the **raisePower()** function and pass the two variables when the user clicks the button.

4.   Save the file in your text editor and refresh your browser.

5.   Enter the number 10.

6.   Enter the number 2.

7.   Click the Calculate button.

FIGURE 7.28

8.   Check your answer. You should receive 100 as the result.

FIGURE 7.29

9. Click OK to acknowledge the alert box.

10. Keep the file open in your browser and text editor for the next exercise.

3. Use an External File to Store the Function

In the previous exercise, you created a button and used inline JavaScript to trigger a function when the user clicked a button. In this exercise, you modify the code so you can use it in an external function.

1. In the open skillsimple.html in your text editor, create a second instance of your text editor with a blank file.

2. In the blank file, insert the function you created in the first Skill Drill, which should match the following code.

```
function raisePower(number,power) {
calculation=Math.pow(number,power);
alert("The result is "+calculation);
}
```

3. Save the file as "raisepower.js" in your WIP_07 folder.

4. Return to the open skillsimple.html in your text editor.

5. Change the **<script>** tag in the head of the document to include a **src** attribute. Specify **raisepower.js** as the value assigned to this attribute.

   This creates a link to the external file.

6. Delete the function from the skillsimple.html file.

7. Save the skillsimple.html file in your text editor and refresh your browser.

8. Test your file.

   It should work as before.

9. Close all files in your text editor and browser.

4. Call a Function within a Function

In the previous Skill Drill, you created a function in an external file. You also created a link to the external file in your HTML document. In this exercise, you invoke a function within a function. This technique is often used to break down a problem into component parts according to their specific functions.

1. In your text editor, open WIP_07>skillcurrency.html. Find the following line of code in the body of the HTML document.

```
// invoke function
```

2. Insert the following to start a line of code and create a variable.

```
. . .
<body>
<script language="JavaScript" type="text/javascript">
// invoke function
mySum=
document.write(mySum);
</script>
</body>
. . .
```

3. Complete the new line of code by inserting the following code to invoke a function named "**computeTotal()**" and to pass three numbers to the function.

```
mySum=computeTotal(32,43,84);
```

The result of the **computeTotal()** function will be stored in the **mySum** variable.

4. In the head of the document, find the following line of code.

```
// create function
```

5. On the next line, create a function named "**computeTotal()**." The function should accept three variables named "**item1**," "**item2**," and "**item3**."

6. Inside the function, insert the following code.

```
. . .
<script language="JavaScript" type="text/javascript">
// create function
function computeTotal(item1,item2,item3 ) {
var total=item1+item2+item3;
total=makeCurrency(total)
return total;
}
</script>
</head>
<body>
. . .
```

Notice that the variable is passed to and returned from the **makeCurrency()** function after the value is computed. You construct the **makeCurrency()** function in the next step.

7. After the closing brace for the function, create another function named "**makeCurrency()**." This function should accept a variable named "**total**."

8. In the **makeCurrency()** function, insert the following code.

```
total="$"+String(total);
return total;
```

This code turns the result into a string value and adds a dollar sign.

9. Save the file in your text editor and open it in your browser.

FIGURE 7.30

A value of $159 returns.

10. Change the values of the 3 numbers sent to the function. Test the file.

    You should get different results, depending on the values entered.

11. Close the file in your browser and text editor.

CHALLENGE

Challenge exercises expand on, or are somewhat related to, skills presented in the lessons. Each exercise provides a brief introduction, followed by instructions presented in a numbered-step format that are not as detailed as those in the Skill Drill exercises. You should work through these exercises in the order provided.

1. Create an Averaging Function

You were asked to complete a script that averages three numbers. We started a Web page for you, and we partially completed the scripts. Your task is to write the function to complete the calculation and write the code to invoke the function.

1. In your text editor, open challengeaverage.html from the WIP_07 folder.

2. Find the following line of code.

    ```
    // invoke function
    ```

3. Insert a line of code that calls on a function named "**getAverage()**." The function call should pass the three variables from the **prompt()** statements in the order they were created.

4. In the head section of the HTML document, we started a script for you. Create the function you invoked in Step 3. Make sure the names match exactly and the function can accept the three variable values.

5. In the function, create a variable named "**total**" that adds the three numbers.

For example, if you named the numbers **number1**, **number2**, and **number3** in the function declaration, you could write the following line of code.

```
total=number1+number2+number3;
```

6. Insert the following statement to create a variable named "**average**."

```
average=total/3;
```

7. Output the value of the **average** variable in a **document.write()** statement.

8. Save and test your file. Use **1** for the first number, **2** for the second number, and **3** for the third number.

The result should be 2.

FIGURE 7.31

Your output may look slightly different, depending on how you wrote the **document.write()** statement in Step 7.

9. Keep the file open in your browser and text editor for the next exercise.

2. Adapt a Function to Share among Pages

This challenge tasks you with creating code that can be used by multiple pages. This simple technique allows you to share code among multiple pages or even among multiple sites. This also gives you a simple way to guarantee consistency in calculations.

1. In your text editor, create a new file named "average.js" and save it in your WIP_07 folder.

2. In the average.js file, insert the function you created in the previous Challenge.

3. Delete the function from the challengeaverage.html file.

4. Create a link to the external file in challengeaverage.html so you can access the function.

5. Change the function call in challengeaverage.html to send a fourth value that represents the number of items averaged. Insert the number "**3**" for this variable.

Your code probably matches the following.

```
getAverage(number1,number2,number3,3);
```

6. Return to average.js in your text editor.

7. Change the function in average.js to accept a fourth variable named "**numItems**."

8. Change the line of code that computes the average to the following.

    ```
    average=total/numItems;
    ```

    This code allows the function to adapt to any number of items being passed from any page.

9. Save both files and test challengeaverage.html in your browser.

10. Close the files in your browser and text editor.

3. Create a Constructor Function

In this Challenge, you play the part of a Web developer for a car company. You develop a constructor function that creates objects in the programming environment. These objects will store information about vehicles within a script.

1. In your text editor, open WIP_07>challengeconstructor.html.

2. Enter the following code in the head section of the document.

    ```
    . . .
    <title>challengeconstructor.html</title>
    <script language="JavaScript" type="text/javascript">
    // create function
    function Car(carMake, carModel, carYear) {
    this.make=carMake;
    this.model=carModel;
    this.year=carYear;
    }
    </script>
    </head>
    <body>
    . . .
    ```

    This code creates a constructor function.

3. In the body section of the document, insert the following code in the script.

    ```
    . . .
    <body>
    <script language="JavaScript" type="text/javascript">
    // create new object
    myCar=new Car("Pontiac","Aztec","2001");
    </script>
    </body>
    </html>
    ```

    This code creates an object based on the constructor function you created in Step 2.

4. Insert the following code to output a property of the object you created in Step 3.

```
...
<script language="JavaScript" type="text/javascript">
// create new object
myCar=new Car("Pontiac","Aztec","2001");
document.write(myCar.model);
</script>
</body>
</html>
```

5. Save the file in your text editor and open it in your browser.

FIGURE 7.32

6. Return to your text editor and delete the following line of code.

```
document.write(myCar.model);
```

7. Insert a statement to create another object named "**yourCar**." This object is a 1970 Buick Road Master. Make sure you store the make, model, and year in the object when you create the object.

Use the statement you created in Step 3 as a guide.

8. Save the file in your text editor and keep the file open for the next Challenge.

4. Create a Custom Method for a Custom Object

In the previous challenge, you created a constructor function. This allowed you to create multiple objects based on this function (class). Assume you will often need to output the properties of the objects created from this class. To make this process easier, you write a custom method.

1. In the open challengeconstructor.html in your text editor, insert the following function into the script in the head section of the HTML document.

```
...
this.make=carMake;
this.model=carModel;
this.year=carYear;
}
function outputCarProps(){
document.write(this.make+"<br />");
document.write(this.model+"<br />");
```

```
document.write(this.year+"<br />");
}
</script>
</head>
<body>
. . .
```

2. In the **Car** constructor function, insert the following code to make the **outputCarProps()** function a method of objects based on the **Car** class.

```
. . .
this.make=carMake;
this.model=carModel;
this.year=carYear;
this.display=outputCarProps;
}
function outputCarProps(){
document.write(this.make+"<br />");
. . .
```

3. Find the **</script>** tag near the bottom of the page. Insert code to call on the custom function. Type the following code directly before the **</script>** tag.

```
. . .
// create new object
myCar=new Car("Pontiac","Aztec","2001");
yourCar=new Car("Buick","Roadmaster","1970");
myCar.display();
</script>
</body>
</html>
```

4. Save the file in your text editor and refresh your browser.

FIGURE 7.33

5. Return to your text editor. Directly before the last **</script>** tag on the page, create a line of code that uses the **display()** method of the **yourCar** object to display the properties of the **yourCar** object.

Use the code you inserted in Step 3 as a guide.

6. Save the file in your text editor and refresh your browser.

FIGURE 7.34

7. Return to your text editor. Add the following line of code directly before the final **</script>** tag to change the **make** property of the **myCar** object to "**Honda**."

```
...
yourCar=new Car("Buick","Roadmaster","1970");
myCar.display();
yourCar.display();
myCar.make="Honda";
</script>
</body>
</html>
```

8. Add one more line of code to output the properties of the **myCar** object a second time.

9. Save and test your file.

FIGURE 7.35

10. Close the file in your browser and text editor.

PORTFOLIO BUILDER

Add Scripts to Calculate Exchange Rate

In this Portfolio Builder, you add scripting to the North American Currency Converter page (convert.html). Before you begin, look at the page in your browser. Notice that the page doesn't calculate any monetary conversions. To complete the page, you need to add functions, create variables to store values, and perform calculations.

1. Begin by creating prompts to collect user input. Ask the user to do the following:

    "Please enter an amount of money in U.S. dollars."

    "Please enter the current exchange rate."

2. Store the data in the following variables: "**amount**," "**exchangeRate**."

3. Once the values have been stored, use the values in a calculation to determine the converted amount. Store the converted amount in a variable named "**convertedAmount**."

4. Create the calculation using the following pseudocode.

    ```
    convertedAmount equals amount multiplied by exchangeRate
    ```

Using **amount** and **exchangeRate** in a calculation, you can convert from one currency to another. To test the program, use 11.4393 as the exchange rate.

The variable **convertedAmount** should be written to the page in the appropriate place, along with the **amount** and **exchangeRate** variables that you used in the calculation.

CHAPTER **8**

Reacting to Events

OBJECTIVES

In this chapter, you learn how to:

- Detect mouse events
- Use events with the <body> tag
- Apply blur and focus event handlers
- Detect keyboard events

- Utilize form events
- Add selection events
- Apply advanced features of event handlers

Why Would I Do This?

Events are critical elements in object-based environments. Simply put, events are occurrences the programming environment can detect and react to accordingly. A common event is pressing a key on your keyboard; every time you press a key, an event occurs.

As you might remember from an earlier chapter, event handlers are keywords that allow JavaScript to detect and react to events. Event handlers are occasionally referred to as *listeners* in advanced programming applications. Event handlers tell JavaScript how to handle an event by describing what code to use when an event occurs. Most event handlers are quite easy to understand: when you click the mouse button, an event occurs; when you move the mouse over an object (such as an image), an event occurs; when an HTML document finishes loading, an event occurs.

As an analogy, consider a security guard who guards a gate and waits for visitors to drive up and request entry. Using pseudocode, you might describe this activity in the following fashion:

```
oncardriveup="askForIdentification();"
```

In the pseudocode example, the event handler is **oncardriveup**, which simply means, "when a car approaches the gate." In this example, the security guard performs an action after he detects the event (a car driving up to the gate). An event handler is JavaScript's security guard: the event handler tells JavaScript to "watch" (or "listen") for an event to occur. If you remember from Chapter 2, when an event occurs, programmers say it *fires*. Using our pseudocode, when a car drives up to the gate, you would say the **oncardriveup** event fires.

Event handlers are usually used to bind (attach) HTML and JavaScript code. When Web pages load, the HTML interpreter usually displays the page as the characters from the HTML document load into the browser. You can use JavaScript event handlers to trigger actions when certain events are detected. Most practical uses of JavaScript require the detection of a specific event — such as when the user rolls over an image or submits a form.

In this chapter, you explore event handlers and discover how to use them in your JavaScript code. You investigate the most common event handlers and integrate them into HTML documents. You also learn how to use event handlers in JavaScript without using HTML attributes.

VISUAL SUMMARY

Event handlers are usually used inline with HTML tags. For example, the following code causes an alert box to appear when the user clicks the mouse button over the words contained between the **<p>** and **</p>** tags.

```
<p onclick="alert('hi!');">Welcome to my site.</p>
```

The **onclick** event handler appears to be an HTML attribute of the **<p>** tag. Students who are learning JavaScript might wonder whether the word "**onclick**" is part of the HTML or JavaScript language. In reality, most JavaScript event handlers are also considered HTML tag attributes — they belong to both languages.

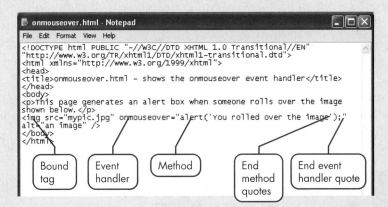

FIGURE 8.1

Event handlers always start with the word "**on**" followed by the event. This is typical of most object-oriented languages. Unlike most of JavaScript, event handlers aren't case sensitive when used inline in HTML. In this context, the inline JavaScript becomes an extension to and a part of the HTML language. As such, the code is case insensitive because HTML is case insensitive.

Event handler statements are typically written in one of three ways.

Type	Example
Method	onclick="alert('hi');"
User-Defined Function	onmouseover="myFunction();"
Multiple Statements	onkeypress="window.open(); x=10;"

In object-oriented languages, events are tied to particular objects. This simply means that an object can detect certain events, based on the definition of the object. Even though this may seem confusing, it is actually simple. Consider a button on a Web page. You might expect that a button could respond to a mouse click or a mouse rollover (because those are typical functions that buttons perform). You might not expect a button to detect whether the page had finished loading. As a more abstract example, consider a car as an object. You would probably want the car to detect when the brake pedal was pressed (because that is a key function of a car), but you wouldn't need the car to detect whether you had eaten breakfast that morning.

In JavaScript, event handlers are bound to an HTML tag or to the object that represents the HTML tag. The term **bound** simply means the event handler is attached to the object. For instance, if you bind an **onclick** event to an **<a>** tag, it simply means the event will fire when a user clicks the content of the **<a>** tag.

Each HTML tag has a list of event handlers it can detect and to which it can respond. In many cases, browsers aren't consistent in the tags they allow for a specific event. As an example, consider the **onload** event that detects whether a page has finished loading. You can bind this event to a **<body>** tag in virtually every browser. In many versions of Netscape Navigator, the **onload** event can also be used with the **<layer>** tag, but this is not the case in all browsers. For best results, consult a good reference book when you are unsure of whether an event handler and an HTML tag will work together in most browsers. In the following sections, you consider many of the most common event handlers as well as discover which tags work in most browsers with the event handler described.

LESSON 1   Detecting Mouse Events

When it comes to mouse events, HTML is rather limited: it allows the user to click the mouse on a hyperlink to go to another page and click a button to submit or reset a form. This is not a very impressive list of functions. In answer to HTML's limitation, event handlers related to using a mouse were among the first added to JavaScript. With mouse-related event handlers, developers can trigger any number of actions when the user rolls over an object, when the user clicks an object, or when the user double-clicks an object.

Mouse-related events are among the most popular event handlers. Newer versions of JavaScript contain event handlers to detect such things as the roll of a mouse wheel. A number of common event handlers are described below.

Onclick and Ondblclick

The **onclick** event fires when a user clicks an object. The **ondblclick** event fires when a user double-clicks an object. The **onclick** and **ondblclick** event handlers work on virtually any element that can be displayed on the screen. For instance, if you want users to be able to double-click an image to go to another page, you can write the following code.

```
<img src="mypic.jpg" ondblclick="alert('You double clicked!');" alt="my
picture" />
```

In many browsers, you can use the Tab key to move through the links on a page, or you can press the Enter/Return key to choose a link. The **onclick** event reacts to the user clicking the mouse or to the user pressing the Enter/Return key. This is in contrast to the **onmousedown** event, which only fires when the user clicks the mouse.

Onmousedown, Onmousemove, Onmouseout, Onmouseover

The **onmousedown** event fires when the user clicks the mouse on an object. The **onmousemove** event fires when the mouse moves while over an element. The **onmouseover** handler fires when the mouse initially moves over the edge of an element. The **onmouseout** event fires when the user moves the mouse off of an element. These handlers work on most display elements.

These event handlers are useful for creating image rollovers that have associated hyperlinks. This is one of the most common uses of JavaScript. Using pseudocode, you can probably guess how image rollovers use these event handlers.

```
<img src="normal version of the image;"
onmouseover="switch the normal image with a rollover version;"
onmouseout="remove the rollover image and return the original image;"
onmousedown="go to the associated URL;" />
```

Use onclick

1 **Copy the content of the Chapter_08 folder into the WIP_08 folder.**

You use these files throughout this chapter.

2 **In your text editor and browser, open WIP_08>onclick.html.**

This file displays text in a **<p>** tag, an image, and a hyperlink.

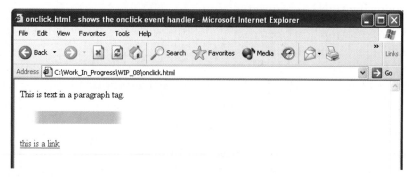

FIGURE 8.2

3 **Find the following line of code in the document.**

```
<p>This is text in a paragraph tag.</p>
```

4 **Insert the `onclick` event handler in the `<p>` tag as follows.**

```
<p onclick="eventTest()">This is text in a paragraph tag.</p>
```

The event handler triggers a function that hasn't yet been created. Event handlers are often used to trigger functions.

5 **Find the following line of code.**

```
<img src="mypic.jpg" alt="my picture" />
```

This code displays an image on the page.

6 **Insert the `onclick` event handler into the `<img>` tag as follows.**

```
<img src="mypic.jpg" alt="my picture" onclick="eventTest()" />
```

7 **Find the following line of code.**

```
<a href="#">
```

This hyperlink does not link to a file.

8 **Insert the `onclick` event handler as follows.**

```
<a href="#" onclick="eventTest()">
```

This code binds the event handler to the hyperlink.

9 **Find the following code in the head of the document.**

```
<script language="JavaScript" type="text/javascript">
// insert function here

</script>
```

10 **Insert the following code to create a function.**

```
<script language="JavaScript" type="text/javascript">
// insert function here
function eventTest() {
    alert("The function has been activated");
}
</script>
```

11 **Save the file in your text editor and refresh your browser.**

12 **Move your mouse pointer over each item and click to select the item. Click OK to acknowledge each alert box that appears.**

FIGURE 8.3

13 Keep the file open in your text editor for the next exercise. Close the file in your browser.

Detect Double Mouse Clicks

1 In the open onclick.html, delete the following line of code.

```
<title>onclick.html - shows the onclick event handler</title>
```

2 Replace the line of code you deleted in Step 1 with the following line of code.

```
<title>ondblclick.html - shows the ondblclick event
handler</title>
```

3 Find the following line of code in the document.

```
<p onclick="eventTest()">
```

4 Change the event handler to the **ondblclick** event handler by changing the line as follows.

```
<p ondblclick="eventTest()">
```

To use this event handler, you must use Internet Explorer 4.0 or higher or Netscape Navigator 6.0 or higher, as your browser.

5 Find the following line of code in the document.

```
<img src="mypic.jpg" onclick="eventTest()" alt="my picture" />
```

6 Change the event handler to the **ondblclick** event handler by changing this line as follows.

```
<img src="mypic.jpg" ondblclick="eventTest()" alt="my picture" />
```

7 Find the following line of code in the document.

```
<a href="#" onclick="eventTest()">this is a link</a>
```

8 Change the event handler to the **ondblclick** event handler by changing the line as follows.

```
<a href="#" ondblclick="eventTest()">this is a link</a>
```

9 Save the file as "ondblclick.html" in the WIP_08 folder. Open the file in your browser.

10 Single-click your mouse on the items on the page.

Nothing happens.

11 Double-click each item to generate the alert box. Click OK to acknowledge each alert box as it appears.

FIGURE 8.4

12 Close the file in your browser and text editor.

To Extend Your Knowledge . . .

THE ONDBLCLICK EVENT

The `ondblclick` event handler is rarely used in Web pages because users do not expect that they must double-click an item to perform an action.

Detect Rollovers

1 In your text editor, open onmouseover.html from the WIP_08 folder.

2 Find the following line of code.

```
<img src="mypic.jpg" alt="an image" />
```

This tag displays an image.

3 Change the tag by inserting the following code.

```
<img src="mypic.jpg" onmouseover="alert('You rolled over the
image');" alt="an image" />
```

This code triggers an alert box when the user rolls over the image.

4   Save the file in your text editor. Open the file in your browser.

FIGURE 8.5

5   Move your mouse over the image.

FIGURE 8.6

An alert box appears.

6   Click OK to acknowledge the alert box.

7   Close the file in your browser and text editor.

To Extend Your Knowledge . . .

EVENT HANDLER CAPITALIZATION

Many reference books capitalize the second word in event handlers, such as `onClick`. The process of starting the second word of an event handler or variable name with a capital letter is called **camel-back notation**. This book uses all lowercase letters when spelling event handlers. Both camelback and lowercase styles should work correctly in your browser, because event handlers are part of HTML (which is case insensitive). Bugs in older browsers may occasionally cause error messages related to event handler capitalization.

LESSON 2 Using Events with the `<body>` Tag

The `<body>` tag is a display tag that represents every item displayed in the active part of the browser window. Since the `<body>` tag represents the page displayed, you can use event handlers such as `onclick` or `onmouseover` with the `<body>` tag. Consider the following code as an example.

```
<body onclick="alert('The page has been clicked')">
```

As you have seen with other display tags (such as `<p>`, `<a>`, and `<img>`), this code triggers an alert box when the user clicks anywhere on the page. Despite this functionality, mouse events such as `onclick` and `onmouseover` rarely have practical applications when used with the `<body>` tag. (Designers are rarely interested in carrying out instructions when the mouse rolls over any area of the page or when the user clicks anywhere in the browser window.)

You can use other (more useful) event handlers with the `<body>` tag. For example, the `onload` event handler triggers an event when an HTML page has finished loading into the browser. Other event handlers determine if a file is unloading from the browser or if a page is unloading from memory.

Onload

The `onload` event handler fires after the last character of the HTML page loads. In HTML, the code loads first, and then related files (images and/or animations) load. This is an important distinction: the event fires when the source code finishes loading, which is before the supporting files load.

This event is typically used with the `<body>` or `<frameset>` tag, but may also be attached to the `<applet>`, `<embed>`, `<link>`, `<script>`, or `<style>` tags. The following example demonstrates the use of an alert box that appears when the source code of the page has finished loading.

```
<body onload="alert('The page has finished loading.');">
```

Onresize

This event handler indicates the page is being resized. This event is typically used with the `<body>` tag, as shown in the following example.

```
<body onresize="alert('page resized');">
```

This event handler offers many options to Web designers. For example, you can use it to change the way items display, depending on the current width or height of the browser window.

Onunload

The `onunload` event fires when the browser is leaving the current document in a window or frame. To be more specific, the event occurs if you click a hyperlink that loads a new document or if you try to close the browser window. The event also fires when you click the Refresh button, since the Refresh button unloads the current document and loads a new version of the file. You can use the `onunload` event with the `<body>` or

<frameset> tag. For example, if you want to generate an alert box when a page unloads, you can use the following code.

```
<body onunload="alert('the page is unloading');">
```

The alert would generate when the user closes the browser window or tries to navigate to a different Web page.

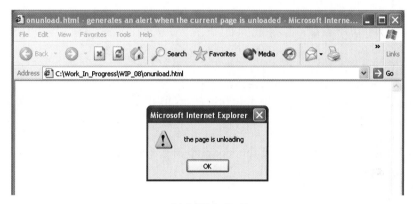

FIGURE 8.7

Use onresize

1   In your text editor, open resizefunction.html from the WIP_08 folder.

2   Examine the source code.

```
<!DOCTYPE html PUBLIC "-//W3C//DTD XHTML 1.0 Transitional//EN"
"http://www.w3.org/TR/xhtml1/DTD/xhtml1-transitional.dtd">
<html xmlns="http://www.w3.org/1999/xhtml">
<head>
<title></title>
<script language="JavaScript" type="text/javascript">
function setSize() {
setTimeout("self.resizeTo(640,480)",1000);
}
</script>
</head>
<body>
<p>This page will automatically resize to a resolution of 640*480, one
second after the user tries to resize it. </p>

</body>
</html>
```

FIGURE 8.8

The function defined in the head of the document resizes the current document to a resolution of 640 × 480 approximately one second after the function invokes.

3   **Open the file in your browser and resize the window.**

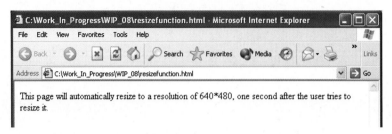

FIGURE 8.9

At this point, nothing happens — the function exists in the document, but hasn't been invoked in the code.

4   **Return to your text editor and find the `<body>` tag. Change the tag to the following.**

```
<body onresize="setSize()">
```

This calls the function when you resize the window.

5   **Save the file in your text editor and refresh your browser.**

6   **Resize the browser window.**

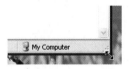

FIGURE 8.10

After you resize the window, the window should resize itself to a resolution of 640×480 approximately one second after you resize it. Depending on your browser's security settings, you may get an "Access Denied" message.

7   **Keep the file open in your browser and text editor for the next exercise.**

Curious students may wonder why the **setTimeout()** method was used in the function. The answer lies in the circumstances under which the **onresize** event fires. You investigate this further in the following exercise.

Correct Event Detection Issues

1   **In the open resizefunction.html, find and delete the following code in the function.**

```
setTimeout("self.resizeTo(640,480)",1000);
```

2   **Replace the line of code you deleted in Step 1 with the following line of code.**

```
self.resizeTo(640,480);
```

This removes the **setTimeout()** method, which causes the one-second delay.

3   **Save the file in your text editor and refresh your browser.**

4   **Resize the window.**

You may notice a jerky effect as the window constantly resizes while you resize it. Technically, the code works; but this version isn't nearly as user friendly as the one that uses the **setTimeout()** method. Without the **setTimeout()** method, the event is constantly detected and acted upon.

5   **Close the file in your text editor and browser.**

In this exercise, you created a problem associated with an event being detected and acted upon too quickly. This type of problem can be troublesome when creating code. Other problems that can occur may include code that does not allow an event to occur or code that is written in such a way that an event cannot be detected.

To Extend Your Knowledge . . .

THE ONUNLOAD HANDLER

Programmers often use the **onunload** handler for questionable purposes. For example, this handler can trigger a pop-up window when a user leaves your page. The handler can also keep a user from leaving your page by forcing the page to reload when the **onunload** event is detected. Because these techniques prove annoying to virtually all users, you should avoid including them in your code.

LESSON 3   Applying Blur and Focus Event Handlers

As you know, the **focus()** method draws focus to a **window** object, and the **blur()** method blurs the current object by removing focus. You can apply these events to form elements. The user can also create these events by clicking an object with his mouse. In this lesson, you learn how to detect these events when they occur.

Onblur and Onfocus

If a window or frame has focus, any keystrokes a user types are directed to that window or frame. A window can gain focus in a number of ways, such as clicking in or on the window, or using the **focus()** method. If you give focus to one window, any other windows blur (only one window can have focus at any given time). Depending on your operating system, blurred windows are often shown with lighter colored title bars.

If an item blurs, the item no longer has focus and keystrokes are not directed to that window. The **onblur** event fires when focus is given to another window. The **onfocus** event fires when the user clicks the specified window. You can extend the idea of focus to other elements in a page besides the **window** object. For instance, in a form, the user can often tab between form elements or click in a text box to activate (focus) that box.

You can apply the **onblur** event to the following tags: `<a>`, `<area>`, `<body>`, `<ilayer>`, `<button>`, `<input>`, `<label>`, `<select>`, `<textarea>`, `<applet>`, `<area>`, `<div>`, `<object>`, `<span>`, `<table>`, and `<td>`.

You can apply the **onfocus** event to the following tags: `<a>`, `<applet>`, `<area>`, `<button>`, `<div>`, `<embed>`, `<hr>`, `<img>`, `<input>`, `<label>`, `<marquee>`, `<object>`, `<select>`, `<table>`, `<td>`, `<tr>`, and `<textarea>`.

Take a moment to examine the following source code that includes the **onblur** event handler. This code generates an alert box whenever the window blurs.

```
<title>onblur.html - shows the onblur event handler</title>
</head>
<body onblur="alert('You have blurred the window.');">
<p>This page generates an alert box when the page is blurred.</p>
</body>
</html>
```

If you open this page in a browser and click another window, the **onblur** event fires, and the alert box appears. The window is already blurred when the alert box appears and may not be visible behind the window that currently has focus. For this reason, you would need to return focus to the blurred window to see the alert box.

FIGURE 8.11

Detect the Blur of a Window Object

1 In your text editor, open onblur.html from the WIP_08 folder.

2 Insert the following code into the `<body>` tag.

```
<body onblur="alert('You have blurred the window');">
```

3   Save the file in your text editor and open the file in your browser.

FIGURE 8.12

4   Use your mouse to click any area of the screen that is not part of the browser window (the Start button, desktop, or another window).

FIGURE 8.13

The window blurs and an alert box displays.

5   Click OK to acknowledge the alert box.

6   Close the file in your browser and text editor.

Detect the Blur of a Form Element

1   Open WIP_08>blurelement.html in your browser.

FIGURE 8.14

Your cursor should appear in the Comments box. The **focus()** method automatically draws focus to this text area.

2   **Press the Tab key.**

The cursor moves to the next form element (the Your name field).

3   **Open the file in your text editor.**

4   **Find the following line of code.**

```
<textarea name="comments" id="comments" tabindex="1"></textarea>
```

5   **Insert the following code into the `<textarea>` tag.**

```
<textarea name="comments" id="comments" tabindex="1" onblur="if
(this.value=='') { alert('Please Enter a Comment');}"></textarea>
```

Part of the statement **(`this.value=='`)** uses a pair of single quotes to indicate the text string is blank. This is necessary since the **`onblur`** handler uses double quotes in this example. Placing a single double quote in the **`this.value==`"** sequence would generate a syntax error. Placing a space before the **`</textarea>`** tag would also cause an error.

6   **Save the file in your text editor and refresh your browser.**

The cursor appears in the Comments text area because this field has focus.

7   **Press the Tab key to blur the Comments text area and advance to the next frame.**

FIGURE 8.15

An alert box appears.

8   **Click OK to acknowledge the alert box.**

9   **Close the file in your browser and text editor.**

It may be necessary to close the alert box again.

To Extend Your Knowledge . . .

FOCUS AND BLUR EVENTS

The `onblur` and `onfocus` events can effectively stop actions in a window. For example, developers can pause animation when a window blurs or continue playback when the window gains focus.

LESSON 4   Detecting Keyboard Events

Keyboard events refer to a group of events related to keys pressed on the keyboard. A keyboard event usually fires when the user either presses or releases a key. Using advanced techniques, developers can determine the specific key pressed and create actions that are tied to specific keys.

Onkeydown, Onkeypress, Onkeyup

The **onkeydown** event fires if the user presses a key while the element has focus. The event fires as soon as the user presses the key; the key doesn't have to be released for the event to fire. The event fires no matter which key the user presses.

The **onkeypress** event fires if a key is pressed and then released while the element has focus. The event doesn't fire until the user releases the key. The event fires no matter which key the user presses.

The **onkeyup** event fires when the user releases a key when the element has focus. The event doesn't fire until the user releases the key. In other words, if the user continues to press the key down and doesn't release it, the event never occurs. You can use all three of these events with virtually any element that can display in a browser window.

Detect a Key Press

1   **In your text editor, open onkeypress.html from the WIP_08 folder.**

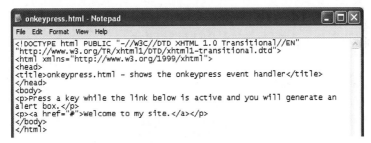

```
onkeypress.html - Notepad
File  Edit  Format  View  Help
<!DOCTYPE html PUBLIC "-//W3C//DTD XHTML 1.0 Transitional//EN"
"http://www.w3.org/TR/xhtml1/DTD/xhtml1-transitional.dtd">
<html xmlns="http://www.w3.org/1999/xhtml">
<head>
<title>onkeypress.html - shows the onkeypress event handler</title>
</head>
<body>
<p>Press a key while the link below is active and you will generate an
alert box.</p>
<p><a href="#">welcome to my site.</a></p>
</body>
</html>
```

FIGURE 8.16

2   **Find the following code.**

```
<p><a href="#">Welcome to my site.</a></p>
```

3   **Insert the onkeypress event handler in the <a> tag.**

```
<p><a href="#" onkeypress="alert('hi!');">Welcome to my
site.</a></p>
```

4 | **Save the file in your text editor and open the file in your browser.**

FIGURE 8.17

5 | **Press the Tab key until the link becomes active.**

In Internet Explorer, a dotted line appears around the link to indicate it is active. Other browsers may give slightly different results.

FIGURE 8.18

6 | **Press any key on your keyboard.**

FIGURE 8.19

An alert box appears.

7 | **Click OK to acknowledge the alert box.**

8 | **Close the file in your browser and text editor.**

To Extend Your Knowledge . . .

KEYBOARD EVENTS

Keyboard event handlers allow you to create interactive experiences for users who may have difficulty controlling a mouse. Standardized methods of applying keyboard shortcuts are common in traditional computer applications where interfaces tend to be standardized. Since users are less likely to understand how a Web site interface works, developers face unique challenges when designing sites that allow keyboard interaction with a Web site.

LESSON 5   Using Form-Related Events

Forms offer practical uses for various event handlers. For example, when a user submits a form, you may want to ensure the form was filled out correctly before the data transmits to the server for processing. Doing so can often avoid costly, time-consuming mistakes. The following event handlers detect whether forms have been submitted or reset.

Onsubmit

The **onsubmit** handler indicates that a form is being submitted, usually by clicking a Submit button. This event is usually bound to the **<form>** tag. The following code creates an alert box when the user clicks the Submit button.

```
<form name="form1" method="post" action="" onsubmit="alert('form
submitted');">
  <p>Name:
    <input type="text" name="name" />
  </p>
  <p>
    <input type="submit" name="Submit" value="Submit" />
<input type="reset" name="Reset" value="Reset">
  </p>
</form>
```

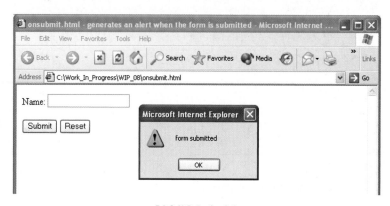

FIGURE 8.20

Onreset

The **onreset** handler indicates that a form is being reset, usually by clicking a Reset button. This event is usually bound to the **<form>** tag. The following code creates an alert box when the user clicks the Reset button. The onreset handler may not work in all browsers.

```
<form name="form1" method="post" action="" onreset="alert('form
reset');" id="form1">
<p>Name:
<input type="text" name="name" />
</p>
<p>
<input type="submit" name="Submit" value="Submit" />
<input type="reset" name="Reset" value="Reset" />
</p>
</form>
```

FIGURE 8.21

Use the onsubmit Event Handler

1   In your browser, open onsubmit.html from the WIP_08 folder.

FIGURE 8.22

2   Enter a name and click the Submit button.

The form clears as it submits.

3   **Open the file in your text editor.**

```
onsubmit.html - Notepad
File  Edit  Format  View  Help
<!DOCTYPE html PUBLIC "-//W3C//DTD XHTML 1.0 Transitional//EN"
"http://www.w3.org/TR/xhtml1/DTD/xhtml1-transitional.dtd">
<html xmlns="http://www.w3.org/1999/xhtml">
<head>
<title>onsubmit.html - generates an alert when the form is
submitted</title>
<script language="JavaScript" type="text/javascript">
function formCheck() {
alert("You entered "+document.form1.name.value);
}
</script>
</head>

<body>
<form action="" method="post" name="form1" id="form1">
  <p>Name:
    <input type="text" name="name" />
  </p>
  <p>
    <input type="submit" name="Submit" value="Submit" />
<input type="reset" name="Reset" value="Reset" />
  </p>
</form>
</body>
</html>
```

FIGURE 8.23

We provided a function in the head of the document. This function returns any value entered into the form field.

4   **Find the following line of code.**

```
<form action="" method="post" name="form1" id="form1">
```

5   **Insert the following event handler to trigger the function.**

```
<form action="" method="post" name="form1" onsubmit="formCheck()"
id="form1">
```

```
With onsubmit="formCheck()" id="form1">
```

6   **Save the file in your text editor and refresh your browser.**

7   **Enter a name into the Name field and click Submit.**

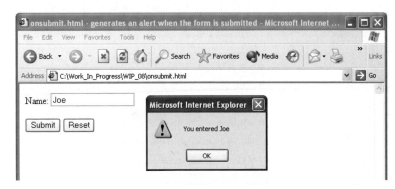

FIGURE 8.24

| 8 | Click OK to acknowledge the alert box. |

| 9 | Close the file in your browser and text editor. |

To Extend Your Knowledge . . .

USING ONSUBMIT

The `onsubmit` event handler detects when the user is ready to submit the content of a form. This handler allows JavaScript to check the user's answers for completeness and correctness and stop the submission of data if the user made a mistake or failed to enter required information. This handler reduces the interaction with the server, since the client-side script can check the form's content before the information is forwarded to the server. This often decreases frustration for the end user — he no longer has to reenter the entire content of a form because he made an error on a single element.

LESSON 6   Using a Selection Event

The primary purpose of event handlers is to allow JavaScript to determine if an element has been selected or changed. Event handlers are used within form elements for a variety of reasons, such as the **onselect** and **onchange** event handlers, which you learn about in this lesson.

Onselect

The **onselect** event handler fires when the user selects text in a form element by highlighting the text. You can use this handler with the **<input>** and **<textarea>** tags. For example, if you want to generate an alert box when the user highlights the content of an input text box in a form, you can modify an **<input>** tag as follows.

```
<input type="text" name="name" onselect="alert('you have selected text
in the input box');" />
```

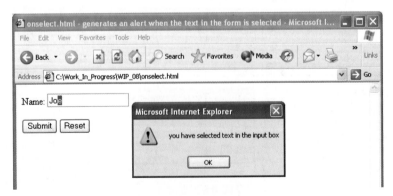

FIGURE 8.25

Onchange

The **onchange** event handler fires when the user modifies the value or content of an HTML select, input, or text area element in a form and then releases the mouse button. This handler is often used to check or confirm changes the user made.

Detect the Selection of Text

1   **In your text editor and browser, open select.html from the WIP_08 folder.**

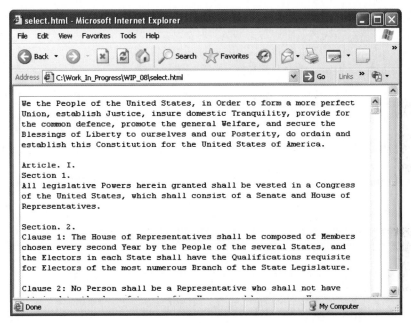

FIGURE 8.26

This page displays the U.S. Constitution in a scrollable text area.

2   **In your text editor, find the following code.**

```
<textarea name="textarea" cols="70" rows="20" wrap="VIRTUAL">
```

This code creates the text area.

3   **Add the following code to include an event handler and alert.**

```
<textarea name="textarea" cols="70" rows="20" wrap="VIRTUAL"
onselect="alert('Copyright, the US Government');">
```

This generates an alert box when the user selects the text. The U.S. Constitution is not copyrighted; this is for demonstration purposes only.

4   Save the file in your text editor and refresh your browser.

5   Click your mouse anywhere in the text and try to drag the mouse to select some of the text.

FIGURE 8.27

An alert box appears.

6   Click OK to acknowledge the alert box.

7   Close the file in your browser and text editor.

Detect the Change of a Form Element

1   In your text editor and browser, open onchange.html from the WIP_08 folder.

FIGURE 8.28

2   In your text editor, find the following code.

```
<input name="shipmethod" type="text" id="shipmethod"
value="USPS" />
```

This code creates a form element.

3   Insert an event handler by inserting the following code.

```
<input name="shipmethod" type="text" id="shipmethod" value="USPS"
onchange="alert('other shipping methods require additional
cost');" />
```

4   Save the file in your text editor and refresh your browser.

5   Replace the default text with any text you prefer.

FIGURE 8.29

6   Press the Tab key or click somewhere else on the page to blur the input text box.

An alert box appears.

FIGURE 8.30

7   Click OK to acknowledge the alert box.

8   Close the file in your browser and text editor.

To Extend Your Knowledge . . .

DETECTING CHANGES IN FORM ELEMENTS

The onchange event handler tells developers when form elements have changed. This allows you to design forms that assist with complicated procedures. For example, technical support forms often ask for a major category in a form element such as "PC Hardware Problem" or "Software Problem." You can detect changes in this element and tailor future questions to solving this specific problem.

LESSON 7   Advanced Use of Event Handlers

So far in this chapter, you have bound event handlers to HTML tags by including the events in the HTML tags. This is the easiest way to use event handlers; it represents the way that event handlers are typically incorporated into an HTML document. You can also use event handlers outside HTML tags by incorporating them directly into scripts. As you know, every HTML element has a corresponding object in JavaScript. For instance, if you want an **onclick** event to activate when the user clicks the content of the first HTML **<a>** tag, you could write the following statement.

```
<!DOCTYPE html PUBLIC "-//W3C//DTD XHTML 1.0 Transitional//EN"
"http://www.w3.org/TR/xhtml1/DTD/xhtml1-transitional.dtd">
<html xmlns="http://www.w3.org/1999/xhtml">
<head>
<title>eventinscript.html - shows how to use an event handler within a
script</title>
</head>
<body>

<p><>a href="#">Panic</a></p>
<script language="JavaScript" type="text/javascript">
window.document.links[0].onclick=new Function("alert('You clicked the
first link in the document')");
</script>
</body>
</html>
```

In this example, the **onclick** event appears to be a property of the object. In a manner of speaking, it is, since you can store an instruction within the property. This code requires you to create a function that does not have a name and is assigned directly to an event handler. This type of function is called an ***anonymous function.***

You can also write code to manually fire JavaScript events without the event actually occurring. For instance, if you want to trigger the **onclick** event shown above, you can invoke it as a method of the object. For example, you could add the following statement in the above script.

```
window.document.links[0].onclick();
```

Adding this line of code to the example file causes the event to fire, even though the user hasn't clicked the link.

FIGURE 8.31

The event handler works in a similar fashion to a conditional evaluation or a flow-of-control statement. The event handler causes JavaScript to evaluate whether the event has occurred. If the answer is **true**, the code assigned to the event handler executes; if the answer is **false**, the code does not execute.

Returning Information from an Event Handler

When you use an event handler as a method, you set the value of the condition to **true**, which allows JavaScript to execute the associated code. You can also set the event to **false**, which stops the associated code from executing, even though the event occurred. For example, consider a situation where a user is entering critically important information into a form. In such a situation, you may want to ask the user if she is sure the information is correct or if she is sure she wants to submit the form.

You can program the Submit button on a form to ask if the user is sure she wants to enter the information before she submits the form. Even though the user clicked the Submit button, the form would not submit unless the user confirms that she wants to submit the information. You can use the **confirm()** method to ensure the user approves the request, as shown in the following example.

```
<body>
<form name="form1" method="post" action="" id="form1">
 <p>Name:
 <input type="text" name="name" />
 </p>
 <p>
 <input type="submit" name="Submit" value="Submit" onclick="return
confirm('Submit form?')" />
 </p>
</form>
</body>
```

Recall that the **confirm()** method returns a value of **true** or **false** when used with the **return** keyword. If you were to place this code into a Web page, fill out the form, and then click the Submit button, you would receive the following result.

FIGURE 8.32

The user must click OK to return a value of **true** and complete the form submission. If the user clicks Cancel, the return value is **false**, which effectively cancels the submit action.

Use Dot Syntax to Create an Event Handler

1   **In your browser, open jsevent.html from the WIP_08 folder.**

FIGURE 8.33

2   **Move your mouse over the image.**

Nothing happens, because no event handler has been assigned.

3   **Open the file in your text editor. Insert the following code into the document.**

```
...
<script language="JavaScript" type="text/javascript">
// insert function here
window.document.images[0].onmouseover=new Function("alert('You
moved your mouse pointer over the image')");
</script>
</body>
</html>
```

4   Save the file in your text editor and refresh your browser.

5   Move your mouse over the image.

The event fires.

FIGURE 8.34

6   Click OK to acknowledge the alert box.

7   Close the file in your browser and text editor.

To Extend Your Knowledge . . .

EVENT HANDLERS AND ANONYMOUS FUNCTIONS

Using event handlers in anonymous functions allows developers to place all event handlers in one section of code, rather than spreading the event handlers throughout the HTML document as they are needed. Most developers prefer to implement handlers using inline JavaScript, but the ability to declare anonymous functions is useful in complex coding tasks.

SUMMARY

In this chapter, you explored events and their associated event handlers. You learned that JavaScript event handlers are usually associated with HTML tags, but may also be assigned directly to JavaScript objects that represent HTML tags. You discovered that event handlers are often associated with user actions, such as when a user clicks a button or presses a key on the keyboard.

You also learned that many events are used with display elements, such as images displayed with the **<img>** tag or links created with an **<a>** tag. Events not associated with display elements are usually associated with other tags, such as the **<body>** or **<frameset>** tag. An event may also be the result of another action, such as when the source code of a page finishes loading. Many events are related to the use of forms and can detect whether the user is attempting to submit or reset a form.

You discovered that you can manually fire most events by calling the event as a method of an object. Additionally, you found that you can use the **return** keyword and **confirm()** method to ask a user to confirm an action before it executes. In this situation, you learned that you can use the **return** keyword to stop an action from occurring by assigning the event handler a **false** value and canceling the event.

You learned that event handlers typically execute a single JavaScript statement, which is often a function. This allows you to accomplish complex actions, such as validating form data when the action is completed. In this chapter, you studied the most common event handlers used in JavaScript, which are available in most versions of common Web browsers. Other event handlers are available in specific Web browsers; due to compatibility issues, we recommend that you avoid using them.

KEY TERMS

Anonymous function	Camelback notation	Keyboard event
Bound	Fire	Listener

CHECKING CONCEPTS AND TERMS

MULTIPLE CHOICE

Circle the letter that matches the correct answer for each of the following questions.

1. Which event handler is commonly used with display elements, such as type or images?
   a. onload
   b. onsubmit
   c. onclick
   d. All of the above.
   e. None of the above.

2. Which event handlers are used to create image rollovers?
   a. onload, onselect
   b. onmouseover, onmouseout
   c. onfocus, onblur
   d. onsubmit, onreset

3. Which event handlers are often used with forms?
   a. onsubmit
   b. onreset
   c. onchange
   d. All of the above.
   e. None of the above.

4. Which event handler can be used to determine if keystrokes are not currently being directed to a Web page?
   a. onblur
   b. onchange
   c. onfocus
   d. onselect

5. Which event handler fires when the user moves the mouse off the edge of a page element?
   a. onchange
   b. onblur
   c. onmouseout
   d. onmouseover

6. The **onunload** event handler can determine if the browser window is being closed.
   a. True
   b. False

7. An event handler can determine if the current browser window is being resized.

a. True

b. False

8. When does the **onload** event fire when attached to a **\<body>** tag?

   a. When the head section of the HTML document finishes loading.

   b. When the last image finishes loading.

   c. When the last character of the HTML page finishes loading.

   d. None of the above.

9. Why is the **onsubmit** event handler useful?

   a. It signals the server that information is being transmitted.

   b. It performs actions before a form is submitted, but after the user enters information.

   c. Both of the above.

   d. None of the above.

10. Why is the **onchange** event used?

    a. To determine if the user changed the browser preferences.

    b. To determine if the user changed the screen resolution.

    c. To determine if the user changed the content of a form element.

    d. To determine if the user stole an image from the page.

DISCUSSION QUESTIONS

1. What is the purpose of the **ondblclick** event handler? Why do you think this event is rarely used?

2. If you can use the **onkeypress** event handler to determine if specific keys have been pressed, how can you use this information to improve impaired users' accessibility to a Web page?

3. Describe two different situations where you might need to use event handlers to improve the design of a Web page.

4. Why is it useful to use the **return** keyword with event handlers? Name two situations where this could improve the functioning of a Web page.

SKILL DRILL

Skill Drill exercises reinforce chapter skills. Each skill reinforced is the same (or nearly the same) as a skill presented in the chapter. Detailed instructions are provided in a step-by-step format. You can work through one or more exercises in any order.

1. Detect the Focus of a Window

In this exercise, you detect whether a browser window has focus. This task requires you to use the **onfocus** event handler with the **\<body>** tag.

1. In your text editor, open skillfocus.html from the WIP_08 folder.

2. Find the following line of code.

```
<body>
```

3. Bind the **onfocus** event handler to the **<body>** tag by adding the following code directly into the **<body>** tag.

    ```
    onfocus="alert('The window has been focused');"
    ```

4. Save the file in your text editor and open it in your browser.

FIGURE 8.35

The alert box appears when the file loads because the window has focus.

5. Click OK to acknowledge the alert box.

6. Click a different window, the desktop, or the Start button to blur the browser window.

    You can also click a different browser window to blur the skillfocus.html file.

7. Click the browser window that contains skillfocus.html.

    This action draws focus to the browser window.

8. Click OK to acknowledge the alert box.

    The alert box should reappear.

9. Close the file in your browser and text editor.

2. Perform Actions While a Page Unloads

In this exercise, you detect whether the current page is unloading from the browser. You use the **onunload** event handler to accomplish the task. This event handler is designed to work with the **<body>** tag.

1. In your text editor, open skillonunload.html from the WIP_08 folder.

2. Find the **<body>** tag.

3. Modify the **<body>** tag to include the **onunload** event handler. The event handler should execute the following code when the **onunload** event is encountered.

    ```
    onunload="alert('Thank you for visiting this page');"
    ```

4. Save the file in your text editor.

5. Open the file in your browser.

6. Click the Refresh button.

FIGURE 8.36

The alert box appears because the current page must unload before the file can reload.

7. Click OK to acknowledge the alert box.

8. Try navigating to another page or closing your browser window.

    The alert box should appear in either case.

9. Close the file in your browser and text editor.

3. Confirm a Hyperlink

In this exercise, you design a hyperlink that asks the user to confirm whether he wants to leave the current page. This requires you to use the **return** keyword with the **onclick** event handler.

1. In your text editor, open skillconfirmlink.html from the WIP_08 folder.

2. Find the following line of code.

    ```
    <a href="http://www.web-answers.com">Go to Web Answers</a>
    ```

3. Bind the **<a>** tag with the **onclick** event handler by inserting the following code directly into the **<a>** tag.

    ```
    onclick="return confirm('Are you sure you want to go to that
    page?');"
    ```

4. Save the file in your text editor.

5. Open the file in your browser.

6. Click the hyperlink.

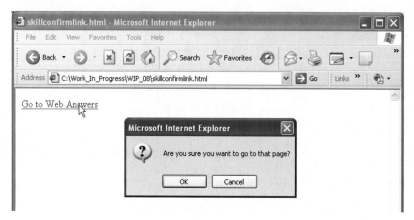

FIGURE 8.37

A confirm box appears.

7. Click Cancel.

    The hyperlink should cancel.

8. Click the hyperlink again.

9. Click OK.

    The page should redirect.

10. Close the file in your browser and text editor.

4. Confirm a Form Reset

In this exercise, you confirm whether a user wants to reset the content of a form. This action is often useful when the user must fill in large, complicated forms. The user could become quite frustrated if he accidentally resets the form by clicking the wrong button.

1. In your browser, open skillreset.html from the WIP_08 folder.

FIGURE 8.38

2. Fill out the form and click the Reset button.

   The form resets.

3. Open the file in your text editor.

4. Find the following code.

   ```
   <form action="" method="post" name="form1" id="form1">
   ```

5. Bind the **onreset** event handler to the **<form>** tag by placing it inside the tag. Set the **onreset** event to trigger the following actions.

   ```
   return confirm('Are you sure you want to reset the form?');
   ```

6. Save the file in your text editor.

7. Refresh the file in your browser.

8. Fill out the form and click the Reset button.

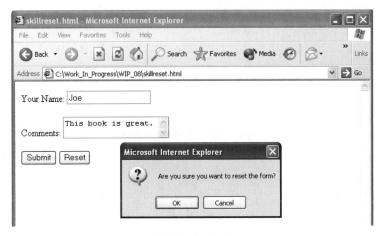

FIGURE 8.39

9. Click Cancel.

   The form submission aborts. Notice how the form content remains intact.

10. Click Reset again.

11. Click OK.

    The form resets.

12. Close the file in your browser and text editor.

CHALLENGE

Challenge exercises expand on (or are somewhat related to) skills presented in the lessons. Each exercise provides a brief introduction, followed by instructions presented in a numbered-step format that are not as detailed as those in the Skill Drill exercises. You should work through these exercises in order.

1. Determine Which Key Was Pressed

You are designing a script to use in various applications. Your code consists of a function that determines which key has been pressed. The function allows you to create different effects as the user presses different keys on the keyboard. In the following exercise, you test this function.

1. In your text editor, open challengekey.html from the WIP_08 folder.

2. Find the following line of code in the document.

    ```
    // insert code here
    ```

3. Insert the following code to create a function.

    ```
    . . .
    <title>challengekey.html - shows the onkeydown event
    handler</title>
    <script language="JavaScript" type="text/javascript">
    // insert code here
    function determineKey() {
    alert('You pressed: '+String.fromCharCode(event.keyCode));
    }
    </script>
    </head>
    <body>
    . . .
    ```

    This function only works in Internet Explorer browsers.

4. Find the **<body>** tag in the document.

5. Insert code directly into the **<body>** tag that will use the **onkeydown** operator to trigger the **determineKey()** function when the user presses any key on the keyboard.

6. Save the file in your text editor.

7. Open the file in the browser.

8. Press the "A" key on your keyboard.

FIGURE 8.40

9. Click OK to acknowledge the alert box.

10. Press other keys on the keyboard and view the results.

11. Close the file in your browser and text editor.

2. Manipulate an Image

Manipulating an image is one of the most common uses of event handlers. In this exercise, you change the source file assigned to an image when the user clicks the image. You use the **onclick** event handler to accomplish the task.

1. In your text editor and browser, open challengeimage.html from the WIP_08 folder.

FIGURE 8.41

You must have buttonup.jpg and buttondown.jpg in the WIP_08 folder for this page to function correctly.

2. Find the following line of code.

```
<img src="buttonup.jpg" width="100" height="40" alt="button" />
```

3. Bind the **onmousedown** event handler to the **<img>** tag by inserting the following code into the **<img>** tag.

```
onmousedown="document.images[0].src='buttondown.jpg';"
```

4. Save the file in your text editor.

5. Open the file in the browser.

6. Move your mouse over the image.

FIGURE 8.42

Nothing happens.

7. Click the mouse button.

FIGURE 8.43

The image changes.

8. Move your mouse off the image.

You continue to see the changed image.

9. Keep the file open in your text editor and browser for the next exercise.

3. Create a Rollover Effect

In the previous exercise, you used the **onclick** event handler to trigger an image change. A more useful effect is to change the image when the user rolls over the image. In this exercise, you use the **onmouseover** event handler to accomplish this task.

1. In the open challengeimage.html, find the following line of code.

```
<img src="buttonup.jpg" width="100" height="40"
onmousedown="document.images[0].src='buttondown.jpg';"
alt="button" />
```

2. Change the event handler to change the image when the user rolls over the image (**onmouseover**) instead of when the user clicks the image (**onmousedown**).

3. Save the file in your text editor.

4. Refresh the file in your browser.

FIGURE 8.44

5. Move your mouse over the image.

    The image changes.

FIGURE 8.45

6. Move your mouse off the image.

FIGURE 8.46

The image remains the same.

7. Keep the file open in your browser and text editor for the next exercise.

4. Detect Roll-Offs

In the previous exercise, you used the **onmouseover** event handler to detect whether the user had moved the mouse pointer over a button. In this exercise, you add to the script by changing the image back when the user moves the mouse away from the image.

1. In the open challengeimage.html, find the following line of code.

    ```
    <img src="buttonup.jpg" width="100" height="40"
    onmouseover="document.images[0].src='buttondown.jpg';"
    alt="button" />
    ```

2. Before the ending bracket (**>**) of the **<img>** tag, insert the following code.

    ```
    <img src="buttonup.jpg" width="100" height="40"
    onmouseover="document.images[0].src='buttondown.jpg';"
    onmouseout="document.images[0].src='buttonup.jpg';"
    alt="button" />
    ```

3. Save the file in your text editor.

4. Refresh the file in your browser.

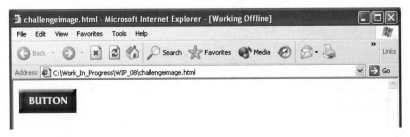

FIGURE 8.47

5. Move your mouse over the button.

The button changes.

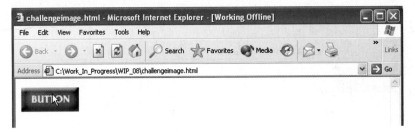

FIGURE 8.48

6. Move your mouse off the button.

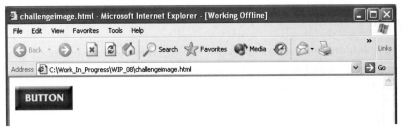

FIGURE 8.49

The image changes to the original image file.

7. Close the file in your text editor and browser.

5. Scroll on Key Press

In this exercise, you work with a page that contains a great deal of text. To simplify the task of scrolling through this large amount of text, you create code that scrolls the page downward whenever the user presses a key on the keyboard.

1. In your browser, open challengescroll.html from the WIP_08 folder.

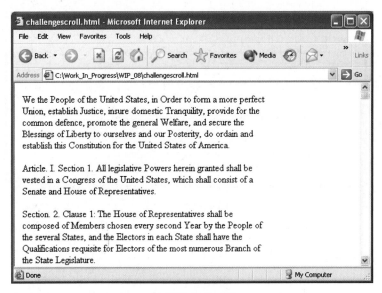

FIGURE 8.50

This page contains the U.S. Constitution, presented in a simple table.

2. Use the vertical scroll bar to scroll to the bottom of the page.

3. Open the file in your text editor.

4. Find the **<body>** tag.

5. Bind the **onkeypress** event handler to the **<body>** tag by inserting the event handler within the **<body>** tag. Carry out the following code when the **onkeypress** event is detected.

```
scrollBy(30);
```

6. Save the file in your text editor.

7. Refresh the file in your browser.

8. Press the Spacebar or any other key.

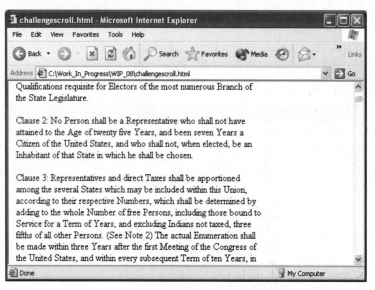

FIGURE 8.51

The page should scroll down 30 lines of text.

9. Close the file in your browser and text editor.

PORTFOLIO BUILDER

Enhance a Home Page Prototype

Integrating client-side scripting into documents allows developers to create truly interactive experiences for users. One of the most common uses of interactivity is to change (swap) images when the user moves his mouse over a navigation image. You can see this effect when text changes color, icons move or change, and images animate (or stop animating). JavaScript's ability to interactively swap images makes all of these effects possible.

In this Portfolio Builder, we provided a home page prototype for you. It contains a grid of images that functions as an interactive navigation structure. From the WIP_08>Portfolio_Builder_08 folder, open home.html in your browser. One of the images (image2_.jpg) changes to another image (image_2_over.jpg) when you move your mouse pointer over the image. This change occurs because of the following line of code.

```
<img src="images/image_2.jpg" width="200" height="150" border="0"
onmouseover="document.images[1].src='images/image_2_over.jpg';"
alt="image two" />
```

Using the **onmouseover** event handler to change image sources, you create an innovative navigation structure that users will want to explore. As a curious user explores the page, the navigation structure is revealed.

To complete this Portfolio Builder, you must use a newer browser — Netscape Navigator versions 6 and earlier cause errors.

1. Start by resizing the Web page to 680 by 640 (**resizeTo(680,640);**) after the page loads. This allows the page to appear at the optimum viewing resolution.

2. Insert an event handler into image 3 to swap the image **onmouseover**. The swapped image should be image_3_over.jpg.

3. Repeat this process for images 4, 5, and 6 — changing the number for each image. Insert the word "_over" into the file name for the over images. Use the code for image 2 as an example.

CHAPTER  **9**

Exploring the Document Object

OBJECTIVES

In this chapter, you learn how to:

- Change color properties
- Use properties of the links object
- Employ the anchors array
- Assign the title property

- Use the location and URL properties
- Control document loading
- Implement history methods

Why Would I Do This?

Within the hierarchy of the JavaScript language, the **document** object is one part of the **window** object. As you know, the **window** object allows you to interact with, control, and measure properties of browser windows. In contrast, the **document** object represents the HTML code that exists within an individual **window** object. The **document** object allows you to interact with various elements of the HTML code.

The **document** object contains many objects that represent various aspects of the HTML code contained in a document. For instance, if a document contains a form, then a **form** object represents the form as a part of the **document** object. A new **form** object is created every time a **<form>** tag is encountered in the HTML code.

Objects are represented by arrays. Similar to a variable, an *array* is a temporary storage space for information; but an array takes on multiple elements, whereas a variable can only take on a single element. For instance, the phrase **games[0]** may represent the first game played by a sports team, and the phrase **games[1]** may represent the second game played.

In JavaScript, the first element of an array is usually referred to as **[0]**, such as referring to the first game as **games[0]**. In JavaScript, most HTML tags are represented by an element in the matching array. For instance, in the **links** array, **links[0]** would represent the first **<a>** tag in the document, and **links[1]** would represent the second **<a>** tag in the document. Using dot syntax in JavaScript, you could refer to the first hyperlink in any HTML document as **window. document.links[0]**.

The objects that exist within the **document** object represent HTML elements:

- **image** objects represent **<img>** tags
- **link** objects represent **<a>** tags
- **form** objects represent **<form>** tags

These objects and their associated methods and properties are among the most-used commands in JavaScript. In this chapter, you take a closer look at the Document Object Model (DOM) as you learn how to describe key objects that exist within the object model and how to apply the primary methods and properties of the **document** object.

VISUAL SUMMARY

The **document** object contains various objects, methods, and properties designed to interact with the HTML document. The following diagram shows the standard subordinate objects that exist as part of the **document** object. Collectively, this group of objects is known as the Document Object Model (DOM).

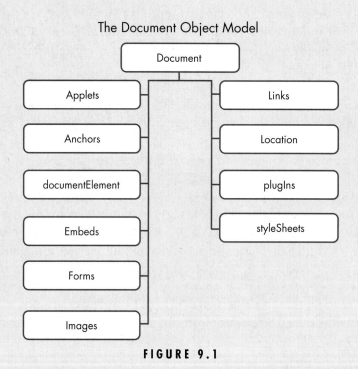

FIGURE 9.1

In earlier chapters in this book, you interacted with various aspects of the DOM to a certain extent, such as when you used the **write()** method of the **document** object. In this chapter, you learn about additional objects that belong to the **document** object, including the **anchors** object, the **links** object, and the **location** object.

You also interact with various properties and methods that belong to the **document** object, as well as learn how to use the subordinate objects mentioned earlier. A complete discussion of every aspect of the DOM is beyond the scope of a single chapter.

LESSON 1 Changing Color Properties

HTML allows the user to set various color properties, including the background color of a Web page and the color of text that displays on the page. Other color properties control the color of hyperlinks. Consider the following HTML code that sets the default background color of a Web page:

```
<body bgcolor="#000033">
```

This statement changes the default background color to dark blue. The color is written as a hexadecimal number, which represents ***RGB*** (red, green, blue) color values. In a ***hexadecimal number***, the first two digits represent the amount of red, the second two digits represent the amount of green, and the third two digits represent the amount of blue in the RGB color. Designers can also choose to represent colors using simple names, such as **<body bgcolor="navy">**.

When you specify a color by name, the color may appear differently in one browser than another. The color "navy" often displays as a lighter shade of blue than the hexadecimal equivalent of the color (#000033). For this reason, most designers prefer to specify hexadecimal color values, which allow them to ensure consistent color display across browser platforms.

Both JavaScript and HTML support hexadecimal and name color values. HTML color attributes (such as **bgcolor**) have matching representation in JavaScript. You can access these attributes through properties of the **document** object.

Modifying Default Link Colors

Every Web browser sets default colors for links, active links, and visited links. In a typical browser, the user can press the Tab key to go from one choice to the next, or advance from one hyperlink to the next. The currently active link is the link currently selected but not yet activated — the user has not yet clicked the link. You can use hexadecimal colors or color names to define link colors.

AlinkColor

The **alinkColor** property displays the active link. The active link is the currently active link that displays if the user clicks his mouse on the link or presses the Enter/Return key. For example, if you want to set the **alinkColor** property to white, you can type the following statement.

```
document.alinkColor="#FFFFFF";
```

LinkColor

The **linkColor** property holds the default color used to display hyperlinks. Hyperlinks not currently selected nor recently visited appear in the color specified by the **linkColor** property.

VlinkColor

The **vlinkColor** property represents links recently visited by the Web browser. Every Web browser keeps a history list of URLs recently visited. If a hyperlink represents a file that is cataloged in the history list, the link appears in the color specified by the **vlinkColor** property.

Changing the Background Color Property

The **bgColor** property allows you to specify the background color of an HTML document. This property represents the same value that you can set with the **bgcolor** attribute of the **<body>** tag. The following command sets the background color to red.

```
document.bgColor="#FF0000";
```

Changing the Foreground Color Property

The **fgColor** property allows you to specify the foreground color of an HTML document. The foreground color represents the default text color specified in the **<body>** tag of an HTML document. The following command sets the foreground color to red.

```
document.fgColor="#FF0000";
```

This property represents the same value as the **text** attribute of the HTML **<body>** tag. The following line of HTML code achieves the same result.

```
<body text="#FF0000">
```

Link Color Properties

1   **Copy the content of the RF_JavaScript_L1>Chapter_09 folder into the Work_In_Progress>WIP_09 folder.**

2   **In your browser, open main.html from the WIP_09 folder and explore the links in the document.**

This mock site contains three simple pages that link to one another. Each page consists of a title and the links to the other pages. In most browsers, the link colors change from blue (the default) to purple to indicate a previously visited site.

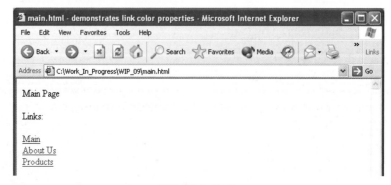

FIGURE 9.2

3   Open main.html in your text editor.

4   Insert the following code.

```
. . .
<script language="JavaScript" type="text/javascript">
// change link color properties
document.alinkColor="#CC0000"; // dark red
document.vlinkColor="#666666"; // dark gray
document.linkColor="#FF0000";  // bright red
</script>
</head>
<body bgcolor="#FFFFFF">
. . .
```

This code changes the default link colors in the Web browser: it makes active links dark red (#CC0000), previously visited links dark gray (#666666), and unvisited links bright red (#FF0000).

5   Save the document in your text editor.

6   Refresh main.html in your browser to see the new colors.

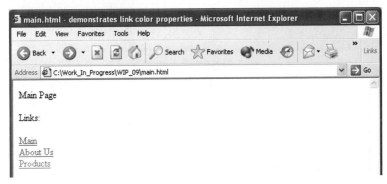

FIGURE 9.3

At this point, it is likely that most links on the main page appear in dark gray because you recently visited these pages.

7   Repeat Steps 3–5 for aboutus.html and products.html to apply these styles to the other documents.

8   View the pages in your browser. Click the Refresh button to see the changes in link colors.

9   Close the files in your browser and text editor.

To Extend Your Knowledge . . .

THE LINKCOLOR PROPERTY

In older versions of Netscape Navigator, you must set the `linkColor` property within the `<head>` and `</head>` tags of the HTML document.

Set Background and Foreground Colors

1   In your text editor and browser, open backgroundcolor.html from the WIP_09 folder.

FIGURE 9.4

2   Click OK to acknowledge the alert box.

3   Find the following code in your text editor.

```
<body bgcolor="#000033" text="#FFFFFF">
```

This code sets the background color to blue (#000033) and the text color to white (#FFFFFF).

4   Find the following code.

```
. . .
<script language="JavaScript" type="text/javascript">
alert("Hello!");
// insert code here

</script>
. . .
```

The alert statement stops the flow of the script, which allows you to easily see the color changes after you acknowledge the alert box.

5   Insert the following code.

```
...
<script language="JavaScript" type="text/javascript">
alert("Hello!");
// insert code here
//set background to white
document.bgColor="#FFFFFF";
// set text to black
document.fgColor="#000000";
</script>
</body>
</html>
```

The "C" in "**Color**" must be capitalized in **bgColor** and **fgColor** for this script to work properly.

6   **Save the file in your text editor.**

7   **Refresh the file in your browser.**

The alert box appears.

8   **Click OK to acknowledge the alert box.**

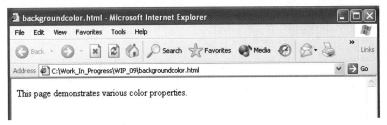

FIGURE 9.5

The background and foreground colors change.

9   **Close the file in your browser and text editor.**

To Extend Your Knowledge . . .

BACKGROUND AND FOREGROUND COLORS

In some versions of Netscape Navigator, you must specify the foreground and background colors within a script located between the **<head>** and **</head>** tags of the HTML document.

HEXADECIMAL NUMBERS

The Windows operating system includes a built-in calculator application that can easily convert hexadecimal numbers to regular numbers.

LESSON 2   Using Properties of the Link Object

Many tags in HTML have matching objects in JavaScript. For example, when an `<img>` tag is found in HTML, JavaScript creates a matching **image** object. This allows JavaScript to access and control various aspects of HTML.

JavaScript also creates an array to keep track of each type of object it creates. JavaScript references each object as an element of an array. For example, JavaScript references an **image** object as an element of the **images** array.

The array that stores information about hyperlinks is known as the **_links array_**, and each object referenced in the array is referred to as a **_link object_**. This may seem confusing, but it is consistent with other objects in JavaScript and their associated arrays — such as the **frames** array and its associated **frame** objects.

The Links Array and Link Object

Whenever you use an `<a>` tag in HTML code to create a link, an entry is also made in the **links** array for the document. Aside from creating an entry in the **links** array, JavaScript also creates a **link** object. Each **link** object contains a variety of properties that describe characteristics of each hyperlink in the HTML document. You use HTML to create hyperlinks with statements such as the following.

```
<a href="http://www.web-answers.com">Web Answers Web site</a>
```

Assuming this link is the first hyperlink in the HTML document, JavaScript refers to the link as:

```
document.links[0]
```

The **link** object has a number of useful properties. For instance, the **link.href** property specifies the entire hypertext reference specified in an HTML hyperlink. The term **_hypertext reference_** is synonymous with the term URL (Uniform Resource Locator), which simply represents the location of a document. In the above example, the **link.href** property would contain the entire address specified within the quotes. Additional examples of link properties include the **link.pathname** property, which includes the path to the file, but does not include the domain name. The following table contains many commonly used link properties.

Property	Represents
`href`	Entire URL entered in hyperlink
`domain`	Domain name in a URL
`hash`	Internal anchor links in a URL (such as #products)
`innerHTML`	Text between the `<a>` and `</a>` tags
`pathname`	Path to the file, not including the domain name
`protocol`	The protocol in a hyperlink, such as `http:`, `ftp:`, or `mailto:`
`search`	A search string appended to a URL, such as `?category=12`
`target`	The target for the link, such as `_blank`, `_parent`, or `_self`

TABLE 9.1

Properties such as **href** and **target** represent the same information as the HTML attributes of the same name. For example, consider the following line of HTML code.

```
<a  href="http://www.secure.com/index.html"  target="_blank">Secure,
Inc.</a>
```

- The **href** property is equal to http://www.secure.com/index.html.

- The **target** property is **_blank**.

- Other properties are usually derived from the **href** property. For example, the **pathname** property is equal to index.html. (A *pathname* is the location of the file relative to the domain name.)

Use Properties of the Link Object

1   In your text editor, open linkshref.html from the WIP_09 folder.

2   Insert the following code.

```
...
<a href="http://www.web-answers.com">Web Answers</a><br />
<script language="JavaScript" type="text/javascript">
// insert code here
document.write("Link object href: " + document.links[0].href);
</script>
</body>
</html>
```

This code outputs the **href** property of the **link** object.

3   Save the document in your text editor and open it in your browser.

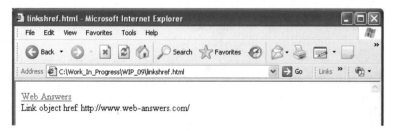

FIGURE 9.6

The **href** property contains the text specified in the **href** attribute of the **<a>** tag.

4   Keep the file open in your text editor and browser for the next exercise.

Use the Pathname Property

1   **In the open linkshref.html in your text editor, find the following line of code.**

```
<a href="http://www.web-answers.com">Web Answers</a><br />
```

2   **Rewrite the statement beginning with the `<a>` tag to change the `href` attribute to the following.**

```
<a href = "http://www.web-answers.com/books/index.html">
Web Answers</a><br />
```

This link is for demonstration purposes only, so you will probably receive an error if you click this hyperlink in the browser window.

3   **Create a new line beneath the `document.write()` statement and add the following two lines of code.**

```
...
<script language="JavaScript" type="text/javascript">
// insert code here
document.write("Link object href: " + document.links[0].href);
document.write("<br />");
document.write("Link object pathname: " + document.links[0].
    pathname);
</script>
</body>
</html>
```

The first statement simply adds a new line to format the document. The second statement displays the **pathname** property of the first hyperlink in the document.

4   **Save the file in your text editor and refresh your browser.**

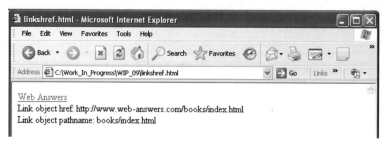

FIGURE 9.7

The pathname is the location of the file; it does not include the domain name.

5   **Close the file in your browser and text editor.**

To Extend Your Knowledge . . .

THE SEARCH PROPERTY

URL parameters pass information from one page to another by including a question mark and additional info at the end of a URL in a hyperlink. Let's use `href="products.html?product=ovens"` as an example. The `link.search` property can access the information entered after the question mark (`product=ovens`). This feature is particularly useful for database-backed Web sites, which often need to pass information from one page to another.

THE INNERHTML PROPERTY

The `link.innerHTML` property holds the text shown in the browser for the link. This useful property is only available in Internet Explorer 5.0 and later and Netscape Navigator version 6.0 and later.

LESSON 3 Employing the Anchors Array

Text anchors are used in HTML to create links to other locations within the HTML document. They work well for pages with long sequences of text, such as a glossary or a frequently asked questions (FAQ) section of a Web site. The point you link to is known as an ***anchor***, which is simply an **<a>** tag that has a **name** attribute. Consider the following example, where the anchor is named "F."

```
<a name="F"></a>
```

You can use the following HTML code to create a link to the "F" section of a glossary page.

```
<a href="#F">go to F section</a>
```

JavaScript creates an ***anchors array*** to represent every text anchor created in the HTML code. Each element in the anchors array is known as an ***anchor object***. You can also link to a named anchor in an external document by specifying the file name in the link. For example, if you want to link to a named anchor for the "F" section in the glossary page, you can create the following hyperlink.

```
<a href="glossary.html#F">F</a>
```

In the anchors array, the **name** property holds the name of each anchor as specified in the HTML code. To output the name of the second anchor object to the screen, you would write the following statement.

```
document.write("Anchors object: " + document.anchors[1].name);
```

Use the Anchor Object

1   **In your text editor and browser, open glossary.html from the WIP_09 folder.**

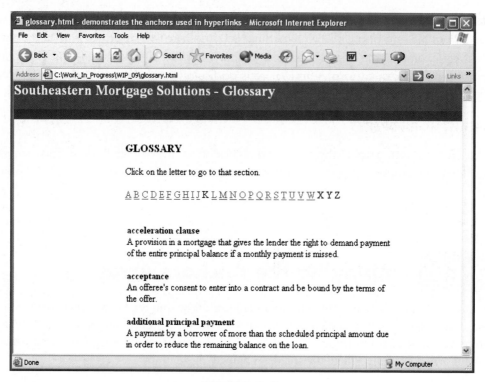

FIGURE 9.8

This file is a glossary page for a mortgage company.

2   **Click the "C" link.**

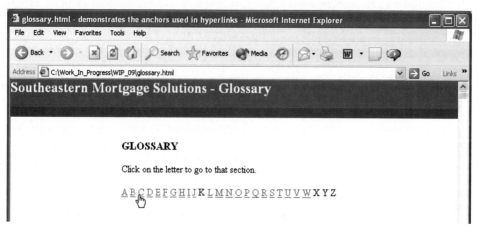

FIGURE 9.9

The page scrolls to the "C" section.

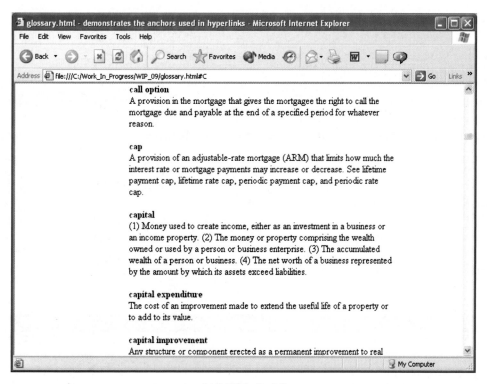

FIGURE 9.10

3   In your text editor, scroll to the bottom of the page.

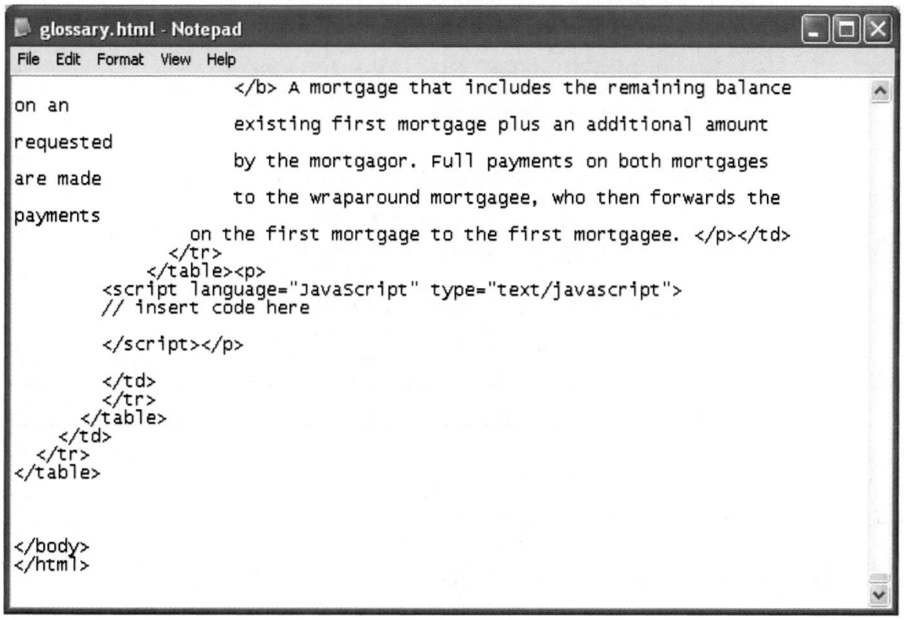

FIGURE 9.11

4   Insert the following code.

```
...
<script language="JavaScript" type="text/javascript">
//insert code here
document.write("Link object href: " + document.links[1].href);
document.write("<br />");
document.write("Anchors object: " + document.anchors[1].name);
</script>
...
```

5   Save the file in your text editor.

6   Refresh the file in your browser.

7   Scroll to the bottom of the page.

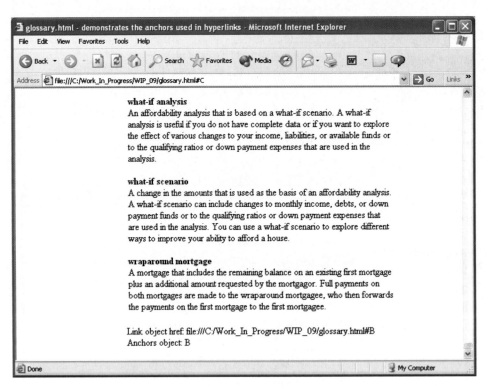

FIGURE 9.12

Information about the second anchor object displays.

8   Close the file in your browser and text editor.

To Extend Your Knowledge . . .

TEXT ANCHORS

You can create text anchors in JavaScript as well as HTML. For example, consider the following code that creates an anchor in HTML.

```
<a name="bookanchor">Book Index</a>
```

The following code creates the same anchor on a string of text (or variable) called myString.

```
var myString = "Book Index";

document.write(myString.anchor("bookanchor"))
```

In this case, the keyword **anchor** is used as a method. (This feature is not supported by earlier versions of Internet Explorer, and we recommend that you avoid using it.)

LESSON 4   Assigning the Title Property

The **title** property holds the title specified within the **<title>** and **</title>** tags of an HTML document. This text element appears in the title bar of most browsers. If you specify the title of a document in the HTML code as "**<title>Home of the JavaScript Master!</title>**," you can use the following statement to output the **title** property to the screen.

```
document.write(document.title);
```

Integrating these statements into a simple HTML document results in the following code.

```
<!DOCTYPE html PUBLIC "-//W3C//DTD XHTML 1.0 Transitional//EN"
"http://www.w3.org/TR/xhtml1/DTD/xhtml1-transitional.dtd">
<html xmlns="http://www.w3.org/1999/xhtml">
<head>
<title>Home of the JavaScript Master!</title>
</head>
<body>
<script language="JavaScript" type="text/javascript">
document.write(document.title);
</script>
</body>
</html>
```

The code shown above results in the following display in a Web browser.

FIGURE 9.13

Similar to other properties, you can change the **title** property by assigning a new text string. In newer browsers, this causes the title bar to change the title message.

In the next exercise, you investigate how to dynamically change the page title by changing the **title** property. To dynamically change the page title after the page loads, you must use Internet Explorer version 5 or above or Netscape Navigator version 6 or above; this exercise does not work in other (older) browsers.

Change the Title of the Page Dynamically

1   **In your text editor, open titleproperty.html from the WIP_09 folder.**

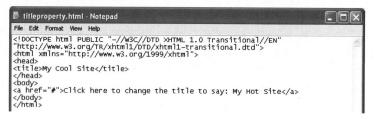

FIGURE 9.14

2   **Change the statement in the `<a>` tag to the following.**

```
<a href="#" onclick="document.title='My Hot Site';">Click here to
change the title to say: My Hot Site</a>
```

3   **Save the file in your text editor and open it in your browser.**

FIGURE 9.15

4   **Click the link.**

The title bar should change to "My Hot Site."

FIGURE 9.16

5 **Close the file in your browser and text editor.**

To Extend Your Knowledge . . .

ANIMATED PAGE TITLES

Using a combination of string methods and the `title` property allows you to create an animated title in the title bar. For example, consider a site where each letter of the title appears one at a time in rapid succession. When the title appears fully, the animation begins again. On first glance, this may appear to be an interesting addition to a site; in reality, however, most users find animated titles distracting and annoying. Most designers believe animated titles distract users from the important information presented in the content of the page. For these reasons, we recommend that you avoid adding this type of script to your Web pages.

LESSON 5   Using the Location and URL Properties

The **document** object contains a number of properties you can use to access the name of the currently loaded document. Changing the values stored in these properties often causes the browser to load a new page. These properties can be particularly useful when writing advanced scripts.

The Location Property

The ***location property*** holds the address of the current HTML document. Changing the `location` property forces the Web browser to load the page stored in the new address. The following example would force the browser to change the current document to the default page of the Web Answers Web site.

```
document.location="http://www.web-answers.com";
```

As of this writing, the **location** and **URL** properties are commonly used in many Web sites. Plans are in place, however, to eventually drop these properties from the language in favor of the **location.href** property, which (essentially) performs the same function.

As programming languages evolve, certain keywords become targeted for removal from the language. Once a keyword is targeted for removal, it is called a ***deprecated command***. Developers try to avoid using deprecated commands whenever possible to avoid future incompatibility issues. Even though the **URL** and **location** properties are considered deprecated commands, we present them in this text, because they exist in a significant number of current Web sites and script examples.

The URL Property

The **URL** property is almost identical to the **location** property. In Internet Explorer, changing the **URL** property forces the browser to load a new page. In Netscape Navigator, changing the **URL** property does not change the current page. For instance, the following statement would force Internet Explorer to redirect to the Web Answers Web site.

```
document.URL="http://www.web-answers.com";
```

Use the Location Property

| **1** | In your browser and text editor, open location.html from the WIP_09 folder. |

FIGURE 9.17

| **2** | Insert the following code. |

```
...
<p>This page will redirect to Web Answers </p>
<script language="JavaScript" type="text/javascript">
// insert code here
document.location="http://www.web-answers.com";
</script>
</body>
</html>
```

| **3** | Save the file in your text editor. |

| **4** | Refresh the file in your browser. |

The page redirects to the Web Answers Web site.

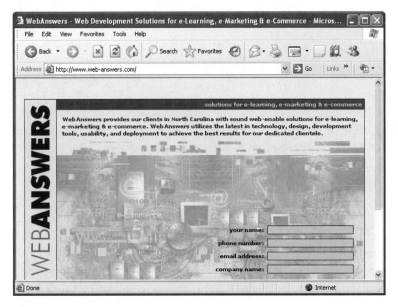

FIGURE 9.18

5　**Close the file in your browser and text editor.**

To Extend Your Knowledge . . .

LOCATION PROPERTY OR URL PROPERTY

To redirect users to a new page, the `location` property is a better choice than the `URL` property, since it is compatible in Netscape Navigator.

LESSON 6 Controlling Document Loading

In the previous lesson, you considered properties that hold the file name or URL of the currently loaded document. The `location` property is more useful than the `URL` property because it is better supported in most browsers. The `location` property is also an object in JavaScript, known as the `location` object. The *location object* allows you to change the browser's URL or reload the current document.

Aside from properties that hold the name of the currently loaded document, you can use methods of the `location` object to change the current URL. The primary methods of the `location` object are `assign()`, `reload()`, and `replace()`. As you see in this lesson, each of these methods is used for a slightly different purpose.

Assign()

The **assign()** method loads a new HTML document. The **assign** statement is written as:

```
location.assign("http://www.web-answers.com");
```

If you were using a relative hyperlink, you would write the statement as:

```
location.assign("index.html");
```

The **href** property performs the same function in JavaScript as the **assign()** method. For example, the statement **location.href="http://www.web-answers.com"** ; performs the same function as **location.assign("http://www.web-answers.com");**.

Reload()

The **reload()** method reloads the current HTML document. This method is primarily used on sites that constantly change content, such as Web sites that report news events. Imagine that you are creating a site that provides details on current weather conditions. You could use the **reload()** method to tell the browser to download a new copy of the page every fifteen minutes. The **reload()** method performs the same function as clicking the Reload button in Netscape or the Refresh button in Internet Explorer.

Using the **reload()** method without arguments causes the page to reload if any changes have been made to the file — in other words, if the file on the server is newer than the file located in the browser's cache.

```
location.reload();
```

You can also write this statement as **location.reload(false);**. Specifying a Boolean value of **false** has the same effect as leaving the parameter blank. You can specify a Boolean argument of **true** to force the browser to reload the page even if the page hasn't changed.

```
location.reload(true);
```

Replace()

The **replace()** method replaces the currently loaded URL with a different URL. Many developers often assume this means the **replace()** method performs the same function as the **assign()** method. To a certain extent, this is true; however, the **replace()** method actually deletes the old page in the browser's cache and replaces the old URL in the browser's history list. The **assign()** method does not replace the current entry in the browser's history list.

```
location.replace("newfile.html");
```

Use the Reload() Method

| 1 | In your text editor, open reload.html from the WIP_09 folder. |

| 2 | Find the <body> tag in the document. |

3 Insert the following code to create a link.

```
. . .
<title>reload.html</title>
</head>
<body>
<a href="#">reload the page</a>
</body>
</html>
```

4 Insert the following inline code into your link.

```
. . .
<title>reload.html</title>
</head>
<body>
<a href="#" onclick='location.reload();'>reload this page</a>
</body>
</html>
```

5 Save the file in your text editor.

6 Open the file in your browser.

FIGURE 9.19

At this point, clicking the link would not create a noticeable change, because the file hasn't changed since it loaded into the browser.

7 Return to your text editor and insert the following code.

```
. . .
<body>
<a href="#" onclick='location.reload();'>reload this page</a>
<p>This text is new.</p>
</body>
</html>
```

8 Save the file in your text editor.

9 In your browser, click the link.

The page should refresh and the change should be visible.

FIGURE 9.20

10 Close the file in your browser and text editor.

To Extend Your Knowledge . . .

FORCING THE BROWSER TO RELOAD

Forcing the browser to reload a page might be useful in situations where the page changes based on the user's choices. For example, if you are building a simple video game in the page, you could use the `reload()` method to start the game over again at the beginning — the browser would return the page to its original state when the page first loaded.

Use the Replace() Method

1 In your text editor, open replace.html from the WIP_09 folder.

2 Insert the following code.

```
...
<body>
<script language="JavaScript" type="text/javascript">
// insert code here
location.replace("http://www.web-answers.com");
</script>
</body>
</html>
```

This code forces the browser to go to a different URL and replaces the current page with the new page.

3 Save the file in your text editor.

4 Open the file in your browser.

You may see the original page before it redirects to the new page.

FIGURE 9.21

5 **After the Web Answers Web page loads, try to click the Back button.**

You can't return to the replace.html page. If replace.html was the first page opened, you can't access the Back button because the page was deleted from the browser's history list.

6 **Close the file in your browser and text editor.**

To Extend Your Knowledge . . .

THE REPLACE() METHOD

The `replace()` method is often useful in e-commerce applications. For security reasons, you may not want to allow a Web surfer to return to the last document — the document may contain sensitive information, or it may contain an e-commerce transaction. For example, let's say that a user entered his credit card information and clicked the Complete button to complete the transaction. Then he realizes he entered the wrong telephone number. He clicks the Back button, corrects the error, and resubmits the form. The user does not realize that when he resubmitted the form, he inadvertently placed a second order, which placed a second charge on his credit card.

LESSON 7 Implementing History Methods

As most Web users know, you can click the Back button to return to a document you viewed earlier; after you click the Back button, you can click the Forward button to return to the page where you started. Providing the user with immediate access to multiple Web pages requires the browser to keep an internal history list of the pages the user has visited.

Each instance of the browser (each browser window) has a unique history list. If you start the browser by choosing it in the operating system, the history list is initially blank (in most browsers). If you create a new browser window by choosing File>New Window, the new browser window copies the history list from the original (already open) browser window.

JavaScript creates a **history** object for each open browser window. The ***history object*** allows you to access and manipulate the content of the browser's history list. You can use the **history** object to create Back and Forward buttons within a Web interface, which perform the same functions as the Back and Forward buttons in the browser.

Back()

The **back()** method of the **history** object allows you to change a browser window to a previous page in the history list. The following command changes the URL in the open browser window to the previous URL in the browser's history list.

```
history.back();
```

Incorporating an event handler with the **back()** method allows you to create a button that performs the same command as the browser's Back button. In the following example, you use the HTML **input** command to create the Back button.

```
<input type="button" value="Back" onclick="history.back()">
```

Forward()

The **forward()** method of the **history** object allows you to change a browser window to the next page in the history list. The following command changes the URL in the open browser window to the next entry in the browser's history list.

```
history.forward();
```

Go()

The **go()** method allows the browser to jump forward or backward anywhere in the history list. Passing a positive integer to the **go()** method allows you to jump forward in the history list. Passing a negative integer to the **go()** method allows you to jump backward in the history list. The following statement forces the browser to go back two pages in the history list.

```
history.go(-2);
```

The **go()** method is problematic in versions 2 and 3 of Netscape and version 3 of Internet Explorer. You should avoid using the **go()** method unless you can ensure that Web surfers will use version 4 or higher of these Web browsers.

In the following exercise, you use methods of the **history** object to create buttons in Web pages. Specifically, you add links to a simple Web site that allow the Web surfer to move backward and forward through the site — just as they would jump backward and forward when clicking the Back and Forward buttons in the Web browser interface.

Use the History Object to Create Buttons

1   In your text editor and Web browser, open page1.html from the WIP_09>history folder.

2   Examine the source code in your text editor and then view the page in your browser.

FIGURE 9.22

This site contains five pages. Each page contains links to the other four pages.

3   Click the links to see all five pages in the site.

Each page displays a title that identifies the page you are currently visiting.

4   Return to the open page1.html file in your text editor. Insert the following code.

```
...
<p><a href="page1.html">Page 1</a> | <a href="page2.html">Page
2</a> | <a href="page3.html">Page 3</a> | <a
href="page4.html">Page 4</a> | <a href="page5.html">Page 5 </a>
</p>
<p>This is page 1. </p>
<input type="button" value="Back" onclick="history.back()">
</body>
</html>
```

This code is using the HTML <input> tag to add a button that serves as a Back button. The same code has already been inserted into the other four pages of the site.

5   Insert the following code.

```
...
<p>This is page 1. </p>
<input type="button" value="Back" onclick="history.back()">
<input type="button" value="Forward" onclick="history.forward()">
</body>
</html>
```

This code creates a button that serves as a Forward button. The same code has already been inserted into the other four pages.

6   **Save the file in your text editor and refresh your browser.**

Back and Forward buttons should now appear on the page.

FIGURE 9.23

7   **Click the Page 2 link.**

The browser advances to the second page. The other pages in this folder have the code already included to create the back and forward buttons.

8   **Click the Back button on the page.**

The browser returns to the previous page in the history list (Page 1).

9   **Experiment by clicking various page links and then clicking the Back and Forward buttons you created.**

10   **Close the file in your text editor and browser.**

To Extend Your Knowledge . . .

SECURITY AND THE HISTORY OBJECT

The `history` object was originally designed to hold the names of all the URLs in the browser's history list. This capability allowed developers to read a list of sites users had recently visited — which quickly prompted privacy concerns from browser users. As one might expect, the feature was removed from newer browsers. In modern browsers, the `history` object does not allow anyone to determine the names of Web pages the user previously visited.

LESSON 8   Recognizing Other Methods and Properties

In previous chapters, you considered a number of methods, objects, and properties that are part of the **document** object. Consider the **document.write()** method as an example. This method outputs text to the browser; it is one of the simplest and most useful JavaScript methods.

A number of the **document** object components have not yet been covered in significant detail in this chapter or previous chapters in this book. A number of these items, such as the **form** and the **image** objects, are commonly used in JavaScript applications and require a great deal of explanation and practical examples — more than we can cover in the confines of this book. Even though complete discussion of the **applets** array, **forms** array, and **images** array, and **lastModified** property is outside the scope of the book, let's take a few moments to briefly review these elements as a matter of reference.

The Applets Array

You can use the Java programming language to create **applets**, which are self-contained computer programs often used on Web sites. The **<applet>** tag was previously used in HTML to use an applet within a Web page. This tag was deprecated in HTML 4.01 and will not be available in future versions of XHTML. The JavaScript **applets array** creates an **applet** element every time the **<applet>** tag is added to an HTML document. Newer scripts will use the **<object>** tag to insert an applet into an HTML page.

The Forms Array

Every time the **<form>** and **</form>** tags are used in an HTML document, JavaScript creates a corresponding object in the **forms** array. The **form** object is a sub-object of the **document** object. The **form** object also has sub-objects associated with each part of the form. These objects are known as **form elements**; each form element represents one portion of a form — such as a radio button or text area.

The Images Array

Whenever you use an **<img>** tag in HTML, a corresponding entry is made in JavaScript within the **images** array. You can use the entries in the **images** array to create image rollovers and manipulate images to create animations. Each element of the **images** array contains information about an **image** object, and each **image** object represents an image shown on the page.

The LastModified Property

When you save an HTML to disk, the date and time are stored within the **lastModified** property. For example, you can write the following code to display the last time a page was updated.

```
document.write("Document last updated: " + document.lastModified);
```

The **lastModified** property is useful for pages containing time-sensitive information. For example, let's consider a Web page that lists employment opportunities. As excellent job opportunities are usually filled quickly, job seekers need to know when a position was posted. With this necessary information, job seekers can decide whether to expend the energy applying for (and getting excited about) the opportunity. Including the **lastModified** property on the page allows users to know when the page was last updated and make educated decisions based on that information.

Document Object Methods

The **document** object has four primary methods: **open()**, **close()**, **write()**, and **writeln()**. Earlier in the book, you examined each of these methods. As you may remember, the **open()** and **close()** methods are also methods of the **window** object.

Even though they are considered methods of both objects, the **open()** and **close()** methods have the same attributes whether they are written as methods of a **window** object, such as **adWindow.close();**, or written as methods of the **document** object, such as **document.close();**.

The first code example closes the window named **adWindow**. The second code example closes the current document. The current document is the document where the code exists.

Write() and Writeln()

You used the **write()** and **writeln()** methods repeatedly throughout this book. Both methods output text to the browser window. Unlike the **write()** method, the **writeln()** method adds a new line character to the end of the text.

```
document.writeln("Hi World!");
```

When using newer browsers, the **writeln()** method may simply add a space instead of inserting a new line. Even though you specifically insert a new line character into a page, the browser ignores the character — just as HTML ignores new line characters when you press the Enter/Return key to go to the start of the next line.

Use the LastModified Property

1   **In your browser, open lastmodified.html from the WIP_09 folder.**

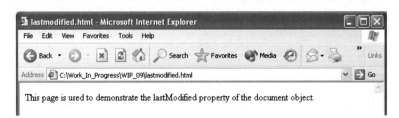

FIGURE 9.24

2   **Open the file in your text editor.**

3   **Insert the following code.**

```
. . .
<p>This page is used to demonstrate the lastModified property of
the document object. </p>
<script language="JavaScript" type="text/javascript">
// insert code here
document.write("This document was last modified
"+document.lastModified);
</script>
</body>
</html>
```

The lastModified property is not supported in the Safari browser.

4 **Save the document in your text editor.**

5 **Refresh the document in your browser.**

FIGURE 9.25

The date and time when the file was last saved to disk appears.

6 **Close the file in your browser and text editor.**

CAREERS IN DESIGN

Document Object Properties

Professional portfolio Web sites include consistent color schemes and themes. For example, you may choose a theme that suggests the rugged feel of an old mining town and then create an interface that supports that theme. As part of this process, you should choose a color scheme that reinforces your theme while it ensures text and hyperlinks remain easy to read.

After you choose a color scheme, you can use properties of the **document** object to improve the consistency, professionalism, and ease of maintenance associated with your online portfolio. Simply create a function in an external file and set the color properties of text, the background color, and hyperlinks (visited, active, and regular links). Then, create a script that links to the external file and triggers the function. Including this script in the head section of every page allows you to ensure the pages are formatted consistently. This method also allows you to quickly modify the pages in your site — simply edit the external file, and the changes take effect on every page.

S U M M A R Y

In this chapter, you explored the organization of the **document** object, as well as the objects that exist within the **document** object. You also considered the methods and properties of the **document** object — which are the most commonly used aspects of JavaScript — including the **title** property, the **lastModified** property, and the **location** property.

You found that properties of a **link** object are used to store information about the link: the **href** property represents the entire URL created by an **<a>** tag; the **innerHTML** property stores the text displayed between the **<a>** and **</a>** tag; and the **target** property represents the **target** attribute of the **<a>** tag.

You discovered that the **anchors** array represents text anchors in the HTML document. Text anchors are useful for creating internal links in HTML documents, which is particularly useful when you create glossaries or FAQ pages. You learned that the **anchors** array and **links** array both represent hyperlinks and can often be used interchangeably.

In the discussion on the **location** object, you learned how to apply several methods to change the file currently loaded into the browser. You learned to use the **reload()** method to force the browser to reload the current document, and you used the **replace()** method to force the browser to load a new document and delete the old document's entry in the browser's history list.

You discovered that the **history** object represents the browser's history list. You learned that the primary methods of the history object are **back()** and **forward()**. You can use these methods to create buttons (or links) that imitate the Back and Forward buttons in the browser's standard interface.

K E Y   T E R M S

Anchor	Form element	Location object
Anchor object	Forms array	Location property
Anchors array	Hexadecimal number	Pathname
Applet	History object	RGB color
Applets array	Hypertext reference	URL parameter
Array	Link object	
Deprecated command	Links array	

CHECKING CONCEPTS AND TERMS

MULTIPLE CHOICE

Circle the letter that matches the correct answer for each of the following questions.

1. Which attribute of the HTML **<body>** tag is represented by the *fgColor* property of the *document* object?
   a. vlink
   b. link
   c. text
   d. alink
   e. None of the above.

2. Which attribute of the HTML **<body>** tag is represented by the **bgColor** property of the **document** object?
   a. background color
   b. link
   c. bgcolor
   d. None of the above.

3. Which attribute of the HTML **<body>** tag is represented by the **vlinkColor** property of the **document** object?
   a. vlink
   b. link
   c. visitedColor
   d. None of the above.

4. What does the **links** array represent?
   a. Images in the HTML page
   b. The **<body>** tag
   c. Every hyperlink in the HTML document
   d. Layers

5. What does the **search** property of a **link** object represent?
   a. Results from a search engine
   b. The content of a text box in a form
   c. A search string appended to a URL
   d. The target attribute of an **<a>** tag

6. What does the **title** property of the **document** object represent?
   a. The object name of a browser window
   b. The **name** attribute of the **<body>** tag
   c. The text between the **<title>** and **</title>** tags in HTML
   d. Text from a text area in an HTML form

7. Why should developers avoid using the **URL** property?
   a. It creates a new browser window before loading a file.
   b. It does not force the browser to change to a new page.
   c. It is not compatible with Netscape Navigator browsers.
   d. It is not compatible with Internet Explorer browsers.

8. What does the **protocol** property of the **links** object represent?
   a. A string method for finding matching text
   b. The protocol in hyperlinks, such as http: or ftp:
   c. The type of Internet connection used by the browser, such as wireless or dial-up
   d. A search string appended to a URL, such as **?item=43**

9. What does the **innerHTML** property of the **link** object represent?
   a. The text between **<a>** and **</a>** tags
   b. The HTML code in an associated Web page
   c. A tag nested within another tag
   d. HTML code contained in a JavaScript event handler

10. In JavaScript, what does the **anchors** array represent?

a. The hide source property

b. The end of each HTML document in the Web site

c. Every text anchor in the HTML document

d. Every image in the document

DISCUSSION QUESTIONS

1. What is the difference between a **link** object and the **links** array? Why are arrays useful for interacting with objects that are part of the DOM?

2. How are properties of objects (such as the **href** property) related to attributes of HTML tags (such as the **href** attribute of the **<a>** tag)?

3. You can force the browser to load a new document by changing the **location** property, **URL** property, or the **location.href** property. If you were asked to write a script that loads a new document, which property would you use? Why?

4. What does the **images** array represent? Why is the **image** object useful?

5. How do the **reload()** and **replace()** methods differ? Name a situation when you would want to use **reload(true)** instead of **reload()**.

SKILL DRILL

Skill Drill exercises reinforce chapter skills. Each skill reinforced is the same (or nearly the same) as a skill presented in the chapter. Detailed instructions are provided in a step-by-step format. You should work through the Skill Drills in order.

1. Change the Default Link Colors

In this Skill Drill, you change the default link colors. These properties of the **document** object allow you to change the default colors for hyperlinks, active links, and visited links. Once changed, all links on the page appear in nonstandard colors.

1. In your browser, open skilllinkcolors.html from the WIP_09 folder.

    This page contains links to various JavaScript resource sites.

FIGURE 9.26

2. Open the file in your text editor and find the following line of code.

```
// insert code here
```

3. On the next line, change the **linkColor** property of the **document** object to "**#990000**" (burgundy).

4. Insert another line and change the **alinkColor** property of the **document** object to "**#990099**" (lavender).

5. Create another line of code that changes the visited links color to "**#CC9900**" (orange).

6. Save the file in your text editor and refresh your browser.

   The link colors should change.

FIGURE 9.27

7. Keep the file open for the next Skill Drill.

2. Use the Target Property

1. In the open skilllinkcolors.html in your browser, click one of the links.

   The page redirects to another site.

2. Click the Back button to return to the skilllinkcolors.html page.

3. Find the following line of code.

```
<p><a href="http://devedge.netscape.com/central/
javascript">JavaScript Central</a> </p>
```

4. Insert the following code. Be careful not to insert a new line character in the code.

```
...
<p><a href="http://www.javascript.com"
target="_self">JavaScript.com</a></p>
<p><a href="http://javascriptkit.com">JavaScript Kit</a></p>
<p><a href="http://www.computerarts.co.uk">Computer Arts</a></p>
<p><a href="#" onclick="document.links[0].target='_blank';
document.links[1].target='_blank';
document.links[2].target='_blank';">Open links in a new
window</a>
</body>
</html>
```

5. Save the file in your text editor and refresh your browser.

6. Click the "Open links in a new window" hyperlink.

7. Click another link.

   The page should open in a second browser window instead of opening in the existing browser window.

8. Close the file in your text editor and close both browser windows.

3. Add Date Content

1. In your browser and text editor, open skilllastmodified.html from the WIP_09 folder.

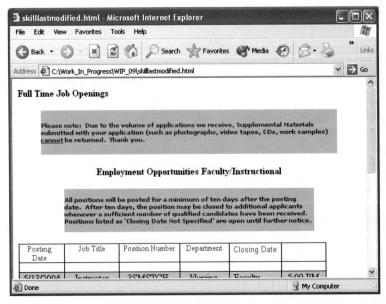

FIGURE 9.28

This page contains a list of job openings at a community college.

2. Find the following code in the head of the document.

```
<script language="JavaScript" type="text/javascript">
// insert code here
```

3. Insert a statement to output the date when the document was last modified, as it appears in the following illustration. You must use the **lastModified** property to complete this task.

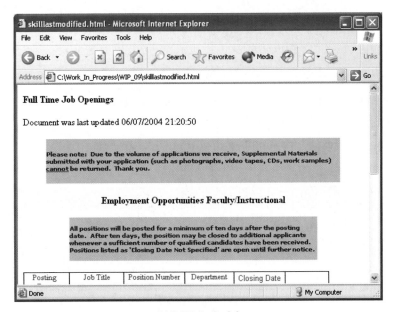

FIGURE 9.29

4. Save the file in your text editor.

5. Refresh the file in your browser to make sure it works correctly.

6. Close the file in your browser and text editor.

4. Use the InnerHTML Property

1. In your text editor, open skillinner.html from the WIP_09 folder.

2. On the line after the **<body>** tag, insert the following code to create a hyperlink.

```
. . .
<title>skillinner.html</title>
</head>
<body>
<a href="#">hyperlink</a>
</body>
</html>
```

3. Create a blank line after the line you just inserted. Insert a script between the `</a>` and `</body>` tags.

4. In the script, insert the following code to create a variable.

```
theLink=prompt("Enter a site you would like to visit","");
```

5. On the next line, insert the following code to set the **innerHTML** property of the hyperlink to the same value as the variable.

```
document.links[0].innerHTML=theLink;
```

6. On the next line, insert the following line of code to add the protocol to the variable value.

```
theLink="http://"+theLink;
```

7. Use the following pseudocode to write the next line of code.

```
make the href property of the first hyperlink equal to the
variable called theLink;
```

8. Save the file in your text editor and open the file in your browser.

FIGURE 9.30

9. Enter "www.web-answers.com" and click OK.

The hyperlink changes to www.web-answers.com.

FIGURE 9.31

10. Click the hyperlink.

The page changes to the Web Answers Web page.

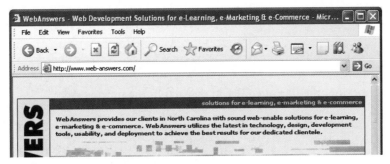

FIGURE 9.32

11. Close the file in your browser and text editor.

CHALLENGE

Challenge exercises expand on (or are somewhat related to) skills presented in the lessons. Each exercise provides a brief introduction, followed by instructions presented in a numbered-step format that are not as detailed as those in the Skill Drill exercises. You can work through one or more exercises in any order.

1. Apply Link Properties

You decided to explore the various aspects of the **link** object. In this Challenge, you write a script to examine a hyperlink. Your script will create a detailed report of the various properties of the link.

1. In your text editor, open challengelink.html from the WIP_09 folder. Examine the code.

2. Open the file in your browser.

FIGURE 9.33

3. Insert the following line of code to output the **href** property of the link to the user.

```
...
<a href="http://www.web-answers.com/booklist.asp?c=3"
target="_blank">Web Answers</a>
<script language="JavaScript" type="text/javascript">
// insert code here
```

```
document.write("href property "+document.links[0].href+"<br />");
</script>
</body>
</html>
```

4. Insert a blank line after the line of code you inserted in the previous step.

5. Using Step 3 as a guide, create a line of code to output the **pathname** property of the link to the user.

6. Insert another blank line. Using Step 3 as a guide, create a line of code to output the **target** property of the link to the user.

7. Insert another blank line. Using Step 3 as a guide, create a line of code to output the **protocol** property of the link to the user.

8. Insert another blank line. Using Step 3 as your guide, create a line of code to output the **innerHTML** property of the link to the user.

9. Insert another blank line. Using Step 3 as a guide, create a line of code to output the **search** property of the link to the user.

10. Save the file in your text editor and refresh your browser.

    Assuming you entered the code correctly, your screen should match the following illustration.

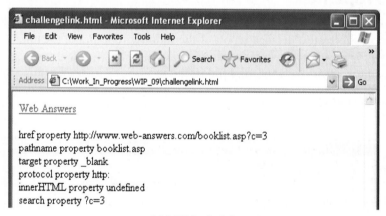

FIGURE 9.34

11. Close the file in your browser and text editor.

2. Use History Object Methods

You are designing a Web site for a college professor. The site will include a main page for each subject, one page for each week of homework, and a page for each project. We included three pages of the site for you to modify. Use **history** object methods to enhance the navigation of this site.

1. In your browser, open fundofauth.html from the WIP_09>challengehistory folder.

   You use the files in this folder throughout this Challenge. This is the main page for a class titled, "Fundamentals of Authoring."

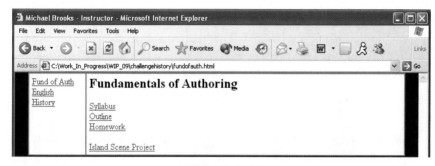

FIGURE 9.35

2. Click the Island Scene Project link.

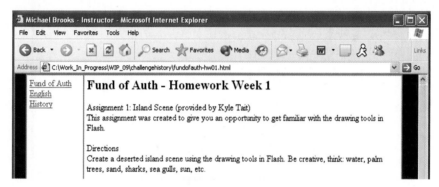

FIGURE 9.36

This page includes the Island Scene assignment, which is also the homework for the first week of class. Links to other subjects (English and History) do not work, since these pages were not included in the resource folder.

3. Click the browser's Back button.

The page returns to the main page of the Fundamentals of Authoring class.

4. Click the Homework link.

The page advances to the main homework page for this subject.

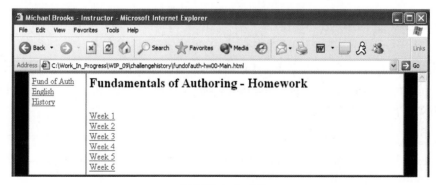

FIGURE 9.37

5.   Click the Week 1 link.

This is the only homework page provided. This returns you to the page for the Island Scene assignment, which is the homework for the first week of class. At this point, you should notice that you can reach the page from the main page for the class or from the main homework page.

6.   Open fundofauth-hw00-Main.html in your text editor.

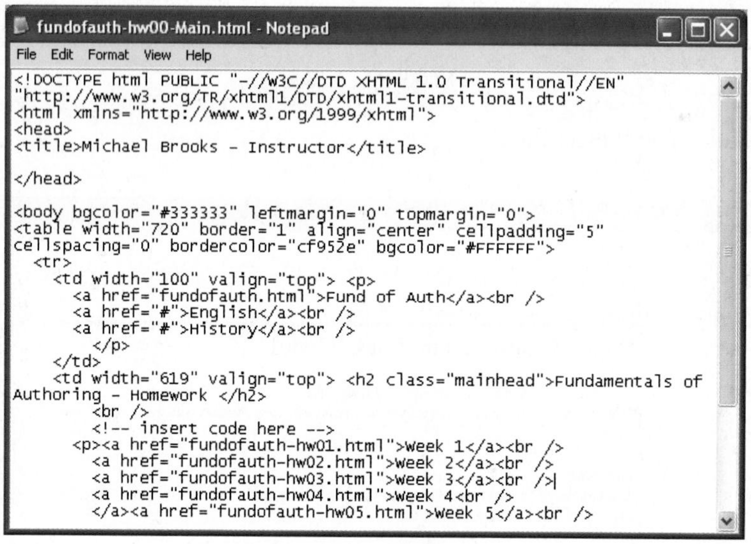

```
 fundofauth-hw00-Main.html - Notepad
File  Edit  Format  View  Help
<!DOCTYPE html PUBLIC "-//W3C//DTD XHTML 1.0 Transitional//EN"
"http://www.w3.org/TR/xhtml1/DTD/xhtml1-transitional.dtd">
<html xmlns="http://www.w3.org/1999/xhtml">
<head>
<title>Michael Brooks - Instructor</title>

</head>

<body bgcolor="#333333" leftmargin="0" topmargin="0">
<table width="720" border="1" align="center" cellpadding="5"
cellspacing="0" bordercolor="cf952e" bgcolor="#FFFFFF">
  <tr>
    <td width="100" valign="top"> <p>
      <a href="fundofauth.html">Fund of Auth</a><br />
      <a href="#">English</a><br />
      <a href="#">History</a><br />
        </p>
    </td>
    <td width="619" valign="top"> <h2 class="mainhead">Fundamentals of
Authoring - Homework </h2>
      <br />
      <!-- insert code here -->
    <p><a href="fundofauth-hw01.html">Week 1</a><br />
      <a href="fundofauth-hw02.html">Week 2</a><br />
      <a href="fundofauth-hw03.html">Week 3</a><br />|
      <a href="fundofauth-hw04.html">Week 4<br />
      </a><a href="fundofauth-hw05.html">Week 5</a><br />
```

FIGURE 9.38

7.   Find the following code, which appears 20 lines down from the top of the page.

```
<!-- insert code here -->
```

8.   At the end of this line of code, insert the following.

```
. . .
<td width="619" valign="top"> <h2 class="mainhead"> Fundamentals
of Authoring - Homework </h2>
     <br />
     <!-- insert code here --> <a href="#">back..</a>
     <p><a href="fundofauth-hw01.html">Week 1</a><br />
     <a href="fundofauth-hw02.html">Week 2</a><br />
     <a href="fundofauth-hw03.html">Week 3</a><br />
. . .
```

9.   Within the **<a>** tag you just created, use inline JavaScript to trigger the **back()** method of the **history** object when the **onclick** event is detected.

10.   Save the file in your text editor.

11.   In your text editor, open fundofauth-hw01.html and find the following line of code. It appears 15 lines down from the top of the document.)

```
<!-- insert code here -->
```

12. Create a hyperlink that takes the user back one step in the history list.

    Hint: use the same code you inserted in Steps 8 and 9.

13. Save the file in your text editor.

14. Refresh the open fundofauth-hw01.html in your browser.

    A back link appears.

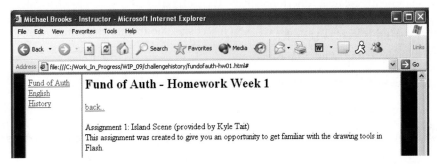

FIGURE 9.39

15. Click the Back link.

    The page returns to the previous page in the history list. A working Back button should also appear on this page. Each Back button takes a user back to the previous page, regardless of how they reached the current page.

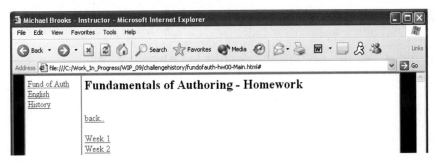

FIGURE 9.40

16. Close all files in your text editor and browser.

3. Add Random Links

You are creating a page that includes hyperlinks to your favorite Web sites. In this Challenge, you write a script that randomly picks one of these links and takes the user to one of the Web sites listed.

1. In your text editor, open challengerandomlink.html from the WIP_09 folder.

2. Find the following line of code.

```
<a href="#">random hyperlink</a>
```

3. In this line of code, use the **onclick** event handler to trigger a function called "**pickLink()**".

   The function does not accept any values.

4. Find the following line of code.

```
// insert function here
```

5. After this statement, create a function called "**pickLink()**".

   The function does not accept any values. You insert statements into the function in the following steps.

6. Insert the following line inside the function.

```
theNumber=Math.round(Math.random()*2);
```

   This code generates the number 0, 1, or 2.

7. On the next line, create an alert to output the value stored in the variable named **theNumber**.

   For example, if the number 1 returns, the user would see the following alert box.

FIGURE 9.41

8. On the next line, insert the following code.

```
document.location=document.links[theNumber];
```

   This code sets the **location** property to one of the three hyperlinks on the page.

9. Save the file in your text editor.

10. Open the file in your browser.

FIGURE 9.42

11. Click random hyperlink.

   The script picks one of the first three hyperlinks at random and redirects to that page.

12. Click the Back button in your browser to return the challengerandomlink.html page.

13. Close the file in your browser and text editor.

4. Create Dynamic Color Schemes

You decided to create a system where a Web page user can pick his own color scheme and customize his online experience. You start by giving the user two choices. When the user picks a color scheme, the page changes to indicate the new scheme — including background color, text color, and link colors.

1. In your text editor and browser, open challengecolorscheme.html from the WIP_09 folder.

FIGURE 9.43

2. Find the following line of code.

   ```
   <p><a href="#">Night</a></p>
   ```

3. Modify this line of code to trigger a function and pass the word "**night**" to the function.

   ```
   <p><a href="#" onclick="changeColor('night')">Night</a></p>
   ```

4. Find the following line of code.

   ```
   <p><a href="#">Lipstick</a></p>
   ```

5. Modify this line of code to trigger the same function when the user clicks the link, but pass the word "**lipstick**" to the function.

6. Find the following line of code in the head of the document.

   ```
   // insert function here
   ```

7. Insert the following code to create a function and to allow the function to receive a variable value.

   ```
   ...
   <title>challengecolorscheme.html</title>
   <script language="JavaScript" type="text/javascript">
   // insert function here
   ```

```
function colorChange(scheme) {
} // end function
</script>
</head>
. . .
```

8. In the function, insert the following code to create a decision statement.

```
. . .
<script language="JavaScript" type="text/javascript">
// insert function here
function colorChange(scheme) {
        if (scheme=="night") {
        document.bgColor="#000066";
        document.fgColor="#FFFFFF";
        document.linkColor="#FF3399";
        document.aLinkColor="#FF33FF";
        document.vLinkColor="#000033";
        } // end if
} // end function
</script>
</head>
. . .
```

This statement sets various color values if the user chooses the night color scheme.

9. Create a second **if** statement before the end of the function that checks to see if the user chooses lipstick as the color scheme.

    Hint: use the code entered in Step 8 as a guide.

10. In the **if** statement you created in Step 9, set the background color to "**#FF3399**", set the foreground color to "**#000033**", set the link color to "**#339933**", set the active link color to "**#006600**", and set the visited links color to "**#000066**".

11. Save the file in your text editor and refresh your browser.

12. Choose the Night color scheme.

FIGURE 9.44

The page changes to the new color scheme.

13. Choose the Lipstick color scheme.

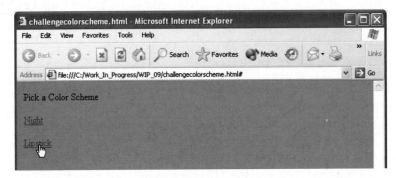

FIGURE 9.45

The color scheme changes again.

14. Close the file in your browser and text editor.

PORTFOLIO BUILDER

Change File Name and Color Scheme

You were hired as the lead designer for a corporate Web site. The company asked you to build a new site to replace their aging and less-than-professional-looking Web site. The site will represent a small company that has enjoyed recent success. Due to this success, you are their first full-time Web designer.

The company recently advertised their existing URL in a number of promotional materials. Your first job is to redirect users to a newer Web page with a different file name. Then, establish a master file to control the color scheme of every page in the new Web site.

1.   Open oldsite.html from the WIP_09>Portfolio_Builder_09 folder. Create a script in this file that changes the currently loaded document to index.html and deletes the old entry from the history list. (Hint: use the **replace()** method).

2.   Create a new text file and save it as "colors.js" in the same directory as the Web site. Create a function named "**setColors()**". The function should perform the following tasks:

- Set the **bgColor** property of the document to black (**#000000**)

- Set the **linkColor** property of the document to silver (**#CCCCCC**)

- Set the **vlinkColor** property of the document to (**#FF0000**)

- Set the **fgColor** property of the document to gray (**#333333**)

3.   Open index.html in your text editor. Add a script to link the external file (colors.js) to the existing file. In this script, call on the **setColors()** function.

4.   Open oldsite.html in your browser. The browser should redirect to index.html and you should see your new color scheme.

5.   As a final step, search the Web for appealing color schemes. Modify your external function to a new color scheme that matches the theme of the site.

CHAPTER 10

Exploring the Window Object

OBJECTIVES

In this chapter, you learn how to:

- Implement status bar properties
- Use screen properties
- Move and resize windows

- Control scrolling
- Work with frames
- Redirect users to a frameset

Why Would I Do This?

The **window** object is the highest level object in the Browser Object Model. For every browser window you create, an instance of the **window** object is also created. In previous chapters, you used JavaScript to generate alert boxes, open new browser windows, and display text information in various windows. You also learned how to apply special attributes to new **window** objects. For example, the following line of code creates a pop-up window with specific **name**, **height**, and **width** properties.

```
myWin=window.open("http://www.web-
answers.com","myWin","height=420,width=760");
```

In the chapter that focused on working with pop-up windows, you discovered how to control several aspects of the **window** object, including its resolution. You learned how to use JavaScript to blur and focus a window, open and close a window, as well as detect when a user moves his mouse over an element on the page.

In another chapter, you learned how to detect events associated with **window** objects. Most events bound to **<body>** tags are associated with the entire browser window. For example, you can use the following code to detect when a page loads and trigger the **myFunc()** function.

```
<body onload="myFunc()">
```

Given the ability to complete all of these varied tasks, you should have a significant appreciation for the usefulness of the **window** object and its associated methods, properties, and event handlers. In this chapter, you consider the advanced features of the **window** object. During this discussion, you learn to resize windows, move windows, control the browser's status bar, partition windows into frames, and manually control scrolling.

VISUAL SUMMARY

Certain objects, such as the **location** and **history** objects, are part of both the **document** object and the **window** object. The **document** object is the most useful aspect of the **window** object. Other useful aspects of the **window** object include the **screen** object and **frames** object. In this chapter, you study these and other aspects of the **window** object.

The *screen object* represents the user's computer screen. You can use properties of this object to determine the current width and height resolution (in pixels) of the user's computer screen. On most Windows machines, you can change the screen resolution by accessing the Display Properties dialog box in the Control panel. The Display Properties dialog box varies slightly from one system to the next, depending on the user's video card, exact operating system, and settings.

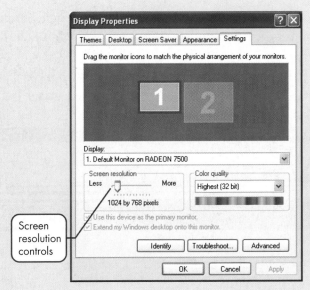

FIGURE 10.1

In this example, the user applied a resolution of 1024 pixels wide by 768 pixels high. The user can raise or lower the screen resolution at any time, depending on personal preferences and the application in use. It remains a challenge to design Web pages that look good at any resolution; using screen properties, however, you can adapt to different screen resolutions and various browser window sizes accordingly. Not only does screen resolution play a part in the appearance of a Web page, it is also a factor when determining proper placement of a pop-up window.

A single browser window can contain multiple HTML documents. A *frameset* is an HTML file that divides the browser window into sections and displays different HTML files in each of the sections. A

FIGURE 10.2

frame is an HTML page displayed with other HTML pages in a single browser window. Consider the figure shown on the previous page (independencehummer.com) as an example of a frameset site.

The first file loaded on this site is the frameset file. This file causes the other pages to load, including the top navigation page.

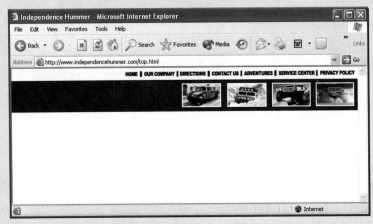

FIGURE 10.3

The frameset also causes the left navigation page to load.

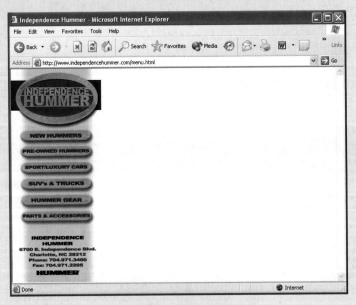

FIGURE 10.4

The content of the site loads last. The content is placed in a separate file that includes no branding and no navigation structures.

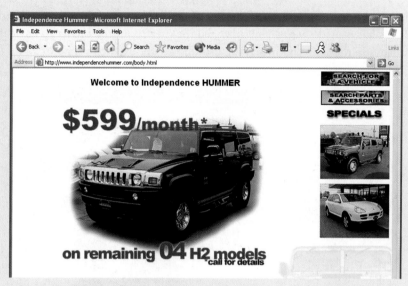

FIGURE 10.5

Frames offer several advantages, as well as several disadvantages. In this chapter, you study the positive and negative aspects of frames and frameset pages and learn how they interact with JavaScript.

LESSON 1 Implementing Status Bar Properties

Most browsers have a status bar that appears in the lower-left corner of the browser window. In newer browsers, the status bar is turned off by default. In Internet Explorer 6, you can turn on the status bar by choosing View>Status Bar.

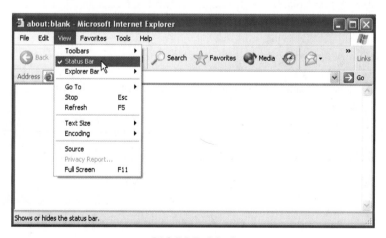

FIGURE 10.6

The status bar is designed to enhance the *usability* of Web pages — which simply means to make Web pages easier to use. The status bar provides visual clues that tell the user about the browser's navigation. In most Web browsers, a URL displays in the status bar when the user moves her mouse over a link.

FIGURE 10.7

HTML does not allow the user to change or control aspects of the status bar. In contrast, JavaScript allows developers to manipulate the messages that display in the status bar. To do so, programmers use the **status** and **defaultStatus** properties of the **window** object. Mac users should note that status bar properties do not work on Internet Explorer 5.2 for the Mac.

The DefaultStatus Property

The **defaultStatus** property places text messages within the status bar. The following line of code places the message "Welcome to our site" as the default message in the status bar:

```
window.defaultStatus="Welcome to our Site";
```

As you might expect, the property can also be detected and used in JavaScript code.

```
document.write("The message in the status bar is "+defaultStatus);
```

Using these two statements together, you receive the following result in the browser.

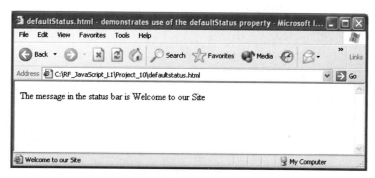

FIGURE 10.8

The Status Property

The **status** property consists of a string that temporarily displays in the browser's status window. After a brief period, the string in the **defaultStatus** property replaces the temporary message. This feature is especially useful when you want to add explanatory copy to a choice the user can make.

For example, let's assume you rent hotel rooms from your Web site. The rooms come in three varieties, each of which has its own price. The user can choose from three options: Ocean Front, Ocean View, or Adjoining. When the user rolls over a button, you can detect the mouse rollover and set the **status** property to display additional explanatory copy. Assuming the user rolls over the button for an Adjoining room, you could provide the following explanation in the status bar.

```
status = "Adjoining rooms are a short walk to the beach."
```

When you place a status message on an image or hyperlink, you control the message temporarily — such as when the user moves the mouse over a hyperlink. This action requires the **return** keyword to work correctly, the event handlers to trigger, and the event handlers to reset the original message. Consider the following code as an example.

```
<a href="products.html" onmouseover="window.status='Learn About Our
Products!';return true" onmouseout="window.status='';">Products Page</a>
```

Notice how the **status** property is assigned two single quotes when the **onmouseout** event is detected. These quotes set the status message to a null value when the **ononmouseout** event is detected. In computer language terms, *null* means that the property or value exists, but has no assigned value. When the **status** property is set to null, the **defaultStatus** property displays in the browser.

Implement a Default Status Message

1   **Copy the content of the RF_JavaScript_L1>Chapter_10 folder to the Work_In_Progress>WIP_10 folder.**

2   **In your text editor, open status.html from the WIP_10 folder.**

3   Insert the following code.

```
...
<script language="JavaScript" type="text/javascript">
// insert code here
defaultStatus="Welcome to our site!";
</script>
</body>
</html>
```

This code creates a default message that displays in the browser's status bar.

4   Save the file in your text editor and open it in your browser.

FIGURE 10.9

A default message appears in the status bar. You must turn on the status bar in your browser to see this message. In IE 6, you can turn on this feature by choosing View>Status Bar. Some status bar properties, including this one, may not work on Mac versions of IE.

5   Keep the file open in your browser and text editor for the next exercise.

Create Temporary Status Messages

1   In the open status.html in your browser, move your mouse over the About Us Page link.

FIGURE 10.10

The browser displays the URL of the hyperlink. Most browsers do this by default.

2   Move your mouse away from the link.

FIGURE 10.11

The default message you created in the previous exercise reappears.

3   In your text editor, find the following line of code.

```
<a href="aboutus.html">About Us Page</a>
```

4   **Insert the following inline code into this statement.**

```
<a href="aboutus.html" onmouseover="window.status='Learn About
Us';return true" onmouseout="window.status='';">About Us Page</a>
```

Make sure you use two single quotes to set the status for the **onmouseout** event (**window. status='';**).

5   **Save the file in your text editor.**

6   **Refresh the file in your browser.**

7   **Move your mouse over the About Us Page hyperlink.**

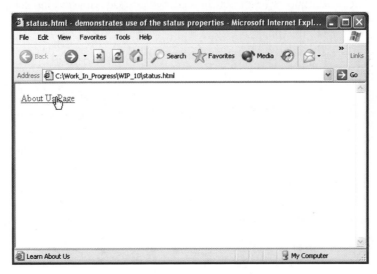

FIGURE 10.12

While your mouse is over the link, the status message should change.

8   **Move your mouse off the hyperlink.**

The message should revert to the default message.

9   **Close the file in your browser and text editor.**

To Extend Your Knowledge . . .

STATUS MESSAGES IN NETSCAPE NAVIGATOR

Due to event-firing issues, Netscape Navigator 6.x browsers do not use the `status` property correctly. To use this property in Netscape browsers, you need a timer to offset the firing problem. For example, in the `onmouseover` event, you can trigger the following code.

```
setTimeout("status='Hello'",0);
```

When the user moves the mouse off the link (`onmouseout`), you can trigger the following code.

```
setTimeout("status=''",0);
```

This fix requires an understanding of timers and loops, which goes beyond the scope of this chapter.

LESSON 2   Moving and Resizing Windows

Various methods in JavaScript allow you to resize and move browser windows, which in turn provide new possibilities for browser interaction. For example, consider that pop-up windows usually appear by default in the upper-left corner of the browser window. Once open, a pop-up window hides the content presented on the main browser page. In the following illustration, a vision-care facility added a pop-up window to their Web site to advertise a special sale. Notice how the pop-up interferes with the user's ability to see the company logo and the primary content on the page.

FIGURE 10.13

One possible solution involves multiple **window** object methods and properties. For example, you could change the size of the main window to use more of the available screen resolution. You could also move the pop-up window to a more attractive (and effective) location.

FIGURE 10.14

Window sizes and window locations are measured in pixels. You can place a window in a precise location by specifying x-coordinates and y-coordinates. An ***x-coordinate*** represents the number of pixels from the left corner of the screen. A ***y-coordinate*** represents the number of pixels from the top of the screen. For example, using pseudocode, you can move a window in the following fashion.

```
moveTo(x-coordinate, y-coordinate);
```

The upper-left corner of the screen is position (**0,0**), with both the x- and y-coordinate equal to "**0**." If you move a window 10 pixels to the right, the new position would be (**10,0**), with the x-coordinate equal to "**10**," and the y-coordinate remaining at "**0**." In this lesson, you consider methods that allow you to move and resize **window** objects.

ResizeBy()

The **resizeBy()** method resizes a window by a specific number of pixels. For example, the following statement makes the browser window 15 pixels wider and 10 pixels taller.

```
self.resizeBy(15,10);
```

The following statement reduces the size of the browser window by the same number of pixels.

```
self.resizeBy(-15,-10);
```

ResizeTo()

The **resizeTo()** method allows you to change the browser window to a width and height that you specify. The entire browser window, including toolbars and buttons, reset to the width and height you specify in the code. It is important to note this, since the values you specify include all areas of the browser window, not only the display area.

```
//the next statement changes the width to 300 and height to 350
self.resizeTo(300,350);
```

As a general rule, it's a good idea to size the window when it opens, rather than resize the window after the user starts reading the page (but the latter method can be useful in certain situations).

MoveBy()

The **moveBy()** method allows you to move the current browser window by a specific number of pixels. The following command moves the current browser window by 40 pixels to the right and 35 pixels down from its current position.

```
self.moveBy(40,35);
```

When you specify negative numbers, you move the browser window to the left and up. For security purposes, most Web browsers do not allow you to move a window off the edge of the screen.

MoveTo()

The **moveTo()** method moves the browser window to a specific location on the screen. Assuming you want to place the current window in the upper-left corner of the screen, you could specify the following.

```
self.moveTo(0,0);
```

Resize a Window

| **1** | In your text editor, open resize.html from the WIP_10 folder. |

| **2** | Insert the following code statement. |

```
...
<a href="#">Make Larger</a>
<script language="JavaScript" type="text/javascript">
//insert code here
self.resizeTo(250,200);
</script>
</body>
</html>
```

| **3** | Save the file in your text editor. |

| **4** | Open the file in your browser. |

The window resizes to 250 pixels wide and 200 pixels high.

FIGURE 10.15

5   Keep the file open in your text editor and browser for the next exercise.

Resize a Window Incrementally

1   In the open resize.html file in your text editor, find the following line of code.

```
<a href="#">Make Larger</a>
```

2   Insert the following inline code into the statement.

```
<a href="#" onclick="resizeBy(15,10);">Make Larger</a>
```

3   Save the file in your text editor.

4   Choose View>Refresh to refresh the file in your browser.

FIGURE 10.16

5   Click the hyperlink.

The browser window gets 15 pixels wider and 10 pixels taller.

6   Continue to click the link until you can see the entire URL in the Address field.

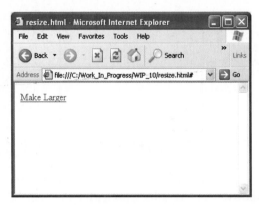

FIGURE 10.17

| **7** | **Close the file in your browser and text editor.** |

To Extend Your Knowledge . . .

SIZING WINDOWS

As a general rule, you should use the `width` and `height` parameters of the `open()` method to size windows when they open. Using the `resizeTo()` method can confuse some users.

LESSON 3   Using Screen Properties

The **screen** object represents the user's computer screen. This object contains useful properties designed to determine information about the screen settings on the client's computer. Using advanced techniques, you can use JavaScript to determine the size of the client's current screen resolution and load a page that looks best at that particular screen size.

You can use the following code to ask JavaScript to display the dimensions of the current screen resolution. Figure 10.18 shows you that the client's monitor is set at a resolution of 1024 by 768. (Some of the screen area was used for the Windows task bar at the bottom of the screen, which reduced the reported number by 30 pixels.)

```
document.write("The screen width is "+screen.availWidth);
document.write("The screen height is "+screen.availHeight);
```

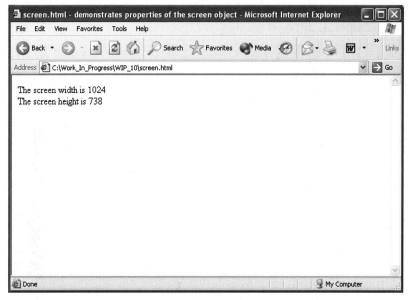

FIGURE 10.18

Use Screen Properties

1   In your text editor, open screen.html from the WIP_10 folder.

2   Insert the following lines of code.

```
...
<body>
<script language="JavaScript" type="text/javascript">
// insert code here
document.write("The screen width is " +screen.availWidth+"
<br />");
document.write("The screen height is "+screen.availHeight);
</script>
</body>
</html>
```

3   Save the file in your text editor.

4   Open the file in your browser.

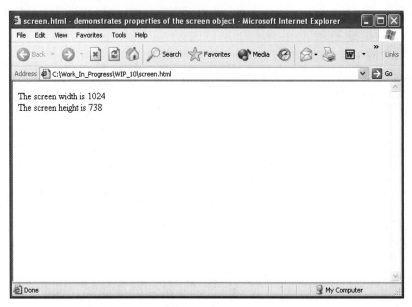

FIGURE 10.19

The screen properties return to the user. Your results may vary slightly, depending on your screen resolution and the amount of space used by the Windows task bar.

5   **Close the file in your browser and text editor.**

To Extend Your Knowledge . . .

THE SCREEN OBJECT

Don't confuse screen properties such as `availHeight` and `availWidth` with the actual size of the browser window. These properties are only relevant to the size of the browser window if the browser window occupies the entire screen.

LESSON 4   Controlling Scrolling

In addition to many other useful features, Web pages can expand as necessary to include additional information. In normal HTML pages, scroll bars automatically appear when they are needed, such as when the browser resolution does not allow the user to see the entire page.

To control where the user scrolls in a document, you can use the **`scrollBy()`** and **`scrollTo()`** methods. Both methods allow you to specify where to scroll in terms of width (x-coordinates) and height (y-coordinates). Using pseudocode, you would specify the x- and y-coordinates as follows.

```
scrollTo(x,y);
```

If you want to go 500 pixels down in the document (the y-coordinate), you could use the following code.

```
scrollTo(0,500);
```

These methods prove especially useful for pages that are longer or taller than the browser window. For instance, if you had a large map, you could use these commands to take the user to a specific portion of the map; from there, the user could choose a spot on a smaller version of the map or click the name of a specific building.

ScrollBy()

The **scrollBy()** method allows you to move the current scroll position up or down by a specific number of pixels. Doing so changes where the user is currently scrolled in the document. This is in contrast to the **scrollTo()** method, which requires you to specify absolute positions. To scroll the user up 100 pixels, you would type the following.

```
scrollBy(0,-100);
```

To move the user 100 pixels to the right, you would type the following.

```
scrollBy(100,0);
```

Use JavaScript to Control Scrolling

1   **In your browser, open scroll.html from the WIP_10 folder.**

This is a frequently asked questions (FAQ) page for a skin care clinic.

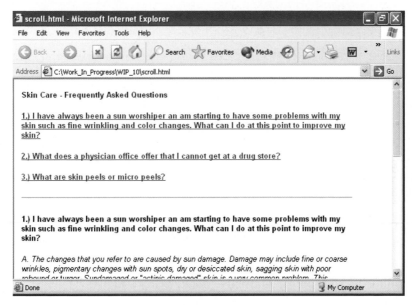

FIGURE 10.20

2   **Scroll to the bottom of the page.**

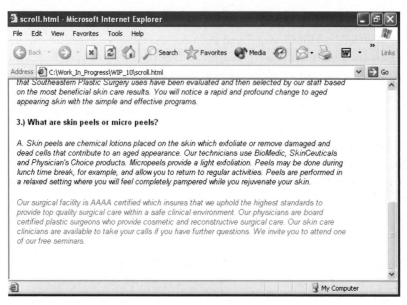

FIGURE 10.21

There is currently no mechanism to take the user back to the top of the page.

3   **Open the file in your text editor and scroll to the bottom of the page.**

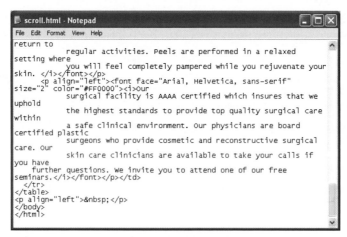

FIGURE 10.22

4   **Insert the following code on the line above the `</body>` tag.**

```
...
</tr>
</table>
```

```
<p align="left"> </p>
<form action="" method="POST" id="myForm">
<input type="Button" name="" value="Back to Top" id="myButton"
    onclick="self.scrollTo(0,0);">
</form>
</body>
</html>
```

5   Save the file in your text editor.

6   Refresh the file in your browser.

7   In your browser, scroll to the bottom of the page.

The change you made in Step 4 made the page longer, so you may need to scroll down a short distance farther, even if your browser is already near the bottom of the page.

FIGURE 10.23

8   Click the Back to Top button.

The page scrolls back to the top.

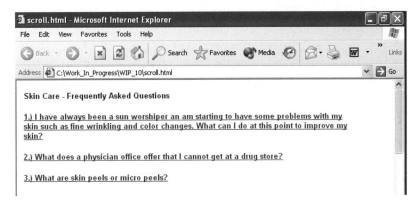

FIGURE 10.24

9   Close the file in your browser and text editor.

To Extend Your Knowledge . . .

SCROLL METHODS

Using text anchors to control scrolling is usually easier than using JavaScript to scroll pages to specific points.

LESSON 5   Working with Frames

Even though many HTML students have difficulty learning how to use frames, frames are actually very easy to use. Frames allow Web designers to divide the content area of the browser window into sections and display a different Web page within each section. JavaScript offers greater control over frames than HTML provides.

To ensure that you fully understand the concept of frames, this lesson discusses how to use HTML to create frames. The next lesson explains how to use JavaScript to manipulate frames.

HTML Frames Explained

A Web surfer who visits a site may see a top navigation area, a left navigation bar, and content in the bottom-right area of the browser window. If the Web surfer were to look at the source code of that page, he might wonder why the code he sees contains only a small portion of the page's content, such as the code that displays the left navigation bar.

The most likely explanation of this scenario is that the page uses a frameset design. As you learned earlier, a frameset is an HTML file that divides the browser window into sections. The frameset file tells the browser to create frames, which are portions of the browser window that display individual HTML pages.

In developing such a site, it is likely the designer started by creating an HTML frameset file. The frameset file:

- Instructed the browser to create a top frame, a left frame, and a frame for the main content area of the page.
- Told the browser how much space to allocate for each frame.
- Applied a window name to each frame.
- Told the browser which HTML file to display in each frame.

It's important to remember the frameset file loads first and then tells the browser which file to load in each frame. In many ways, HTML and JavaScript treat each frame as a separate browser window.

Creating a Frameset

Creating a frameset is as simple as creating any other HTML file. The **<frameset>** tag splits the browser window into sections. The **<frame>** tag names the frame area, specifies which HTML page to display in the area, and sets the properties of the area. The following code creates the frameset page previously described.

```
<!DOCTYPE html PUBLIC "-//W3C//DTD XHTML 1.0 Transitional//EN"
"http://www.w3.org/TR/xhtml1/DTD/xhtml1-transitional.dtd">
<html xmlns="http://www.w3.org/1999/xhtml"> <head>
<title>Frameset Page</title>
</head>

<frameset rows="*" cols="130,*" frameborder="yes" border="0"
    framespacing="0">
  <frame name="leftFrame" scrolling="yes" noresize src="leftNav.html">
  <frameset rows="100,*" frameborder="yes" border="0"
      framespacing="0">
    <frame name="topFrame" noresize scrolling="yes" src="topNav.html">
    <frame name="mainFrame" src="main.html">
  </frameset>
</frameset>

<noframes>
<body>
This page uses frames. You need a frame-enabled browser to view this
page correctly.
</body>
</noframes>
</html>
```

Use the asterisk character (*****) when you want to leave a dimension unspecified for the width or height of a frame. The browser will use the available space when it encounters an asterisk. In the sample code, the first **<frameset>** tag splits the page into a left section of 130 pixels.

A second **<frameset>** tag tells the browser to split the remaining part of the browser window into a 100-pixel top section. A third **<frame>** tag creates the **mainFrame** and allows the browser to use the remainder of the available space. The following illustration shows the result of the sample code.

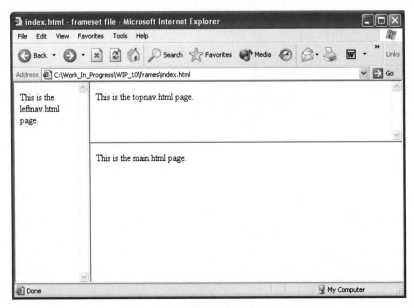

FIGURE 10.25

Several aspects of the frameset code are noteworthy. First, you use the **<frame>** tag to name each frame. Second, you can turn on/off several characteristics of the frame command. In the sample code, frame borders and scroll bars were turned on, making the various frames easy to identify.

The leftnav.html page displays in the **leftFrame** part of the frameset. The page consists of a simple text message that the browser formats to fit within the frame. It is possible to make the page wider or longer than the space allowed by the frame; if you turn off the **scrollbar** attribute, however, the user will not have access to the content.

The frames used in many current Web pages do not include borders or scroll bars. Returning to the sample code, you can turn off the **frameborder** attribute by changing the **frameborder="yes"** statement to **frameborder="no"**. You can turn off the **scrollbar** attribute by changing the code from **scrollbar="yes"** to **scrollbar="no"**. When you view the frameset page in a browser, you can see the results of these changes.

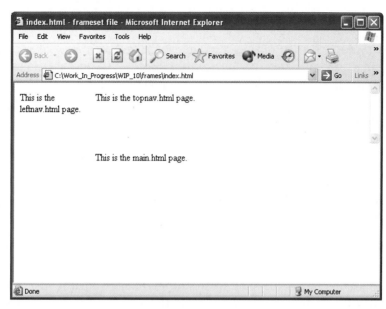

FIGURE 10.26

Turning off the scroll bars and frame borders creates a clean, professional appearance while eliminating the visual clues that tell users they are actually looking at several pages at once. Using borderless frames, designers can create elaborate interfaces from multiple frames, which they can align to create a seamless appearance.

Frame sites tend to work especially well for e-commerce sites, which are often generated with data from external databases and may incorporate content from multiple Web sites. Framesets offer the powerful advantage of allowing designers to separate content from navigation and branding. For instance, by placing the left navigation structure in a file named leftnav.html and then incorporating the file into a frame-based design, you can ensure the navigation structure looks and behaves the same on every Web page in a site.

Let's assume a site contains over 100 pages of content and every page uses leftnav.html for the navigation structure. The design team decides to add another link to the navigation structure throughout the Web site. Adding the code for the left navigation structure into every page of the site would require a change in every page of the site — a tedious and time-consuming process. Instead, you could use a frame-based design to make the change in a single file, eliminating hours of needless work.

Now you know about many of the advantages of using frames; but frames also have disadvantages:

- Imagine that a user chooses File>Print on a frames-based page. Which file prints? Usually, the file in the active frame prints. For instance, if the user clicks within **leftFrame**, then **leftFrame** becomes active, and the file within **leftFrame** prints when the user chooses File>Print.

- Similarly, when a Web surfer views the source code in his browser, he may see the code for the frameset file or a frame displayed within the frameset, depending on which window is currently active.

- Another common problem is when a hyperlink on an external site links to a frame — when it should link to a frameset file.

Frame Attributes

Frame attributes refer to the properties of the **<frame>** tag. These attributes allow you to control various aspects of the frame. You specify frame attributes in the **<frame>** tag of the frameset file that creates the frame. Frame properties are also represented with matching properties in JavaScript.

The **src** attribute specifies which HTML page appears within the frame. You add the **src** tag to the **<frame>** tag as follows.

```
<frame src="leftNav.html">
```

Linking a frame to an external URL is often desirable. To do so, simply specify an absolute location, such as the following.

```
<frame src="http://www.web-answers.com/leftnav.html">
```

JavaScript and HTML use the **name** attribute to refer to the frame created by the code. Don't confuse the **name** attribute with the **src** attribute, which sets the HTML file to display. The **name** attribute addresses the frame in HTML or JavaScript code, as shown below.

```
<frame name="leftFrame" src="leftNav.html>
```

The **noresize** attribute stops the end user from moving the borders between frames and resizing the amount of space allocated to each frame.

```
<frame name="leftFrame" noresize src="leftnav.html">
```

As you might imagine, the **scrolling** attribute turns scroll bars on or off in the frame. If the **scrolling** attribute isn't used, the browser will activate the scroll bars when/if they are needed. The **scrolling** attribute takes a "**yes**" or "**no**" parameter.

```
<frame name="leftFrame" noresize scrolling="no" src="leftnav.html">
```

The **marginheight** parameter specifies the top and bottom margins of the frame in pixels.

```
<frame name="leftFrame" noresize marginheight=50 scrolling="no"
src="leftNav.html">
```

The **marginwidth** parameter specifies the left and right margins of the frame in pixels.

```
<frame name="leftFrame" noresize marginwidth=50 scrolling="no"
src="leftNav.html">
```

Create the Frameset File

1   **In your browser, open each file from the WIP_10>frames folder, and then examine each file.**

The index.html file has no content. You use this file to create the frameset file. You use the files in this folder throughout this exercise.

2   **In your text editor, open index.html.**

3   **Insert the following code between the </head> and <body> tags.**

```
<!DOCTYPE html PUBLIC "-//W3C//DTD XHTML 1.0 Transitional//EN"
"http://www.w3.org/TR/xhtml1/DTD/xhtml1-transitional.dtd">
<html xmlns="http://www.w3.org/1999/xhtml">
<head>
<title>index.html - frameset file</title>
</head>
<frameset rows="*" cols="130,*" frameborder="YES" border="0"
framespacing="0">
  <frame name="leftFrame" scrolling="yes" noresize
      src="leftNav.html">
    <frameset rows="100,*" frameborder="yes" border="0"
        framespacing="0">
      <frame name="topFrame" noresize scrolling="yes"
          src="topNav.html">
      <frame name="mainFrame" src="main.html">
    </frameset>
</frameset>
<body>
</body>
</html>
```

It's a common mistake to try to put the frameset code within the **<body>** and **</body>** tags. This is not allowed by most HTML interpreters and causes your code to malfunction. Always place the frameset code between the **</head>** and **<body>** tags.

4   **Save the file in your text editor.**

5   Open the file in your browser.

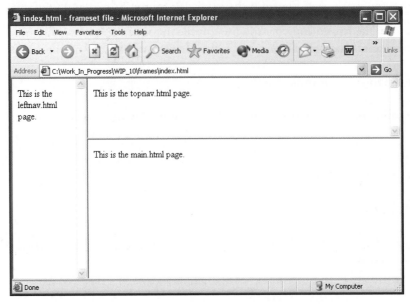

FIGURE 10.27

6   Keep the file open in your text editor and browser for the next exercise.

Load an HTML Document into Another Frame

In this exercise, you create a link that loads an HTML document into another frame in the frameset.

1   In the open index.html in your text editor, examine the source code.

This is the frameset file. The name assigned to the main content area is **mainFrame**.

2   Close index.html and open leftnav.html in your text editor.

3   Create a link in leftnav.html by inserting the following command before the **</body>** tag.

```
...
</head>
<body>
This is the leftnav.html page.
<a href="content2.html" target="mainFrame">Content Page 2 </a>
</body>
</html>
```

4   Save the file in your text editor.

5 Refresh your browser to reload the files, including the newest version of the leftnav.html page.

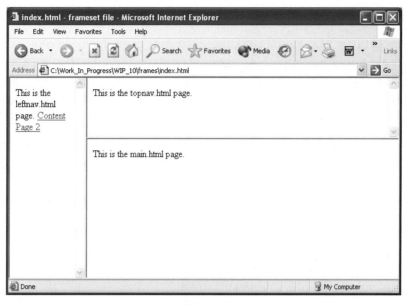

FIGURE 10.28

6 Click the Content Page 2 hyperlink to see the result of the targeted link.

The content2.html page should load into the **mainFrame** area.

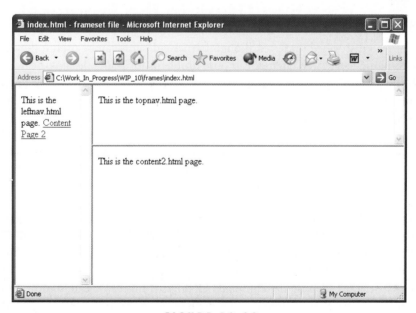

FIGURE 10.29

7 Close the file in your text editor and browser.

To Extend Your Knowledge . . .

TARGET NAMES

If you specify a target name that doesn't exist, most browsers open the file in a new browser window. If you don't specify a target name, the new page appears in the same frame as the hyperlink that opened it. Predefined target names in HTML (such as `_blank` and `_parent`) always include an underscore as the first character in the name. Don't confuse the underscore with a dash or leave the underscore off of the name.

HTML includes certain predefined target names for links to frames. For instance, `_blank` opens a new browser window when used in the `target` attribute. The `_self` qualifier loads the referenced page in place of the current document; this can also be accomplished by leaving off the `target` attribute. The `_parent` qualifier loads the window that contains the parent of the current document. If you use `_parent` as the target, the page replaces the frameset file; in other words, the new page loads in the entire browser window instead of loading within a frame.

OPENING A FRAMESET WITHIN A FRAME

It is a common mistake for designers to specify the name of the frameset file when they actually want to open a content page in a frame. This error causes the frameset to load a second time within a frame and show the same pages again (such as when two mirrors repeat the same nested reflection). Try to avoid opening a frameset within a frame of an existing frameset whenever possible.

LESSON 6   Redirecting Users to the Frameset

Earlier in this chapter, you discovered that even though frameset designs can be useful, they can also (occasionally) confuse users. In particular, search engines can pose problems for frame designs. Search engines often use *spiders* or *bots*, which are simply automated programs that explore Web pages, record the hyperlinks used, and index the content of the pages. The term "bot" is short for *robot* — another term used to describe these automated programs.

Imagine that you created a Web site on skateboarding. A bot visits the site and notices that a page named "content.html" contains significant information on skateboarding. The bot does not realize this page is meant to display as part of a frameset. The bot records this page as a reference for skateboarding.

Along comes an end user who uses a popular search engine to search for information on skateboarding. When the user clicks a particular link, content.html appears. Since the page is not being viewed through the frameset, the navigation structure does not appear on the page and the user cannot visit other pages in the site. To make matters worse, the company name, logo, and branding are not included in content.html (they appear in a separate frame), so the user can't identify the company. Obviously, this can create significant confusion for the user. Feeling frustrated, the user goes to the next company listed in the search engine results, and your client loses a potential sale.

Rather than accept this problem, you can use JavaScript to detect and control frames and provide a solution to this problem. First, consider how JavaScript deals with the frameset. When frames are used, JavaScript creates one **window** object to represent the frameset file and other **window** objects to represent each of the frames. You can refer to the frameset file as "**parent**" in the code. JavaScript creates an array to represent the frames in the document. Each element of the array represents a **<frame>** tag in the HTML document.

For instance, **frames[0]** would represent the first frame created, and **frames[1]** would represent the second frame created. Using this terminology, to send a command from a frame to the first frame, you would write the following.

```
parent.frames[0].document.write("hi");
```

Framesets can be nested within other framesets. The keyword **top** differs slightly from the keyword **parent** in that **top** always represents the highest-level frameset. Assuming you want to print a message in the first frame of the highest-level frameset, you can write the following.

```
top.frames[0].document.write("hi");
```

You can call the frames by the names assigned in the code. This gives you multiple ways to address a frame. Assuming you named the frame **mainFrame**, either one of the following statements would be acceptable.

```
top.frames["mainFrame"].document.write("hi");
top.mainFrame.document.write("hi");
```

Even though we have shown you several ways to address a frame (which helps you learn to read several methods of code writing), remember that dot syntax is the preferred method of writing code. For this reason, it is preferable to refer to the frame as **top.mainFrame** instead of **top.frames["mainFrame"]**.

If no frameset is encountered, JavaScript refers to the current document as **top**. Knowing this, you can work around the problem of users going to an individual page that should be viewed within a frameset. Placing code in the individual pages that appear within the frames allows you to verify that the page is being viewed in the frameset; if not, you can send the user back to the frameset, so he can see the site as intended. When you remember that no individual page should be the **top** page (except the frameset, of course), you can use pseudocode to describe how the code should work.

```
If the current page is the top document then change the browser's
current page to be the frameset file.
```

This script accomplishes your goal if you place it in the individual pages that should be viewed in the frameset, since the frame pages will never be the **top** document if they are viewed within a frameset. The code is not necessary within the frameset file. Assuming the frameset file is index.html, you would write the actual JavaScript as follows.

```
<script language="JavaScript" type="text/javascript">
if (this.document == top.document) {
location.replace("index.html");
}
</script>
```

You could have used **location.assign()** or **location.href** to change the URL, but **location.replace()** has the added benefit of erasing the entry in the history list and keeping users from clicking the Back button to return to the frame page. This avoids confusion, since many users expect to return to the search engine (or other referring URL) when they click Back.

Use a Frame-Redirect Script

1   **In your browser, open index.html from the WIP_10>frames2 folder.**

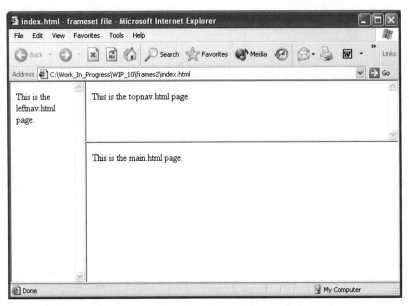

FIGURE 10.30

This simple frameset file displays three separate HTML pages. You use the files in this folder throughout this exercise.

2   **Open main.html in your browser.**

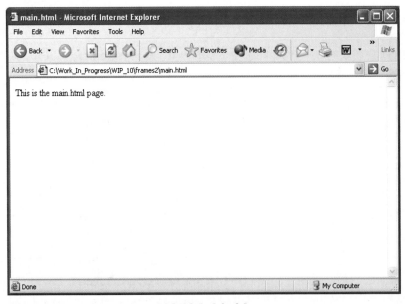

FIGURE 10.31

Assume this page would contain the first page of content on the Web site.

3   **Open main.html in your text editor. Add the following code before the `</body>` tag.**

```
...
</head>
<body>
This is the main.html page.
<script language="JavaScript" type="text/javascript">
if (this.document == top.document) {
location.replace("index.html");
}
</script>
</body>
</html>
```

4   **Save the file in your text editor.**

5   **Refresh main.html in your browser.**

The browser redirects to the frameset.

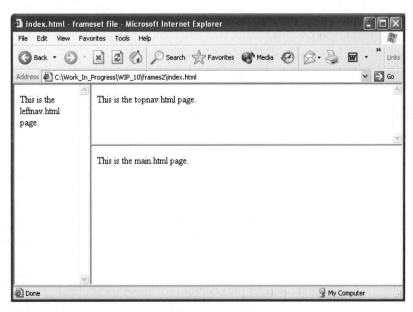

FIGURE 10.32

6   **Close the files in your text editor and browser.**

To Extend Your Knowledge . . .

FRAME-REDIRECT SCRIPTS

A frame-redirect script has the added benefit of stopping users from viewing the source code of individual frame pages.

SPIDERS

Bot (spider) programs were originally designed to gather lists of Web sites for early Internet users; they were later modified to gather information on the content of Web sites. Many search engines and search engine companies are named for different species of spiders, such as Inktomi and Lycos.

S U M M A R Y

In this chapter, you learned additional aspects of the **window** object. In previous chapters, you learned how to create **window** objects using the **open()** method and how to delete **window** objects using the **close()** method. You learned new methods of the **window** object, including **resizeTo()** and **moveTo()**. These methods, along with others, allow you to move and resize browser windows after they open on the screen. These features allow developers to place pop-up windows in specific areas of the screen.

You learned that the **status** and **defaultStatus** properties allow developers to control messages placed in the browser's status bar. Messages created with the **status** property only appear for a few seconds, whereas messages created with the **defaultStatus** property appear by default in the status bar whenever temporary messages are not displayed.

You discovered that the **screen** object represents the user's computer screen; it allows developers to determine the current size of the end user's screen. With this information, you can size browser windows or elements of an HTML page to a specific resolution. The **screen** object has two properties — **availHeight** and **availWidth**—which represent the height and width of the user's screen resolution.

You also found that using JavaScript, you can control scrolling in the browser window. You do this with the **scrollTo()** or **scrollBy()** method. The **scrollTo()** method takes the page to a specific area of the browser window. The **scrollBy()** method scrolls the browser a certain amount in a specified direction.

You learned that a frameset is an HTML file that divides the browser window into sections and displays a different HTML file in each section. The frameset file contains no visible content and is not seen by the user. You learned that an HTML file shown within a frameset is called a frame. Frames can have visible or invisible borders, and developers can allow scroll bars to appear in the frameset when necessary.

You found that JavaScript tracks the use of frames through the **frame** object and **frames** array. The **frames** array represents each frame created in the HTML document. For example, the third frame created in an HTML document is called **frames[2]** in JavaScript code.

You discovered that in JavaScript, a frameset file is referred to as **parent**. Since framesets can be nested within other framesets, the keyword **top** refers to the highest-level frameset (the first HTML document loaded).

When viewing a file meant to be seen in a frameset, the document represented by the keyword **top** should be the frameset. Using these naming rules allows you to write simple scripts to determine if a file is being viewed in a frameset; if not, you can use JavaScript to load the frameset file.

KEY TERMS

Bot	Robot	X-coordinate
Frame	Screen object	Y-coordinate
Frameset	Spider	
Null	Usability	

CHECKING CONCEPTS AND TERMS

MULTIPLE CHOICE

Circle the letter that matches the correct answer for each of the following questions.

1. Which property can you use to temporarily change the browser's status bar message?
   a. `defaultStatusMessage`
   b. `screen`
   c. `status`
   d. `temporaryStatus`
   e. None of the above.

2. Which object represents the user's monitor resolution in JavaScript?
   a. `monitor`
   b. `status`
   c. `screen`
   d. `resolution`

3. A frameset file contains visible content that displays in the browser window.
   a. True
   b. False

4. Which term describes how easy a Web page is to use?
   a. Clickability
   b. Easiness
   c. Usability
   d. Frustration factor

5. Where will the statement **moveTo (0,0)** place a browser window on the user's computer screen?
   a. Mid-point of the screen
   b. Upper-left corner of the screen
   c. Lower-right corner of the screen
   d. Off the visible area of the screen

6. Why is the **availHeight** property of the **screen** object often smaller than the current screen resolution?
   a. Because of the space devoted to the browser interface
   b. Because of space devoted to the Windows task bar
   c. Because of blank content on the Web page
   d. Because of a bug in JavaScript

7. In computer technology, what is a spider?
   a. A script that prevents access to inappropriate material
   b. A software bug
   c. An automated program used by a search engine to index content
   d. An animation program used for Web development

8. Why can a frameset-designed Web site be problematic to users?

   a. The wrong frame may get keyboard focus in a frameset-viewed page

   b. Users may print a single frame, instead of the whole page

   c. Users may accidentally load a page that should be seen in a frameset

   d. All of the above.

   e. None of the above.

9. In the command `resizeTo(640,480)`, what is resized to 640 pixels by 480 pixels?

   a. The entire browser window

   b. The live area of the browser where content is displayed

   c. The user's screen resolution

   d. A frame in a frameset

10. What are search engine companies (such as Inktomi) and search engines (such as Lycos) named after?

    a. Ancient scribes

    b. Greek gods

    c. Ancient libraries

    d. Species or types of spiders

DISCUSSION QUESTIONS

1. What are the advantages and disadvantages of using frames?

2. Why do frame-based Web sites often create problems for Web surfers using search engines? How can JavaScript minimize this problem?

3. Why is it better to size a browser window through the `open()` method when the window is created than through the `resizeTo()` method?

4. In your own words, explain how the frame-redirect script presented in this chapter works.

SKILL DRILL

Skill Drill exercises reinforce chapter skills. Each skill reinforced is the same (or nearly the same) as a skill presented in the chapter. Detailed instructions are provided in a step-by-step format. You should work through these exercises in order.

1. Scroll on Key Press

In this Skill Drill, you use the `scrollBy()` method. This method allows you to create a scrolling effect anytime the user presses a key on the keyboard.

1. In your browser, open skillscroll.html from the WIP_10 folder.

   This is essentially the same file you used in a previous exercise.

2. Open the file in your text editor.

3. Find the `<body>` tag in the code.

4. Modify the `<body>` tag by inserting the following inline code.

```
<body bgcolor="#FFFFFF" onkeypress="scrollBy(0,23);">
```

5. Save the file in your text editor.

6. Refresh the file in your browser.

7. Press the Spacebar.

    The page should scroll down each time you press any Spacebar. (The browser window must have focus.)

8. Keep the file open for the next Skill Drill.

2. Manipulate Status Bar Messages

1. In the open skillscroll.html, find the **</head>** tag.

2. Directly before the **</head>** tag, insert the following lines of code to create a script.

```
<!DOCTYPE html PUBLIC "-//W3C//DTD XHTML 1.0 Transitional//EN"
"http://www.w3.org/TR/xhtml1/DTD/xhtml1-transitional.dtd">
<html xmlns="http://www.w3.org/1999/xhtml">
<head>
<title>skillscroll.html</title>
<script language="JavaScript" type="text/javascript">

</script>
</head>
...
```

3. Insert a line of code into your script to make the **defaultStatus** property equal to "Press a key to scroll down".

    This command makes the status bar display this message by default, as shown below.

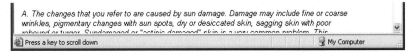

FIGURE 10.33

4. Save the file in your text editor.

5. Refresh the file in your browser to make sure the message displays correctly in the status bar.

6. Close the file in your browser and text editor.

3. Use a Frame-Redirect Script

1. In your browser, open index.html from the WIP_10>skillframes folder.

You use the files in this folder throughout this exercise. This is a Web site for a college instructor. The index.html file is the frameset that displays the other pages.

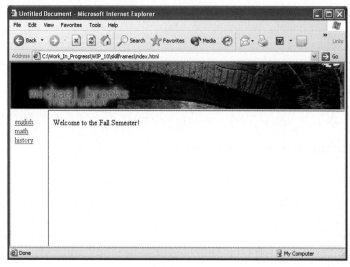

FIGURE 10.34

2. Open topnav.html in your browser.

   This is the top page; it contains a branding image for the site. Plans include a second navigation structure in this area.

3. Open main.html and leftnav.html in your browser. Examine the files.

4. In your text editor, open main.html.

5. Insert the following code before the **</body>** tag.

```
. . .
</head>
<body>
Welcome to the Fall Semester!
<script language="JavaScript" type="text/javascript">
if (this.document == top.document) {
location.replace("index.html");
}
</script>
</body>
</html>
```

   This code redirects the browser to the frameset if this file opens in the browser.

6. Save the file in your text editor and open it in your browser.

   The page redirects to the frameset.

7. Add code to leftnav.html and topnav.html to redirect the browser to the frameset if these files open.

8. Test each file individually in your browser. Each of the three pages (main.html, leftnav.html, and topnav.html) should redirect to the frameset.

9. Keep index.html open in your browser for the next exercise. Close any open files in your text editor.

4. Resize a Window

1. With index.html open in your browser, try to resize the browser window to a larger size.

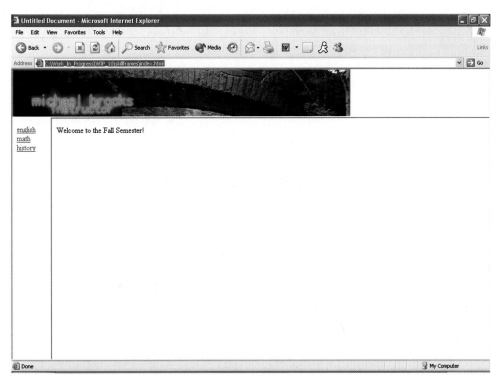

FIGURE 10.35

This site was designed for viewing at an 800 by 600 screen resolution. The illustration above shows the site at 1024 by 768.

2. Open index.html in your text editor.

3. Create a script in the head section of the HTML document.

4. In the script, insert a line of code that uses the **resizeTo()** method to resize the browser window to 640 pixels wide and 480 pixels high.

5. Save the file in your text editor.

6. Open the file in your browser.

    The window should resize itself to a resolution of 640 by 480.

7. Close the file in your browser and text editor.

CHALLENGE

Challenge exercises expand on (or are somewhat related to) skills presented in the lessons. Each exercise provides a brief introduction, followed by instructions presented in a numbered-step format that are not as detailed as those in the Skill Drill exercises. You should work through these exercises in order.

1. Resize Browsers to Full Screen

In this Challenge, you create a script to resize the browser to occupy the full size of the screen. This is tricky, since many different screen resolutions are possible. Design your script to figure out the size of the screen and resize the browser window accordingly.

1. In your browser, open challengescreen.html from the WIP_10 folder.

   The script for this page determines the available width and height of the browser window and outputs this information to the screen. Your results may vary slightly, depending on your computer's current screen resolution.

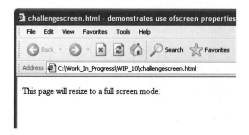

FIGURE 10.36

2. Open the file in your text editor.

3. Insert the following code.

```
...
<p>This page will resize to a full screen mode.</p>
<script language="JavaScript" type="text/javascript">
// insert code here
if (screen.availWidth>1000&&screen.availWidth<1100) {
     alert("screen size is approximately 1024");
}
</script>
</body>
</html>
```

   This code checks to see if the screen resolution is approximately 1024 pixels wide. Several factors affect the exact number of pixels, so the **if** statement was designed to verify that the width is between 1000 and 1100 pixels wide.

4. Save the file in your text editor.

5. Open the file in your browser.

   Assuming your resolution is 1024 × 768, you receive an alert message.

6. If you see the alert box, click OK.

7. In your text editor, find and delete the following statement in your code.

   ```
   alert("screen size is approximately 1024");
   ```

8. Replace the code you just deleted with the following lines of code.

   ```
   . . .
   <p>This page will resize to a full screen mode.</p>
   <script language="JavaScript" type="text/javascript">
   // insert code here
   if (screen.availWidth>1000&&screen.availWidth<1100) {
   resizeTo(1024,768);
   moveTo(0,0);
   }
   </script>
   </body>
   </html>
   ```

   This code resizes the browser window to a resolution of 1024 pixels wide by 768 pixels high and places the window in the upper-left corner of the screen.

9. Save the file in your text editor and test the page in your browser.

   If your resolution is 1024 by 768, the browser occupies the entire screen.

10. Return to your text editor and find the following lines of code.

    ```
    </script>
    </body>
    </html>
    ```

11. Directly before this code, create another **if** statement that verifies that the screen resolution is between 750 pixels of available width and 850 pixels of available width. If so, change the browser window size to 800 pixels wide by 600 pixels high.

    Hint: use the existing **if** statement as a guide.

12. Create a third **if** statement that determines if the screen resolution is approximately 640 by 480 and, if so, resizes the browser window to a 640 by 480 resolution.

13. Test the file in your browser.

14. Close the file in your browser and text editor.

2. Resize to Test Resolution

In this Challenge, you use the **resizeTo()** method for a particularly practical purpose. A design firm asked you create JavaScript code to resize browser windows to common screen resolution sizes, including 640 by 480,

800 by 600, and 1024 by 768. This code will allow the firm to test Web pages to ensure they look good at specific screen resolutions.

1. In your browser, open challengeresize.html from the WIP_10 folder.

2. Open the file in your text editor.

3. Find the following line of code.

    ```
    <a href="#">Resize to 640 × 480</a>
    ```

4. Remove the hash symbol (#) from this statement and replace it with the following code.

    ```
    <a href="javascript:resizeTo(640,480)">Resize to 640 × 480</a>
    ```

5. Save the file in your text editor and refresh the file in your browser.

6. Click the hyperlink.

    The browser window changes to a resolution of 640 pixels wide and 480 pixels high.

7. Hold down your mouse button on the hyperlink and drag the link onto the Favorites pull-down menu. Do not release the mouse button.

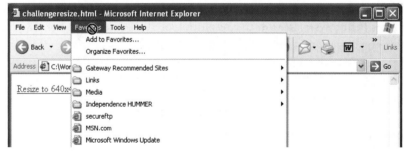

FIGURE 10.37

Your Favorites menu will probably look different than the one shown above.

8. Without releasing your mouse button, drag the link down to add it to your Favorites menu.

9. Release the mouse button over the list of favorites.

    A Security Alert message appears.

10. Click Yes to add the link to your Favorites menu.

11. Click the Favorites pull-down menu to see the list of favorites.

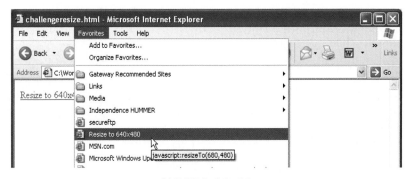

FIGURE 10.38

Whenever you choose this favorite, the current page resizes automatically to the 640 by 480 resolution.

12. Return to your text editor and find the following line of code.

```
<a href="javascript:resizeTo(680,480)">Resize to 640 × 480</a>
```

13. Insert the following lines of code to insert a new line character and create a second hyperlink that resets the screen resolution to 800 by 600.

```
. . .
<body>
<a href="javascript:resizeTo(680,480)">Resize to 640 × 480</a>
<br />
<a href="javascript:resizeTo(800,600)">Resize to 800 × 600</a>
</body>
</html>
```

14. Save the file in your text editor and refresh your browser.

15. Click each hyperlink.

The page should resize to the specified resolution.

16. Create a third hyperlink that changes the screen resolution to 1024 by 768.

17. Test the file in your browser and add the links to your Favorites menu.

18. Close the file in your browser and text editor.

3. Place a Pop-Up Window

Pop-up windows are often used to generate advertisements or hold extraneous content on Web pages. By default, most pop-up windows appear near the upper-left corner of the main browser window. This position often blocks the visibility of logos or other important items on the main page. In this Challenge, you use the **moveTo()** method to place a pop-up window in a more suitable position.

1. In your browser, open challengemoveby.html from the WIP_10 folder.

This file creates a small pop-up window.

2. Close the pop-up window.

3. Open the file in your text editor.

4. Find the following code.

    ```
    // insert code here
    ```

5. On the next line after this comment, insert a **moveTo()** method to move the **myWin** pop-up window to a left margin of zero (0) and 240 pixels down from the top of the screen.

6. Use the **focus()** method to draw focus to the pop-up window after it moves.

7. Save the file in your text editor and refresh your browser.

    The pop-up window moves below the link.

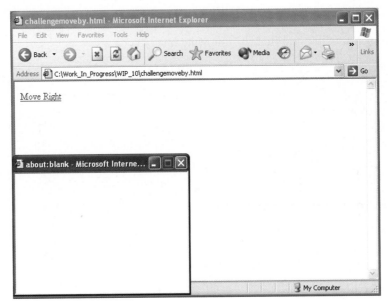

FIGURE 10.39

8. Close the pop-window.

9. Keep the file open for the next exercise.

4. Move a Pop-Up Window Incrementally

In this exercise, you create a pop-up window and build buttons to move the window across the screen. To accomplish the tasks, you use the **moveBy()** method.

1. In the open challengemoveby.html in your text editor, insert a blank line before the following line of code.

    ```
    </script>
    ```

2. In the blank line you just created, insert the following code to create a function.

    ```
    function makeMoveRight() {
    ```

```
}
</script>
</head>
<body>
. . .
```

3. In this function, insert the following lines of code.

```
. . .
function makeMoveRight() {
myWin.moveBy(100,0);
myWin.focus();
}
</script>
</head>
<body>
. . .
```

When invoked, this function moves the pop-up 100 pixels to the right. The **focus()** method ensures the pop-up isn't blurred behind the current window.

4. Find the following line of code.

```
<a href="#">Move Right</a>
```

5. Insert the following inline code to trigger the function when the mouse clicks the hyperlink.

```
<a href="#" onclick="makeMoveRight()">Move Right</a>
```

6. Save the file in your text editor.

7. Refresh the file in your browser.

8. Click the hyperlink to move the window 100 pixels to the right.

9. Click the button repeatedly until the pop-up reaches the right side of the main browser window.

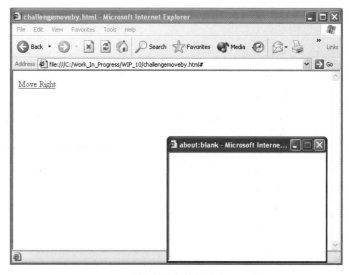

FIGURE 10.40

10. Close the pop-up and return to your text editor.

11. Create a second function named "**makeMoveLeft()**" that (when invoked) moves the pop-up 100 pixels to the left, and then focuses the pop-up window.

     Hint: Use the existing function as a model, but use "-100" for the x-coordinate change, and use "0" for the y-coordinate change.

12. Create a hyperlink that says "Move Left", as shown below.

FIGURE 10.41

13. Use inline JavaScript in the hyperlink you just created to trigger the function you created in Step 11 when the user clicks this link.

14. Save the file in your text editor and test it in your browser.

     The pop-up moves as you click the Move Left and Move Right links.

15. Close the file in both applications.

PORTFOLIO BUILDER

Enhance the Functionality of Pop-Up Windows

The Charlotte College of Art and Design in Charlotte, North Carolina, asked you to finish their Web site. Currently, the opening page on the site shows the branding of the school and offers some basic information. The home page (index.html) launches a pop-up window when it finishes loading. The pop-up window (pop-up.html) encourages students to call the college for more information. The files you need to complete this project are in the WIP_10>Portfolio_Builder_10 folder.

In this Portfolio Builder, your job is to enhance the site as follows:

1.   Set your screen resolution to 800 by 600 pixels. In the pop-up.html file, write an **if** statement to determine if the screen is less than or equal to 800 pixels wide. If this condition evaluates to **true**, place the pop-up window in the bottom-right position of the browser window at this resolution. Experiment with different x- and y-coordinates to determine the best position for the pop-up window.

2.   Set your screen resolution to 1024 by 768 pixels. In pop-up.html, write an **if** statement to determine if the screen is less than or equal to 800 pixels wide. If this condition evaluates to **true**, place the pop-up window in the bottom-right position of the browser window at this resolution. Experiment with different x- and y-coordinates to determine the best position for the pop-up window at this resolution.

CHAPTER **11**

Using Dates, Times, and Numbers

OBJECTIVES

In this chapter, you learn how to:

- Use operators and precedence
- Use Math object methods
- Generate random numbers

- Incorporate math properties
- Get and set time units
- Create timers

Why Would I Do This?

JavaScript has many built-in objects and methods that allow you to work with dates, times, numbers, and timers. Understanding how to manipulate dates, times, and numbers is essential for writing many JavaScript programs. Many objects, methods, and properties are designed to facilitate the use of complex calculations that include dates and numbers. For example, we often use the following types of calculations, which can be made simpler using the following methods:

- Financial transactions require us to round dollar amounts to two decimal places.

- We must often convert a number from one form to another (e.g., meters to feet).

- We must often compute calculations based on units of time (e.g., the date and amount of a car payment).

Learning how to use these objects and methods allows you to complete complex programming tasks in much less time and with reduced effort.

In this chapter, you examine how mathematical calculations are completed in JavaScript and other object-oriented programming languages. As part of the discussion, you consider the methods and properties of the `Math` object, which are used to simplify computations. You also learn how to create and manipulate `date` objects to complete calculations involving time and dates. In addition, you explore the use of timers, which you can use to delay the execution of a JavaScript statement or to tell a JavaScript statement to repeat at various intervals.

VISUAL SUMMARY

When processing complex formulas, programming languages incorporate *rules of precedence* that determine how the formulas are computed. The term *precedence* simply means the order in which operations are completed. Consider the following formula; it computes a temperature in Fahrenheit when given a Celsius value.

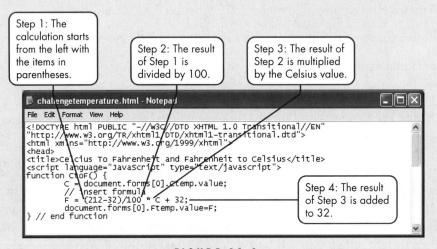

Step 1: The calculation starts from the left with the items in parentheses.

Step 2: The result of Step 1 is divided by 100.

Step 3: The result of Step 2 is multiplied by the Celsius value.

Step 4: The result of Step 3 is added to 32.

```
challengetemperature.html - Notepad
File  Edit  Format  View  Help
<!DOCTYPE html PUBLIC "-//W3C//DTD XHTML 1.0 Transitional//EN"
"http://www.w3.org/TR/xhtml1/DTD/xhtml1-transitional.dtd">
<html xmlns="http://www.w3.org/1999/xhtml">
<head>
<title>Celcius To Fahrenheit and Fahrenheit to Celsius</title>
<script language="JavaScript" type="text/javascript">
function CtoF() {
        C = document.forms[0].Ctemp.value;
        // insert formula
        F = (212-32)/100 * C + 32;
        document.forms[0].Ftemp.value=F;
} // end function
```

FIGURE 11.1

If you were to remove the parentheses, the calculation would change, causing a subsequent error in the calculation.

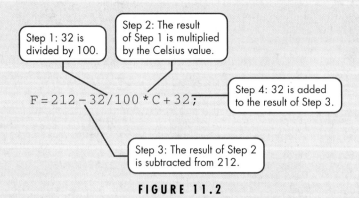

Step 1: 32 is divided by 100.

Step 2: The result of Step 1 is multiplied by the Celsius value.

Step 4: 32 is added to the result of Step 3.

$$F = 212 - 32 / 100 * C + 32;$$

Step 3: The result of Step 2 is subtracted from 212.

FIGURE 11.2

Calculations may often involve the manipulation of dates or time. The date object offers a comprehensive set of methods that can be used to calculate specific dates or times. Methods of the date object can be used in numerous ways. For example, you could insert the current date and time into a Web page or script. You could also calculate the exact amount of time that has elapsed since a specific date.

Consider the following script as an example of the date object and its associated methods.

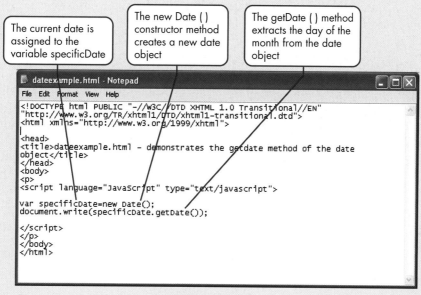

FIGURE 11.3

In this example, the current day of the month is returned to the user. If the current date is January 12, the script will output the number 12 back to the user.

JavaScript also has methods that are designed to create timers. For example, we may want to create a page that reloads automatically every 15 seconds.

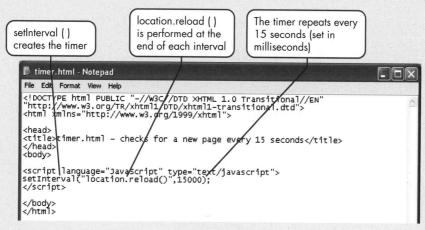

FIGURE 11.4

LESSON 1 Understanding Operators and Precedence

In previous chapters, you considered basic mathematical manipulation in terms of variables and assignment operators, an example of which is shown in the following statement:

```
var calculation=64/5+87*4;
```

At this point in your JavaScript studies, a discussion of mathematical precedence is warranted. If you use the previous statement in a script, JavaScript will report the value of the variable as `360.8`. Assuming you want to double-check the code, you could do the math yourself to check the logic in the formula. Let's start by performing the following calculation:

```
65/5=12.8
```

Next, add 87 to the previous total:

```
12.8+87=99.8
```

Last, multiply the result by 4:

```
99.8*4=399.2
```

This value is different than the JavaScript calculation. Obviously, this could cause a significant problem if you were calculating an important value, such as a mortgage payment or the amount of refund due to a customer. The answer to the discrepancy lies in the operator precedence of the calculations. Rules of precedence require that certain operators be evaluated before others. In general, calculations are made from left to right in the following order:

1. Calculations in parentheses, dots, and brackets ((), .., [])
2. Increment and decrement operations (++, − −)
3. Multiplication, division, and modulus operations (*, /, %)
4. Addition and subtraction (−, +)

Returning to the previous example, you can now see how JavaScript completes the calculation

```
var calculation=64/5+87*4;
```

JavaScript starts at the left, first evaluating the following:

```
64/5=12.8
```

Because multiplication has precedence over addition, the next part evaluated is

```
87*4=348
```

JavaScript then completes the addition of the two calculations

```
12.8+348=360.8
```

Understanding the rules of precedence are simple but can create problems when devising and entering complex formulas. Memorizing the rules of precedence will help you debug and understand complicated formulas. Remember that you can always break down the steps of a complex formula into smaller steps, and then output the values at each step. This process will help you find errors.

Assignment Operators

An assignment operator is a character (or characters) that assigns a value to a variable. In the statement `variableName="value"`, the equal sign is the assignment operator. This is the simplest assignment statement in JavaScript. Other assignment operators are shown in the following statements:

```
A-=B; which is the same as A=A-B;
A+=B; which is the same as A=A+B;
A*=B; which is the same as A=A*B;
A/=B; which is the same as A=A/B;
A++; which is the same as A=A+1;
A--; which is the same as A=A-1;
```

The modulus operator requires a bit more explaining. You use the ***modulus operator*** to find the remainder left over after division. For instance, the following lines of code return a value of 1:

```
A=5;
B=2;
A=A % B;
document.write(A);
```

Other operators affect the status of a single bit of computer memory; these operators are referred to as ***bitwise operators***. Using bitwise operators is a complex process that is beyond the scope of our current discussion. Common bitwise operators include `&=`, `|=` and `^=`. You will occasionally see these operators in complex code examples.

Correct Precedence Errors

1   **Copy the contents of your RF_JavaScript_L1>Chapter_11 folder into your Work_In_Progress>WIP_11 folder.**

2   **In your text editor, open precedence.html from your WIP_11 folder.**

3   **Insert the following code.**

```
...
</head>
<body>
<script language="JavaScript" type="text/javascript">
commission=10+10*.05;
document.write("The sales commission is "+commission);
```

```
</script>
</body>
</html>
```

4   **Save your changes and open the file in your browser.**

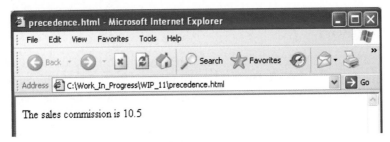

FIGURE 11.5

The script returns the wrong amount because the multiplication occurred before the two numbers were added.

5   **Insert parentheses into your formula as shown here.**

```
...
<body>
<script language="JavaScript" type="text/javascript">
commission=(10+10)*.05;
document.write("The sales commission is "+commission);
</script>
</body>
...
```

The parentheses correct the precedence problem.

6   **Save your changes and refresh your browser.**

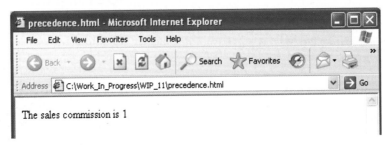

FIGURE 11.6

The calculation executes correctly.

7   **Close the file in your browser and text editor.**

LESSON 2   Using Math Object Methods

The `Math` object is a built-in JavaScript object. It contains various constant values used in mathematical calculations (e.g., pi), as well as numerous methods for calculating many common math functions.

The `Math` object uses various methods to simplify complex mathematical formulas. For instance, to raise 2 to the power of 9 and add 8 to the result, you could devise a statement such as

```
result=(2*2*2*2*2*2*2*2*2)+8;
```

As an alternative, you could simplify the formula by using the `Math.pow()` method:

```
result=Math.pow(2,9)+8;
```

JavaScript supports a number of methods that are used to complete various calculations. The most common `Math` methods are listed as in the following sections.

Math.abs()

The `Math.abs()` method returns the absolute value of any number you pass to it. The result is always positive, regardless of whether the original number is positive or negative. For example, the following code segment outputs the number **27** to the screen, not **-27**, as you might expect:

```
var myNumber=-27;
document.write(.Math.abs (myNumber));
```

Math.max() and Math.min()

These methods allow the programmer to compare multiple numbers and ask for the smallest (min) number or the largest (max) number. For instance, the following script returns the number **6** because **6** is the lowest number in the list:

```
var lowestNumber=Math.min(27,33,54,76,43,23,12,6,78,98);
document.write(lowestNumber);
```

To return the largest number in the list (**98**), you would write the following:

```
var largestNumber=Math.max(27,33,54,76,43,23,12,6,78,98);
document.write(largestNumber);
```

Math.pow()

This method requires two numeric arguments to calculate the result of a specific number raised to a certain power. The first argument is your base number and the second is the exponent. For instance, to calculate **5** to the power of **2**, you would write the following statement:

```
calculation=Math.pow(5,2);
```

Math.round()

This method rounds whatever number it receives to the closest integer value. To round the number `4.343` to the nearest whole number and output the result to the user, you would write the following statement:

```
document.write("The number 4.343 rounded is " + Math.round(4.343));
```

Math.sqrt()

This method returns the square root of whatever number it receives. The following statement returns `2` to the user:

```
document.write ("The square root of 4 is " + Math.sqrt(4));
```

Notice how the method is written with all lowercase letters as `sqrt()`. Similar methods exist that are written differently. For instance, `SQRT2()` returns the square root of the number 2, which is often used in calculations.

Use Math Object Methods

1   **In your text editor, open mathmethods.html from your WIP_11 folder.**

2   **Insert the following code.**

```
...
</head>
<body>
<script language="JavaScript" type="text/javascript">
theRoot=Math.sqrt(20);
document.write("The square root of 20 is " + theRoot+"<br />");
document.write("The number rounded is "+Math.round(theRoot));
</script>
</body>
</html>
```

3   **Save your changes and open the file in your browser.**

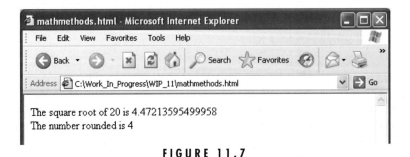

FIGURE 11.7

4   **Close the file in your text editor and browser.**

To Extend Your Knowledge . . .

THE MATH OBJECT

The `Math` object must be spelled as "`Math`" rather than "`math`" to work in most browsers.

LESSON 3   Generating Random Numbers

The `Math.random()` method takes no parameters; it simply returns a random number between 0 and 1. Consider the following code, which generates a random number between 0 and 1:

```
randomNumber=Math.random();
```

The number generated by `Math.random()` is a long decimal. In many common programming problems, it is necessary to produce a random number that occupies a specific range, such as a number between 1 and 10 or a number between 1 and 100. You can do this by mathematically manipulating the number produced by the `Math.random()` method. You will explore this process in the following exercises.

Work with Random Numbers

1   **In your text editor, open mathrandom.html from your WIP_11 folder.**

2   **Insert the following lines of code.**

```
...
</head>
<body>
<script language="JavaScript" type="text/javascript">
randomNumber=Math.random();
document.write("Here is a random number: " + randomNumber);
</script>
</body>
</html>
```

3   **Open the file in your browser and click the Refresh button.**

Every time you click the Refresh button, a new random number between 0 and 1 appears.

FIGURE 11.8

Your results will differ from the illustration, depending on the number your computer generates.

4   **Keep the file open in your text editor for the next exercise.**

Return a 1 or 0 (True or False) Value

1   **In the open mathrandom.html, insert the following code.**

```
. . .
<script language="JavaScript" type="text/javascript">
randomNumber=Math.random();
document.write("Here is a random number: " + randomNumber);
document.write("<br />");
randomNumber=Math.round(randomNumber);
document.write("Rounded version is "+randomNumber);
</script>
</body>
</html>
```

The script returns either 0 or 1, which could later be used to represent a true (1) or false (0) value.

2 **Save your changes and refresh the file in your browser.**

FIGURE 11.9

Every time you click the Refresh button, the random number is updated to either 0 or 1. Depending on your luck, the number could stay as either for a few page refreshes.

3 **Insert the following code to generate a number between 1 and 10.**

```
. . .
randomNumber=Math.random();
document.write("Here is a random number: " + randomNumber);
document.write("<br />");
randomNumber*=10;
randomNumber=Math.round(randomNumber);
document.write("Rounded version is "+randomNumber);
</script>
. . .
```

This statement takes the current value of the number and multiplies it by 10.

4 **Save the file in your text editor.**

5 **Repeatedly click the Refresh button in your Web browser.**

FIGURE 11.10

The code generates random numbers between 1 and 10.

6 **Close the file in your browser and text editor.**

To Extend Your Knowledge . . .

RANDOM NUMBER GENERATION

Computers don't really produce "random" numbers. To operate correctly, a computer processor has an internal clock that completes a full cycle billions or trillions of times each second. When asked for a random number, computer languages check the status of the processor clock and report the position of the processor clock in its current cycle. Because the processor clock completes billions or trillions of cycles per second, the generated number is virtually impossible to predict. This simple fact allows programmers to create complex video games and apply digital encryption.

LESSON 4   Incorporating Math Properties

`Math` object properties are different from the properties of most objects because `Math` object properties cannot be changed. In JavaScript, a property that cannot be changed is referred to as a ***constant property***. Constant properties hold numeric constants that are frequently used in mathematical calculations. JavaScript supports many constant properties, a few of which are described in the following sections.

Math.E

`Math.E` is the constant value `2.718281828459045`, which is used in many common calculations. To compute the value of the number 5 multiplied by the constant "`E`" and store it in a variable named `result`, you would write the following statement:

```
var result=5*Math.E;
```

Math.PI

`Math.PI` is the constant value `3.141592653589793`. For example, consider the following statement that multiplies the number 5 with the constant `PI` and stores the calculation in a variable named `result`:

```
var result=5*Math.PI;
```

Math.SQRT2

`Math.SQRT2` is the constant value given to the square root of 2, which is `1.414213562373091`. To calculate the result of the number 8 divided by the constant number represented by `SQRT2`, you would write the following statement:

```
var result=8/Math.SQRT2;
```

Use Math Properties

1 In your text editor, open mathpi.html from your WIP_11 folder.

2 Insert the following code.

```
...
</head>
<body>
<script language="JavaScript" type="text/javascript">
diameter=prompt("Enter the diameter of the circle","");
diameter=parseInt(diameter);
var circumference=Math.PI*diameter;
document.write("The circumference of the circle is "
+ circumference);
</script>
</body>
</html>
```

The `prompt()` method returns information as a string, so parseInt() is needed to make sure the value is converted to an integer.

3 Save your changes and open the file in your browser.

FIGURE 11.11

A prompt box appears.

4 Enter "5" as the diameter and click OK.

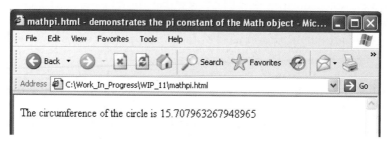

FIGURE 11.12

5 **Refresh the file in your browser and enter different diameters.**

You will receive a response dependent on the numbers you entered.

6 **Close the file in your browser and text editor.**

To Extend Your Knowledge . . .

MATH PROPERTIES

In most browsers, the constant properties of the `Math` object are case sensitive. Typing `Math.PI` as `Math.pi` causes the script to stop working in many browsers.

LESSON 5 Getting and Setting Time Units

The `date` class in JavaScript allows you to create objects that hold date and time information. To insert the current date and time into a variable named `currentTime`, you would write the following statement:

```
var currentTime=new Date();
```

The `newDate()` method is a constructor method that creates a new instance of the `date` object. You can then output the variable to the screen with the following simple statement:

```
document.write(currentTime);
```

It is often necessary to pass a specific date to a `date` object. You can do this by writing the following statement:

```
var specificDate=new Date("October 18, 1969 15:40:00");
```

This code creates a new variable named `specificDate` that creates a new `date` object and stores the date October 18, 1969 and the time 3:40 p.m. Notice that the time must be specified in a 24-hour format. If you prefer, you can specify the date in numeric format. The following pseudo-code shows you how to enter the date in numeric format:

```
var specificDate= new Date(year, month, day, hours, minutes, seconds);
```

More specifically, you could use the following statement to enter the date and time shown previously:

```
var specificDate= new Date(1969, 9, 18, 3, 40, 0);
```

Months start with the number 0 (similar to many other objects in JavaScript), so October is referenced as 9 instead of 10. If you leave off the hours, minutes, and seconds, the computer assumes that you mean midnight, as shown in the following:

```
var specificDate= new Date(1969, 9, 18);
```

Methods of the Date Class

The `date` class includes a large number of methods for manipulating dates. These methods allow programmers to create new dates and change existing dates. Methods of the `date` object are designed to change an aspect of a particular date (e.g., the hour setting) and are often entered as strings or numbers.

Depending on the specific method (when entering the information as a number), you can enter the information in terms of a time (e.g., the 14 of December) or in milliseconds that have elapsed from a certain point (e.g., add 14,523 milliseconds). You can output dates in several ways, depending on the amount of information needed and how user friendly you need the output to be. You explore several of the most common methods of the `date` object in the following sections.

getDate(), setDate()

The `getDate()` and `setDate()` methods apply to the day of the month in a particular `date` object. For instance, the following code outputs 18 as the day in the `date` object:

```
var specificDate=new Date("October 18, 1969 15:40:00");
document.write(specificDate.getDate());
```

The `setDate()` method changes the day of the month in a `date` object. To change the date in the code example to 21, you would write the following statement:

```
specificDate.setDate(21);
```

getDay()

The `getDay()` method returns the day of the week of the day stored in the `date` object. The day of the week returns as a numeric value from 0 (Sunday) to 6 (Saturday). Using the `date` object created in the previous section, you can request the day of the week by writing the following statement:

```
document.write(specificDate.getDay());
```

Using the date October, 25, 1969, the number 6 returns, which indicates that this particular day was a Saturday.

get FullYear(), setFullYear()

These methods allow you to return the year or set the year within the `date` object. The number is specified as a four-digit number (hence, the word "full" in the method name). To return the year from a `date` object named `myDate`, you would write

```
document.write(myDate.getFullYear());
```

To set the year in the same `date` object, you would write

```
myDate.setFullYear(1971);
```

getHours(), setHours()

As you might imagine, these methods get and set the hour stored in the `date` object. Hours are expressed as `0` for midnight and extend to `23` for 11 p.m. To change the hour to 2 p.m., you would write the following statement:

```
myDate.setHours(14);
```

To check the current hour specified in the `date` object, you would write

```
document.write(myDate.getHours());
```

getMinutes(), setMinutes()

To set the `minute` property in a `date` object, you can use the `setMinutes()` method, as shown in the following statement:

```
myDate.setMinutes(10);
```

The previous statement changes the minute setting to `10`. It is important to note that minutes start at `0` for the first minute and end at `59` for the last minute in the hour, which is the way we usually note time (rather than noting the 60th minute at the end of the hour). To check the minute setting in a `date` object, you would write

```
myDate.getMinutes();
```

getMonth(), setMonth()

At this point, the `getMonth()` and `setMonth()` methods are probably obvious to most readers. Remember that months start with `0` for January and end with `11` for December. To change the month to November in a `date` object named `myDate`, and then output the month to the user, you would write the following statements:

```
myDate.setMonth(10);
document.write(myDate.getMonth());
```

toLocaleString()

The `toLocaleString()` method returns the time from a `date` object as an easy-to-understand text string. Browsers often output this information in slightly different fashions, but this method usually offers the most user-friendly version of the date, which includes the day of the week. To create a `date` object and return the object to the user, you would write the following statements:

```
var specificDate=new Date("October 18, 1969 15:40:00");
document.write(specificDate.toLocaleString());
```

Incorporating this code into a Web page with some explanatory copy yields the following result in a browser.

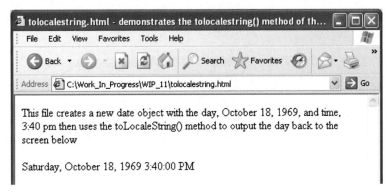

FIGURE 11.13

To Extend Your Knowledge . . .

THE DATE OBJECT

The `newDate()` constructor method and many of the other methods of the `date` object allow programmers to manipulate dates and time in milliseconds. One day is equal to 84,400,000 milliseconds. This level of precision is very useful when working with extremely technical and precise calculations.

Instantiate a Date Object

1   In your text editor, open date.html from your WIP_11 folder.

2   Insert the following code.

```
. . .
<body>
<p>This file creates a new date object with the current day and
time, and then outputs it back to the screen below</p><p>
<script language="JavaScript" type="text/javascript">
var currentTime=new Date();
document.write("The current time is "+currentTime);
</script>
</p>
</body>
. . .
```

3   Save your changes and open the file in your browser.

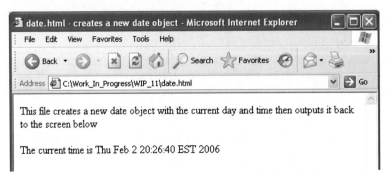

This file creates a new date object with the current day and time then outputs it back to the screen below

The current time is Thu Feb 2 20:26:40 EST 2006

FIGURE 11.14

The current date and time appear.

4   Close the file in your browser and text editor.

To Extend Your Knowledge . . .

MILLISECOND CALCULATIONS FROM INDEX DATES

Dates can also be constructed and manipulated using milliseconds from an index date. This type of date manipulation is more complex than the examples presented in this book. The ability to manipulate dates in this fashion is useful for synchronizing events across different regions or making very precise time measurements. The **index date** is a specific time used in calculations, specifically 12 a.m., January 1, 1970, Greenwich Mean Time (GMT).

When manipulating dates in terms of the index date, date and time information is returned in terms of the amount of time the date occupies from the index date. This can prove confusing to novice programmers because a day has 84,400,000 milliseconds; therefore, a day before the index date would return as −84,400,000, whereas a day after the index date would return as 84,400,000.

Manipulating dates using the index date is quite complex and only useful in technical problem-solving situations. For the sake of simplicity, we describe the most common (and simplest) methods of the `date` object in this chapter and avoid using the index date. In addition, we work with standard dates, such as January 1, 1983, and avoid working with milliseconds wherever possible.

toLocaleString() BROWSER COMPATIBILITY

The text string generated by the `toLocaleString()` method is slightly different in every browser. For this reason, your output may appear slightly different than the screen shots shown in this chapter.

LESSON 6   Creating Timers

Programs often require *timers* to set a waiting period before an action executes. Some JavaScript methods are designed to create a timer, and then carry out a JavaScript statement when the timer expires. Depending on the method used, the method may execute the statement once when the interval expires, or it may start the timer again and repeatedly execute the statement at the end of each interval. Additional methods may also be used to stop the timer (once it starts) and keep the statement from executing. You explore these methods in the following sections.

setTimeout() and clearTimeout()

The `setTimeout()` method requires two parameters. The first is a valid JavaScript statement, and the second parameter is a number that represents the number of milliseconds that should pass before the command executes. The first parameter passes as a string and the second parameter passes as a number. Using pseudo-code, the `setTimeout()` method takes the following form:

```
setTimeout("statement",time in milliseconds);
```

To display a welcome message after 5 seconds, you would write a statement such as

```
setTimeout("document.write('Hi!')",5000);
```

Every timer created by the `setTimeout()` method creates a unique ID, which is returned by the method. This ID can be used by the `clearTimeout()` method to stop the counter before the command in the `setTimeout()` method executes. For instance, examine the following code:

```
var timer=setTimeout("document.write('Hi!')",5000);
document.write(timer);
clearTimeout(timer);
```

These code statements create a timer that writes the string "`Hi!`" after 5 seconds. The timer is created using the `setTimeout()` method, which also places the ID of the timer into the variable named `timer`. The `clearTimeout()` method uses this ID to keep the `document.write()` statement from executing. Placing this code into a script yields the following result in a browser.

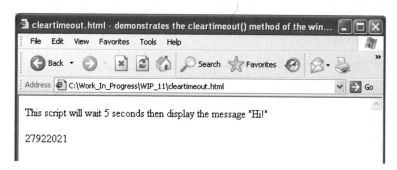

FIGURE 11.15

setInterval() and clearInterval()

The `setInterval()` method is virtually identical to the `setTimeout()` method with one exception: when the time runs out, the command executes and the timer restarts. The code executes repeatedly until the `clearInterval()` method stops the timer.

The `setTimeout()` method executes the statement once — when the timer is finished. The `setInterval()` method loops at the specified interval by executing the statement and restarting the timer.

Timers are used for various purposes in different scripts. Programmers often use timers to allow their users enough time to read a message before an event occurs. In the following exercise, you give the user enough time to read a message before redirecting the browser to another page. Programmers often use this technique when a Web page has been moved to a new location/URL.

Create a Timer

1 **In your text editor, open timer.html from your WIP_11 folder.**

2 **Insert the following code.**

```
. . .
</head>
<body>
<script language="JavaScript" type="text/javascript">
setInterval("location.reload()",15000);
</script>
</body>
</html>
```

This code executes the `reload()` method every 15 seconds. If a new version of the page has been saved, the page automatically reloads.

3 **Open the file in your browser.**

A blank page will appear because the page does not yet have any visible content.

4 **In your text editor, insert the following code:**

```
<body>
<script language="JavaScript" type="text/javascript">
setInterval("location.reload()",15000);
</script>
<p>This file checks for a new file every 15 seconds</p>
</body>
</html>
```

This code creates a noticeable change in the file that can be detected when it reloads.

5 **Save your changes in the text editor.**

6   **Return to your browser and wait.**

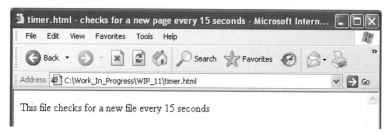

FIGURE 11.16

The file should reload within a few seconds.

7   **Close the file in your browser and text editor.**

To Extend Your Knowledge . . .

MILLISECONDS

A *millisecond* is 1/1000th of a second. Therefore, 5000 milliseconds equals 5 seconds.

SUMMARY

In this chapter, you discovered how JavaScript programmers work with dates, times, and numbers. When working with numbers, it is important to remember that calculations in JavaScript follow a strict precedence. In general, calculations are completed from left to right. You now know that items in parentheses or brackets are calculated first, multiplication or division is completed next, and addition or subtraction is completed last.

You also considered the `date` object and `Math` object in this chapter. Strictly speaking, you can work without either object and still manipulate dates and complete complex calculations — however, the programming would be quite difficult. The `Math` object, in particular, provides methods that convert numbers to absolute values, round numbers to the nearest integer, generate random numbers, raise numbers to powers, take square roots, and pick the largest or smallest number from a list of numbers. The `Math` object also has constant properties that hold constant values, such as the number represented by pi.

The `date` object allows you to easily store and manipulate dates. Various methods of the `date` object allow you to add or subtract time from a date, as well as change part of a date and time, such as the month, day, or hour. In this chapter, you also considered the `setInterval()` and `setTimeout()` methods, which allow you to execute a command after a specific amount of time or to repeatedly perform a command at a specific interval.

KEY TERMS

Bitwise operators

Constant property

Index date

Millisecond

Modulus operator

Precedence

Rules of precedence

Timers

CHECKING CONCEPTS AND TERMS

MULTIPLE CHOICE

Circle the letter that matches the correct answer for each of the following questions.

1. Which list represents the normal order of precedence of mathematical operations in JavaScript?
   a. +, −, /, *, ()
   b. −, +, *, /, ()
   c. (), *, /, +, −
   d. /, *, +, −, ()

2. `Math` properties are different from the properties of most objects because they _____.
   a. represent large text strings
   b. represent very large numbers
   c. represent values (e.g., pi) that cannot be changed
   d. None of the above

3. Which `Math` method can you use to ensure a positive value returns?
   a. `Math.abs()`
   b. `Math.pos()`
   c. `Math.unNeg()`
   d. `Math.makePos()`

4. What is the purpose of the `Math.round()` method?
   a. To calculate the circumference of a round object
   b. To calculate the diameter of a round object
   c. To calculate the area of a round object
   d. To round off a number to the nearest integer

5. What arguments are required by the `Math.pow()` method?
   a. The number to be raised
   b. The number to be raised and the power to raise it to
   c. Four numbers to be multiplied
   d. This method requires no information

6. How does the `getDay()` method of the `date` object return information?
   a. As a day of the week, represented by a text string (e.g., "Saturday")
   b. As a day of the week, represented by a number (e.g., "2")
   c. As a day of the current month (e.g., "25th")
   d. None of the above

7. What is the purpose of the modulus (%) operator?
   a. To convert a string to an integer value
   b. To multiply two numbers
   c. To return the rounded amount after division without a decimal
   d. To return the amount left over after division

8. What type of number does the `Math.random()` method generate?
   a. An integer between 0 and 1000
   b. An integer between 0 and 100
   c. A long decimal between 0 and 1
   d. An integer between 0 and 1000

9. Which method can you use to clear a repeating loop of actions?

   a. `setInterval()`

   b. `setTimeout()`

   c. `clearInterval()`

   d. `clearTimeout()`

10. Which method can you use to create a repeating loop of actions?

   a. `setInterval()`

   b. `setTimeOut()`

   c. `clearInterval()`

   d. `toLocaleString()`

DISCUSSION QUESTIONS

1. Why is the `date` object useful? Can you perform complex time calculations when using `date` objects?

2. Why is the order of precedence important in complex calculations?

3. When would it be useful to work in milliseconds when computing dates?

4. From a conceptual standpoint, what are the steps to calculate a random number between 1 and 10 using JavaScript?

SKILL DRILL

Skill Drill exercises reinforce lesson skills. Each skill reinforced is the same, or nearly the same, as a skill presented in the chapter. Detailed instructions are provided in a step-by-step format. You can work through one or more exercises in any order.

1. Precedence and Math Object Methods

1. In your browser, open skillprecedence.html from your WIP_11 folder.

   This file represents a completed script that returns incorrect answers for a calculation.

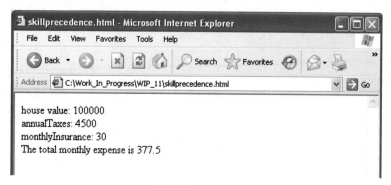

FIGURE 11.17

2. Find the following code in your text editor.

```
houseValue=100000;
annualTaxes=houseValue*0.045;
monthlyInsurance=30;
monthlyExpense=(monthlyInsurance+annualTaxes)/12;
```

Test values were already inserted into the script. The `annualTaxes` value is computed correctly, but the `monthlyExpense` value is incorrect. The `monthlyExpense` value should be the total of the `monthlyInsurance value added to the monthlyTax` value (`annualTaxes` divided by 12).

3. Correct the problem in the `monthlyExpense` calculation.

4. Save and test your file.

    The correct result is 405.

5. Close the file in your browser and text editor.

2. Generate Random Numbers Within a Range

In this exercise, you generate random numbers in a given range. To do so, you create a simple function. You can use this function to generate numbers within any boundaries, such as a number between 50 and 100.

1. In your text editor, open skillrandom.html from your WIP_11 folder.

2. Find the following code in the `<head>` section of the document.

```
. . .
<script language="JavaScript" type="text/javascript">
// insert function here

</script>
. . .
```

3. Create a function named `getBetween`. The function should accept two numbers, named `number1` and `number2`.

4. Insert the following code into the function.

```
. . .
<script language="JavaScript" type="text/javascript">
// insert function here
function getBetween(number1,number2) {
if (number2>number1) {
      return (Math.round(Math.random()*(number2-number1))+number1);
}
else {
return (Math.round(Math.random()*(number1-number2))+number2);
}
}
</script>
. . .
```

5. Insert the following code in the `<body>` section of the document to trigger the function.

```
...
</head>
<body>
<script language="JavaScript" type="text/javascript">
result=getBetween(3,7);
document.write(result);
</script>
</body>
</html>
```

6. Save your file.

7. Test the file in your browser.

   It should return a number between 3 and 7 each time.

8. Change the code to return a number between 10 and 20, and then test the file.

9. Close the file in your browser and text editor.

3. Use Numbered Time Units

1. In your text editor, open datenumbers.html from your WIP_11 folder.

2. Insert the following code.

```
...
<p>This file creates a new date object with the day, October 18,
1969, and time, 3:40 pm, by entering the date as a sequence of
numbers, and then outputs it back to the screen below</p><p>
<script language="JavaScript" type="text/javascript">
// note: months start with month 0 (January) so 9 means October.
var currentTime=new Date(1969, 9, 18, 3, 40, 0);
document.write(currentTime);
</script>
</p>
</body>
...
```

3. Save your changes in the text editor and open the file in your browser.

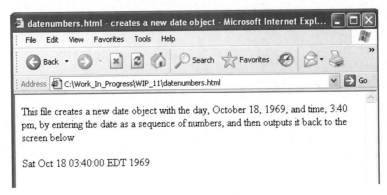

FIGURE 11.18

4. Return to your text editor and change the code to use `January 12, 1985` at `2:30 pm`.

5. Change the explanatory text to match the date you assigned in Step 4.

6. Save and test your file.

7. Close the file in your browser and text editor.

4. Use a Timer Before Redirecting a User to Another Page

1. In your text editor, open skilltimer.html from the WIP_11 folder.

2. Find the following line of code.

    ```
    document.location="http://www.web-answers.com";
    ```

    This file uses the `location` property to redirect users to the Web Answers Web site.

3. Open the file in your Web browser.

    Your browser should immediately redirect to the Web Answers Web site. Users who own computers with fast Internet access may not have seen the initial page — it may not have remained visible long enough to read. You correct this problem by adding a timer that allows you to read the explanatory text on the initial page before being redirected.

4. Return to your text editor. Change the line that starts with `document.location` to the following:

    ```
    setTimeout("document.location='http://www.web-answers.com'",5000);
    ```

    Notice that the code uses single quotes for the location property, nested inside double quotes for the timer.

5. Add some explanatory text to tell the user that the page will redirect after 5 seconds.

6. Save and test your file.

7. Change the code and explanatory text to redirect the user to a Web site of your choice after 4 seconds.

8. Close the file in your browser and text editor.

CHALLENGE

Challenge exercises expand on, or are somewhat related to, skills presented in the lessons. Each exercise provides a brief introduction, followed by instructions presented in a numbered-step format that are not as detailed as those in the Skill Drill exercises. You should work through these exercises in order.

1. Use Precedence

For a class assignment, you are writing a script to change temperature values from Fahrenheit to Celsius and Celsius to Fahrenheit. You partially completed the script. To finish the assignment, you must write the formula that computes the Fahrenheit value when given the Celsius value.

1. In your browser, open challengetemperature.html from the WIP_11 folder.

2. Enter `212` for the Fahrenheit temperature and click elsewhere on the page.

    The Celsius temperature should compute as `100`.

3. Open the file in your text editor.

4. Find the following code.

    ```
    . . .
    function CtoF() {
        C = document.forms[0].Ctemp.value;
        // insert formula

        document.forms[0].Ftemp.value=F;
    } // end function
    . . .
    ```

    You use this function to convert Celsius values to Fahrenheit.

5. Insert the following code to start a calculation for the variable `F`. This variable represents the Fahrenheit value.

    ```
    . . .
    function CtoF() {
        C = document.forms[0].Ctemp.value;
        // insert formula
        F =
        document.forms[0].Ftemp.value=F;
    } // end function
    . . .
    ```

6. Use the following flowchart to write the formula to compute the Fahrenheit value (F) that you started in the previous step.

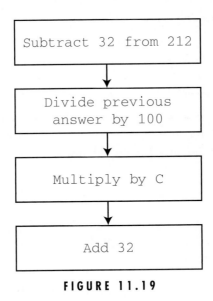

```
Subtract 32 from 212
        │
        ▼
  Divide previous
   answer by 100
        │
        ▼
   Multiply by C
        │
        ▼
      Add 32
```

FIGURE 11.19

7. Save your changes and refresh your browser.

8. Enter `100` as the Celsius value and click elsewhere on the page.

    If you entered the formula correctly, a value of `212` should return as the Fahrenheit temperature.

9. Close the file in your browser and text editor.

2. Determine Maximum and Minimum Values

In this Challenge, you use methods of the `Math` object to determine the largest or smallest number in a string of numbers.

1. In your text editor, open challengemax.html from the WIP_11 folder.

2. Insert the following code.

```
...
<body>
<p>This page uses a simple script to find the largest number in a
list using the Math.max() method.</p>
<script language="JavaScript" type="text/javascript">
var largestNumber=Math.max(27,33,54,76,43,23,12,6,78,98);
document.write("The largest number is "+largestNumber+"<br />");
</script>
</body>
</html>
```

3. Save the file in your text editor and open the file in your browser.

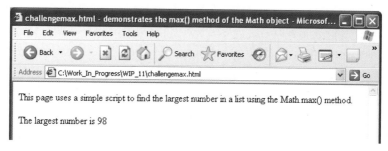

FIGURE 11.20

4. Insert additional code to determine the minimum value from the same list of numbers.

   Hint: Use the `Math.min()` method.

5. Save and test your file.

6. Close the file in your browser and text editor.

3. Use Timers to Create a Clock

In this challenge, you create an online clock, and then place the clock in the title bar of a Web page. This script requires complex use of timers that are triggered by event handlers when the page loads and unloads. You use the `toLocaleString()` method to format the time and date. Please note, this exercise may not work in Mac-based browsers.

1. In your text editor, open challengeclock.html from your WIP_11 folder.

2. Insert event handlers to start the clock when the page loads and stop the clock when the page unloads.

```
...
</script>
</head>
<body onload="startClock()" onunload="stopClock()">
<p>This page creates a clock in the title bar.</p>
</body>
</html>
```

3. Insert the code to initialize the timer and create the function to start the clock.

```
. . .
<script language="JavaScript" type="text/javascript">
// made by: Nicolas - http://www.javascript-page.com
var clockID = 0;

function startClock() {
  clockID = setTimeout("updateClock()", 500);
}
</script>
</head>
<body onload="StartClock()" onunload="StopClock()">
. . .
```

4. Insert the function to update the clock.

```
. . .
function StartClock() {
clockID = setTimeout("UpdateClock()", 500);
}
function updateClock() {
  if(clockID) {
      clearTimeout(clockID);
      clockID = 0;
      } // end if

      var tDate = new Date();
      document.title = tDate.toLocaleString();
      clockID = setTimeout("updateClock()", 1000);
} // end function
</script>
</head>
<body onload="startClock()" onunload="stopClock()">
. . .
```

5. Insert the function to stop the timer when the user closes the page.

```
...
document.title = tDate.toLocaleString();
clockID = setTimeout("UpdateClock()", 1000);
} // end function

function stopClock() {
if(clockID) {
    clearTimeout(clockID);
    clockID = 0;
    }
}
</script>
</head>
<body onload="startClock()" onunload="stopClock()">
...
```

6. Save your changes in the text editor.

7. Open the file in your browser and inspect the title bar to ensure your script is working properly. The clock should change every second.

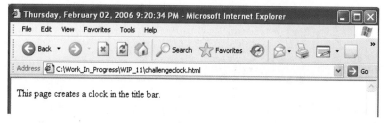

FIGURE 11.21

8. Keep the file open in your browser and text editor for the next challenge.

4. Use Date Object Methods

In the previous exercise, you used timers to constantly create new `date` objects. Using the `toLocaleString()` method, you were also able to output the current date and time as a text string. In this challenge, you use `date` object methods and decision statements to exercise greater control over the information returned to the user.

1. In the open challengeclock.html, find the following line of code in the `updateClock()` function.

    ```
    document.title = tDate.toLocaleString();
    ```

2. Modify this line of code as follows to use `date` methods to format the output of the clock.

    ```
    document.title = ""+ tDate.getHours() + ":" + tDate.getMinutes()
    + ":" + tDate.getSeconds();
    ```

3. Save the file in your text editor and refresh your browser.

    The title bar should be formatted with the hours, minutes, and seconds only.

4. Write a statement to create a variable to hold the current day. Use the `getDay()` method to assign the day to the variable you create.

5. Use `if` statements to translate the day from a number to the name of the day. For example, if the day is 3, convert the day into the string "`Wednesday`".

6. Modify the output to include the day of the week. The formatting of your output should match the following.

FIGURE 11.22

7. Save and test your file.

8. Close the file in your browser and text editor.

PORTFOLIO BUILDER

Calculate a Pizza Order

Designers commonly build forms to calculate e-commerce transactions. This requires users to build forms using various calculations to compute the cost of an online transaction. In this Portfolio Builder, you will build a form that allows customers to order pizza online by using a simple Web page. From your Chapter_11>Portfolio_Builder_11 folder, open the file named pizzacalculator.html in your browser. On the left side of the window, you see a form that allows a user to choose the following options when ordering a pizza:

- What size of pizza?

- What type of pizza?

- How many pizzas?

You need each item to accurately calculate the total cost of the order. Simulate a typical user and make some choices on the form, and then click the Calculate Total button. An alert dialog box appears. Notice that the values are incorrect.

In this Portfolio Builder, your task is to create mathematical calculations that allow a typical user to see accurate values.

1.   As you create your calculations, remember to control the order of operation. The correct order of operation will result in correct results, which will in turn allow users to trust the site and its processes.

2.   Use the following pseudo-code to create the actual calculations:

  - subtotal = (type * 4) + (size * quantity)

  - total = subtotal + delivery

3.   The value type is multiplied by the value of 4, which represents a fixed mark-up based on the type of pizza. Depending on business profit margins, this value could change so a variable should be used to represent the fixed mark-up in the code. The value of the fixed mark-up can be initialized to a value of 4, which represents the current fixed mark-up margin.

4.   After creating both the subtotal and total calculations, the resulting value should be correct in the alert dialog box.

5.   The alert should also tell you whether you are paying a delivery fee.

6.   Use a calculator to check the result to ensure your script is functioning correctly.

CHAPTER 12

Adding Forms and Images

OBJECTIVES

In this chapter, you learn how to:

- Use form elements and properties
- Validate form elements
- Use image properties

- Preload images
- Create rollover scripts
- Use advanced image scripts

Why Would I Do This?

The `form` object and `image` object are probably the most useful objects within JavaScript's Document Object Model because these objects allow you to manipulate HTML forms and images in ways not possible using HTML alone. Most practical applications of JavaScript usually incorporate one of these two objects.

HTML forms allow programmers to gather data from users for various purposes. Designing forms in HTML is particularly practical because it allows designers to create forms that are easy for end users to understand. JavaScript enables you to greatly extend the power and flexibility of HTML forms by allowing you to check the quality of the information entered and perform other tasks before the form data is sent to the server.

JavaScript allows you to use images in many ways, including rollover buttons (images that change in response to user choices). In HTML, you use the `<img>` tag to display images, as shown in the following example:

```
<img src="boy.jpg">
```

Using HTML, you can display an image; in contrast, JavaScript provides several new ways of manipulating images. For example, you can **preload** image files, which means you load the file before the user sees the image. In many situations, this enables images to appear more quickly when the user wants to see them. In this chapter, you learn how to use JavaScript to add and manipulate forms and images, allowing you to extend the complexity, depth, and functionality in your Web page.

VISUAL SUMMARY

Recall from your work with HTML that you use the `<form>` tag to create a form. When you use this tag, JavaScript creates a matching `form` object that can be referenced from the `forms[]` array. For example, the first form in a page would be referred to as `forms[0]`, and the second form in a page would be referred to as `forms[1]`.

To create an element in a form, you use the `<input>` tag. The `type` attribute specifies the type of `form` element that you want to create. The `type` attribute can include the following: `text`, `password`, `radio`, `checkbox`, `reset`, `button`, `submit`, `image`, and `hidden`. Consider the code for the following form, which allows a user to request a service appointment for her vehicle.

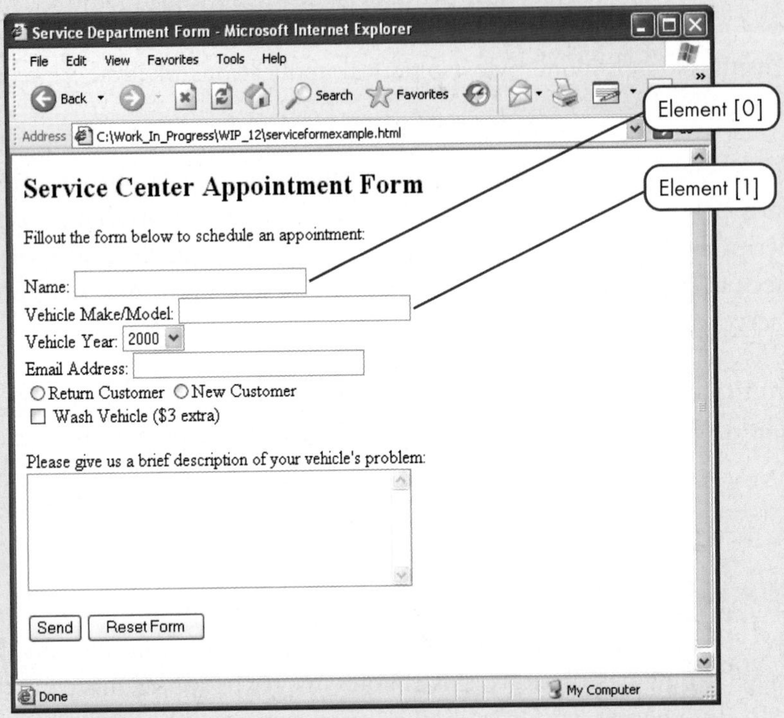

FIGURE 12.1

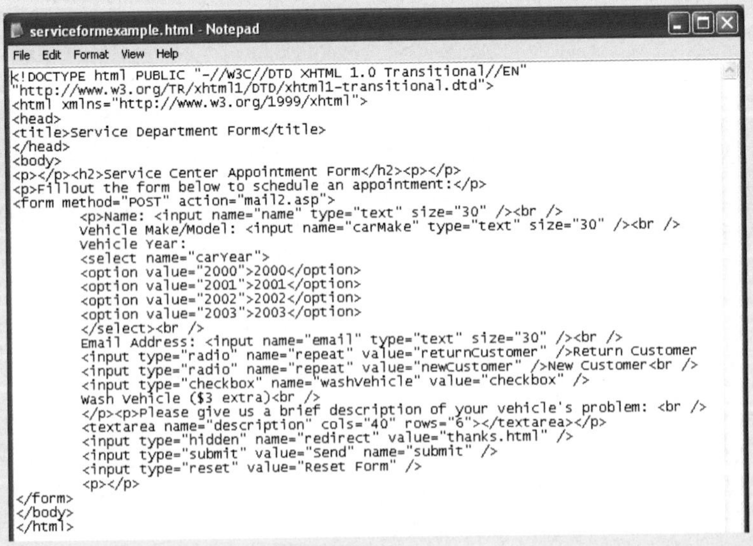

```
<!DOCTYPE html PUBLIC "-//W3C//DTD XHTML 1.0 Transitional//EN"
"http://www.w3.org/TR/xhtml1/DTD/xhtml1-transitional.dtd">
<html xmlns="http://www.w3.org/1999/xhtml">
<head>
<title>Service Department Form</title>
</head>
<body>
<p></p><h2>Service Center Appointment Form</h2><p></p>
<p>Fillout the form below to schedule an appointment:</p>
<form method="POST" action="mail2.asp">
        <p>Name: <input name="name" type="text" size="30" /><br />
        Vehicle Make/Model: <input name="carMake" type="text" size="30" /><br />
        Vehicle Year:
        <select name="carYear">
        <option value="2000">2000</option>
        <option value="2001">2001</option>
        <option value="2002">2002</option>
        <option value="2003">2003</option>
        </select><br />
        Email Address: <input name="email" type="text" size="30" /><br />
        <input type="radio" name="repeat" value="returnCustomer" />Return Customer
        <input type="radio" name="repeat" value="newCustomer" />New Customer<br />
        <input type="checkbox" name="washVehicle" value="checkbox" />
        Wash Vehicle ($3 extra)<br />
        </p><p>Please give us a brief description of your vehicle's problem: <br />
        <textarea name="description" cols="40" rows="6"></textarea></p>
        <input type="hidden" name="redirect" value="thanks.html" />
        <input type="submit" value="Send" name="submit" />
        <input type="reset" value="Reset Form" />
        <p></p>
</form>
</body>
</html>
```

FIGURE 12.2

In this form, the `<input>` tag creates various `form` elements. In the Email Address and Name fields, the `text` type is used. A `checkbox` type is used for the Wash Vehicle check box. The `radio` type is used to create the Return Customer and New Customer radio buttons, and the `<textarea>` tag is used to gather the description of the vehicle.

In this form, the information is sent to a server-side script named mail2.asp using the `post` method. The server-side script is an ASP script that accepts the information and sends an e-mail to the service manager. A hidden field is also sent to the script; it contains the URL of a Thank You page that the user will see after the server-side script accepts the information.

Recall from HTML that you use the `post` or `get` method to submit a form. The `get` method appends the data to the end of the URL specified in the `action` attribute of the `<form>` tag. The `post` method sends the data as part of the HTTP protocol, which effectively hides the information from the end user.

If you do not specify a file in the `action` attribute, the information is sent back to the file that contained the `<form>` tag. If you do not specify a method for the `<form>` tag, the `get` method sends the information. Most server-side scripts are designed to receive information sent by the `post` method. (The ability to set up a server-side script to process form data requires an understanding of a server-side scripting language, as well as an understanding of the server's configuration. An explanation of these items is beyond the scope of this book. Most Web hosting companies offer free scripts and detailed explanations on how to set up form-processing scripts on their servers.)

The `document` object represents the HTML code in a Web page. The `forms[]` array represents each `<form>` tag in the document. Similarly, the `elements[]` array represents each `form` element within the form. The first element in the `elements[]` array would represent the first item in the form. For instance, to reference the first element in the first form, you would write

```
document.forms[0].elements[0]
```

To reference the second element in the first form, you would write

```
document.forms[0].elements[1]
```

The keyword `value` outputs the value stored in the `form` element. For instance, if you want to see what a user entered into the third element in the form, you would write the following:

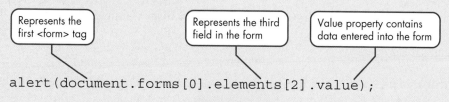

```
alert(document.forms[0].elements[2].value);
```

FIGURE 12.3

Whenever you use an `<img>` tag, JavaScript creates an `image` object to represent the image. Similar to other JavaScript objects, an image can be represented by the name assigned to it in HTML. Similarly, `image` objects in JavaScript are represented by the `images[]` array. The `images[]` array is part of the `document` object. Each element in the `images[]` array contains an `image` object. One `image` object is created for every `<img>` tag found in the HTML code. This is consistent with the way JavaScript handles other HTML tags, as you may remember from previous examples. For instance, if you assume the `<img>` tag example shown previously is the first one in the HTML document, you could reference the image as

```
document.images[0]
```

If the HTML tag includes the name of the image, you can also refer to the image by name in JavaScript. For instance, consider the following line of code:

```
<img src="boy.jpg" name="boyPic">
```

Knowing this, you can also refer to the image in the following ways within JavaScript:

```
document.images['boyPic']
document.boyPic
```

LESSON 1   Using Form Elements and Properties

As you know, JavaScript creates an entry in the `forms[]` array for each `<form>` tag encountered in the document. Each `form` element within a form creates an entry in an `elements[]` array for that form. As you have seen, the forms and elements are numbered in the order in which they appear in the HTML document.

You can also name forms and elements, and then refer to the objects by their assigned names or ids. For instance, you can name a form and an element in the following fashion:

```
<form action=" "name="serviceForm" id="serviceForm">
Name: <input name="name" id="name" type="text" size="30" />
```

In this situation, you can refer to the value of the element of the form as follows:

```
serviceForm.name.value
```

Assuming that `serviceForm` is the first form in the document, you could also refer to the value of this field as

```
forms[0].name.value
```

Assuming that you are referring to the value stored in the first element of the form, you could type

```
serviceForm.elements[0].value
```

Depending on your specific needs, you can choose to use the `forms[]` array or the `elements[]` array to refer to any form or element. As you learned in previous lessons, referring to the number of the element is useful when creating loops, but it is usually easier to use the name of an individual element when checking the value of a single field.

If more than one element has the same name, JavaScript creates an array to hold the values. This is useful with radio buttons that must have the same name because only one button can be chosen at a time. The following code establishes radio buttons that allow you to know whether a customer is new or returning:

```
<input type="radio" name="repeat" value="returnCustomer" />Return Customer
<input type="radio" name="repeat" value="newCustomer" />New Customer<br />
```

To access the value of the first radio button in the `repeat[]` array, you would type

```
forms[0].repeat[0]
```

Similar to radio buttons, multiple check boxes can also have the same name. In this case, you would create an array for all check boxes that have the same name.

The `form` object contains several properties that primarily contain the aspects assigned in the HTML `<form>` tag. These properties include the `name` property assigned to the `<form>` tag and names assigned to individual `<input>` tags. They also include a property that enables you to find out if a particular check box or radio button has been selected. In the following sections, you examine the primary properties of the `form` object.

Name

The `name` property returns the name assigned to each `<form>` tag or each element within the form. Consider the following statements in an HTML form:

```
<form method="post" name="serviceForm" action="mail2.asp">
<p>Name: <input name="name" type="text" size="30"/>
```

To generate an alert box with the name of the first form in the HTML document, you would write

```
alert(document.forms[0].name);
```

Similarly, if you want to determine the name of the first element in the first form, you would write

```
alert(document.forms[0].elements[0].name);
```

Checked

With check boxes or radio buttons, you are usually only interested in the item that was checked (selected). Whenever you have multiple radio buttons or check boxes with the same name, HTML allows you to check only one of the items, and then JavaScript creates an associated array. You can use the `checked` property to discover which element was checked. For instance, to determine whether the first radio button in the example file was checked, you would write

```
document.forms[0].repeat[0].checked;
```

If the first radio button was checked, a value of `true` returns. This creates interesting possibilities. For instance, you might want to trigger a specific action if the second radio button was checked:

```
if (document.forms[0].repeat[1].checked) {
    alert("You chose the second radio button.");
} // end if
```

Action

The `action` property of the `form` object holds the URL where the information in the form will be sent when the user clicks the Submit button. If a form named `serviceForm` sends the information to a server-side script named `formmail.pl`, your `<form>` tag might be written as

```
<form name="serviceForm" action="formmail.pl">
```

In this situation, you could refer to the file in the `action` attribute within JavaScript in the following fashion:

```
document.serviceForm.action
```

In this example, the value of the `action` property is `formmail.pl`.

Method

The `method` property holds the same information specified in the `method` attribute of the `<form>` tag. You may recall from HTML that the `method` is specified as `post` or `get`. For instance, assume that the following `<form>` tag is within an HTML document:

```
<form name="serviceForm" method="post" action="formmail.pl">
```

In this situation, the `method` property of the document returns a value of `post`. You can reference this property as

```
document.serviceForm.method
```

Access Form Elements in JavaScript

1   **In your text editor, open seeelements.html from the WIP_12 folder.**

This file is essentially the same form shown as an example in the preceding text. In the following steps, you write a function to display the content of each `form` element when the form is submitted. The function was started for you.

2 **Insert the following code in the function in the head of the HTML document.**

```
function seeElements() {
alert(document.forms[0].elements[0].value);
} //end seeElements
```

This code will display the first value in the form when the form is submitted.

3 **Add the following code to the `<form>` tag.**

```
<form action="" method="post" onsubmit="return seeElements()">
```

This code triggers the function.

4 **Save the file in your text editor and open it in your browser.**

5 **In the Name field, type your name and click the Send button at the bottom of the page.**

An alert box appears with the name you entered into the field. If your name were Joe Smith, the alert would resemble the following illustration.

FIGURE 12.4

6 **Click OK to close the alert box. Close your browser.**

Next, you change the function to display all the elements.

7 **Return to the text editor. Change the function to the following.**

```
. . .
function seeElements() {
for (x=0; x<11; x++) {
     alert(document.forms[0].elements[x].value);
} //end for
     return false;
} //end seeElements
. . .
```

The `for` statement creates a loop that will cycle through the various elements in the form.

8 **Save your changes in the text editor and reopen the file in your Web browser.**

9 Enter information in the fields on the form, and then click the Send button.

As you click OK to move through each element, match the element value shown in the alert box with the element in the original HTML file. The value of the hidden element is thanks.html, which is the name of the redirect file shown after the form is submitted. The last element shown is the Reset button.

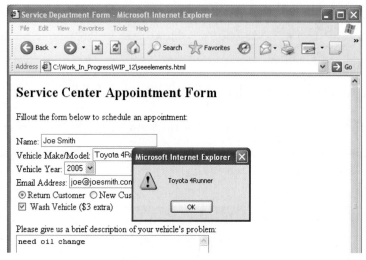

FIGURE 12.5

10 Close the file in your Web browser and text editor.

Your sample form contains a hidden element that also has an entry in the `elements[]` array.

To Extend Your Knowledge . . .

USING SCRIPTS TO CREATE E-MAILS

Active Server Pages (ASP) and Perl are technologies often used to process form data. Students are often curious about how to set up a server-side script to send an e-mail message with the content of an HTML form. You can accomplish this task in a number of ways using different technologies, including ASP and Perl. A Perl script, known as `formmail.pl`, is often used to accomplish this task, and the Common Gateway Interface (CGI) protocol is often used to communicate between the HTML form and a server-side script. CGI is a server-side technology that allows different languages to pass information to one another.

LESSON 2 Validating Forms

The ability to validate form data was one of the primary reasons that JavaScript was created. The term **validate** means to ensure the user entered his or her information completely and correctly, and that the information is in the proper format. Form validation can take on a variety of different aspects. In many cases, you may simply want to ensure the user entered a value in a required field.

Form validation methods vary according to the specific needs of the information you want to receive. In one case, you may want to ensure the user entered an e-mail address or a phone number into a form field. On another form, you may need to ensure the user entered a number or value of a specific length.

Form validation requires a number of concepts previously discussed in this book. The event handler usually calls on a function to validate the data. The function itself may call on various `form` properties, and then use Boolean logic with flow-of-control statements to analyze the information submitted.

Throughout the following sections, you examine a number of simple scripts that validate form data. These scripts demonstrate many basic validation methods that are useful in a number of programming situations.

Validating E-Mail Addresses

Online users often choose to ask questions or investigate products because they like the anonymity associated with using the Internet. They may also buy products from another country or conduct business after hours. Using a Contact form is the method of choice for most users who investigate products online, and many businesses pay particular attention to leads generated from the Contact forms on their Web sites.

Many users inadvertently enter their e-mail addresses incorrectly when filling out forms. When this happens, the user enters his or her e-mail address and submits the form but never receives a response. This error can result in a lost sale or other significant miscommunications.

Many simple forms gather user information. Consider the following form used for a new-user sign-up page:

```
<form action="">
<p>Name: <input name="name" type="text" size="30" /><br />
Email Address: <input name="email1" type="text" size="30" /><br />
<input type="submit" value="Send" name="submit" />
     <input type="reset" value="Reset Form" />
</form>
```

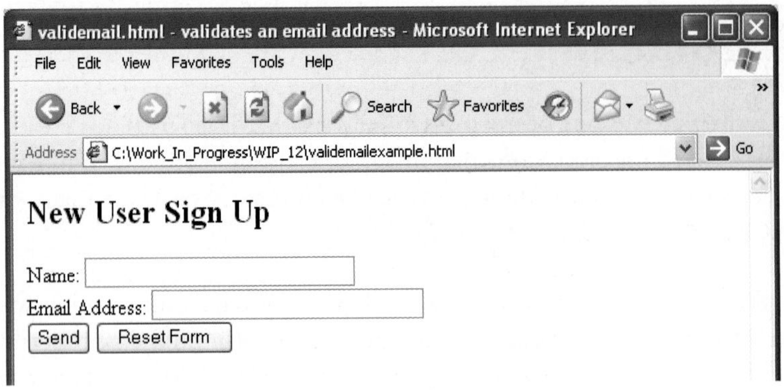

FIGURE 12.6

With JavaScript's ability to read and respond to form data, you can provide solutions to such problems as entering incorrect e-mail addresses. First, you can ensure the user entered a valid e-mail address. Let's start by modifying the `<form>` tag so it uses a function when the form is submitted:

```
<form action="" onsubmit="return validEmail()">
```

By returning a `true` or `false` value to the `onsubmit` event, you can cancel the submission (if the value is `false`) or confirm the submission (if the value is `true`). When you create the function, design the code so it ensures the e-mail address is valid. You can do this by searching through the user's information for the "@" symbol and a final period for the associated domain. (Remember that you can use the `indexOf()` method to search through a string for a specific character or phrase.) If the character doesn't exist, a value of "`-1`" will return from the method. The following code searches for the "@" sign:

```
function validEmail() {
    var atLocation=document.forms[0].email1.value.indexOf("@");
    if (atLocation == -1) {
        alert("The email address entered isn't a valid email address.
        Please resubmit.");
    } // end if
    return false;
} //end function
```

A valid e-mail address also has a period after the @ sign. You can search for the period by using the `lastIndexOf()` method. (Remember that the `indexOf()` and `lastIndexOf()` methods return a value of "`-1`" if the search string cannot be found.) The `lastIndexOf()` method works exactly like the `indexOf()` method, but the `lastIndexOf()` method starts searching at the end of the string, rather than the beginning. The `lastIndexOf()` method is the most appropriate method because an e-mail address can include more than one period:

```
var dotLocation=document.forms[0].email1.value.indexOf(".");
```

You also need to modify your `if` statement to make two comparisons instead of one and perform actions if either statement evaluates to `true`. The logical OR (`||`) operator would satisfy this purpose:

```
if (atLocation == -1 || dotLocation == -1) {
```

This statement ensures both characters are present in the text entered. If you try this in your browser, it will work well in most situations. If a user enters "joe.smith@massivecorporation" into the Email field, the script will not realize that the ".com" part of the address is missing, nor will it know that this is an invalid e-mail address. Your current script will always fail in situations where the user enters a period before the "@" sign.

This may appear to be a lot of worry and work for a few rather unimportant details, but the opposite is actually true. Imagine that you work for a very large company whose Web site receives millions of inquiries every day. You submitted your form to the Webmaster who immediately placed it on the corporate Web site (he assumed it contained error-free code). Within an hour, more than a thousand invalid e-mail addresses had been received. The company had to hire two full-time employees to call the users to obtain their correct information. When the company's president asked the Webmaster what went wrong, he identified the new online form as the culprit.

The business of programming (or scripting) often means that you must consider every mistake a user can make and proactively prevent as many of those errors as possible. The following change to your `if` statement fixes the problem with the period in the e-mail address:

```
if (dotLocation <= atLocation||atLocation==-1) {
```

In this example, the code works as follows:

Situation	Variable Values	Condition
Address entered without dot	`dotLocation = -1`	`true`
Field left blank	`dotLocation = -1;` `atLocation = -1`	`true`
Address entered without @	`atLocation = -1`	`true`
Dot entered before @	`dotLocation<atLocation`	`true`

Even if the user entered an e-mail address that has the @ sign and the final period (dot), the user can still create a typographical error when entering his or her e-mail address. Knowing this to be true, many Web sites ask the user to enter the information twice, and then compare the two entries to ensure they are identical — which is as simple as using the equality operator (`==`). Assuming that you have two Email fields (named `email1` and `email2`), you could write a function such as

```
function compareEmail() {
     if (document.forms[0].email1.value!=
     document.forms[0].email2.value) {
          alert("The email addresses entered don't match.
          Please resubmit.");
     } // end if
     return false;
} //end function
```

Checking for Blank Fields

Making sure the user has entered information into a field is easy to do in JavaScript. You simply need to add a flow-of-control statement to ensure the value isn't blank. The `if` statement works well for this type of work, as demonstrated in the following example:

```
function checkBlank(field)
{
    if (field.value =="")
    {
    alert("You must enter a phone number.");
    return false;
    }
    else
    return true;
}
```

Here is the code to access the form validation:

```
<form action="" onsubmit="return checkBlank(this.phone)">
Phone: <input type="text" name="phone" id="phone">
<input type="submit" value="Submit">
<form>
```

Checking for Numeric Values

It is often necessary to check a value to ensure it is a number. You can do this in a number of ways, including using the `isNaN()` method. This method returns `true` if the submitted value is a number, and it returns `false` if the submitted value is not a number. This method takes a single attribute, which is the value to be considered. The following simple script creates a form that allows a user to enter a number.

```
<form action="" onsubmit="return checkNumber()">
    <input name="number" type="text" size="12" />
    <br />
    <input type="submit" value="Send" name="submit" />
    <input type="reset" value="Reset Form" />
</form>
```

Viewing this code in a Web browser yields the following result.

FIGURE 12.7

You create the necessary `isNaN()` method with the following code:

```
function checkNumber() {
     num=document.forms[0].number.value;
     if (isNaN(num)) {
          alert("You must enter a number. Please resubmit.");
     } // end if
     return false;
} //end function
```

The function simply assigns the value of the `form` element to the variable `num`, and then verifies that the variable is a number. This script does not accept numbers with spaces or dollar signs. Elaborate scripts for number validation are available at no charge at various JavaScript enthusiasts' Web sites.

Submitting and Resetting Forms

Methods of the `form` object allow you to manually trigger the actions of a form. The primary methods of the `form` object are `reset()` and `submit()`. As you might imagine, these actions allow you to reset or submit the content of a form. The `submit()` method does not cause the `onsubmit` event to fire. This is in contrast to the `reset()` method, which causes the `onreset` event to fire.

Reset()

The `reset()` method performs the same action as clicking a Reset button on a form. This method clears all values the user entered into the form and resets the default values. Clever readers might ask why this is necessary because you can click the Reset button to perform the same action. This is true, but being able to manually trigger the event gives you more control over when the event triggers. To reset a form when the user clicks a Reset button, you would write

```
<a href="#" onclick="document.serviceForm.reset();">Reset</a>
```

Submit()

The `submit()` method has the same effect as clicking the Submit button on a form with one minor exception: the `onsubmit` event doesn't fire. This may seem a little confusing, so let's consider the method more carefully. The `onsubmit` event allows you to validate the form data before the data are actually submitted. In this situation, you can use the `onsubmit` event to call on a function that will validate the form data. The `submit()` method is designed to be used within a form validation script, after the data have been successfully validated.

Validate a Form Element

1 | **In your text editor and browser, open checkforblank.html from your WIP_12 folder.**

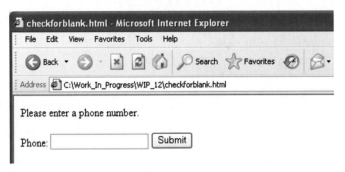

FIGURE 12.8

2 | **Find the following line of code.**

```
<form action="">
```

3 | **Modify the code as follows.**

```
<form action="" onsubmit="return checkBlank(this.phone)">
```

4 | **Insert the following function into the head of the document.**

```
...
<head>
<title>checkforblank.html</title>
<script language="JavaScript" type="text/javascript">
function checkBlank(field) {
     if (field.value =="")
     {
     alert("You must enter a phone number.");
     field.focus();
     return false;
     }
     else
          return true;
} // end function
```

```
</script>
</head>
<body>
. . .
```

5   **Save your changes in the text editor and refresh your browser.**

6   **Leave the Phone Number field blank and click the Submit button.**

FIGURE 12.9

An alert box appears.

7   **Click OK.**

The form submission is canceled.

8   **Enter a value into the field and click Send.**

The form clears, which indicates it was submitted.

9   **Close the file in your browser and text editor.**

To Extend Your Knowledge . . .

USING EVENT HANDLERS TO TRIGGER VALIDATION

You can use event handlers such as onblur or onchange with individual form elements to trigger a function, but the onsubmit handler is usually the easiest and most user-friendly way to trigger form validation.

FORMMAIL SCRIPTS

Most Web hosting providers offer scripts to process information from an HTML form. Other scripts can often be downloaded from various Web sites for this purpose. For example, the Perl script formmail.pl has been a traditional favorite used to set up scripts that process information from an HTML form. You can download this script from Matt's script archive, located at www.scriptarchive.com/formmail.html. Some knowledge of the hosting server is needed to configure this script.

LESSON 3 Using Image Properties

In HTML, `<img>` tags often accept many attributes. Consider the following code statement from an HTML page:

```
<img src="topslice0.jpg" width="720" height="121" border="0"
alt="Bridge Picture" name="bridgePic" />
```

This statement includes many of the attributes common in `<img>` statements. Here, we use pseudo-code to review the purpose of this statement:

```
Display the image topSlice0.jpg at a width of 720 pixels and a height of
121 pixels. Name the picture bridgePic and make sure no border appears
around the image. The text "Bridge Picture" should be shown if the image
hasn't finished loading or if the user rolls his mouse over the image.
```

The attributes shown in the code example represent the most common attributes used to display images, but additional attributes can also be used. You already know that every HTML `<img>` tag is represented by an `image` object in JavaScript. The attributes specified in the `<img>` tag are represented by an associated property of the `image` object. Conveniently, the property in JavaScript is named as it appears in the HTML code. For instance, the `align` property of the `image` object holds the value assigned in the `align` attribute of the HTML `<img>` tag. Take a moment to review the list of properties of the `image` object.

Property	Description
`align`	Can take on several different values, but is usually set to left or right.
`alt`	The alternative text shown if the image hasn't loaded or the user rolls over the image. Set by the `alt` attribute in the `<img>` tag.
`border`	The border (in pixels) shown around the image.
`complete`	A Boolean value that indicates whether the image has finished loading.
`height`	The height of the image in pixels. This can be a percentage value (of the table cell or browser window), but this is rare.
`hspace`	The horizontal space around the image.
`longDesc`	The `longdesc` attribute from the `<img>` tag, which represents a longer description than the `alt attribute`.
`lowSrc`	The `lowsrc` attribute of the `<img>` tag, which specifies a low-resolution file that can temporarily display while a higher-resolution file loads.
`name`	Represents the `name` attribute of the `<img>` tag.
`src`	The URL of the image.

useMap	The URL of the client-side image map if the `<img>` tag has a `useMap` attribute.
vspace	The vertical space in pixels around the image.
width	The width of the image in pixels. This can also be a percentage value (of the table cell or browser window), but this is rare.

Use Image Properties

1   In your text editor and browser, open imageproperties.html from your WIP_12 folder.

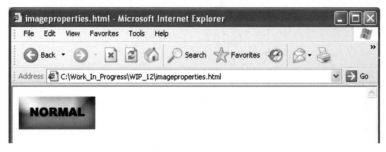

FIGURE 12.10

2   Insert the following code.

```
...
<a href="#">
<img name="imageOne" id="imageOne" src="normal.jpg" border="0"
width="120" height="50" />
</a>
<br />
<script language="JavaScript" type="text/javascript">
document.write("name is " + document.images[0].name+"<br />");
document.write("ID is "+ document.images[0].id+"<br />");
document.write("src is "+document.images[0].src+"<br />");
document.write("width is "+document.images[0].width+"<br />");
</script>
</body>
</html>
```

3   Save your changes in the text editor and refresh the file in your browser.

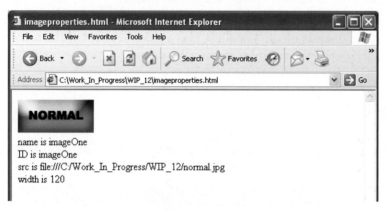

FIGURE 12.11

4   Close the file in your browser and text editor.

To Extend Your Knowledge . . .

TIPS FOR USING IMAGES

It's a good idea to include the `border="0"` statement in your `<img>` tags. If you omit this statement, some browsers display a border around the image by default.

The browser will make your pictures smaller or larger if you set the `width` or `height` attributes different than the actual picture. Doing so distorts the image, however, and should be avoided. If you need to resize an image, do so in an image manipulation program such as Adobe Photoshop or Macromedia Fireworks, and then use a sharpen filter before adding the image to your Web page.

Even if your image is sized correctly, you should always include the width and height statements in the `<img>` tag. This allows the Web browser to format the page correctly (even if the picture hasn't finished loading) and allows users to read text and see most hyperlinks without waiting for the picture to load.

LESSON 4   Preloading Images

Most HTML users are familiar with the concept of image maps. Image maps allow designers to create areas of an image that contain hyperlinks (hotspots). Rollover effects are preferable to image maps because they provide a very visible method of letting the user know he or she can click an image to do something. If nothing occurs when the user moves the mouse over an image, he or she may not realize the image is a link. Most Web designers realize that when the mouse pointer turns into a pointing finger, a hyperlink is present; novice users often miss this detail.

Rollover effects are much more intuitive than image maps, but they have one major disadvantage: rollover effects add significantly to the size of a Web page because a different image must load each time the user rolls over the button.

The use of rollovers creates another issue in terms of usability and file size. Consider the sample rollover effect you created earlier. The `<img>` tag creates an `image` object in JavaScript that you can manipulate. The `image` object has a `src` property that holds the file name of the image represented by the `image` object. By changing the `src` attribute, you force the Web browser to download a new image to display.

In a simple rollover script, you must wait for the rollover image to download once you move the mouse over the original image. When using complex images, the user must wait for several seconds before seeing the rollover effect, which creates the appearance of a sluggish browser or a problem with the page. Worse still, some browsers display a missing image box when it takes more than a few seconds to download an image.

An easy way to work around this problem is to create an `image` object for each image and to set the `src` attribute of each object. This causes the image to preload before the user rolls over the image. You typically add this code in the head section of an HTML document between the `<head>` and `</head>` tags.

Remember that you can create objects by using the keyword `new` and specifying the class to which the object belongs. The object is also created as a variable. For instance, to write a statement that creates a new `image` object named `homeOver`, you would write

```
var homeOver = new Image();
```

Strictly speaking, it isn't necessary to pass any parameters to the constructor that creates the `image` object. However, it is considered good form to pass the `width` and `height` parameters in the following fashion:

```
var homeOver = new Image(width, height);
```

Assuming that your image has a width of 120 pixels and a height of 25 pixels, you would write

```
var homeOver = new Image(120, 25);
```

Next, you set the `src` attribute of the `image` object you created, which causes the image to preload:

```
homeOver.src = "images/homeover.gif";
```

By creating an image object and setting the `src` attribute, we are forcing the browser to load the image, even though it has not yet been displayed. Assume we have already created another image object by using an `<img>` tag in the HTML document. At this point, we can change the src attribute of the `<img>` tag, using JavaScript, to force the browser to exchange the displayed image for the preloaded image. You explore this method in the following exercise.

Use Preloaded Images

1   **In your text editor, open start.html from your WIP_12>preload folder.**

2   **Insert the following code in the head of the document.**

```
<title>start.html</title>
<script language="JavaScript" type="text/javascript">
// preload the images
var offHome = new Image(44,20);
offHome.src = "images/homenormal.gif";
var onHome = new Image(44,20);
onHome.src = "images/homeover.gif";
// turn the button on
function buttonOn ()
{
```

This will create two image objects and preload the files they will contain.

3   **Find and examine the following code.**

```
// turn the button on
function buttonOn ()
{
document.images.home.src = onHome.src;
}
```

This changes the source of the image on the page to the source file of the preloaded image when the user moves over the button. A similar function is used to change the button back when the user moves off the button. Event handlers have been inserted to trigger the functions when needed.

4   **Save your file.**

5   **Open the file in your browser and move your mouse across the button.**

The image should change. You explore techniques to create rollovers in the next lesson.

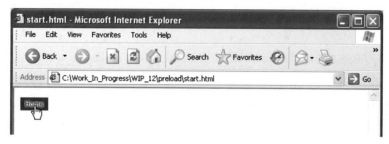

FIGURE 12.12

6   **Close your file in the browser and text editor.**

To Extend Your Knowledge . . .

IMAGE ROLLOVERS

Older browsers may not allow developers to use event handlers such as `onmouseover` and `onmouseout` in `<img>` tags. You can circumvent this problem by enclosing the `<img>` tag within an `<a>` tag and placing the event handler code within the `<a>` tag.

LESSON 5   Creating Rollovers

Creating image rollovers is probably the most popular way to use JavaScript. A rollover effect is created when one image changes to another image when the user moves the mouse pointer over a button. Rollover buttons can have two or three states. A **state** is an image that displays when a particular event occurs.

When creating buttons using JavaScript, designers usually include a normal state and an over state. The **normal state** refers to the image that displays when the user is not interacting with the button. The **over state** refers to the image that displays when the user moves the mouse button over the image.

Using a combination of event handlers and `image` objects, you can change an image when the user clicks it, rolls over it, or rolls off it. For instance, consider the following simple rollover script:

```
<img name="imageOne" id="imageOne" src="normal.jpg" border="0"
width="120" height="50" onmouseover="document.imageOne.src='over.jpg'"
onmouseout="document.imageOne.src='normal.jpg'">
```

Although this script works correctly in most browsers, it has some negative aspects. In the event handler, there is a single quote inside a double quote, which is likely to result in typing errors. In versions 3 or 4 of the Netscape browser, `onmouseover` and `onmouseout` event handlers cannot be used, so this script would not work in those browsers.

Using functions for the normal and over states of the buttons would make the script easier to type and use:

```
function buttonOn()
    {
    //change button to over state
    document.imageOne.src = 'over.jpg'
    } // end function
function buttonOff()
    {
    // change button back to normal state
    document.imageOne.src='normal.jpg'
    }
```

Typically, you want the image rollover to act as hyperlink. You can accomplish this by enclosing the `<img>` tag within an `<a>` tag:

```
<a href='newpage.html'>
<img name="imageOne" id="imageOne" src="normal.jpg" border="0"
width="120" height="50" onmouseover="buttonOn()"
onmouseout="buttonOff()" />
</a>
```

Using the `<a>` tag enables you to add a greater degree of compatibility by allowing you to use event handlers with the `<a>` tag instead of the `<img>` tag. This simple change allows older versions of the Netscape browser to work correctly with this rollover effect:

```
<a href='newpage.html' onmouseover="buttonOn()"
onmouseout="buttonOff()">
<img name="imageOne" id="imageOne" src="normal.jpg" border="0"
width="120" height="50" />
</a>
```

Our current rollover script works well, but you can make additional improvements. If you were to add multiple rollover buttons, you would need multiple rollover functions because the functions are designed to work with only one button. Using variables, however, you can reuse the functions you already created. For instance, if you modify the functions in the following manner, you can pass information to the function as necessary:

```
function buttonOn(imageName,overImage)
    {
    //change button to over image
    document[imageName].src = overImage;
    } // end function
```

```
function buttonOff(imageName,normalImage)
    {
    // change button back to normal image
    document[imageName].src= normalImage;
    } // end function
```

This requires you to also change the HTML code in order to pass the information to the function:

```
<a href='newpage.html' onmouseover="buttonOn('imageOne','over.jpg')"
onmouseout="buttonOff('imageOne','normal.jpg')">
<img name="imageOne" id="imageOne" src="normal.jpg" border="0"
width="120" height="50" />
</a>
```

Let's examine this code more closely. Consider the following statement:

```
onmouseover="buttonOn('imageOne','over.jpg')"
```

Using pseudo-code, you can describe the statement in the following fashion:

```
When the mouse rolls over the current image, call on the buttonOn() func-
tion. For the first parameter, pass the name of the image as specified in
the name attribute of the <img> tag. For the second parameter, pass the name
of the image to show when the mouse is over the image.
```

Incorporating the script into an easily reusable function allows you to use as many rollover buttons as you prefer.

Create a Simple Rollover Effect

1   **In your text editor and browser, open rollover.html from your WIP_12>rollover folder.**

FIGURE 12.13

2   **Find the following code.**

```
<img name="imageOne" id="imageOne" src="normal.jpg" border="0"
width="120" height="50" />
```

3   **Insert the following into the code you found in the previous step.**

```
<img name="imageOne" id="imageOne" src="normal.jpg" border="0"
width="120" height="50" onmouseover="document.imageOne.src=
'over.jpg'" onmouseout="document.imageOne.src='normal.jpg'"/>
```

The file name is enclosed within a set of single quotes, but the entire sequene associated with the event is placed within double quotes.

4   **Save your changes in the text editor and refresh your browser.**

5   **Move your mouse pointer over the button.**

FIGURE 12.14

The button changes as you move the mouse pointer on and off.

6   **Close the file in your browser and text editor.**

To Extend Your Knowledge . . .

DEFINING DOWN STATES

It is possible to define a ***down state*** for a button in JavaScript, which is an image that displays when you click the button. This isn't necessary, however, because you usually go to another page when you click a button.

LESSON 6   Using Advanced Image Scripts

Advanced scripts using the `image` object can be incorporated into Web pages to create stunning effects. For example, you could create a slideshow, complete with Back and Forward buttons, within a single Web page. Using techniques that you learned in previous lessons, you could preload the images, and then change the source file of the `image` object each time the user clicks the Forward or Back button.

Similarly, you could create a portfolio gallery where users could click a thumbnail image to see a larger version of the same image. Changing the event handler associated with the change to the `image` object allows a developer to automatically change one image when the user rolls over a different image — which is called a *disjointed rollover*.

Using loops, you can use JavaScript to create animations. You can create a *keyframe animation*, which is a series of still images played in rapid succession. For instance, if you want to create an animation of a circular logo rolling across a surface, you might create the seven images shown here.

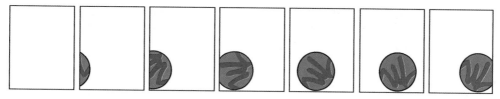

FIGURE 12.15

When using multiple images in a sequence, such as in a slideshow or animation, it is usually best to use a consistent naming scheme or a numbered sequence, such as pic1.jpg, pic2.jpg, and so forth.

Showing these images at short intervals in the same place on the screen creates the illusion of movement. At this point in your JavaScript studies, you have the requisite skills to create an animated sequence. Let's start the sequence by assigning a name to each image — a name easily manipulated in a JavaScript loop. The images in the sample code were created using a naming scheme that uses the word "ball" as the base, and then inserting the image number. For instance, the first image is named ball0001.gif, the second image is ball0002.gif, and the last image shown is ball0007.gif.

Next, you create the code to preload the images. An array provides a simple way to work with the images in JavaScript:

```
//setup array to hold and preload images
ballImage = new Array(7)
ballImage[1] = new Image();
ballImage[1].src="ball0001.gif";

ballImage[2] = new Image();
ballImage[2].src="ball0002.gif";

ballImage[3] = new Image();
ballImage[3].src="ball0003.gif";
```

```
ballImage[4] = new Image();
ballImage[4].src="ball0004.gif";

ballImage[5] = new Image();
ballImage[5].src="ball0005.gif";

ballImage[6] = new Image();
ballImage[6].src="ball0006.gif";

ballImage[7] = new Image();
ballImage[7].src="ball0007.gif";
```

A loop could be used to preload the objects, but that would add a little more complexity to the script. You can use an HTML `<img>` tag to name the image and place the first image on the page, as shown:

```
<img name="slide" src="ball0001.gif" border="0" width="160" height="200">
```

After you preload the images and display the first image, you can create a loop to display each image at a specified interval. You need a counter to keep track of which image is being displayed:

```
function changeSlide(){
    if (counter<7)
        counter++;
    else
        counter=1;
    document.slide.src=ballImage[counter].src;
    timerID = setTimeout("changeSlide()", 200);
} // end function
```

Consider the intent of this code. When the function invokes, it displays each image for 200 milliseconds. The function invokes repeatedly, and each time, 1 is added to the variable named `counter`, and the image is switched to display the image represented by this variable. If the `counter` is already at 7, the last image has already been displayed and the `counter` is reset to 1, causing the animation to loop.

A complete version of this code is shown in the file named animation.html, located in the WIP_12>animation folder. This file includes buttons designed to start and stop the animation.

A script designed to animate a sequence of images is one example of a complex image script. You can use similar techniques to create disjointed rollover effects, gallery pages, click-through slideshows, and other interesting effects. You explore these types of scripts in the following exercises.

Create Disjointed Rollovers

1   **In your text editor, open disjointed.html from the WIP_12>disjointed folder.**

2   **Examine the following code.**

```
// preload the images
var pic1 = new Image(720,121);
pic1.src = "pic1.jpg";
var pic2 = new Image(720,121);
pic2.src = "pic2.jpg";
var pic3 = new Image(720,121);
pic3.src = "pic3.jpg";
```

This code preloads the large images used in the page.

3   **Find the following code that triggers the rollover code for the first image.**

```
<a href="#" onmouseover="changePic1()">
```

Code to trigger the rollover event has been included within the `<a>` tag of each thumbnail image. By examining the `<a>` tag of each thumbnail, you can see that the page uses three functions — one for each image that displays. The names of these functions are `changePic1()`, `changePic2()`, and `changePic3()`.

4   **Insert the following code in head of the document.**

```
...
var pic3 = new Image(720,121);
pic3.src = "pic3.jpg";
// change the main picture
function changePic1 () {
    document.mainPic.src = pic1.src;
}

function changePic2 () {
    document.mainPic.src = pic2.src;
}

function changePic3 () {
document.mainPic.src = pic3.src;
}
</script>
</head>
<body>
...
```

5 | Save the file in your text editor and open it in your browser.

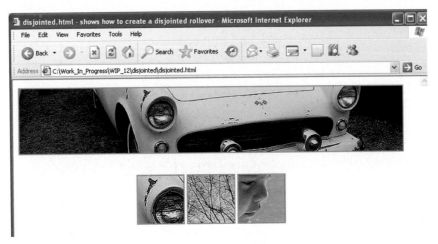

FIGURE 12.16

6 | Roll your mouse pointer over each thumbnail image.

The larger picture changes accordingly.

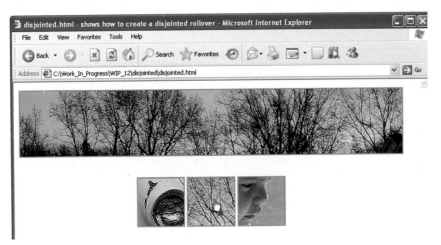

FIGURE 12.17

7 | Close the file in your browser and text editor.

Create a Click-Through Slideshow

1 | In your Web browser, open slideshow.html from the WIP_12>disjointed folder.

This is the finished version of the file that you create in this exercise.

2 Click the Back and Next buttons to move through the available images.

Notice that the slides go back to the beginning when you reach the end.

FIGURE 12.18

3 Close the file in your Web browser.

4 In your Web browser and text editor, open slideshowstart.html from the WIP_12>disjointed folder.

5 Add the following code after the head of the document.

```
...
<head>
<title>slideshowstart.html-creates a slideshow using
JavaScript</title>

<script language="JavaScript" type="text/javascript">
// start by initializing the variables
imageNumber = 1;
totalImages = 3;
// change the slide

</script>
</head>
...
```

This code initializes the variables in the slideshow script.

6 Insert the function that allows users to click through the slides.

```
...
imageNumber = 1;
totalImages = 3;
// change the slide
     function changeSlide(direction) {
     imageNumber = imageNumber + direction;
     if (imageNumber < 1) {
```

```
            imageNumber = totalImages;
        }
        if (imageNumber > totalImages) {
            imageNumber = 1;
        }
        document.mainImage.src = "pic" + imageNumber + ".jpg";
    } // end function
</script>
</head>
<body bgcolor="#FFFFFF">
    . . .
```

The function allows the user to move forward or backward in the list of photos. The file name of the image is written dynamically whenever a user clicks the Back or Next button. The condition (`imageNumber>totalImages`) evaluates whether you have reached the end of the list and, if so, returns to the first image. The condition (`imageNumber < 1`) evaluates whether you have reached the beginning of the list if you are moving backward.

7 **Insert the following code to create the buttons.**

```
    . . .
<body bgcolor="#FFFFFF">
<img name="mainImage" src="pic1.jpg" width="720" height="121"
border="0"><br>
<!-- buttons for changing slides, -->
<!--        -1 means go backward -->
<!--         1 means go forward -->
<a href="javascript:changeSlide(-1)">back</a> |
<a href="javascript:changeSlide(1)">next</a>
</body>
</html>
```

The direction determines whether you go to the previous slide or to the next slide.

8 **Save your changes in the text editor and refresh your browser.**

9 **Click through the Back and Next buttons several times to ensure your page works correctly.**

If you receive an error, check your code against the finished file and search for typing errors.

10 **Close the file in your Web browser and text editor.**

To Extend Your Knowledge . . .

ANIMATION IN JAVASCRIPT

It is possible to create animation in JavaScript by showing a sequence of images with a short delay between each, but this is impractical in most situations. Animation packages (e.g., Macromedia Flash) offer more efficient methods of animating sequences.

IMAGE ROLLOVER SCRIPTS

Image rollover scripts usually use functions to change the image from one state to another.

SUMMARY

In this chapter, you learned that interacting with forms and validating form information are two of the most popular uses of JavaScript. Whenever you add a `<form>` tag to an HTML page, JavaScript creates an entry in the `forms[]` array. For every `form` element created, JavaScript adds an entry in an `elements[]` array for that particular form.

You learned that the `form` object in JavaScript has several properties that are useful in a variety of situations: for check boxes and radio buttons, you can use the `checked` property to determine if a specific element has been checked; the `value` property of the element contains the information submitted by the user; and the `name` property contains any name assigned to the form or element in HTML.

You learned that the methods of the `form` object include `submit()` and `reset()` — not to be confused with the `onsubmit` or `onreset` event handlers — which allow you to manually submit or reset a form. You can use these methods whenever you want within JavaScript, but they are often used after form validation.

In this chapter, you discovered that in general, most form validation scripts exist in functions that are triggered by the `onsubmit` event handler. Many of these scripts cancel the `onsubmit` method by returning negative values when the information entered doesn't meet your specifications.

You learned that JavaScript creates an `image` object for every `<img>` tag created in HTML, which allows you to manipulate images in ways not possible in HTML, including creating rollover effects and click-through slideshows. You also discovered how to create `image` objects in JavaScript. When you assign a `src` attribute to an `image` object, the image preloads before it needs to display. You found that when you change the `src` attribute of an image shown on the screen, you can change to a different image without loading a new page. Finally, you learned how to combine various JavaScript techniques to create advanced scripts to generate animated sequences and portfolio gallery pages.

KEY TERMS

Disjointed rollover	Normal state	State
Down state	Over state	Validate
Keyframe animation	Preload	

CHECKING CONCEPTS AND TERMS

MULTIPLE CHOICE

Circle the letter that matches the correct answer for each of the following questions.

1. The first form in an HTML document can be referred to as _____ in JavaScript code.
   a. `form[0]`
   b. `form[1]`
   c. `form1`
   d. `forms[0]`
   e. `forms[1]`

2. The first image in an HTML Web page can be referred to as _____ in JavaScript code.
   a. `image[0]`
   b. `image[1]`
   c. `image1`
   d. `images[0]`
   e. `images[1]`

3. What does the `elements[]` array represent in JavaScript?
   a. The attributes of an image
   b. Each element or form in an HTML document
   c. Each part of a form in an HTML document
   d. None of the above

4. When using radio buttons or check boxes, what does the keyword `checked` represent in JavaScript?
   a. Data entered into a text field
   b. A Boolean value indicating whether an element was selected
   c. Whether users have read text in a scrolling text field
   d. Whether a borderline appears around a form element

5. What is the purpose of using code such as `onsubmit="return validate()"` in a `<form>` tag?
   a. You can use the `post` protocol method to send the information from the form.
   b. The server can return information from a form-processing script.
   c. A function can be triggered to check information when the form is submitted.
   d. The content of the form can be encrypted on the client's browser.

6. What does the `method` property of the `form` object represent in JavaScript?

  a. The name of the form

  b. The file name of the server-side script where the form information is sent

  c. Whether the form will be submitted by the `post` or `get` method

  d. The type of operating system the user is currently using

7. What does the `action` property of the `form` object represent in JavaScript?

  a. The name of the form

  b. The file name of the server-side script where the form information is sent

  c. Whether the form will be submitted by the `post` or `get` method

  d. The type of operating system the user is currently using

8. To use JavaScript to preload an image, a user must _____.

  a. create an `image` object and assign a file name to the src attribute

  b. use the `preload()` method

  c. put the images into the JavaScript source folder on the server

  d. load each pixel using a `for` loop

9. What happens to an image created by an `<img>` tag when a developer changes the `src` attribute of the matching `image` object to a different image file?

  a. The image shown on screen changes to a different image.

  b. The browser generates an error.

  c. A green box appears over the image.

  d. The `image` object is deleted from memory.

10. Why is JavaScript usually used for form validation?

  a. Because most server-side processing scripts also use JavaScript

  b. Because no other language contains similar tools for validation

  c. Because JavaScript is primarily a client-side language and the processing can be done before the form is submitted to the server

  d. JavaScript is not usually used for form validation

DISCUSSION QUESTIONS

1. Why is the `form` object useful in JavaScript? How can you use this object to enhance HTML Web pages?

2. Why is the `image` object useful in JavaScript? How could you use the `image` object in JavaScript to improve the usability of an HTML Web page?

3. Describe two different situations where it might be useful to validate data submitted in an HTML form.

4. A portfolio Web site could use a sequence of identical pages to show a thumbnail gallery with links to pages that show larger versions of the thumbnail images. Why do you think it would be useful for a developer to build a single page using JavaScript to change the main image when a user clicks a thumbnail image?

SKILL DRILL

Skill Drill exercises reinforce chapter skills. Each skill reinforced is the same, or nearly the same, as a skill presented in the chapter. Detailed instructions are provided in a step-by-step format. You should work through the exercises in order.

1. Trigger a Form Validation Script

Creating scripts to validate form data is one of the primary uses of JavaScript. In this exercise, you use the `onsubmit` event handler to trigger a form validation. This page allows the user to enter a password to set up a new account.

1. In your text editor, open skilllength.html from your WIP_12 folder.

2. Find the following line of code, which creates the form.

    ```
    <form action="">
    ```

3. Insert the following code to trigger a function before the form is submitted.

    ```
    <form action="" onsubmit="return checkLength()">
    ```

4. In the head of the document, create a function named `checkLength()`.

    The function will not accept any values.

5. Inside the function you created in Step 4, insert the following lines of code.

    ```
    var passLength=document.forms[0].password.value.length;
    alert(passLength);
    ```

6. Open the file in your browser.

7. Type three letters into the Password field and click Send.

    An alert box should appear with the number "3." This alert is meant to trace (examine) the number of characters to see if our code is working correctly.

8. Click OK to acknowledge the tracing alert.

9. Keep the file open for the next exercise.

2. Check for Field Length

When creating new user accounts, it is common practice to require users to enter a password and to ensure the password is of minimum length. In this exercise, you check the length of a new user password.

1. In the open skilllength.html, find the beginning of the `checkLength()` function, which is shown in the following code:

    ```
    function checkLength() {
        var passLength=document.forms[0].password.value.length;
        alert(passLength);
    ```

2. After the last line of code in Step 1 and before the end of the function, create an `if` statement to evaluate whether the password length is less than six characters. If so, the following lines of code should execute:

```
alert("Password must be at least 6 characters.
Please resubmit.");
// stop form submission
return false;
```

3. Add an `else` statement to the `if` statement you created in Step 2. When the `if` statement evaluates to `false`, the following statement should execute:

```
// continue form submission
return true;
```

4. Save your changes in the text editor and refresh your browser. Test the file in your browser.

   An alert box should tell you the number of characters that were submitted. If you enter less than six characters, a second alert box should display a warning message and the form submission should stop. If you enter six characters, the password field should clear to indicate the form was successfully submitted.

5. Remove the tracing alert that reveals the number of characters submitted.

6. Save and close the file in your browser and text editor.

3. Create a Gallery Page

1. In your browser, open skillgallery.html from your WIP_12>disjointed folder.

   This is the beginning of a portfolio gallery page.

2. Open the file in your text editor and find the following code, which, when triggered, changes the main image to the first picture:

```
// change the main picture
function changePic1 () {
    document.mainPic.src = pic1.src;
}
```

3. Find the following code, which is the function that changes the main image to the second picture:

   This function is incomplete.

```
function changePic2 () {
}
```

4. Insert code into the `changePic2()` function to change the source of the `mainPic` image object to the file named `pic2.src`.

   Hint: Use the `changePic1()` function as your guide.

5. Insert code into the `changePic3()` function to change the source of the `mainPic` image object to the file named `pic3.src`.

6. Save your changes in the text editor.

7. Refresh in the browser and test the file by moving your mouse over each image. The main picture should change.

8. Keep the file open in your browser and text editor for the next exercise.

4. Use Onclick Events to Change Image Sources

1. In the open skillgallery.html, find the following line of code, which triggers the `changePic1()` function when the mouse moves over the thumbnail image.

```
<p align="center"><a href="#" onmouseover="changePic1()"><img
src="smallpic1.jpg" width="90" height="90" border="0" /></a>
```

2. Change the code in Step 1 to use the `onclick` event to trigger the function, instead of using the `onmouseover` function.

3. Insert code to trigger the `changePic2()` function when the second thumbnail is clicked.

4. Insert code to trigger the `changePic3()` function when the third thumbnail is clicked.

5. Save your changes in the text editor.

6. Test the file in your browser.

As you click each thumbnail, the main image should change.

7. Close the file in your browser and text editor.

CHALLENGE

Challenge exercises expand on, or are somewhat related to, skills presented in the lessons. Each exercise provides a brief introduction, followed by instructions presented in a numbered-step format that are not as detailed as those in the Skill Drill exercises. You should work through these exercises in order.

1. Validate Multiple Fields

Many corporate Web sites collect significant amounts of data through HTML forms. For example, a car repair shop may want to allow customers to schedule service appointments online, which means that scheduling can take place after business hours. This practice saves the company money because the receptionist is not required to be in the office to schedule appointments. Gathering correct information is extremely important in a situation such as this; it contributes significantly to a positive customer experience. In this exercise, you validate the information submitted by the user.

1. In your text editor, open checkblank.js from the WIP_12>external folder.

This file contains a simple script that determines whether a form field is blank. If the field is blank, the function returns `false`. If the field contains information, the function returns `true`.

2. Close the file in your text editor.

3. In your Web browser and text editor, open serviceform.html from the WIP_12>external folder.

   This is essentially the same form you used in the examples throughout this chapter.

4. In the head of the HTML document, create a `<script>` tag that has the `src` attribute set to an external file named `checkblank.js`.

5. Add the following code in the head of the document to create a function to validate two fields from the form:

```
<title>Service Department Form</title>
<script language="JavaScript" src="checkblank.js">
</script>
<script language="JavaScript" type="text/javascript">
function validate() {
      check1=checkBlank(serviceForm.Name);
      check2=checkBlank(serviceForm.Model);
      check3=checkBlank(serviceForm.Email);
}// end function
</script>
</head>
```

6. Add another line of code to create a variable named `check4`. Using code from the previous step as your example, assign the result of a `checkBlank()` function performed on the Description field of the form.

   The code you just added creates four Boolean variables by validating each of the form elements where users are required to type text into a field. You also need to cancel the form submission if any of the fields returns a `false` value from the `checkBlank()` function. You need to add a flow-of-control statement using logical AND operators to ensure every value is `true`.

7. Add the following lines of code to the function you created in Step 5, below the lines you entered in Step 6:

```
if (check1&&check2&&check3&&check4) {
    return true; }
    else
    return false;
```

8. Find the `<form>` tag in the HTML document and change the line to the following:

```
<form name="serviceForm" method="post" action="" onsubmit="return
validate()">
```

9. Save your changes in the text editor and refresh your browser.

10. Click Send without filling out any values on the form.

11. Click OK to close the alert box.

12. Enter various values in the form and leave one or two of the text fields blank to test the validation script.

13. Close the file in your browser and text editor.

2. Incorporate External Rollover Scripts into a Web Page

Rollover scripts are one of the most common and useful ways to use JavaScript. When designing a Web page, it is useful to use these scripts on every page to create a consistent, easy-to-use navigation structure. In this challenge, you will incorporate an external rollover script into a Web page. By repeating this process for all Web pages in a site, you could share the script among many different Web pages.

1. In your text editor, open rollover.js from the WIP_12>externalrollover folder. Examine this script carefully.

   Two functions are defined: one for when you want to change the image of the button (when the user rolls over the button), and one for when you want to return the button to normal (when the user rolls off the button).

2. In your text editor and Web browser, open start.html from the WIP_12>externalrollover folder. Examine the source code.

   The page consists of a simple table that displays three images.

3. Insert the following code into the head section of the HTML document:

```
<!DOCTYPE html PUBLIC "-//W3C//DTD XHTML 1.0 Transitional//EN"
"http://www.w3.org/TR/xhtml1/DTD/xhtml1-transitional.dtd">
<html xmlns="http://www.w3.org/1999/xhtml">
<head>
<title>start.html</title>
<script language="JavaScript" type="text/javascript">
</script>
</head>
<body>
<table width="23%" border="0" cellpadding="0" cellspacing="0"
bordercolor="#336666">
```

4. Modify the code from Step 3 to set the `src` attribute of the `<script>` tag to rollover.js, which gives you access to the functions enclosed.

5. Save your changes and keep the file open in your browser and text editor for the next exercise.

3. Add a Rollover Function

In this exercise, you insert the code to create a rollover effect when the user moves the mouse pointer over the first button.

1. Find the following code in the open HTML document:

    ```
    <a href="#"><img src="images/homenormal.gif" name="home"
    width="44" height="20" border="0" id="home"></a>
    ```

2. Change the code to the following to create the rollover effect:

    ```
    <a href="#"><img src="images/homenormal.gif" name="home"
    width="44" height="20" border="0" id="home"
    onmouseover="buttonOn('home','images/homeover.gif')"></a>
    ```

    Don't forget to use matching pairs of both single and double quotes.

3. Save your changes in the text editor and refresh your browser.

4. Roll your mouse over the Home button.

    The image should change to the rollover image. At this point, the image doesn't change back when you move the mouse off the image.

5. Find the following code, which creates the About Us button:

    ```
    <a href="#"><img src="images/aboutusnormal.gif" name="aboutus"
    width="63" height="20" border="0" id="aboutus" /></a>
    ```

6. Modify the code for the About Us button to use the `buttonOn` function when the user triggers the `onmouseover` event. The event should send two text strings to the function: "aboutus" and "images/aboutusover.gif" to capture the id and location of the image.

    Hint: Use Step 2 as a guide.

7. Modify the `<img>` tag for the Contact Us button to use the `onmouseover` event to trigger the `buttonOn` function. The event should send two text strings to the function: "contactus" and "images/contactusover.gif" to capture the id and location of the image.

8. Save and test your file.

    Each image should change as you move your mouse over it.

9. Leave the file open for the next exercise.

4. Apply a Rolloff Effect

In this exercise, you modify the page to change the images back to the original images when the user rolls off the rollover images.

1. In the open file in your text editor, find the following code:

    ```
    <a href="#"><img src="images/homenormal.gif" name="home"
    width="44" height="20" border="0" id="home"
    onmouseover="buttonOn('home','images/homeover.gif')"
    onmouseout="buttonOff('home','images/homenormal.gif')" /></a>
    ```

2. Modify this code to create a rolloff effect:

    ```
    <a href="#"><img src="images/homenormal.gif" name="home"
    width="44" height="20" border="0" id="home"
    onmouseover="buttonOn('home','images/homeover.gif')"
    onmouseout="buttonOff('home','images/homenormal.gif')" /></a>
    ```

3. Save your changes in the text editor and refresh you browser.

    When you move the mouse off the Home button, the button changes back to the normal image.

4. Find the code for the About Us button, which is shown as follows:

    ```
    <a href="#"><img src="images/aboutusnormal.gif" name="aboutus"
    width="63" height="20" border="0" id="aboutus"
    onmouseover="buttonOn('aboutus','images/aboutusover.gif')" /></a>
    ```

5. Using Step 2 as your guide, change the code for the About Us button to use the `onmouseout` event handler to trigger the `buttonOff` function. The event handler should send two text strings to the function: "aboutus" and "images/aboutusnormal.gif" to capture the id and location of the image.

6. Modify the code for the Contact Us button to change the button back to the normal image when a user moves the mouse off the button.

7. Save your change in the text editor and refresh your browser.

    You should be able to move your mouse over any button and see the rollover and rolloff effects for each.

8. Close the file in your Web browser and text editor.

PORTFOLIO BUILDER

Create Image-Swap Effects

In this chapter, you learned how to create rollover effects with images and how to create disjointed rollover effects. The true skill of a successful developer is combining multiple effects to create an effect greater than any of the individual parts. If the user sees the combination of effects as seamless, the illusion is complete.

Open swapimages.html in your browser. You see five images. Four are obvious because they are colored and numbered; the fifth image appears as text. Currently, the images have no effects applied to them. Your job is to create the image swap effects for the numbered images, as well as a disjointed rollover for the "text" image. There are corresponding text images for each numbered image.

1. Use the following pseudo-code to create a function to swap images on mouse over:

    ```
    swap image 1 for overstate image1 and swap text image for
    text image over 1
    swap image 2 for overstate image2 and swap text image for
    text image over 2
    swap image 3 for overstate image3 and swap text image for
    text image over 3
    swap image 4 for overstate image4 and swap text image for
    text image over 4
    ```

2. Use the following pseudo-code to create a function to restore original images on mouse out:

    ```
    swap overstate image 1 for image1 and swap text image over
    1 for text image
    swap overstate image 2 for image2 and swap text image over
    2 for text image
    swap overstate image 3 for image3 and swap text image over
    3 for text image
    swap overstate image 4 for image4 and swap text image over
    4 for text image
    ```

3. Use the following example to combine the event handlers for both swap image functions:

    ```
    onMouseOver="swapImage(),swapTextImage()"
    onMouseOut="restoreImage(),restoreTextImage()"
    ```

4. After you create and apply the functions, two images should swap at the same time: a numbered image and the text image. (Consider that users with slow Internet connections will have to wait for the swap image to download.)

5. Create a function to preload the images. You may not notice a difference because the files are local, but users with slow Internet connections will certainly appreciate that you added this feature to the page.

CHAPTER 13

Exploring DHTML

OBJECTIVES

In this chapter, you learn how to:

- Manipulate inline styles

- Interact with style sheets

- Control positioning dynamically

- Create a drop-down menu effect

- Use text style properties

- Incorporate background and display properties

Why Would I Do This?

Dynamic HTML (DHTML) is not a technology per se. More accurately, DHTML is a marketing term used by major browser companies to describe the integration of Cascading Style Sheets (CSS), HTML, and JavaScript. In the last few years, XHTML, CSS, and JavaScript have become the de facto standard for building Web sites. DHTML combines the best aspects of all three technologies to allow advanced interactivity.

CSS is usually taught alongside XHTML to students learning to build Web sites. For this reason, this chapter assumes a basic knowledge of CSS. Some basic information and terminology on CSS is provided. Students who do not have formal training with CSS should still be able to complete the lessons without difficulty.

Because DHTML is a voluminous subject, we cannot cover all aspects of the "technology" in the confines of this book. Instead, this chapter serves as a general introduction to DHTML, illustrating how CSS and JavaScript work together. In this chapter, you discover how to change CSS styles dynamically through JavaScript. You also learn how to create animated sequences and drop-down menus.

Aspects of DHTML have been slow to be adopted by many browser manufacturers and, in many cases, have not been consistently implemented. Versions of Internet Explorer for Windows are the most compatible browsers to use with DHTML code. Netscape-based browsers such as Firefox may have particularly difficult issues with much of the code covered in this chapter. For more information on using DHTML, you may want to consult a comprehensive DHTML reference guide.

VISUAL SUMMARY

Consider a Web site that uses CSS to format the page. For example, the EyeCareCenter.com site (shown as follows) uses CSS to position a background image in the upper right-hand corner of the browser window. Regardless of how the screen is resized, the image always remains in position in this area.

FIGURE 13.1

The placement of the background image is accomplished by a style sheet contained in an external file, which is shown as follows.

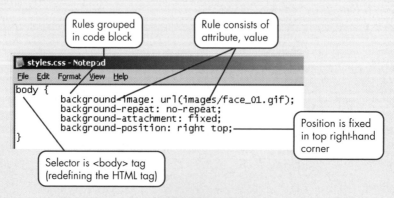

FIGURE 13.2

CSS code consists of *declarations*, which are chunks of CSS that consist of selectors and rules. The *selector* is the class to which the rule is applied. The selector can be an HTML tag, such as all `<table>` tags. When HTML tag names are used as selectors, the rule applied overwrites the default display styles of the tag. This process is known as *redefining HTML tags*.

Let us use pseudo-code to explain the structure of CSS statements, which always follow this syntax:

```
selector { property: value; }
```

CSS commands establish rules for selectors. A *rule* is a guideline for how the selector will display on the page. A rule consists of a *property*, such as `background-color` or `font`, followed by a colon, and then the *value* assigned to the property. Depending on the property, the value can take on a number of values, such as `hidden`, `visible`, or `blue`.

CSS rules are incorporated into a Web page in three ways:

- As an *inline style sheet*, which works as an attribute within an HTML tag.

- As an *embedded style sheet*. Using this method, CSS rules are defined in the HTML document using the `<style>` tag.

- As a *linked (external) style sheet*. Using this method, the style sheets are saved as external documents, using the ".css" extension. The `<link>` tag links the HTML document to the external file. This is the most powerful way to use style sheets because a single file can control the appearance of an entire Web site or even multiple Web sites.

Selectors can also be custom classes that you can apply to any tag in the document. A class has much the same meaning in CSS as it does in JavaScript. A *custom class* is a rule (or rules) that tells the browser how to display any item to which the selector is applied. In other words, any member assigned to the class takes on the characteristics of the class.

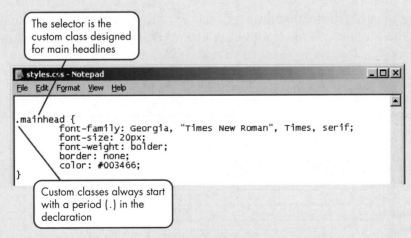

The selector is the custom class designed for main headlines

```
styles.css - Notepad
File  Edit  Format  View  Help

.mainhead {
        font-family: Georgia, "Times New Roman", Times, serif;
        font-size: 20px;
        font-weight: bolder;
        border: none;
        color: #003466;
}
```

Custom classes always start with a period (.) in the declaration

FIGURE 13.3

Inline styles are created with the `style` attribute of HTML tags. The `style` attribute is an extension to HTML that allows you to directly apply styles to a single HTML tag. You create inline styles as follows.

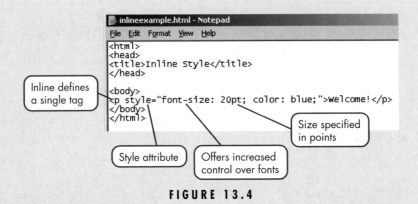

FIGURE 13.4

DHTML refers to the way JavaScript interacts with CSS. For each CSS style defined, a matching `style` object is also created in JavaScript. The properties of the `style` object represent the same attributes that you can set or modify in CSS declarations. With DHTML, you can use JavaScript to change the CSS rules created as inline styles or with `ID` selectors.

Remember that the Document Object Model (DOM) is a term that describes the hierarchy of the JavaScript language. The DOM provides a method for interacting with HTML elements (because JavaScript creates a matching object for every HTML tag found in a document). Employing various aspects of the DOM, you can use JavaScript to access or change the HTML code.

Newer versions of the DOM also create objects in JavaScript to reference CSS declarations and properties. This is the true strength of JavaScript: it allows users to access and manipulate the markup, styles, and properties of HTML and CSS with the power of a traditional programming language.

Consider an e-commerce Web site that displays a table of products. Visitors use the table to purchase products online. You can use CSS to set the colors of the table, as shown in the following example.

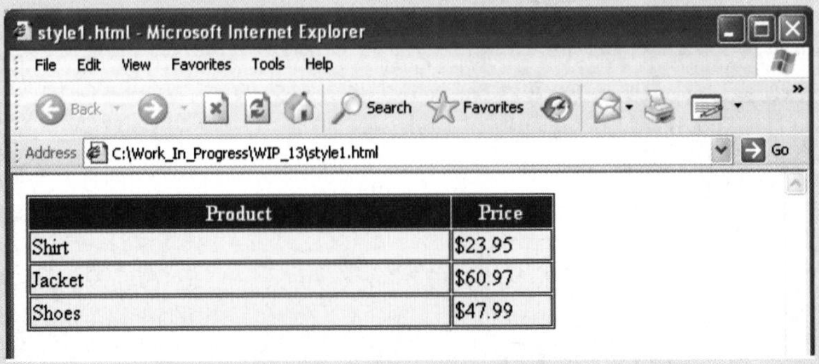

FIGURE 13.5

Whenever an HTML tag is encountered in the code, a corresponding object (otherwise known as an element or element object) is created in JavaScript. Likewise, a JavaScript `style` object is created for any element that has CSS styles attached. The `style` object has properties that represent CSS attributes. Using JavaScript to manipulate these CSS properties, you can change the corresponding CSS code in the same way you used JavaScript to manipulate HTML code.

DHTML provides exciting new options for improving usability. For example, you could change the color of the table row when the user moves the mouse pointer over one of the products.

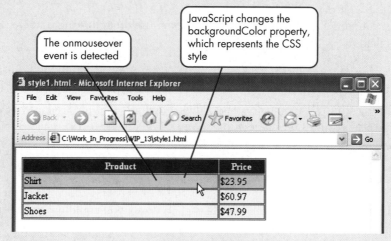

FIGURE 13.6

This code effectively creates a rollover effect by changing the background colors in the table. The code to accomplish this task is very simple.

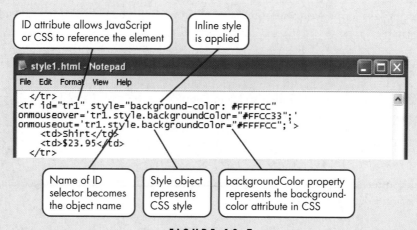

FIGURE 13.7

This method of changing styles works well for inline styles. When using style rules created in style sheets, however, you need to use the `getElementById()` method. The `getElementById()` method is a subordinate method of the `document` object.

LESSON 1 Manipulating Inline Styles

You can control CSS styles through JavaScript and the document object, which is similar to the way you manipulate HTML code through JavaScript. For example, to use JavaScript to access HTML tags, you can use the `name` or `id` attribute in the HTML tag. Either attribute is used to assign a unique name for the tag. The `name` attribute is being phased out, but is still required for forms because of compatibility issues with server side scripts. The following tag creates a form:

```
<form name="theForm" id="theForm">
```

Assume that the form contains a field named `phone`. You can use the following statement to access the value stored in the `phone` field:

```
document.theForm.phone.value
```

In some cases, the `name` attribute is required to access the content of an HTML tag, such as with the `<form>` tag. DHTML, in contrast, requires developers to use the `ID` attribute to reference elements. Consider the following HTML tag:

```
<p id="content">This is a sentence.</p>
```

Assume that you want to access the text of the HTML tag. To do so, you could use the `innerHTML` property of the tag, as shown in the following statement:

```
content.innerHTML
```

The Style Object

The `style` object in JavaScript represents the `style` property of an HTML tag. Consider the following inline style as an example:

```
<p id="content" style="color: red"> This is a sentence.</p>
```

To change the CSS attributes set in the inline style, you could use the `style` object. For example, to change the text to blue, you would write the following line of code in JavaScript:

```
content.style.color="blue"
```

This technique raises interesting possibilities. For instance, you could change the color of the text when a user moves the mouse pointer over the content of the tag:

```
<p id="content" style="color: red" onmouseover='
content.style.color="blue";'> This is a sentence.</p>
```

This technique works for most HTML tags, but it only works for inline styles. In other words, you cannot access styles created in style sheets, as shown in the following example:

```
<style type="text/css">
#myStyle {
      color: white;
}
</style>
```

The `style` object supports a variety of appearance changes, including background color, text spacing, font sizes, and visibility. Properties exist for other CSS categories, such as padding, margins, scroll bars, and cursor styles. You explore these and other style properties throughout this chapter.

Use Style Object Properties

1   Copy the content of the Chapter_13 folder to your Work_In_Progress>WIP_13 folder.

2   In your text editor and browser, open style1.html from your WIP_13 folder.

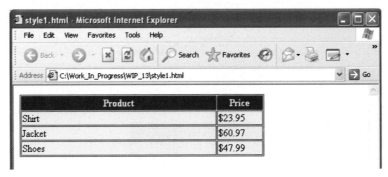

FIGURE 13.8

3   Find the following lines of code.

```
...
<tr>
    <td>Shirt</td>
    <td>$23.95</td>
  </tr>
...
```

These lines of code create the first product row, which currently shows the default background color.

4   Modify the code as follows.

```
...
<tr id="tr1" style="background-color: #FFFFCC">
    <td>Shirt</td>
    <td>$23.95</td>
  </tr>
...
```

This code creates an `ID` and applies an inline style.

5 **Insert the following code.**

```
. . .
<tr id="tr1" style="background-color: #FFFFCC" onmouseover='
tr1.style.backgroundColor="#FFCC33";'
onmouseout='tr1.style.backgroundColor="#FFFFCC";'>
    <td>Shirt</td>
    <td>$23.95</td>
  </tr>
. . .
```

Rollover effects now apply to the first table row.

6 **Save the file in your text editor and refresh your browser.**

7 **Move your mouse over the first product.**

The background of the table row changes color.

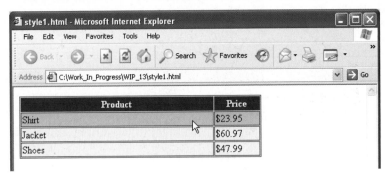

FIGURE 13.9

8 **Close the file in your browser and text editor.**

To Extend Your Knowledge . . .

STYLE PROPERTIES

JavaScript element object properties do not always precisely match CSS properties. For instance, although they represent the same property, the `background-color` property in CSS is known as `backgroundColor` in JavaScript. This minor discrepancy is primarily related to different semantic rules. CSS properties that contain two words are written as all lowercase with a hyphen between the words. You do not use hyphens (or spaces) when you write JavaScript properties, and the second word in a two-word JavaScript property is usually capitalized, which is referred to as **camelback notation**.

LESSON 2 Interacting with Style Sheets

In the previous lesson, you learn how to directly interact with properties of the `style` object by using the same style of dot syntax notation that is always used in JavaScript. This method is useful for changing CSS properties dynamically, but it only works for inline styles. Styles created in style sheets with the `<style>` tag or placed in external style sheet files require a different method of access.

The `getElementById()` method of the `document` object allows you to access information about a particular element. By passing the `ID` of an element to this method, you can access the matching object in JavaScript. When you use an `ID` selector to apply a style to a particular HTML element, the `ID` selector can also be referenced in JavaScript. For instance, you can use the following code to create an `ID` selector to place an object at an absolute position:

```
<style type="text/css">
#eddieImage {
    position: absolute;
    top: 80px;
    left: 10px;
    visibility: visible;
}
</style>
```

Next, you can apply the `ID` selector style by using an `ID` attribute within an HTML tag. For instance, the following code applies the style to an image:

```
<img src="eddie.jpg" ID="eddieImage" >
```

By accessing the element object through the DOM using the `getElementById()` method, you can change any aspect of the element's styles using properties of the `style` object. For instance, to change the `left` CSS property of the element, you would write

```
document.getElementById('eddieImage').style.left=130;
```

Any property that can be used in a style declaration can be accessed or changed with this method. The properties are named in a similar fashion to how they appear in the CSS code, in the same way that other object properties have matching HTML attributes. Bear in mind that the `getElementById()` method must be spelled correctly. It is a common mistake to spell this method as `getElementByID()` or `getElementbyId()`, both of which cause errors in many (but not all) browsers.

Reference Style Attributes in JavaScript

1   **In your text editor and browser, open colorchange.html from the WIP_13 folder.**

This page uses the `background-color` attribute in an `ID` selector to create a blue background behind a short sentence.

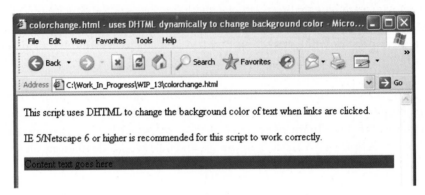

FIGURE 13.10

2   **Insert the following code to create links to change the background color of the text.**

Notice how an `onclick` event triggers the function and how the color value passes to the function.

```
. . .
<p ID="content">Content text goes here</p>
<p>
<!-- ***color links go here*** -->
<a href="#" onclick="colorChange('red')"> Red </a><br />
<a href="#" onclick="colorChange('blue')"> Blue </a>
</p>
</a>
</body>
. . .
```

3   **Insert the following code in the `<head>` section of the document.**

```
. . .
<!-- ***color change script goes here*** -->
<script language="JavaScript" type="text/javascript">
function colorChange(color) {
document.getElementById('content').style.backgroundColor = color;
} // end function
</script>
. . .
```

This code creates the color-change function.

4   **Save the file in your text editor and refresh your browser.**

5   **Click the links at the bottom of the page.**

The background color changes as the `background-color` property changes.

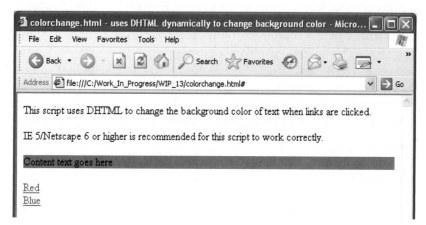

FIGURE 13.11

6   **Close the file in your browser and text editor.**

To Extend Your Knowledge . . .

PROPERTIES OF THE STYLE OBJECT

For a complete list of the properties of the `style` object, visit http://www.w3.org/TR/REC-CSS2, which is the official page for the newest CSS specification.

LESSON 3   Control Positioning Dynamically

In Chapter 12, you used JavaScript to create a simple animation by changing the source file of an `image` object at a short interval. In other words, you showed a slightly different image at short intervals in the same location on the screen, which resulted in a basic animation. This method is rather inefficient because you must load multiple images to create the animated sequence. As you know, multiple images lead to large file sizes and an intensive use of computer resources.

A more efficient method is to animate a single image. For instance, you could make the image larger, smaller, or move it across the screen. You already explored many of the building blocks necessary to accomplish these image changes. You can use HTML to create an image object, load the file, and display the image on the screen. Then, you can use CSS to control the placement of the image and move it to any absolute position. Next, you can use JavaScript to create a loop to animate the object.

To move an object from the left of the screen to the right, follow these three simple steps:

- Place the image in a CSS style.

- Use absolute positioning to place the image in a starting position.

- Use JavaScript to change the x,y coordinates of the image to create the illusion of movement.

This sequence creates simple results: the image seems to disappear from one position and appear elsewhere on the screen. You can create a more complex animation by including a loop that repeatedly moves the object across the screen. To ensure the animation is smooth, you could include a timer that controls the interval between each movement. For instance, you could create a JavaScript loop that moves the object 10 pixels to the right every 500 milliseconds.

Animate an Element

In this exercise, you create a simple animation by manipulating CSS positioning properties through JavaScript.

1   **In your browser and text editor, open move.html from the WIP_13>move folder.**

This file displays an image of a dog named Eddie. The file uses absolute positioning to initially place the image on the page.

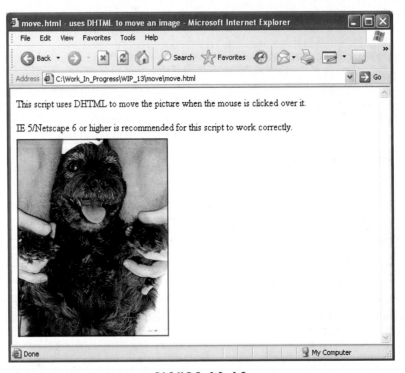

FIGURE 13.12

2 **In your text editor, find the following code.**

```
. . .
<a href="#" ID="eddieImage" width="250" height="315">
<img src="eddie.jpg" border="0" />
</a>
. . .
```

Because the goal is to move the image to a new location when the user clicks the image, the `<img>` tag was placed between the `<a>` and `</a>` tags. An `ID` attribute applies the style to the content of the `<a>` tag. The style that positions the image is in the head of the document.

3 **Change the code to read as follows.**

```
. . .
<a href="#" ID="eddieImage" width="250" height="315"
onclick="moveObject()">
<img src="eddie.jpg" border="0" />
</a>
. . .
```

This code adds the event handler to trigger the function that moves the image.

4 **Insert the following code in the head of the document.**

```
. . .
<title>move.html - uses DHTML to move an image</title>
<script language="JavaScript" type="text/javascript">
// *** insert function below ***
function moveObject() {
        document.getElementById('eddieImage').style.left=130;
        document.getElementById('eddieImage').style.top=100;
} // end function
</script>
<style type="text/css">
#eddieImage {
. . .
```

This function moves the element object when the user clicks the image.

5 **Save the file in your text editor and refresh your browser.**

6   **Click the image.**

The image moves to a different position on the screen.

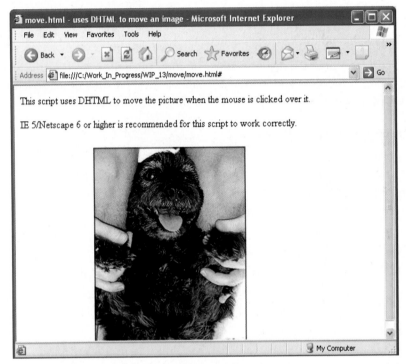

FIGURE 13.13

7   **Close the file in your text editor and browser.**

You now know how to access and change properties of an element through the `style` object. You also know how to move an element dynamically by changing the CSS properties through JavaScript. To animate the element, you would add a loop to move the object incrementally. You could also use a timer to control the smoothness and speed of the animation.

To Extend Your Knowledge . . .

INCORPORATING ANIMATION

Always remember that a small amount of animation goes a long way. Where a small amount of animation adds a bit of zest to a site, too much animation ruins a page by taking attention away from the branding and content.

LESSON 4   Creating a Drop-Down Menu Effect

Many modern Web sites involve the use of drop-down menus to create striking effects. These menus are similar to traditional modern software interfaces; they allow designers to place several links, organized by category, into an easy-to-understand navigation scheme. When the user rolls the mouse pointer over a category name, a list of links appears, as shown in the following example.

FIGURE 13.14

You cannot use HTML to create drop-down menus, but DHTML provides the necessary power to create this type of navigation structure. DHTML drop-down menus have recently begun to appear in various Web sites, but the adoption rate for this technology is rather slow.

DHTML drop-down menus have two primary disadvantages. First, incompatibility issues result in many browsers displaying drop-down menus incorrectly. This problem is partially mitigated by the forgiving nature of browsers — they tend to ignore code that they do not understand. Second, code for DHTML drop-down menus is complex and requires significant understanding of both CSS and JavaScript.

When creating DHTML drop-down menus, developers typically want to apply significant customization to the appearance and style of the menus for a particular project. Given this fact and the other disadvantages associated with using drop-down menus, it makes sense to follow certain guidelines when creating them:

- Use drop-down menus for informational sites where the information fits into easy-to-understand categories.

- The target audience should use newer browsers that can support the technology.

- Older browsers should be able to ignore the code, and the user should be able to navigate to all sections, regardless of whether the drop-down menus appear on the screen.

For these reasons, it typically makes sense to use a Web design program (e.g., Macromedia Dreamweaver or Fireworks) to create drop-down menus. Both programs contain easy-to-understand interfaces that allow users to create and customize drop-down menus that work well across most browser platforms.

To better understand the fundamental concepts of DHTML, you create a basic drop-down script in the following exercise. A basic drop-down menu script uses several concepts that you read about earlier. First, you use CSS properties to create and hide the drop-down menus. Then, you use JavaScript to detect when a user rolls over the menu's trigger area. Next, you use JavaScript to reveal the CSS layer and change the CSS properties. Finally, you use JavaScript to hide the CSS layer (after a certain interval) when the user moves the mouse off the trigger area.

Hide Navigation Menus

1   **In your text editor and browser, open dropdown.html from the WIP_13>dropdown folder.**

2   **Examine the file in your Web browser and try rolling over the links.**

The links are for display only and will not go to a page if clicked.

FIGURE 13.15

3   **Examine the source code in your text editor.**

The file uses some simple CSS commands to create a gray box with a blue stroke. The box has three hyperlinks. The `a:hover` pseudo-class creates a rollover style for the links. Notice how the `<div>` tag separates the grey box in the HTML code, and that an `ID` selector named `menu` applies the styles.

```
<div ID="menu">
```

4   **Find the CSS declaration that creates the `menu` style, as shown in the following.**

```
. . .
#menu {
      visibility: visible;
      z-index: 100;
      background-color: #cccccc;
      width: 75px;
      border: thin solid #330099;
      padding: 5px;
}
. . .
```

5 Change the `visibility` attribute to "`hidden`", as shown in the following code.

```
. . .
#menu {
     visibility: hidden;
     z-index: 100;
     background-color: #cccccc;
     width: 75px;
. . .
```

This value renders the menu invisible when the page initially loads.

6 Save the file in your text editor and refresh your browser.

The box is now hidden from view.

FIGURE 13.16

7 Keep the file open in your browser and text editor for the next exercise.

Show and Hide Menus

1 In the open dropdown.html, find the line of code that displays the word "`products`," as shown.

```
<p><font color="#000099">products</font>
```

2 Change this code to trigger functions when the mouse rolls over or off the text.

```
<p onmouseover="showMenu()"
onmouseout="timer=setTimeout('hideMenu()',2000)"><font
color="#000099">products</font>
```

This timer tells the box to remain visible for 2 seconds. Without the timer, users would find it difficult to click the drop-down options before they disappeared.

3   **Insert the following function into the head of the document.**

```
. . .
// showMenu function goes here
function showMenu() {
       document.getElementById('menu').style.visibility = "visible";
} // end function
// hideMenu function goes here

</script>
</head>
. . .
```

This function causes the menu to appear.

4   **Insert the following function to hide the menu.**

```
. . .
       document.getElementById('menu').style.visibility = "visible";
} // end function
// hideMenu function goes here
function hideMenu() {
       document.getElementById('menu').style.visibility = "hidden";
       clearTimeout(timer)
} // end function
</script>
</head>
<body>
. . .
```

5   **Save the document in your text editor and refresh your browser.**

A drop-down menu appears when you move your mouse over the word "products" and disappears 2 seconds after you move off the word.

6   **Close the file in your browser and text editor.**

To Extend Your Knowledge . . .

DROP-DOWN MENUS

Drop-down menus work well for Web sites that have a significant amount of informational content, and the information is easily separated into categories that a user can understand.

LESSON 5   Using Font and Text Properties

As a designer, you must use text and font styles appropriately to create engaging and interesting visual experiences for your Web visitors. Graphic designers who become Web designers are often frustrated by the lack of flexibility that HTML offers in regard to font styles and sizes. CSS alleviates these restrictions by providing designers with greatly increased control of fonts and the appearance of text elements on the page.

DHTML offers additional flexibility in this area by allowing JavaScript to control fonts as the page loads or as the user interacts with the page. For example, you can use JavaScript to determine the size of the screen, and then size the text appropriately to complement that particular resolution.

A number of CSS attributes and their matching JavaScript properties are listed in the following table.

CSS attribute	JavaScript property	Description
color	Color	Sets or retrieves the color of the text of the object.
font	Font	Sets or retrieves a combination of separate font properties of the object. Alternatively, sets or retrieves one or more of six user preference fonts.
font-family	FontFamily	Sets or retrieves the name of the font used for text in the object.
font-size	FontSize	Sets or retrieves a value that indicates the font size used for text in the object.
font-style	FontStyle	Sets or retrieves the font style of the object as italic, normal, or oblique.
font-variant	FontVariant	Sets or retrieves a value that states whether the text of the object is in small capital letters.
font-weight	FontWeight	Sets or retrieves the weight of the font of the object.
letter-spacing	letterSpacing	Sets or retrieves the amount of additional space between letters in the object.
line-height	LineHeight	Sets or retrieves the distance between lines in the object.

(Continued)

CSS attribute	JavaScript property	Description
text-decoration	textDecoration	Sets or retrieves a value that indicates whether the text in the object has blink, line-through, overline, or underline decorations.
	textDecorationLineThrough	Sets or retrieves a Boolean value indicating whether the text in the object has a line drawn through it.
	textDecorationNone	Sets or retrieves the Boolean value indicating whether the textDecoration property for the object has been set to none.
	textDecorationOverline	Sets or retrieves a Boolean value indicating whether the text in the object has a line drawn over it.
	textDecorationUnderline	Sets or retrieves a Boolean value that indicates whether the text in the object is underlined.
text-indent	textIndent	Sets or retrieves the indentation of the first line of text in the object.
text-justify	textJustify	Sets or retrieves the type of alignment used to justify text in the object.
text-transform	textTransform	Can be set to capitalize, uppercase, or lowercase.
word-spacing	wordSpacing	Sets or retrieves the amount of additional space between words in the object.
word-wrap	wordWrap	Sets or retrieves a value that states whether to break words when the content exceeds the boundaries of its container.

Imagine how you might use these properties to enhance accessibility to a Web site. In the following exercise, you use DHTML to make text larger when the user clicks a button. This simple change makes the site much more accessible to those users who have poor vision.

Use Text Properties

1 **In your text editor and browser, open text.html from your WIP_13 folder.**

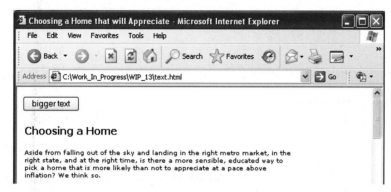

FIGURE 13.17

This page offers advice on buying a new home.

2 **Find the following CSS style in the head of the document.**

```
...
#myBody {
      font-family: Verdana, Arial, Helvetica, sans-serif;
      font-size: 10px;
}
...
```

This style sheet sets the page content to 10-pixel text. An `ID` attribute in the `<table>` tag applies the style.

3 **Find the following line of code.**

```
<p> <input type="button" name="bigger text" value="bigger text" />
```

This code establishes the button at the top of the page.

4 **Modify the button code as follows.**

```
<p> <input type="button" name="bigger text" value="bigger text"
onclick="getBigger()" />
```

This code triggers the function when the user clicks the button.

5 **Insert the following function in the head of the document.**

```
...
</style>
<script language="JavaScript" type="text/javascript">
// insert getBigger function
```

```
        function getBigger() {
        document.getElementById("myBody").style.fontSize = '20px';
}
</script>
</head>
<body bgcolor="#FFFFFF" text="#000000">
. . .
```

6   Save the file in your text editor and refresh your browser.

7   Click the bigger text button.

The text size increases.

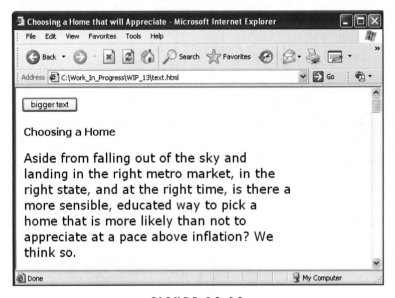

FIGURE 13.18

8   Close the file in your browser and text editor.

To Extend Your Knowledge . . .

FULL LIST OF STYLE OBJECT PROPERTIES

Microsoft provides a comprehensive list of `style` object properties supported by Internet Explorer at http://msdn.microsoft.com/library/default.asp?url=/workshop/author/dhtml/reference/objects/obj_style.asp.

LESSON 6   Incorporating Background and Display Properties

JavaScript contains several properties that allow you to use a style sheet to control the positioning and display of objects. CSS offers excellent flexibility when you position items on the page. Using JavaScript properties to control matching CSS attributes, you can easily move an item from one position to another position.

A number of properties allow you to specify background images, as well as position background images. For example, you can use the `background-image` attribute to specify a background image in CSS. The `backgroundImage` property in JavaScript allows you to change this property and effectively change the source of the background image.

CSS also allows you to layer objects. Using the `z-index` property in CSS, you can stack elements on the page however you prefer. JavaScript takes this feature one step further by allowing you to use the `zIndex` property to change the `z-index` setting, which means you can change the stacking order of objects on the page. For example, you could design a page that showed numerous manila folders stacked on a desk. When you click the tab on one of the file folders, that folder would move to the top of the stacking order because it would assume a higher `z-index` value.

CSS also allows you to hide objects by manipulating the `display` or `visibility` property. Again, JavaScript allows you to take this feature one step further: you can hide or unhide items as necessary while the user interacts with the page.

The following table includes a number of common CSS attributes and their matching JavaScript properties. You can use these attributes and properties to manipulate the visibility, background, and positioning of various items on the page.

CSS attribute	JavaScript property	Description
background-attachment	backgroundAttachment	Sets or retrieves how the background image is attached to the object within the document.
background-color	backgroundColor	Sets or retrieves the color behind the content of the object.
background-image	backgroundImage	Sets or retrieves the background image of the object.
background-position	backgroundPosition	Sets or retrieves the position of the background of the object.
background-position-x	backgroundPositionX	Sets or retrieves the x-coordinate of the backgroundPosition property.
background-position-y	backgroundPositionY	Sets or retrieves the y-coordinate of the backgroundPosition property.

(Continued)

CSS attribute	JavaScript property	Description
background-repeat	backgroundRepeat	Sets or retrieves how the backgroundImage property of the object is tiled.
cursor	cursor	Sets or retrieves the type of cursor to display as the mouse pointer moves over the object.
display	display	Sets or retrieves whether the object is rendered (visible).
position	position	Sets or retrieves the type of positioning used for the object.
	posLeft	Sets or retrieves the left position of the object in the units specified by the left attribute.
	posRight	Sets or retrieves the right position of the object in the units specified by the right attribute.
	posTop	Sets or retrieves the top position of the object in the units specified by the top attribute.
	posWidth	Sets or retrieves the width of the object in the units specified by the width attribute.
visibility	visibility	Sets or retrieves the value that states whether the content of the object displays on screen.
width	width	Sets or retrieves the width of the object.
z-index	zIndex	Sets or retrieves the stacking order of positioned objects.

In the following exercise, you create a script that changes the stacking order of items on the page. Combining this technique with JavaScript event handlers allows an item to appear to move to the front of the stack or move farther back in a stack of objects. Developers often refer to the process of changing the stacking order of objects as *swapping depths* because one object appears to go behind another exposed object.

Swap Depths

1   **In your browser and text editor, open changedepth.html from your WIP_13>depth folder.**

This document uses CSS absolute positioning to display two images. The `z-index` property was used to overlap the objects.

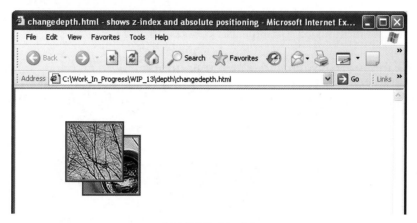

FIGURE 13.19

2   **Insert the following function.**

```
. . .
</style>
<script language="JavaScript" type="text/javascript">
// insert function here
function swapDepth(myLayer) {
     document.getElementById(myLayer).style.zIndex = '20';
}
</script>
</head>
. . .
```

This function changes the depth of the `ID` selector to `20`, which forces the image to appear above the other image.

3   **Find the following code.**

```
<a href="javascript:void(0)"><img src="smallpic1.jpg" width="90"
height="90" id="pic1" ></a>
<a href="javascript:void(0)"><img src="smallpic2.jpg" width="90"
height="90" id="pic2"></a>
```

This code creates the image and applies the style sheet properties. Notice that the images are enclosed within hyperlinks so the users' mouse pointers will change to pointing fingers to indicate that they can click the images.

4 **Insert the following code.**

```
. . .
<a href="javascript:void(0)"><img src="smallpic1.jpg" width="90"
height="90" id="pic1" onclick="swapDepth('pic1');" /></a>
<a href="javascript:void(0)"><img src="smallpic2.jpg" width="90"
height="90" id="pic2" onclick="swapDepth('pic2');" /></a>
. . .
```

This code triggers the function when the user clicks either image.

5 **Save the file in your text editor and refresh your browser.**

6 **Click the image located behind the top image.**

The images change positions.

FIGURE 13.20

7 **Close the file in your browser and text editor.**

To Extend Your Knowledge . . .

OTHER PROPERTIES

A number of other properties allow you to control the color of the browser's scroll bars, padding, borders, margins, and more.

SUMMARY

In Chapter 13, you learned how to use DHTML to create interesting and complex visual effects. You found that the DHTML "technology" integrates JavaScript, CSS, and HTML to create striking effects that are not otherwise possible. You learned that the `getElementById()` method allows JavaScript to access and change CSS styles dynamically. In addition, you found that the `style` object contains a number of JavaScript properties that represent CSS attributes.

You discovered that DHTML is often used to create simple animated sequences and effects, including drop-down menus. Most mainstream Web designers have been slow to adopt DHTML because of compatibility issues that exist between different browsers; however, most of these issues have been corrected in newer browsers. This has led to wider adoption and use of DHTML. A number of large corporate Web sites have embraced DHTML, which suggests that it will soon become a mainstream technology.

KEY TERMS

Camelback notation	ID selector	Rule
Custom classes	Inline style sheet	Selector
Declarations	Linked (external) style sheet	Style object
DHTML	Property	Swapping depths
Embedded style sheet	Redefining HTML tags	Value

CHECKING CONCEPTS AND TERMS

MULTIPLE CHOICE

Circle the letter that matches the correct answer for each of the following questions.

1. You need to use the `getElementById()` method to access _____.
   a. Netscape 3.0 styles
   b. styles created with `<style>` tags
   c. inline styles
   d. styles created with `<text=attribute>` tags
   e. None of the above

2. How are properties of the `style` object similar to CSS attributes?
   a. They both use all lowercase letters.
   b. They both use camelback notation.
   c. They both use dots to separate parts of names.
   d. None of the above

3. The `getElementById()` method is a method of the _____ object in JavaScript.

a. `document`

b. `style`

c. `CSS`

d. `window`

4. _____ uses the `ID` parameter to reference a particular HTML tag.

a. CSS

b. JavaScript

c. Both of the above

d. None of the above

5. How can you use DHTML in Web pages?

a. To create rollover effects in table rows

b. To move an object across the screen

c. To temporarily hide items, such as drop-down menus

d. All of the above

e. None of the above

6. Why should you use a timer when creating drop-down menus in DHTML?

a. To allow users enough time to read menu choices

b. To allow users enough time to make choices

c. Both of the above

d. None of the above

7. Which items use camelback notation?

a. JavaScript style properties

b. CSS attributes

c. Both of the above

d. None of the above

8. Which items use a hyphen to separate two-word names?

a. JavaScript style properties

b. CSS attributes

c. Both of the above

d. None of the above

9. Which CSS attribute and JavaScript property controls the stacking order of objects?

a. `position-number` and `positionNumber`

b. `z-index` and `zIndex`

c. `stack` and `stackingOrder`

d. `vector-position` and `vectorPosition`

10. DHTML properties control the color and style of the browser's scroll bars.

a. True

b. False

DISCUSSION QUESTIONS

1. How are inline styles and styles defined in style sheets treated differently in DHTML?

2. What types of tasks can you accomplish with DHTML that you cannot accomplish using CSS or HTML alone?

3. How can you use DHTML to improve the accessibility of a Web page?

4. What are the major categories of CSS attributes that can be controlled by DHTML?

SKILL DRILL

Skill Drill exercises reinforce chapter skills. Each skill reinforced is the same, or nearly the same, as a skill presented in the chapter. Detailed instructions are provided in a step-by-step format. You should work through these exercises in order.

1. Create Smooth Animation

In this Skill Drill, you use JavaScript to control CSS positioning to create a smooth animation. Smooth animation requires at least 10 frames per second. Since a millisecond is 1/1000 of a second, intervals greater than 100 milliseconds usually result in jerky motion and poor animation.

1. In your text editor and browser, open skillanimation.html from your WIP_13>move folder.

    This is essentially the same file you used in a previous exercise.

2. Modify the following line of code near the bottom of the page.

    ```
    <a href="#" ID="eddieImage" width="250" height="315"
    onclick="moveObject(10,80)">
    ```

    This code passes starting x,y coordinates to the function.

3. Find the following function in the head of the document.

    ```
    . . .
    // *** insert function below ***
    function moveObject() {
        document.getElementById('eddieImage').style.left=130;
        document.getElementById('eddieImage').style.top=100;
    } // end function
    . . .
    ```

4. Change the function code to the following.

    This change adds a loop, timer, and statements to increment the x,y variables each time the function is called.

    ```
    . . .
    function moveObject(x,y) {
    if (x<300) {
        document.getElementById('eddieImage').style.left = x;
        document.getElementById('eddieImage').style.top = y;
        x=x+3;
        y++;
        setTimeout('moveObject('+x+','+y+')',20);
    } //end if
    } // end function
    . . .
    ```

5. Save the file in your text editor and refresh your browser.

6. Click the image.

   The image should move smoothly to the lower right-hand area of the browser window. Notice that the image moves 3 pixels to the right for every 1 pixel it moves down.

7. Return to your text editor and find the timer statement that sets the interval between movements. Change the number of milliseconds from `20` to a larger or smaller number, and see how this change affects the speed and smoothness of the animation.

8. Find the statements that increment the x,y variables. Change the numbers to make the animation faster, and then change the numbers to move the animation in a straight line from left to right with no downward movement.

9. Close the file in your browser and text editor.

2. Add JavaScript Event Handlers to Change CSS Styles

JavaScript event handlers allow you to detect user events and respond accordingly. In this exercise, you create rollover style effects for tabular data to improve the usability of an e-commerce Web site.

1. In your text editor and browser, open skillstyle.html from the WIP_13 folder.

   This is essentially the same file you used earlier.

2. Move your mouse over the table row for the first product.

   The table row changes color as you move your mouse over or off the row.

3. In your text editor, find the inline JavaScript code that triggers the rollover effect for the Shirt row.

4. Add the same rollover effect to the other two product rows (Jacket and Shoes).

5. Save your changes in the text editor. Test the file in your browser.

   Each of the three rows should change color as your mouse moves on and off the row.

6. Close the file in your browser and text editor.

3. Manipulate Text Properties

CSS offers a number of new ways to work with text, and DHTML offers new ways to interact with users. In this exercise, you create a page that offers new accessibility options to users: you allow users to dynamically change the size of the content that displays on the screen.

1. In your browser and text editor, open skilltext.html from the WIP_13 folder.

   This is essentially the same file you used in a previous exercise, but a "smaller text" button was added to the page.

2. Create a function named `makeSmaller()` that changes the font size of the `myBody ID` selector to `10px`.

   Hint: Use the `getBigger()` function as a guide.

3.   Create inline JavaScript to trigger the `makeSmaller()` function when the user clicks the smaller text button.

4.   Save your changes and test the file in your browser.

The text should become larger when you click the bigger text button, and then the text should shrink when you click the smaller text button.

5.   Close the file in your browser and text editor.

4. Change Layering

In this exercise, you change the stacking order of layered objects, making some objects appear closer or farther away than other objects. To accomplish this task, you use the `zIndex` property to change `z-index` values created by CSS.

1.   In your text editor and browser, open skilldepth.html from the WIP_13>depth folder.

This file is similar to the file you created in a previous exercise, but a third image has been inserted onto the page. If you click one of the first two images, the image appears above the other images.

2.   Two `ID` selectors appear in the existing style sheet. Create a third `ID` selector named `pic3` in the existing `<style>` tag. Position the `pic3` object at a top setting of `70px` and a `left` setting of `100px`. Set the `pic3` object's initial `z-index` value to `3`.

The `ID` attribute was already included in the `<img>` tag to link the tag to the style sheet.

3.   Save the file in your text editor and refresh your browser.

The image moves to a different position on the screen.

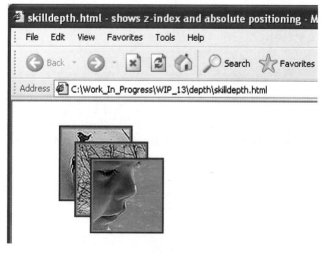

FIGURE 13.21

4. Find the following line of code.

```
<a href="javascript:void(0)"><img src="smallpic3.jpg" width="90"
height="90" id="pic3" /></a>
```

5. Modify the code you found in Step 4 to trigger the `changeDepth()` function when the user clicks the image to change the position of this image.

6. Save and test your file.

7. Close the file in your browser and text editor.

5. Modify the Class Associated with an Object

In this chapter, you used DHTML properties to change the CSS attributes of an object to create a rollover effect. The `className` property offers a different way to change attributes. The `className` property allows you to change the entire class of styles associated with an object. You use the `className` property in this exercise.

1. In your browser and text editor, open skillswapclass.html from the WIP_13 folder.

2. Roll your mouse pointer over the menu items.

    You see no effect.

3. Insert the following code.

```
. . .
</head>
<body>
<div id="menu" class="menu">
<div class="navMenu"
onmouseover="this.className='navMenuOver'">Home</div>
<div class="navMenu" id="menuItem">Products</div>
<div class="navMenu" id="menuItem">Services</div>
<div class="navMenu" id="menuItem">Contact</div>
. . .
```

4. Refresh the page in your browser.

    When the mouse rolls over the Home menu item, the background and text colors change, and the text becomes underlined because the class changes.

5. Insert code to change the class of the same `<div>` so it changes back to the `navMenu` class when the `onmouseout` event occurs.

    Hint: Use the code in Step 3 as a guide, but change the event handler and class name.

6. Refresh the page in your browser and test the file to ensure the rollover effect appears when the mouse pointer moves on or off the first menu item.

7. Save and close the file in your browser and text editor.

CHALLENGE

Challenge exercises expand on, or are somewhat related to, skills presented in the lessons. Each exercise provides a brief introduction, followed by instructions presented in a numbered-step format that are not as detailed as those in the Skill Drill exercises. You should work through these exercises in order.

1. Use DHTML to Create an Interactive Button

In Chapter 12, you used JavaScript to create image rollovers. You can accomplish the same effect with CSS and JavaScript by using background images.

1. In your text editor, open challengebutton.html from the WIP_13 folder.

2. Use the `onmouseover` event handler to change the class, as shown.

```
...
</style>
</head>
<body>
<div class="button" onmouseover="this.className='buttonOver'" >
</div>
</body>
</html>
```

3. Use the `onmouseout` event handler to change the class back to the `button` class.

4. Save and open the file in your browser.

   The image should change as you move over and off the button.

5. Close the file in your text editor and browser.

2. Open (Show) a Menu

In this challenge, you use `<div>` tags to create menu effects: `button`, `menu`, and `closer`. The `button` effect adds an `onmouseover` effect to a navigation button. The `menu` effect opens or shows a div by changing visibility. The `closer` effect collapses the menu. Start the exercise by adding code to make the menu visible.

1. In your browser and text editor, open challengemenu.html from the WIP_13 folder.

2. Find the following code.

```
function showMenu() {
        document.getElementById('closer').style.visibility =
        "visible";
} // end function
```

The code currently changes the `closer` object to `visible`.

3. Modify the `showMenu` function to change the visibility of `menu`. Use the following pseudo-code as a guide.

    ```
    change the visibility of the div with id=menu to visible
    ```

4. Find the following code.

    ```
    <a href="#">
    ```

5. Modify the code you found in Step 4 to use the `onmouseover` event handler to trigger the `showMenu()` function.

6. Save and refresh the file in your browser.

    The menu appears as you move the mouse pointer over the image.

7. Keep the file open for the next challenge.

3. Collapse (Hide) a Visible Menu

In this challenge, you write code to collapse a menu.

1. In the open challengemenu.html, find the following code.

    ```
    // hideMenu function goes here
    function hideMenu() {
          document.getElementById('closer').style.visibility =
          "hidden";
    } // end function
    ```

    This function currently modifies the `closer` object.

2. Modify the `hideMenu()` function to change the visibility of `menu`. Use the following pseudo-code as a guide.

    ```
    change the visibility of the div with id=menu to hidden
    ```

3. Find the following code.

    ```
    <div id="closer" >
    <img src="images/closer_trigger.gif" width="100%"
    height="100%" />
    </div>
    ```

4. Use the `onmouseover` event to trigger the `hideMenu()` function when the user moves the mouse pointer over the closer_trigger.gif image.

5. Save and refresh the file in your browser.

The `div (id="closer")` has its `visibility` value changed from `hidden` to `visible` when the `onmouseover` event occurs. This `div` contains a single image set to 100% wide and 100% tall. When the mouse rolls over the image or off `menu`, the `menu` visibility changes. The `closer` must be below the `menu` and the `button` in `z-index`, which assures the `hideMenu()` function does not trigger while the mouse is over the `button` or `menu`.

6. Close this file in your browser and text editor.

4. Style Menu Items

In this challenge, you will create a pull-down menu effect by changing the class of the div when the user moves their mouse over a link. Essentially, this file is the same as the one you created in a previous exercise, but a timer has been added to keep the pull-down menu visible for 2 seconds.

1. Open challengemenu2.html in your text editor and browser and find the following code.

```
<div id="menu" class="menu">
    <div class="navMenu">Home</div>
    <div class="navMenu">Products</div>
    <div class="navMenu">Services</div>
    <div class="navMenu">Contact</div>
</div>
```

This code creates a menu (of class `menu`) and four menu items in the `navMenu` class.

2. Add `onmouseover` events to the four menu items to change the class to "`navMenuOver`" when the user moves the mouse pointer over the contents of the `<div>` tags.

Hint: Use `this.className` in your code.

3. Add `onmouseout` events to the four menu items to change the class to "`navMenu`" when the user moves the mouse pointer off the contents of the `<div>` tags.

4. Save and refresh the file in your browser.

The `button` image swaps, the menu appears and disappears, and menu items change when a user rolls the mouse pointer over them. Combining multiple effects allowed you to create a dynamic menu system.

5. Close the file in your browser and text editor.

PORTFOLIO BUILDER

Create a Navigational System

Creating an effective navigational (menu) system is of critical importance because the menu system has a direct impact on the user. The most common navigational control element a user experiences is the horizontal menu bar located along the top of virtually every application's interface. Leveraging such well-known conventions allows designers to develop systems that users find familiar and comfortable, which results in freely browsing the content of the sites — rather than trying to figure out what to do and how to do it.

In this Portfolio Builder, your task is to complete a menu system for a Web site. To finish the job, follow these steps:

1. Open WIP_13>multiplemenus.html in your text editor and browser. The file is nearly complete.

2. Attach the multiplemenus.css style sheet (also in the WIP_13 folder) and refresh the Web page in your browser. Most of the styling is complete.

3. Move your mouse over the products link. The menu that appears is out of place. Look for the `ID` rule in the style sheet for the menu (`#productsMenu`). Adjust the positioning until the menu is centered below the products in the menu bar.

4. Examine the `showMenu()` and `hideMenu()` functions in multiplemenus.html. The function changes the visibility of `productsMenu`. The `showMenu()` function is triggered by an `onmouseover` event that makes two layers visible. The layers are named `productsMenu` and `closer`. The `hideMenu()` function triggers when the mouse moves off the menu and over the layer named `closer`. The only purpose of the `closer` selector is to close menus.

5. Two additional menus have a `visibility` value of `hidden` in the multiplemenus.html file. You need to correct the positions of these menus. In addition, you must adapt the `showMenu()` and `hideMenu()` functions to accept values passed by the `onmouseover` and `onmouseout` events to tell the function which menu needs to be visible.

6. Once the menu system is working correctly, examine the CSS styles. Make additional adjustments to perfect the overall look and feel of your menu system.

INTEGRATING PROJECT

As a junior Web developer for a small marketing firm, you have been asked to use frames and JavaScript commands to finish and enhance a Web site that has been partially completed. The site you will create is a simplified version of Optometric Eye Care Centers actual site, which is located at www.EyeCareCenter.com.

The site is designed to be viewed in a frameset design. This allows several advantages, including ease of maintenance and the ability to keep branding and navigation structures visible at all times. For purposes of this project, assume that you are part of the design team that is building the site. The site structure and site design has been approved by the client. Content has been gathered and many of the components of the site have been built.

HTML pages have been built for the top and left navigation structures. Content pages have also been built. Every content page has been built using a standard template to ensure consistency and professionalism. In addition to the creation of the content pages, members of the project team have used JavaScript to create image rollovers for the navigation buttons, created artwork for a pop-up ad, and designed a Flash animation to show the steps involved in laser vision surgery.

As a Web developer, it will be your job to create the frameset that will bind the pages together in the browser window. Additionally, you will create the code to open a pop-up ad when the frameset is loaded and the code to create a pop-up window to display the Lasik animation. Lastly, you will use JavaScript to improve the usability of the site by adding links to close the ad pop-up window and to create "back" links on several pages.

Setting up the site

1 Copy the RF_JavaScript_L1>IP folder to your Work_In_Progress>WIP_IP folder.

2 Begin to explore the completed components of the site by opening WIP_IP>menu.html in your Web browser.

This is the page that will form the left navigation structure. From this point forward, when asked to open a file, it is assumed the file will be located within the Work_In_Progress>WIP_IP folder

3 Repeat step 2 with top.html and main.html to see the top navigation structure and main content page of the site.

At this point, astute students will notice no file is named index.html since this name is reserved for the frameset file. Pages in the site use Cascading Style Sheets (CSS) to place background images and control other formatting. Additionally, JavaScript code has been included to allow rollover images for buttons.

4   Look at the files in your site to see how the site is organized.

All images are placed within the images folder. A number of pages exist to explain common eye conditions such as conjunctivitis and dry eyes. Feel free to open a few of these pages in your Web browser and explore more of the site.

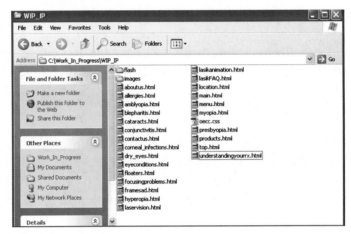

FIGURE IP.1

At this point, you've become familiar with the components that will comprise the site. Our next step will be to create the frameset file to bind the pages together in the browser window. The frameset file will be the default Web page for the site since we want it to be the first page loaded.

Create the Frameset File

1   Open your text editor and start a new file. Save the file as "index.html" in your WIP_IP folder.

Insert the following code for the primary HTML tags; specifically:

```
<!DOCTYPE html PUBLIC "-//W3C//DTD XHTML 1.0 Transitional//EN"
"http://www.w3.org/TR/xhtml1/DTD/xhtml1-transitional.dtd">
<html xmlns="http://www.w3.org/1999/xhtml">
<head>
<title>Eye Care Center</title>
</head>
<body>
</body>
</html>
```

2   Create a blank line after the **\</head\>** tag and before the **\<body\>** tag. Insert the following code to create an area that is 180 pixels wide for the left navigation area:

```
<head>
<title>Eye Care Center</title>
</head>
<frameset rows="*" cols="180,*" frameborder="NO" border="0"
framespacing="0">
</frameset>
<body>
</body>
</html>
```

3   In-between the **\<frameset\>** and **\</frameset\>** tags you just created, insert the following line of code to set the characteristics for the left frame:

```
<title>Eye Care Center</title>
</head>
<frameset rows="*" cols="180,*" frameborder="NO" border="0"
framespacing="0">
<frame name="leftFrame" scrolling="no" noresize src="menu.html">
</frameset>
<body>
</body>
```

4   Now, you can add the code to split the right side of the browser window into a top area for navigation and a bottom area for content. After the line that uses the **\<frame\>** tag, insert a line and add the following lines of code before the **\</frameset\>** tag.

```
</head>
<frameset rows="*" cols="180,*" frameborder="NO" border="0"
framespacing="0">
<frame name="leftFrame" scrolling="no" noresize src="menu.html">
<frameset rows="57,*" frameborder="no" border="0"
framespacing="0">
<frame name="topFrame" noresize scrolling="no" src="top.html">
<frame name="mainFrame" src="main.html">
</frameset>
<body>
</body>
```

5   Save your file.

6   Open index.html in the Web browser to see the completed frameset file.

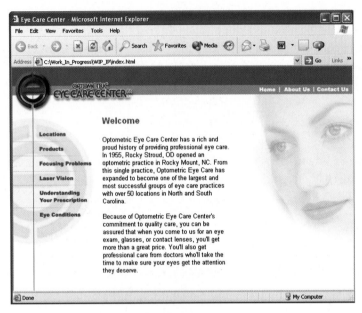

FIGURE IP.2

7   Close the file in your text editor.

Now that you've created the frameset file, you can program the navigation buttons. The code to display the buttons exists in the top.html and menu.html files. In the next part of the project we will add the links for these pages and specify where the new pages will appear.

Programming Targeted Links for the Frameset

1   In your text editor, open top.html in your text editor and examine the code within the **<body>** and **</body>** tags.

The code generates a table for the top navigation structure. The code also includes some inline JavaScript within the **<a>** tags to create image rollovers for the buttons. Notice how the HTML comments are placed so that any carriage returns that are needed for easy reading of the code are placed within the **<!--** and **-->** tags. This is necessary to ensure proper formatting of the HTML page.

FIGURE IP.3

2 Look for the HTML comment statement that marks the beginning of the code for the home button. It will be written as:

```
<!--
************************************************
**** code for home button starts here ******
************************************************
-->
```

3 Find the next statement, which will start with the anchor (`<a>`) tag and will define the button; you will see the HTML comment end tag (`-->`) appear at the beginning of the same line. A return character cannot be inserted between the `<a>` statement and the comment statement (`<--`); this would make the source code easier to read but change the formatting of the table.

```
--><a href="#" onmouseout="MM_swapImgRestore()" onmouseover=
"MM_swapImage('Image12','','images/na01b.gif',1)"><img
src="images/na01a.gif" name="Image12" width="64" height="57"
id="Image12" alt="home button"/></a><!--
```

4 Change this statement to link to the main.html file and to target the mainFrame area of the browser window. The revised statement should read as follows:

```
--><a href="main.html" target="mainFrame" onmouseout=
"MM_swapImgRestore()" onmouseover="MM_swapImage
('Image12','','images/na01b.gif',1)"><img src="images/na01a.gif"
name="Image12" width="64" height="57" id="Image12" alt=
"home button"/></a><!--
```

5 Find the comment in the source code that has the following message:

```
* * * * * * * * * * * * * * * * * * * * * * * * * * * * * * * * * * * * * * * * *
**** code for about us button starts here*********
* * * * * * * * * * * * * * * * * * * * * * * * * * * * * * * * * * * * * * * * *
```

6 An anchor statement will follow that starts with **`<a href="#"`**, change this statement to link to the aboutus.html page and target the frame named mainFrame. Hint: use step 4 as a guide.

7 Using steps 4 and 5 as your example, program the Contact Us button by finding the comment in the code that begins the code for the button and changing the hyperlink to link to the contactus.html file. As in the previous examples, the target should be the mainFrame window.

8 Save your file in your text editor. You should have your frameset file loaded in the Web browser. Choose refresh to load the changes and try choosing the buttons in the top navigation structure to ensure you entered the code changes correctly.

9 Close the top.html file in your text editor. Open the menu.html file to see the code that establishes the left navigation structure.

10 Find the **`<body>`** tag in the source code and look for the code that establishes the buttons on the left side of the browser window. The code is virtually identical to the top.html file but the filenames of the linked documents have already been specified as well as the **`target="mainFrame"`** part of the statement. Another member of the design team has already completed this task in accordance with the project plan and no additional work is necessary.

FIGURE IP.4

11 Close your file in the text editor.

In this section, we've added the hyperlinks necessary to load the proper pages into the mainFrame area of the frameset. In the next section, we'll create the code to open and close the pop-up windows needed in the site. Two HTML pages have already been created to display the content needed in the pop-up windows.

Create a Command to Close the Ad Window

1 Open the framesad.html page in your web browser. This is a simple page that displays a graphic for a currently advertised special.

FIGURE IP.5

2 Since we are going to have the page appear in a pop-up window, you should include a close window button to make the page more user-friendly. Open the framesad.html page in your text editor.

3 Find the following comment in the code.

```
<!--
*************************************************
***** window close command needed here *******
*************************************************
-->
```

4 Insert a line just after the **—>** statement and insert the following code to add a button to close the window.

```
<!—
*************************************************
***** window close command needed here *******
*************************************************
—>
<font face="Verdana, Arial, Helvetica, sans-serif" size="1"
onclick="window.close()"><a href="#">close window</a></font>
<br />
</div>
</body>
```

Note how the JavaScript is used inline within the **<font>** tag to trigger the **close()** method when the text is clicked. The anchor tag (**<a>**) isn't needed, strictly speaking, but has the advantage of making the browser treat the text as a hyperlink. This will make the mouse pointer change to a hand when the user rolls over the linked text.

5 Save your file and refresh in the browser. You should see a link to close the window at the bottom of the window.

FIGURE IP.6

6 Try choosing the close window command.

Since the operating system (and not the JavaScript code) generated the browser window, it is likely you will get a confirmation box asking if you are sure you want to close the window.

7 Choose no to keep the page open.

The link appears in the default link colors, which are difficult to read on the blue background we have chosen. For this reason, it would make sense to change the link colors to white or another light color that will be easier to see on the chosen background. In the next section, you will change the default link colors to make them more readable.

Change the Default Link Colors

1 Return to the open framesad.html in your text editor.

2 Create a script in the head of the document.

3 In the script you created in the previous step, change the **linkColor** property of the document object to white by inserting the following line of code.

```
document.linkColor="#FFFFFF";
```

4 Using the last step as a guide, create another statement to change the **vlinkColor** property to white also.

5 Create another statement to change the **alinkColor** property to white also.

6 Save your file and refresh in the Web browser.

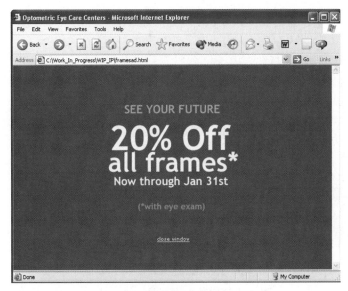

FIGURE IP.7

7 Close the file in your text editor.

A Lasik animation page has been built to also be displayed in a second pop-up window. A link to close the window has been included in the code of the second page as well as code to change the default link colors to white. In the next section you will write the code to open the pop-up windows for the frames ad.

Create the Code to Display the Pop-Up Ad

The marketing department of the client would like the framesad.html page to appear whenever a new Web surfer visits the site. You could place the code on the main content page, but the pop-up window would reappear every time a user returned to the homepage. Placing the code in the frameset file is a better choice since the pop-up window will only appear when the site is initially loaded by the frameset file.

1 Open index.html in your text editor and in your Web browser.

2 Insert a blank line between the **</title>** tag and the **</head>** tag and insert the following code.

```
...
<html xmlns="http://www.w3.org/1999/xhtml"><head>
<title>Eye Care Center</title>
<script language = "JavaScript" type="text/javascript">
var adWindow=open("framesad.html","","width=300, height=370");
</script>
</head>
<frameset rows="*"cols="180,*" frameborder="NO" border="0"
framespacing="0">
<frame name="leftFrame" scrolling="no" noresize src="menu.html">
...
```

3   Save the file and refresh in your Web browser.

FIGURE IP.8

4   Close the file in your text editor and close the popup window in your browser.

Inserting the code into the frameset file allows the page to appear when the user loads the frameset. A second page has been created to display an animation regarding Lasik surgery. This pop-up window will be displayed when the user chooses a link to view the animation, requiring the use of the **onclick** event handler.

Open a Window Using the Onclick Event

1   Open the lasikanimation.html file in your Web browser. This file consists of a simple HTML page with a Flash animation displayed in the center of the page.

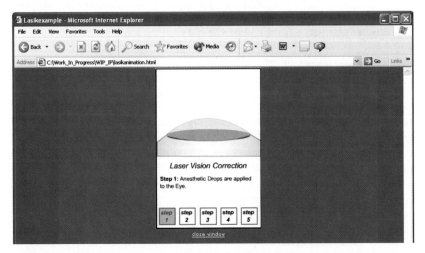

FIGURE IP.9

The Flash 4.0 or higher browser plug-in is required to view the animation shown in this project. This Flash plug-in is included in most browsers and can be downloaded for free from macromedia.com.

2 Open the laservision.html page in your browser and text editor. Links to the animation page will be triggered from the laservision.html and lasikFAQ.html pages.

3 In your text editor, find the HTML comment that marks where the links for the Animation and Lasik FAQ pages are located. It will contain the following comments to mark the proper location.

```
* * * * * * * * * * * * * * * * * * * * * * * * * * * * * * * * * * * * * * * * * * *
* * * * * * Start code for Animation, FAQ Links * * * * * *
* * * * * * * * * * * * * * * * * * * * * * * * * * * * * * * * * * * * * * * * * * *
-->
```

4 On the next line after these statements, change the statement that is written as **<a href="#">** and replace it with the following code.

```
* * * * * * Start code for Animation, FAQ Links * * * * * *
* * * * * * * * * * * * * * * * * * * * * * * * * * * * * * * * * * * * * * * * * * *
-->
<a href="#" onclick = 'window.open("lasikanimation.html","
","toolbar = no,location = no,directories = no,status =
no,menubar = no,scrollbars = no,resizable = no,width = 250,height
= 384")'> Animation</a>  | <a href="lasikFAQ.html">
 FAQs</a></font>
<h3>Laser Vision</h3>
<table width="100%" border="0">
```

5 Save your file and refresh in the browser.

6 Choose the animation link to see the results your code changes.

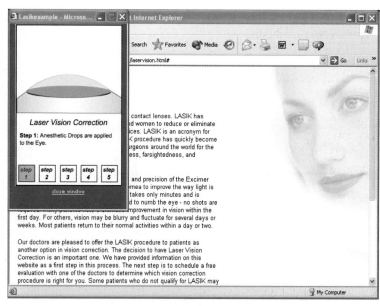

FIGURE IP.10

7   Close the lasik animation window. Close the laservision.html file in your text editor.

8   Open the lasikFAQ.html file in your text editor and your browser.

Repeat steps 3, 4, and 5 to insert the code to trigger the pop-up window when a user chooses the animation link.

9   Close any open pop-up windows and close any open files in your text editor.

10   Open the index.html file in your browser window. Navigate to the Laser Vision page and choose the animation link to test your code within the frameset file.

In most PC browsers, you can right-click with your mouse within a non-image area of a frame and choose refresh to reload the page without reloading the entire frameset. The same menu options can be seen on the Mac by holding down the control key and clicking the mouse button.

11   Close any open pop-up windows.

At this point, you have written code to open and to close the pop-up windows. The site is basically finished. In the next section, we'll use the history object to make site navigation easier.

The project team has decided that a back link would work well on the eye conditions sub pages. Since we can't be sure where the user found the link to the page, you will use the history object to create the back links. The text for the back links has been added to the bottom of each page along with an anchor tag to add the same visual clues as any hyperlink. It will be your job to add the code to allow the link to use the history object to go to the previous page.

Add a Back Link to the Eye Conditions Pages

1   Open the index.html page in your Web browser if it isn't already open and choose the link to the eye conditions section. A list of links will appear to pages for various eye conditions. It is important to note that some conditions are linked to from the eye conditions page and also from the focusing problems page.

2   Open allergies.html in your text editor and scroll down until you find the following code.

```
<!--
***** back link code begins *****
********************************
-->
<p><font face="Verdana, Arial, Helvetica, sans-serif" size="1"
><a href="#">Back</a></font></p>
```

3   Change the code that says **`<a href="#">`** to read as follows.

```
<p><font face="Verdana, Arial, Helvetica, sans-serif" size="1"
><a href="#" onclick="history.back()">Back</a></font></p>
```

4   Save the file.

5   In your browser, choose the allergies link and choose the refresh button. This may also refresh the frameset file and open the adWindow pop-up. If the pop-up window appears, close it.

6 Choose the back link at the bottom of the allergies page. You should be returned to the Eye Conditions page.

7 Now insert the code necessary for the other eye conditions pages. This will require you to complete steps 2, 3, and 4 for the following files: amblyopia.html, blepharitis.html, cataracts.html, conjunctivitis.html, corneal_infections.html, dry_eyes.html, floaters.html, hyperopia.html, myopia.html, and presbyopia.html.

8 Test the files in your browser to make sure you entered the code correctly.

9 Close all files in your browser and text editor.

This project should have given you a feel for the construction of a complex, professional quality site. The actual site for Optometric Eye Care Centers is a larger and more complex site that includes much additional content and database search capabilities for specific doctors, products, and locations. The actual site required a strong plan and individuals with proficiency in Flash animation, JavaScript interactivity, database connectivity, Cascading Style Sheets, graphic design, and HTML. The ability to understand the complexity of the site and complete the final aspects of the site is an indicator that you would have much to contribute to a design team on a similar project.

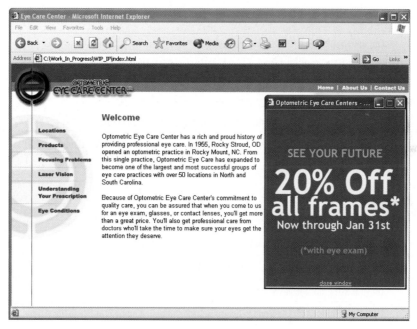

FIGURE IP.11

ECMAScript REFERENCE

Operations

Operator	Description
ARITHMETIC	
+	Adds 2 numbers.
++	Increments a number.
–	As a unary operator, negates the value of its argument. As a binary operator, subtracts 2 numbers.
--	Decrements a number.
*	Multiplies 2 numbers.
/	Divides 2 numbers.
%	Computes the integer remainder of dividing 2 numbers.
STRING	
+	Concatenates 2 strings.
+=	Concatenates 2 strings and assigns the result to the first operand.
LOGICAL OPERATORS	
&&	(Logical AND) Returns true if both logical operands are true. Otherwise, returns false.
||	(Logical OR) Returns true if either logical expression is true. If both are false, returns false.
!	(Logical negation) If its single operand is true, returns false; otherwise, returns true.
BITWISE OPERATORS	
&	(Bitwise AND) Returns a one in each bit position if bits of both operands are ones.
^	(Bitwise XOR) Returns a one in a bit position if bits of one but not both operands are one.
|	(Bitwise OR) Returns a one in a bit if bits of either operand is one.
~	(Bitwise NOT) Flips the bits of its operand.
<<	(Left shift) Shifts its first operand in binary representation the number of bits to the left specified in the second operand, shifting in zeros from the right.
>>	(Sign-propagating right shift) Shifts the first operand in binary representation the number of bits to the right specified in the second operand, discarding bits shifted off.
>>>	(Zero-fill right shift) Shifts the first operand in binary representation the number of bits to the right specified in the second operand, discarding bits shifted off, and shifting in zeros from the left.

Operations (continued)

Operator	Description
ASSIGNMENT	
=	Assigns the value of the second operand to the first operand.
+=	Adds 2 numbers and assigns the result to the first.
—=	Subtracts 2 numbers and assigns the result to the first.
*=	Multiplies 2 numbers and assigns the result to the first.
/=	Divides 2 numbers and assigns the result to the first.
%=	Computes the modulus of 2 numbers and assigns the result to the first.
&=	Performs a bitwise AND and assigns the result to the first operand.
^=	Performs a bitwise XOR and assigns the result to the first operand.
|=	Performs a bitwise OR and assigns the result to the first operand.
<<=	Performs a left shift and assigns the result to the first operand.
>>=	Performs a sign-propagating right shift and assigns the result to the first operand.
>>>=	Performs a zero-fill right shift and assigns the result to the first operand.
COMPARISON	
==	Returns true if the operands are equal.
!=	Returns true if the operands are not equal.
>	Returns true if left operand is greater than right operand.
>=	Returns true if left operand is greater than or equal to right operand.
<	Returns true if left operand is less than right operand.
<=	Returns true if left operand is less than or equal to right operand.
SPECIAL	
?:	Performs simple "if ? then : else"
,	Evaluates two expressions and returns the result of the second expression.
delete	Deletes an object property or an element at a specified index in an array.
new	Creates an instance of an object.
this	Refers to the current object.
typeof	Returns a string indicating the type of the unevaluated operand.
void	Specifies an expression to be evaluated without returning a value.

Statements

Statement	Description
break	Terminates the current while or for loop and transfers program control to the statement following the terminated loop.
continue	Terminates execution of the block of statements in a while or for loop, and continues execution of the loop with the next iteration.
delete	Deletes an object's property or an element of an array.
do ... while (*condition*)	Executes its statements until the test condition evaluates to false. Statement is executed at least once.
for (*init; condition; increment*)	A loop that consists of three optional expressions, enclosed in parentheses and separated by semicolons, followed by a block of statements executed in the loop.
for (*var* in *object*)	Iterates a specified variable over all the properties of an object. For each distinct property, JavaScript executes the specified statements.
function	Declares a JavaScript function name with the specified parameters. Acceptable parameters include strings, numbers, and objects.
if (*condition*) ... else	Executes a set of statements if a specified condition is true. If the condition is false, another set of statements can be executed.
labeled	Provides an identifier that can be used with break or continue to indicate where the program should continue execution.
return	Statement that specifies the value to be returned by a function.
switch (*expression*) case label:	Evaluates an expression and attempts to match the expression's value to a case label.
var	Declares a variable, optionally initializing it to a value.
while (*condition*) ...	Creates a loop that evaluates an expression, and if it is true, executes a block of statements.
with (*object*) ...	Establishes the default object for a set of statements.
//	Defines comment until end of the line.
/* ... */	Defines comment within the operators.

Core Objects

Property/Method	Description
ARRAY OBJECT	
length	Size of the array.
index	Position of matched substring (from RegExp object)
input	Original string for matching (from RegExp object)
concat(array1)	Joins two arrays into one array.
join(separator)	Joins array element into a string, separated by separator (Defaults to ",")
pop	Removes last element from an array and returns that element.
push(e1, e2 ...)	Adds one or more elements to the end of the array and returns the last element.
reverse	Reverses the elements in the array.
shift	Removes the first element from an array and returns that element.
slice(begin, end)	Extracts elements from index begin to end and returns a new array.
sort	Sorts the elements of an array
splice	Change content of array by adding and removing elements.
toString	Returns string representation of array
unshift(e1, e2 ...)	Adds one or more elements to the beginning of the array and returns new array length.
BOOLEAN OBJECT	
toString	Returns string representation of Boolean.

Core Objects (continued)

Property/Method	Description
DATE OBJECT	
getDate	Returns the day of the month.
getDay	Returns the day of the week.
getHours	Returns the hour.
getMinutes	Returns the minutes.
getMonth	Returns the month.
getSeconds	Returns the seconds.
getTime	Returns the numeric value corresponding to the time.
getTimezoneOffset	Returns the time-zone offset in minutes for the current locale.
getYear	Returns the year.
parse	Returns the number of milliseconds in a date string since January 1, 1970, 00:00:00, local time.
setDate	Sets the day of the month.
setHours	Sets the hours.
setMinutes	Sets the minutes.
setMonth	Sets the month.
setSeconds	Sets the seconds.
setTime	Sets the value of a Date object.
setYear	Sets the year.
toGMTString	Converts a date to a string, using the Internet GMT conventions.
toLocaleString	Converts a date to a string, using the current locale's conventions.
UTC	Returns the number of milliseconds in a Date object since January 1, 1970, 00:00:00, Universal Coordinated Time (GMT).

Core Objects (continued)

Property/Method	Description
MATH OBJECT	
E	Euler's constant, approximately 2.718.
LN10	Natural logarithm of 10, approximately 2.302.
LN2	Natural logarithm of 2, approximately 0.693.
LOG10E	Base 10 logarithm of E, approximately 0.434.
PI	Pi, approximately 3.14159.
SQRT1_2	Square root of 1/2, approximately 0.707.
SQRT2	Square root of 2, approximately 1.414.
abs	Returns the absolute value of a number.
acos	Returns the arccosine (in radians) of a number.
asin	Returns the arcsine (in radians) of a number.
atan	Returns the arctangent (in radians) of a number.
atan2	Returns the arctangent of the quotient of its arguments.
ceil	Returns the smallest integer greater than or equal to a number.
cos	Returns the cosine of a number.
exp	Returns E^{number}, where number is the argument, and E is Euler's constant, the base of the natural logarithms.
floor	Returns the largest integer less than or equal to a number.
log	Returns the natural logarithm (base E) of a number.
max	Returns the greater of two numbers.
min	Returns the lesser of two numbers.
pow	Returns base to the exponent power, that is, baseexponent.
random	Returns a pseudo-random number between 0 and 1.
round	Returns the value of a number rounded to the nearest integer.
sin	Returns the sine of a number.
sqrt	Returns the square root of a number.
tan	Returns the tangent of a number.

Core Objects (continued)

Property/Method	Description
NUMBER OBJECT	
MAX_VALUE	The largest representable number.
MIN_VALUE	The smallest representable number.
NaN	Not a number value.
NEGATIVE_INFINITY	Negative infinite value for overflow.
POSITIVE_INFINITY	Infinite value for overflow.
toString	Returns string representation of a number.
OBJECT OBJECT	
eval	Evaluates a string of ECMAScript in the context of this object.
toString	Returns the string representation of this object.
valueOf	Returns the primitive value of the specified object.
STRING OBJECT	
length	Returns length of the string.
charAt	Returns the character at the specified index.
charCodeAt	Returns a number indicating the ISO-Latin-1 codeset value of the character at the given index.
concat	Combines the text of two strings and returns a new string.
fromCharCode	Returns a string from the specified sequence of numbers that are ISO-Latin-1 codeset values.
indexOf	Returns the index within the calling String object of the first occurrence of the specified value.
lastIndexOf	Returns the index within the calling String object of the last occurrence of the specified value.
match	Matches a regular expression against a string.
replace	Finds a match between a regular expression and a string, and replaces the matched substring with a new substring.
search	Executes the search for a match between a regular expression and a specified string.
slice	Extracts a section of a string and returns a new string.
split	Splits a string into an array of strings by separating the string into substrings.
substr	Returns the characters in a string beginning at the specified location through the specified number of characters.
substring	Returns the characters in a string between two indexes into the string.
toLowerCase	Returns the calling string value converted to lowercase.
toUpperCase	Returns the calling string value converted to uppercase.

Core Objects (continued)

Property/Method	Description
REGEXP OBJECT	
$1...$9	Parenthesized substring matches, if any.
global	Whether or not to test the regular expression against all possible matches in a string, or only against the first.
ignoreCase	Whether or not to ignore case while attempting a match in a string.
input or $_	The string against which a regular expression is matched.
lastIndex	The index at which to start the next match.
lastMatch or $&	The last matched characters.
lastParen	The last parenthesized substring match, if any.
leftContext or $`	The substring preceding the most recent match.
multiline or $*	Whether or not to search in strings across multiple lines.
right Context or $'	The substring following the most recent match.
source	The text of the pattern.
compile	Compiles a regular expression object.
exec	Executes a search for a match in its string parameter.
test	Tests for a match in its string parameter.

GLOSSARY

absolute path　The location of a file or Web page beginning with the root. Includes all necessary information to find the file or page. In the case of a Web page, called "absolute URL." See *relative path*.

absolute reference　The complete path of the file you want to open.

action　The location that receives data from a form.

ActionScript　The scripting language used in Macromedia Flash MX.

algorithm　A specific sequence of mathematical steps to process data. A portion of a computer program that calculates a specific result.

anchor　A location within an HTML document that can be reached with a hyperlink.

anchor object　Represents a text anchor created in the HTML code. Anchor objects can be referenced by the anchors array.

anchors array　Represents every text anchor created in the HTML code. For example, anchors[0] represents the first text anchor in the document.

animation　The technique of simulating movement by creating slight changes to an object or objects over time.

anonymous function　A function that does not have a name and is assigned directly to an event handler.

applet　Self-contained computer programs, created in the Java programming language, often used on Web sites.

applets array　In JavaScript, represents each Java applet, or HTML <applet> tag, added to an HTML document.

array　A collection of separate objects or values represented by a single name.

ASP　Active Server Pages. A specification for a dynamically created Web page that contains either Visual Basic or JavaScript code. When a browser requests an ASP page, the Web server generates a page with HTML code.

aspect ratio　The width-to-height proportions of an image.

assignment operator　A character or characters that assign a value to a variable.

bit (binary digit)　A computer's smallest unit of information. Bits can have only two values: 0 or 1.

bitmap image　An image constructed of individual dots or pixels set to a grid-like mosaic. The file must contain information about the color and position of each pixel, which requires significant amounts of disk space.

bitwise operators　An assignment operator that affects the status of a single bit of computer memory.

blur　When keystrokes redirect to another object.

bookmark　HTML feature that allows you to save a link to a Web page.

boolean values　Data type set to either true or false.

bots　Automated programs that explore Web pages, record any hyperlinks used, and index the content of the pages. The term "bots" is short for "robots," another term used to describe these programs. See *spider*.

bound　When the event handler is attached to the object.

browser　Software program that allows you to surf the Web. The most popular browsers are Netscape Navigator and Microsoft Internet Explorer. The very first browsers, such as Lynx, only allowed users to see text. Also called "Web browser."

browser compatibility　A term that compares the way a Web page functions on different browsers. Incompatibilities often exist due to the way a browser interprets HTML. The differences may be slight or significant.

browser objects　JavaScript objects that control specific aspects of the Web browser.

built-in objects　Objects included in the JavaScript language.

camelback notation　The process of starting the second word of an event handler or variable name with a capital letter.

case sensitive　Languages that distinguish between uppercase and lowercase letters.

CGI　Common Gateway Interface. Interface that allows scripts to run on a Web server. CGI scripts put the content of a form into an e-mail message, perform a database query, and generate HTML pages on the fly.

CGI-Bin　The most common name of a directory on a Web server in which CGI scripts are stored.

CGI script　A CGI program used to process a form or provide other dynamic content.

class　Represents the definition of an object.

comparison operators　In computer languages, specific characters or phrases that make comparisons between values.

concatenating　Combining two text strings.

constant property　A property that cannot be changed.

constructor method　A method used to generate a new object.

custom classes　In CSS, a rule (or rules) that tell the browser how to display any item to which the selector is applied.

data type　Determines the kind of information the variable can hold.

data type errors　Errors involving data types.

decision statements　Questions the interpreter must answer based on the relationship of the variables.

declarations　Chunks of CSS that consist of selectors and rules.

decrement　To decrease the value of a variable by 1.

deprecated   The status of a tag or attribute that can still be used, but will eventually be removed, so you should avoid using it, if possible.

DHTML   Dynamic HTML. JavaScript code that dynamically changes cascading style sheet properties, allows parts of a Web page to be hidden, shown, or animated.

directories option   Allows developers to specify whether directory buttons appear in Web browsers.

disjointed rollover   When one image changes when the user rolls over a different image.

div   A block of content that can be positioned on the page.

DNS   Domain Name Server or Domain Name System. Maps IP numbers to a more easily remembered name. When you type http://www.somedomain.com into a browser, the DNS searches for a matching IP address (228.28.202.95).

document   The general term for a computer file containing text and/or graphics.

document object   Represents the HTML document loaded into the browser window.

document objects   Allow the developer to control aspects of HTML and cascading style sheet (CSS) code.

document root   The main directory for a Web site.

DOM   Document Object Model. The most useful part of the complete object model; provides direct control over HTML and CSS coding.

domain name   A unique name used to identify a Web site, FTP site, and/or e-mail server. A domain name always points to one specific server, even though the server may host many domain names.

dot syntax   Periods used within the JavaScript code to note how items relate to one another.

down state   An image that displays when you click a button.

dpi   Dots Per Inch. The measurement of resolution for page printers, phototype-setting machines, and graphics screens. Currently graphics screens use resolutions of 72 to 96 dpi; standard desktop laser printers work at 600 dpi.

DSL   Digital Subscriber Line. A means for gaining high-speed access to the Internet using phone wiring and a specialized phone connection.

DSN   Data Source Name. Used to access a database.

dynamic   Content that changes according to client-side or server-side scripting.

ECMA   European Computer Manufacturers Association.

ECMAScript   An official standardized version of JavaScript maintained by ECMA.

e-commerce   Electronic commerce. Conducting business online, including product display, online ordering, and inventory management. The software, which works in conjunction with online payment systems to process payments, resides on a commerce server.

element object   Individual fields in a form.

e-mail address   An electronic mail address. E-mail addresses are in the form of user@domain.com.

embedded style sheet   CSS rules are defined in the HTML document using the <style> tag.

embedding   Including a complete copy of a text file or image within a document, with or without a link.

empty string   A unit of zero characters.

equality operator   The "==" operator, which means "are the values equal?"

event handler   A keyword that allows the computer to detect an event.

exclusive OR operator   Returns a value of true if, and only if, one of the values is true. Programmers typically refer to this operator as XOR (pronounced "ex or").

external URL   A page outside the local Web site.

features   Attributes of the browser window.

features parameter   Allows developers to turn on menu bars, toolbars, and scroll bars, as well as control the width and height aspects of the pop-up window within the open() method.

file extension   The suffix used to identify file types under the Macintosh and Windows operating systems, separated from the rest of the file name by a period.

file:///   A protocol used by browsers to access information available on the local computer.

fires   When an event occurs, programmers say that it fires.

flag   A Boolean variable that determines whether an event has occurred.

flowchart   A diagram that shows how a script progresses during execution.

flow-of-control statements   Decision statements.

focus   The state of being active. Usually the last object clicked currently has focus.

font   The complete collection of all the characters (numbers, uppercase and lowercase letters, and in some cases, small caps and symbols) of a given typeface in a specific style; for example, Helvetica Bold.

font class   In Web design, the type of font (serif, sans serif, monospace, cursive, or fantasy) that will be used if the user's computer does not have any of the font-family members.

font family   In Web design, a grouping of (supposedly) similar fonts, used to display text in the Web page.

form   A page that enables a user to type information and send it to a site via form elements such as text boxes and pull-down menus.

form element   Objects that represent one portion of a form — such as a radio button or text area.

form method   See *get* and *post*.

form object   Represents a form in the HTML document.

form validation   The process of making certain a Web form contains all required data and no invalid data.

forms array   Collection of objects that represent every <form> tag encountered in an HTML document.

frame   An HTML page, displayed with other HTML pages in a single browser window.

frameset   HTML file that divides the browser window into sections and displays various HTML files in the sections, which are known as frames.

FTP   File Transfer Protocol. Internet method of transferring files through the Internet from one computer to another. FTP allows you to download files from another computer, as well as to upload files from your computer to a remote computer.

functions   Named, reusable sections of code that can exist in the head or body section of an HTML document or in an external file.

get   A method for sending form data by appending it to the URL of the action. See *post*.

GIF   Graphics Interchange Format. A popular graphics format for online clip art and drawn graphics. Graphics in this format are acceptable at low resolution. See *JPEG*.

global scope   Variables that can be used anywhere.

global variables   Variables declared outside functions.

height option   Used to specify a value for the height of a browser window.

hex values   Numbers specified in the hexadecimal system, commonly used for specifying colors on Web pages.

hexadecimal number   Method of writing numbers where each digit represents a number between 1 and 16. Also known as base-16.

history object   JavaScript object that represents the browser's history list. Used to return to pages previously visited by the browser.

home page   Main page of a Web site. A Web site containing only one page is also called a home page.

hyperlink   An HTML tag that directs the computer to a different anchor or URL. A hyperlink can be a word, phrase, sentence, graphic, or icon. A hyperlink can also cause an action, such as opening or downloading a file.

hypertext   An organization of content that enables the user to select related content.

hypertext reference   Synonymous with the term URL (Uniform Resource Locator), which simply represents the location of a document.

hypertext reference attribute   The location of the information to which a browser should link.

ID selector   Used to create a single element that can be referenced in JavaScript, CSS or other languages.

if-then statement   A programming construction that executes one section of code if a particular expression is true, and a second section if it is false.

IIS   Internet Information Server. Microsoft's Web server that runs on Windows NT platforms. IIS comes bundled with Windows NT 4.0. IIS is tightly integrated with the operating system, so it is relatively easy to administer.

image map   A graphic containing "hot areas," or areas of an image defined as links. When a viewer clicks the hot area, he is actually clicking a link.

increment   To increase the value of a variable by 1.

index date   The index date is 12 a.m., January 1, 1970, Greenwich Mean Time (GMT), this date is used to synchronize events across different regions or making very precise time measurements.

inequality operator   The "!=" operator, which means "the values are not equal."

initialize   To assign a beginning value to a variable.

inline code   A single JavaScript command or multiple commands that appear inside an HTML tag.

inline style sheet   Works as an attribute within an HTML tag.

internal style sheet   Style information included within a Web page.

interpreter   The program that executes instructions in a computer language.

Java   A platform-independent programming language invented by Sun Microsystems that Web developers use to create applets. Java-enabled Web pages can include animations, calculators, scrolling text, sound effects, games, and more.

JavaScript   A scripting language, originally designed by Netscape, that you can embed into HTML documents.

JavaScript Object Model   A map of how objects are categorized in JavaScript.

JPEG   A compression algorithm that reduces the file size of bitmapped images, named for the Joint Photographic Experts Group that created the standard. JPEG is "lossy" compression; image quality is reduced in direct proportion to the amount of compression.

Jscript   Microsoft's version of JavaScript.

keyboard event   Refers to a group of events related to keys pressed on the keyboard.

keyframe animation   A series of still images played in rapid succession.

language   The common set of words, including definitions and pronunciations, and the methods of combining those words shared for the purpose of communication among a group of people.

language attribute   Specifies the scripting language that appears within an HTML <script> tag.

link object   Object that represents a hyperlink.

linked (external) style sheet   See *external style sheet*.

links array   The array that stores information about hyperlinks in an HTML document.

listener   Another term for event handler.

LiveScript   The original name for JavaScript.

local scope   A variable that only exists within a function.

local variable   A variable created within a function, only available within the function.

location   The address of a particular Web page or file.

location object   Allows you to change the browser's URL or reload the current document.

location option   Includes the URL location box.

location property   Holds the address of the current HTML document. Changing the location property forces the Web browser to load the page stored in the new address.

logical AND operator   Evaluates whether both variables are set to true.

logical NOT operator   Negates a Boolean value.

logical operators   Special operators designed to compare two true or false values.

logical OR operator   Returns a value of true if any of the variables compared is equal to true.

loosely typed language   Since JavaScript does not require you to declare the data type when you create the variable, the JavaScript language is described as a loosely typed language.

mailto: A protocol used to tell the browser to create a new e-mail message.

math object   Used to complete various calculations.

menu bar option   Turns on the browser's menu bar.

meta tag   An optional HTML tag that specifies information about a Web document. Some search engines index Web pages by reading the information contained within meta tags.

methods   Commands that perform actions.

millisecond   1/1000th of a second. Therefore, 5000 milliseconds equals 5 seconds.

MIME   Multipurpose Internet Mail Extensions. Standard for attaching non-text files (formatted word-processing files, spreadsheets, pictures, executable files) to e-mail messages.

MIME type   An indication of the kind of data being sent to the browser. Used by the browser so it knows what to do with the data.

modulus operator   An assignment operator (%) used to find the remainder left over after division.

mouseover   The event triggered at the moment the user rolls the mouse (cursor) over an area or item on a Web page. Typically used to tell the browser to do something, such as execute a rollover script.

multimedia   The combination of sound, video images, and text to create an interactive document, program, or presentation.

named target   A frame that has a designated name, allowing links to specify that content should be displayed within that frame.

naming convention   A standard way to create variable names.

negated   Opposite.

nested frameset   A frameset contained within another frameset.

nested tag   A tag contained within another tag.

normal state   The appearance of a button when the user is not interacting with the button.

null   Means the property or value exists, but has no assigned value.

object   A reference to a collection of properties and methods.

object method   A function executed by an object.

object model   A map of the organizational structure of an OOP environment.

object property   A unit of information about an object.

objects   As a simple analogy, think of objects as nouns that you can use in the JavaScript language.

OBL   Object-Based Language. A style of programming that relies on reusing objects in multiple computer programs.

ODBC connectivity   A standard database access method developed by Microsoft. The goal of ODBC is to make it possible to access any data from any application, regardless of which database management system (DBMS) handles the data.

OOP   Object-Oriented Programming. A style of programming that relies on reusing objects in multiple computer programs.

OS   Operating System. The software that allows your computer to function. Examples of operating systems include Mac OS X and Microsoft Windows XP.

over state   The image that displays when the user moves the mouse pointer over an image.

page properties   In Web design, the characteristics of a layout page, including default background and text colors, page width, and background image.

page title   Text that appears in the title bar of the user's browser when the page is viewed.

parsing   When you view a Web page in a browser, an interpreter decides how to display the HTML or JavaScript code, and then returns information to the screen.

pathname   The location of the file relative to the domain name.

PHP   A server-side HTML-embedded scripting language used to create dynamic Web pages. The strength of PHP lies in its compatibility with many types of databases. PHP can talk across networks using IMAP, SNMP, NNTP, POP3, and HTTP.

PNG   Portable Network Graphics. A graphics format similar to GIF. It is not widely supported by older browsers.

pop-under windows   Using various JavaScript techniques, designers often create pop-up windows that display behind the main browser window.

pop-up blockers   Software packages designed to stop scripts from generating pop-up windows without the user's permission.

pop-up windows   Used for a wide variety of purposes in Web development, the most common being online advertisements.

post   A method for sending form data using headers. See *get*.

precedence   The order in which operations are completed.

preload   Loading the file before the user sees the image.

program   A sequence of instructions, encoded in a specific computer language, for performing predetermined tasks.

programmer's comments   Messages that programmers insert directly into their source code to explain how the code was written.

property   An aspect or quality of an object.

protocol   A set of rules and conventions that describe the behavior computers must follow in order to understand each other.

radio button   A Web-page form field; users can choose one of several defined options.

raster graphics   A class of graphics created and organized in a rectangular array of bitmaps. Often created by paint software or scanners.

redefining HTML tags   When HTML tag names are used as selectors, the rule applied overwrites the default display styles of the tag.

redirect   To cause the browser to load a different page without intervention from the user. A particular HTML code in the heading of a Web page seamlessly redirects the visitor to another Web page.

relative path   The location of a file or Web page that uses the location of the current file or page as a reference. In the case of a Web page, called "relative URL." See *absolute path*.

relative reference   A path to a file that is written relative to the current document.

reserved words   Names of commands used in the programming language.

resizable option   Determines whether the user is allowed to resize the window once it is opened.

RGB   1. The colors of projected light from a computer monitor (Red, Green, and Blue) that, when combined, simulate a subset of the visual spectrum. 2. The color mode of most digital artwork.

robots   See *bots*, and *spiders*.

root   1. Top-level directory from which all other directories branch out. 2. On a UNIX system, the system administrator's account (also called a "superuser account"). For security reasons, only the system administrator is allowed to log in as root.

rule   Consists of an attribute and a value.

rules of precedence   Rules that determine the order in which mathematical operations are completed.

screen object   Represents the user's computer screen and allows developers to determine the current size of the end user's screen.

script   Written document that tells what the computer or browser what to do.

script tag   Allows JavaScript to be inserted into an HTML document.

scripting   The process of adding programming capabilities to a program (AppleScript), file (ActionScript), or Web page (JavaScript).

scripting language   Similar to a traditional programming language, but is usually less powerful and often designed for a specific function.

scrollbars option   Determines whether the scroll bars appear.

search engine   A Web site that allows users to search for keywords on Web pages. Every search engine has its own strategy for collecting data.

search engine optimization   Judicious incorporation of keywords and alt text in creating Web sites to maximize the likelihood that those sites will be found by various search engines.

select list   A list of potential choices that display as a menu that appears when the user clicks it, or as a box with its own scroll bar.

select option   A potential choice listed in a select list.

selection   The currently active objects in a window. Often made by clicking with the mouse or dragging a marquee around the desired object/s.

selector   Can be an HTML tag that you are redefining; it can also be a special situation, which is a name you assign to a rule that you can apply to specific HTML elements.

self   Using frames, a value for the target attribute. This value causes the browser to place the linked content into the frame containing the current document when the user follows the associated link.

server-side scripting   The Web server (not the user's computer) processes the JavaScript.

shopping cart   A piece of software that acts as the interface between a company's Web site and its deeper infrastructure, allowing consumers to select merchandise, review what they selected, make necessary modifications or additions, and purchase the merchandise.

spider   Also known as a robot or bot, a program used by search engines to index Web sites. Spiders search the Web to find URLs that match the given query string.

state   An image that displays when a particular event occurs; the current condition or situation.

status option   Turns on the browser's status bar, which appears at the bottom of the window in most browsers.

strictly typed languages Require you to specify the data type used with a specific variable when you create the variable.

string methods Ways to control a string object variable.

string object A variable that stores a text string.

string variables Variables that possess string values.

style object A defined set of formatting instructions for font and paragraph attributes, tabs, and other properties of text.

style sheet A defined set of formatting instructions for font and paragraph attributes, tabs, and other properties of text.

sub-object Part of another object.

swapping depths The process of changing the stacking order of objects.

syntax The set of rules that dictates how the language is written.

target The page or part of a page to which a link points.

TCP/IP Transmission Control Protocol/ Internet Protocol. A suite of communications protocols that defines the way information transmits over the Internet.

text The characters and words that form the main body of a publication.

text box A box into which users can type.

text editor An application used to create or make changes to text files.

text field A Web page form element in which users can enter information, such as name, address, or other data.

timer Used to set a waiting period before an action executes or to repeat an action at specific intervals.

tokens Keywords or other items that have significance to the interpreter.

toolbar option Used to specify whether the window displays toolbars.

top When using frames, a value for the target attribute. This value causes the browser to place the linked content into the current browser window, rather than an individual frame, when the user follows the associated link.

type attribute In a <script> tag, the type attribute specifies the type of information and language, such as type="text/javascript".

uppercase The capital letters of a typeface as opposed to the lowercase (small) letters. When type was hand composited, the capital letters resided in the upper part of the type case.

URL Uniform Resource Locator. Address of any resource on the Web.

URL parameter Passes information from one page to another by including a question mark and additional information at the end of a URL in a hyperlink.

usability The ease with which a user can access, navigate, and achieve goals on a Web site.

user-defined objects Created by programmers to bring consistent structure to specific programming tasks.

validate To ensure the user entered information completely and correctly and the information is in the proper format.

validation Making certain input fields, particular types of information, or information is in a specific format mandatory for that form to be successfully submitted.

value In a rule, the value assigned to a property.

variable A unit of information that can be referred to by name.

VBScript A Microsoft scripting language used for client-side scripting.

vector graphics Graphics defined by coordinate points and mathematically drawn lines and curves, which may be freely scaled and rotated without image degradation in the final output.

Web designer The aesthetic and navigational architect of a Web site, determining how the site looks, the site design, and what components the site contains.

Web developer A person who builds the technical architecture of Web sites, providing the programming required for a particular Web product to work.

Web directory A site that contains categorized listings of Web sites.

Web host A company that provides access to a server on which you can place Web site content. This server is connected to the Internet, allowing the general public to access the Web site.

Webmaster The person responsible for the Web server (usually the sysadmin).

Web page A single file or Web address containing HTML or XHTML information. Web pages typically include text and images, but may include links to other pages and other media.

Web-safe color A color palette used for images that will be displayed on the Internet. The Web-safe color palette is a specific set that accurately displays on most computer operating systems and monitors.

Web site A collection of HTML files and other content that visitors can access by means of a URL and view with a Web browser

white space Includes tabs and spaces; often used to make code easier to read.

width option Specifies a value for the width of a browser window.

window object Represents the browser window.

World Wide Web Consortium (W3C) The group responsible for defining HTML Standards (www.w3c.org).

WYSIWYG Web page editor A Web page editor that allows an author to directly manipulate items on a page, so that "what you see is what you get."

x coordinate In JavaScript, represents the number of pixels from the left side of the screen.

XHTML An acronym for eXtensible HyperText Markup Language. The reformulization of HTML 4.01 in XML.

XHTML elements An emerging specification for defining the handling of events on a Web page.

XHTML Frameset A version of XHTML that includes all tags that are part of HTML 4.01, including those involving frames.

XHTML Strict A version of XHTML that does not include any presentational tags or attributes.

XHTML Transitional The most common version of XHTML. Includes all tags and attributes that are part of HTML 4.01 except those involving frames.

XML An acronym for eXtensible Markup Language.

XOR See *exclusive OR operator*.

XSL An acronym for eXtensible Stylesheet Language.

y coordinate In JavaScript, represents the number of pixels from the top of the screen.